AN INTRODUCTION TO THE SOCIOLOGY OF LAW

(third edition)

(previous title: "A Primer in the Sociology of Law")

by

Dragan Milovanovic

Criminal Justice Press

Monsey, New York

2003

ISBN: 1-881798-40-2.

Preface to the Third Edition

The third edition of *Sociology of Law* has been updated. It includes more illustrative examples and some new sections. I have benefited greatly from many critical discussions about the book with numerous friends since the last edition. Bruce Arrigo and Stuart Henry have been especially supportive of this undertaking in their continuous critical dialogues. I have also benefited from the continuous input from students who have used this book for their course. The book is still meant to be read sequentially. The earlier chapters lay the groundwork for understanding in the later chapters. This book offers a basic understanding of key concepts in the sociology of law. It does not conduct an exhaustive review of the literature, particularly historical developments traced back to the dawn of civilization. It does not do systematic critiques of the various perspectives. Rather, it is meant for the student to enter the fascinating area of the development, functions, and perseverance of law in its various forms. The book can be used by undergraduates or graduates. It can also be used in substantive courses in law schools. Those already in the field will be provided a short overview of the various areas in the sociology of law, and the book can be used as a valuable reference text. Not all perspectives have been covered in this book. An author picks and chooses amongst the many. Certainly this has been the case here also. However, those who work their way through this book will find their understanding of what law is will be greatly expanded. It is a book meant to suggest pursuing further reading in the area of interest of the reader.

There is no conclusion to this book because that is the nature of law. It is more of a beginning, not ending. The reader is encouraged to pursue further inquiry in this area, for much exciting analysis and many discoveries await.

Dragan Milovanovic
August 14, 2002

ACKNOWLEDGMENTS

A number of people made contributions to this book in ways I am sure they don't even realize. Special thanks to Graeme Newman for always being there. To Hi and Julia Schwendinger, thanks for pointing the way. To Richard Quinney, thanks for all those peaceful moments at your farm together. To Stuart Henry, our collaboration over the years has been stimulating, productive, and rewarding. You have taught me much. To Bruce Arrigo, thanks for the endless discussions and insights on things that matter. A very special thanks to Richard Allinson for his many useful comments, suggestions and support for the third edition. To Mike McCarthy, thanks for showing me that the impossible can be done.

Thanks to an anonymous medic in Vietnam who, with total abandon, darted through a vicious cross-fire to pull me out of an inferno as my life seemed for a moment to have ended as my blood poured forth from the wounds. Thanks for giving me the extra precious years. Wherever you are out there, keep the peace.

And thanks to all my really good friends who have made the difference.

CONTENTS

continued...

continued...

ABOUT THE AUTHOR

Dragan Milovanovic is Professor of Criminal Justice at Northeastern Illinois University. He has written over 15 books and numerous articles on critical criminology and law from a postmodern perspective. He is Editor of the *International Journal for the Semiotics of Law*. His recent book is *Critical Criminology at the Edge* (2002). His practical experiences include work in a juvenile institution, maximum-security jail, and a mental hospital. He has been a member of a prison/jail inspection team for the John Howard Association since 1987. Dr. Milovanovic served as a paratrooper, squad leader, and company point-man during the Vietnam War. His current research is focused on a critically informed psychoanalytic semiotics, chaos, topology theory, catastrophe theory, edgework, and constitutive criminology and law. In 1993 he was the recipient of the Distinguished Achievement Award from the Division on Critical Criminology of the American Society of Criminology for his research and service in critical criminology and law.

FOREWORD

Some 50 years ago Georges Gurvitch said the sociology of law was in its infancy and suffered from a lack of exact definition. In spite of the publication of thousands of studies, articles, books and several journals devoted to the area, today Dragan Milovanovic is still able to make the same observation. Why this is so probably has more to do with the fact that, like the sociology of medicine and the sociology of religion, the sociology of law challenges professional orthodoxy and questions its neutrality and independence from the wider socio-political context.

The challenge from the sociology of law appears in several guises but all have to do with demonstrating the connections between law and other social forms. For the classical sociological theorists such as Marx, Weber and Durkheim, the essential connection was to structural conditions that appear to give rise to different kinds of law and legal systems. Their insights challenged the accepted views of positive law philosophers such as Austin and Kelsen, who assumed that the law contains essential and irreducible elements. Sociologists also relieve natural law theorists, such as St Thomas Aquinas and Justice Clarence Thomas, of their embarrassing inability to explain how the "natural" is articulated. They enable us to peer behind the discursive mask to see who decides what counts as "natural," "essential" and "moral," and to expose the social processes through which law is legitimated by reference to gods, common sense notions of right, or the general will.

Sociology of law clearly demonstrates that: law is born of socio-political contexts, themselves existing in different historical eras; that it serves some interests rather than others; that different societal structures or forms of organization give rise to different laws and legal systems; and that a combination of coercive and ideological processes are at work to ensure the continuation of existing legal systems and through these, existing structures of domination.

The sociology of law also draws sustenance from the fertile soils of anthropology, jurisprudence, and legal realism. Indeed, the struggle by positive law philosophers to separate law from other rules such as morals and customs met an early challenge from those like Ehrlich, Ross, Pound, Llewellyn, Hoebel and Malinowski. In their different ways these scholars demonstrated that law was a part of, rather than separate from, the wider phenomenon of social control. For Ehrlich, the root of law was to be found not in logical and consistent rules, but in the "living law" of the social association that exercises sanctions more forcibly than law and which dominates life itself. For Ross the law was just one of as many as 33 forms of social control, while Pound showed us that without a consideration of the context and application of law, any analysis of it, or even lawmaking itself was meaningless. But it was the legal realism of those like Holmes, Frank, Llewellyn, and Hoebel that struck a javelin blow to the heart of the positivist distinction between law and social context, with their demonstration that the law in practice was not the same as "law in the books." This fundamental reconception led to years of research on the "gap" problem of law and its application that is manifest in numerous studies such as those on police discretion, plea bargaining, and bias in sentencing.

Nor was the anthropological evidence from those like Malinowski in his famous study of the Trobriand Islanders, *Crime and Custom in Savage Society*, any less damaging to the pure legal formalist position since it showed the range of sanctions and systems of social control embodied in the customs and psychological fabric of non-industrial societies. Pospisil laid out the legal pluralist case first formulated by the likes of Krause, Gierke, and Weber, that there are as many legal orders as there are groups. He pointed out that membership in more than one group places competing and conflicting legal demands on individuals. More recent work of anthropologists has moved us from the law-centered approach of Western societies, where all rules are seen as laws and all peacemakers as judges, to Moore's notion of "law as process." Here law is seen as part of the social matrix that provides just one form of dispute settlement among many for restoring breached social relations.

Not only do studies of the social context of law show that it is inextricably linked to a multiplicity of social forms and political interests, but social theorists from Gurvitch to Nelken and Fitzpatrick have showed the depth of law from its formal rules to its informal spontaneity. They have demonstrated that the sociology of law is not simply the study of law *and* society, but the study of the interrelationship of law *with* society, such that each is a part of the other.

Others like Selznick and Fuller have stressed the importance of law as an instrument or even the embodiment of justice through the establishment of rational and accountable procedures for processing offenders. These sociologists emphasize how law cannot be restricted to government social control for to do so allows government to be beyond the law. In contrast, others like Zinn, Unger, Kennedy and Abel of the critical legal studies movement see law as a mask of justice, the very denial of the social process identified by Malinowski, and even go so far as to claim law creates injustice.

What then can be expected of a text in the sociology of law? Clearly it must give some sense of the history of its discipline and the development and evolving nature of its key concepts. It must also explain these concepts and present the leading perspectives on the law-society connection with enough detail that they are understandable but not so much that essential clarity is swamped. In this book, Dragan not only assists us with definitions and examples, but he avoids the pitfalls of other sociology of law texts that draw excessively on research studies to the exclusion of theory and analysis. Milovanovic presents us with the right balance of materials to serve as a guide to reading the original theory and research literature.

Sociology of law has suffered over the years from a paucity of texts and a dearth of good ones. Only Robert Kidder's *Connecting Law and Society*, and Alan Hunt's *The Sociological Movement in Law* made the grade of excellent, but even Hunt's book is limited to the classics, and unlike Professor Milovanovic's comparable work does not include the latest theorizing from critical legal studies, through postmodernism, feminism, and semiotic theory.

The sad truth about many textbooks is that like hamburgers, they are wrapped and ready to consume. But such "knowledge on a bun" lacks subtleties of taste and flavor, leaving us wanting. Professor Milovanovic's work, in contrast, is like a mid-afternoon meal in a French restaurant, to be enjoyed in small bites over many courses, during many hours; to be experienced, discussed and debated over; to be re-tasted and relished. Here knowledge is a journey of discovery. The book is not a quick read but one that patience and engaging thought will handsomely reward.

Professor Milovanovic is eminently qualified to have undertaken the task of writing this book. Apart from being a leading authority and proponent of postmodernist and semiotic theories of law, having authored and edited 17 books and over 100 articles in the area, he is former editor of the journal *Humanity and Society*, former editor of *Human Justice*, and current editor of the *International Journal for the Semiotics of Law*, and, for his contribution to the field was awarded in 1993 with the Distinguished Achievement Award by the Division of Critical Criminology of the American Society of Criminology. But as you learn from this work, perhaps what should be remembered is that Professor Milovanovic has lived in the socio-legal context of three different societies: Australia as a child; the United States as a teenager, adult, student and professor; and Vietnam as a U.S. Army paratrooper. And it is as a sergeant, squad leader, and company point-man in the jungles of South East Asia, a grunt of the U.S. military machine, that this veteran of law order and society was informed about the sociological realities of state power, the fragility of legitimation and the ugliness of human intolerance for difference. It is from these roots that he teaches us about law, justice and humanity.

Stuart Henry
Professor and Chair
Department of Interdisciplinary Studies
Wayne State University

INTRODUCTION

To study law is to study the evolving structures of society in a developing political economy. In addressing the question "What is law?" one responds to the question of how society is organized. In this introductory text, our goal is to introduce interested readers to some of the dominant thoughts in Western Society on the subject of the sociology of law.

To this end we will present, in Part 1, the classical theorists: Emile Durkheim, Max Weber and Karl Marx. We will be particularly concerned with their views concerning the development of society, the form of law and legal thought, the juridic subject (the so-called "reasonable man in law"), the contract, and the idea of private property rights. An understanding of the classical theorists provides us a foundations for understanding emerging perspectives in the sociology of law. In Part 2, we will examine some contemporary perspectives in the sociology of law, focusing on sociological jurisprudence, legal realism, the critical legal studies movement, feminist jurisprudence, critical race theory, the structural approach, the autopoietic view, the behavioristic perspective of Donald Black, legal semiotics, a Marxist semiotic approach, and a postmodern view in law with two specific examples — postmodernist feminism and the constitutive approach.

These theorists and perspectives have been chosen because of their centrality in current trends in the sociology of law. Because this is an introductory text, many less central theories relating to the diverse facets of law have been necessarily excluded. Nor have we embarked on a lengthy history of the sociology of law. Empirical studies have also been avoided in favor of concentrating intensively on the key thoughts in a discipline that is still in its infancy. In fact, one of the major problems is to establish what falls within the sociology of law, and what does not.

Defining the Domain of Inquiry

There are two general approaches to the study of law. One approach we may call *jurisprudence* (or, alternatively, legal science, sociological jurisprudence or legal dogmatics). The second approach is the *sociology of law*. Since the latter part of the 1980s, perhaps a third approach, *legal semiotics*, has taken form, and it is unclear whether in fact it will eventually be a subdivision of jurisprudence or the sociology of law, or retain some autonomous standing.

Members of the legal profession are most often concerned with jurisprudence. Social scientists, on the other hand, are more likely to identify with sociology of law. For the sake of clarifying domains of inquiry (that which is the focal point of inquiry), let us provide a working definition of each and then some explanatory remarks.

Jurisprudence is the study of:

(1) the existing system of written rules, established in codified form by the state (statutory and case law);

(2) their ongoing systematization into a body of relevant law by some coordinating principle of justification;

(3) the application of doctrinal legal discourse that is structured by a relevant morphological structure (word meanings) and syntactical structure (linear constructions of narratives and texts) in doing "correct" reasoning in law;

(4) the formal, logical application of abstract and general legal propositions and doctrines by the use of doctrinal legal discourse to "factual" situations by a specialized staff which provides a high degree of probability of resolution of the issue(s) in controversy; and

(5) the analysis of how all conflicts can be inevitably subsumable (self-referencing) to some absolute postulates, which provide the body of core premises and criteria for the correct resolution of differences in a self-regulating (homeostatic) formal system.

Members of the legal profession, be they practitioners or law professors, due to their educational experience provided in law schools and the continuous affirmation in everyday practice, internalize this emphasis in law. (We should add, too, that many legislators are legally trained.) It becomes the focal point of their practice. Rules promulgated by the legislative branch are taken as a given. Abstract legal propositions are applied to "factual" situations (the "what happened?") in an attempt to resolve different conflicts (e.g., one learns how to apply an "equal protection" or a "due process" analysis that is rooted in the Fourteenth Amendment to the U.S. Constitution). Precedents, or *stare decisis*, provide a background that constrains decision-making processes. A specialized staff — lawyers, trained in a specific discourse — apply their learned skills to points of controversy.

The doctrinal legal discourse in use is structured by two axes: the morphological structure and the syntactical structure.

The morphological structure is the repository of correct legal meanings of words (e.g., words such as intent, duress, reckless, person, etc., have legally bestowed meanings). The syntactical structure provides the correct method of linear construction of these words in narratives and text. In other words, within legal practice there is a particular way of constructing narratives: for example, in cross-examination there are particular methods of not leading witnesses, of introducing evidence, etc. (see Tiersma, 1999).

Any situation is said to be resolvable in law. One only needs to find the appropriate rule and premise(s), and by the use of formal logic — specifically, syllogistic reasoning and deductive logic — to proceed step by step toward the correct conclusion. "Truth" is said to exist independently of discourse, politics, and subjective evaluations. It can be discovered by the correct legal reasoning. It can be objectively obtained by the clash of two opposing sides, the prosecutor and the defense in criminal cases, or the plaintiff and the defense in civil cases. The legal system is seen as a potentially self-regulating (homeostatic) formal system, providing internal criteria and premises for resolving disputes. That is, the legal system not only deals with all points of controversy, but also is said to be adaptable as it grows (legal precedents).

Practitioners of law and law professors who do attempt to go beyond mere doctrinal legal analysis most often find the basis of their philosophical inquiry in the works of such exemplary theoreticians as Hart (1958, 1961, 1983) and Kelsen (1970), with their conceptualizations of law as a system of rules positively developed (legal positivism); Finnis (1980, 1983), with his reliance on "natural law" based on some deep structures of human nature and moral thought and the ultimate necessity of coercion in law; or in Dworkin (1978, 1985, 1986), with his liberal conception of rights and interpretive theory of reading the legal text (hermeneutics). Arguably Dworkin is at the borders of doing jurisprudence and has one foot in a sociology of law.[1]

Within jurisprudence, therefore, several schools of thought exist: legal positivism, classical natural law theory, rights theory, sociological jurisprudence, realist theory, critical legal studies, critical feminist analysis, critical race theory and various persuasions of legal semiotics. As cases in point, we shall develop some of these in Part 2, chapter 4. In chapter 6 we will present two representative examples from the legal semiotics perspective.

Academic jurisprudes who focus on doctrinal legal analysis find their main conduit for dissemination in law school classes and university law journals. Most law schools of repute support or subsidize a university law journal. Here one finds critique, comparison, and comment on how cases could have been decided otherwise, alternative ways of constructing the issues and "facts," an examination of the consistency or inconsistency of a decided case, etc. It is this body of material, as well as published case material, that is the focal point of study for the law student. The neophyte jurisprude is likely to receive a very limited introduction to the classic and progressive philosophers and sociologists. Consequently, those within the jurisprudence school of thought are more likely to continue to do doctrinal legal analysis, to be more technician than theoretician. Most often, those from the sociology of law tradition would argue, some internalized but yet uncritically examined theory of society, social order, and the human being (referred to as a meta-narrative) is the basis of much of their analysis and critique of law.

Sociology of law, on the other hand, is the study of:

(1) the evolution, stabilization, function, and justification of forms of social control;

(2) the forms of legal thought and reasoning as they relate to a particular political economic order;

(3) the legitimation principles and the effects that evolve with them;

(4) the "causes" of the development of the form of social control and staff of specialists that are its promoters;

(5) the transmission of "correct" methods of legal reasoning;

(6) the creation of the juridic subject with formal, abstract and universal rights;

(7) the evolution of the juridico-linguistic coordinate system (legal discourse) in use and its nexus with the political economic sphere; and

(8) the degree of freedom and coercion existing in the form of law.

Rather than taking rules, forms of law, rights and abstract notions of the legal subject (juridic subject) as a given, this approach examines the evolution of these forms and how they become the dominant factors in legal thinking and in the resolution of conflicts in society. The emphasis is on specifying the causes of law, legitimation principles, the specific legal discourse and forms of legal reasoning that arise, the development of a specialized staff to use it, the evolution of the so-called juridic subject (the "reasonable man" in law), and the degree of coercion and freedom that exist in law. Finally, this approach examines the connection (nexus) between the form of law and the political and economic sphere.

Sociologists of law would generally argue that jurisprudes — as well as scholars like Finnis, Hart and Dworkin — operate within a horizon of thought that has been pre-constituted (Poulantzas, 1973:207; Kerruish; 1991:147, 157-160); see our chapter below on "constitutive law," which is especially focused on this issue. In other words, the form of law, the basis of rights, and the nature of the legal subject in law (the juridic subject) are said to be, in the first instance, connected to socio-economic relations (Pashukanis, 1980, 2002; Beirne, 1979b; Beirne and Quinney, 1982; Beirne and Sharlet, 1980; Kerruish, 1991; Milovanovic, 1981, 1987, 1997). Thus, sociologists of law would criticize jurisprudes for uncritically accepting categories generated from historically-specific socio-economic relations. Jurisprudes would respond by saying that "[t]he appearance...*is* the reality of rights and law" (Kerruish, 1991:158; my emphasis). In other words, that law can be analyzed on its own terms and not as a reflection of other societal institutions. And herein lies the core difference between jurisprudes and sociologists of law.

Those doing sociology of law are more likely to find themselves in criminology, sociology, legal studies, political science, and criminal justice departments within colleges and universities. Although they occasionally have their work published in university law journals, more often their work appears in social science journals. They are also active in presenting their analysis in many social science conferences.

Beyond the two general approaches we have outlined, a third perspective, *legal semiotics*, is beginning to unfold, particularly since the late 1980s. The claim by those in legal semiotics — the study emphasizing semiotics in jurisprudential analysis — for the existence of an autonomous semiotic approach in the study of law is problematic. There is no doubt that we can approach the study of law by the use of the tools provided by semiotics; thus we do have semiotic perspectives.[2] In fact, a semiotic perspective has been neglected for far too long in the literature. The critical question will pivot on whether legal semiotics can stand on its own as an umbrella under which other fields are subsumed, or whether semiotics is one element, be it one of the most important, that needs to be integrated with other social theories in studying law.[3]

Be that as it may, in this book we are more interested in introducing some recent works in the sociology of law tradition, in which semiotics is one of the key elements. Thus, for example, we will include a Marxist view that makes heavy use of a linguistic determinism. We will also include postmodern views and how they have incorporated a perspective on semiotics derived from Jacques Lacan (see chapter 7). We will also include two of the most dominant legal semiotics approaches that have developed, one Peircian, the other Greimasian (see chapter 6).[4]

Several approaches in a critically grounded sociology of law, we shall see, make heavy use of semiotic analysis: postmodernist, feminist, Marxist (of the Structural Interpellation variety), and the constitutive approach.

Since the turn of the 20th century, the jurisprudence school of thought has dominated the analysis of law. Members of the legal profession have continued to operate within its more narrowly construed domain (formalism). Thus, within law schools, but also within liberal arts programs of universities, the emphasis in the study of law has been on legal science. The middle 1970s has been marked, however, by an increased sociological emphasis in law. Many critical scholars have returned to the classical theorists — Durkheim, Weber and Marx — in order to develop more sociologically-oriented approaches. Law is increasingly seen as intimately connected with the internal dynamics of a political economic order. It is to this second approach that this book is dedicated.

Definition of Law

Definitions of law vary widely. At one end of the continuum is the classic statement of Rousseau in the *Social Contract* (1954) that law is but the reflection of the will of all derived by a mythically established contract by members in a social body to end the "war of all against all" (that which Hobbes, in *Leviathan* [1946], posits as the "state of nature"). At the other end of this spectrum stands one variant of the Marxist's perspective, which states that law is class rule, or bourgeois law. We shall develop this in chapter 3. Between these extremes many alternative definitions arise. Take for example Hoebel, an anthropologist who, in *The Law of Primitive Man* (1974) offered the following: "A social norm is legal if its neglect or infraction is regularly met, in threat or in fact, by the application of physical force by an individual or group possessing the socially recognized privilege of so acting."

The key elements of his definition are: "social norm," by which is meant regularity in behavior; "regularly met," by which we mean with a high degree of probability; "application of physical force," which means that some external body will administer force against defined lawbreakers; and "an individual or group possessing the socially recognized privilege of so acting," which implies that a particular individual or staff are in the accepted position of administering punishment. The enforcer, too, can assume, can expect as a right, no legal retaliation. This definition, then, would exclude such behavior as the Bible's *lex talionis* — an eye for an eye, a tooth for a tooth — but would also have problems with such behavior as that of Bernhard Goetz, who shot several youths in a New York City subway, arguing that it was a preventive strike. It would also have problems with the Red Brigade (rebels operating in Italy who kidnap members of the upper class and subject them to a "people's trial" and then, upon conviction, inflict punishment). Other problem areas would include "bandits" (the Robin Hood types) that Hobsbawm (1969) has studied, or even the situation where, in times of an economic downturn, a robber enters a social security or an unemployment office and robs it in front of the recipients while the recipients cheer. Clearly, the question of "possessing the socially recognized privilege of so acting [application of physical force]," runs into a problem here, particularly because of substantial open or tacit support by some segments of the population in these situations.

Let's take a more classic definition. Weber has attempted to clarify the difference between mere customary behavior and law. "An order will be called... *convention* so far as its validity is externally guaranteed by the probability that deviation from it within a given social group will result in a relatively general and practically significant reaction of disapproval" (Weber, 1978:34).

Notice that within this definition no externally defined specialized group is given the power to enforce deviation from an order. An "order" he defines as a regular orientation to rules of conduct ("maxims") (Weber, 1978:31). On the other hand, "an order will be called... *law* if it is externally guaranteed by the probability that physical or psychological coercion will be applied by a *staff* of people in order to bring about compliance or avenge violation" (Weber, 1978:34, emphasis in the original).

Note the emphasis on a "staff" of people given the responsibility of assuring compliance or for avenging violations. Notice, too, that psychological coercion is included. Weber's definition, then, would seem to include "laws" of bodies such as the American Bar Association, the American Medical Association, etc., in that they, too, have codes of ethics and disciplinary procedures enforced by a staff to bring about compliance.

Other theorists have offered us a behavioral definition of law. Black, for example, defines law as "governmental social control" (1976, 1989). For Black, in explaining such things as crime, one need not get into the question of the motivation of the deviant. Law, as a quantitative variable (it varies in time and space) and as a qualitative variable (different styles of law can be applied, even to the same situation) can be fruitfully investigated in terms of the mobilization of law. In other words, the more law that is mobilized, the more serious is the perceived event. The seriousness of the offense, the definition of crime, who the offenders are, and official crime statistics can all be explained by how much law is mobilized. We shall return to Black in chapter 5.

Malinowski, an anthropologist, has noted that laws are not necessarily written (1976). The Trobiander of Melanesia, for example, found her/himself in a web of continuous relationships. The subjects depended on each other and found themselves in reciprocal relationships. There existed an intricate network of privileges, duties and benefits within which identity was centered. The bond of reciprocity and the felt obligations were so strong that for all intents and purposes these intricate relationships also constituted the law.

Anarchists would take Malinowski's analysis one step further. For them stateless societies have been shown to successfully exist, and can thus be duplicated in a society of the future. Kropotkin (1902, 1913) has argued that a society can function perfectly well guided by the principle of "mutual aid" and shared responsibility. In his words, the principle of mutual aid "grants the best chance of survival to those who best support each other in the struggle for life" (ibid., 115; see also Morland, 1997). It is unclear, however, if stateless societies have no law. For Black (1976), by definition, a stateless society has no law ("law is governmental social control"). For others, such as Luhmann (1985), law exists in every society (it is a generalization of expectations, see chapter 5). Thus, anarchists may argue, on the one hand, that without a state, no law exists, but on the other, they can equally argue, by the definition given, that law in fact exists. (For additional information on stateless societies, see, Michalowski, 1985:45-68; Black, 1976:123-137; Kennedy, 1976; Tifft and Sullivan, 1980; Ferrell, 1995, 1997, 1999; Williams and Arrigo, 2001.)

Sir Henry Maine wrote one of the first classic social science oriented books on the evolution of law. In his treatise, *Ancient Law* (1861), he observed that the movement in the orientation of law has been from the centrality of the family in ancient society, to the individual in modern society.

As Maine has noted, in ancient society, when an individual sins, the punishment extends to his children, his kinfolk, his tribesmen — and even as a substitute for him, in his absence (1861:75). Thus, for the ancient, collective responsibility and liability existed. Law, then, was directed to the family as a unit, rather than to an individual. Primitive societies were characterized by membership in some group. (We shall see that Durkheim, in chapter 1, and Weber in chapter 2 will have more to say about this.) It was within the group that rights, privileges and duties were defined. Individuality as we know it today was totally out of accord with the organizational structure of primitive society. Property, too, belonged to the family. The father was the supreme authority (*patria potestas*). Even his spouse was treated more as a daughter, not as an equal in law (1861:91).

Commentators such as Gibbs (1967) have noted that many definitions of law assume a coercive form. Gibbs offers a "composite" definition of law, which is a grand synthesis of all the coercive forms. The elements include:

(1) an evaluation of conduct held by at least one person in a social unit; and

(2) a high probability that, on their own initiative or at the request of others, persons in a special status will attempt by coercive or non-coercive means to revenge, rectify, or prevent behavior that is contrary to the evaluation; with

(3) a low probability of retaliation by persons other than the individual or individuals at whom the reaction is directed (Gibbs, 1967:431).

In his composite definition, rather than using such words as norm or order, he substitutes "evaluation" of conduct, which is not necessarily collective. "Special status," rather than necessarily implying an official, court, or state, implies that someone must occupy a status, which is universally accepted. And finally, his definition relies on the idea that this enforcing party is immune from retaliation ["when a perpetrator can rely on other parties to rally to his cause...law does not exist" (Gibbs, 1967:433)].

The autopoeitic (Luhmann, 1992; Teubner, 1993; and chapters 5 and 7 of this book) as well as the constitutive perspective (Henry and Milovanovic, 1996, 1999) view the emergence of a particular definition of law more in terms of a relatively stabilized manifestation at historical junctures of otherwise more hidden complex interrelated elements at work. It is not just the economic that is determinative, nor just the ideological sphere. Thus law is not simply class rule, nor the product of enlightened, rational thought. Law is both constituted by and constitutive of socially constructed reality. Law appears in a trial court setting, legislative discussion, police encounter, and so forth, as well as in individual dealings with everyday conflict situation. The "micro" exists in the "macro" and the "macro" exists in the "micro."

At this point in our introduction to the sociology of law we merely wish to indicate the varying positions on the definition of law. This is not merely an academic exercise. Take for example, the instrumental Marxists. They argue that even under the "first phase of communism," that is, socialism, law will still be dictatorial, or class rule, be it in the form of proletarian law. For Marxists, it is only in the "higher phases" that the state and law will "wither away" (see chapter 3). Here, by definition, absent a state and a staff, no law exists. Clearly the accepted definition of law dictates the scope of the analysis of law. It also defines, or even "creates" crime (see the various discussions in Henry and Lanier, 2001).

Functions of Law

Let us now turn to the functions of law. Put simply: what does law do? Law has repressive, facilitative and ideological dimensions. Any given system of laws will probably have aspects of all three within them. However, one may be dominant. The *repressive function* of law addresses the question of coercion in law. Thus, legal repression is variable. Law can be more or less coercive. By repressive functions we mean the degree of mobilization of physical force in the service of social control. There are some theorists who rest their argument on the necessity of repression on particular ontological assumptions (the philosophy of essential being). For example, there are those from a Freudian or Hobbesian perspective (acknowledged or not), who assume that because of strong hedonistic, self-centered (egoistic) or biological impulses, a person left to him/herself in a state of nature would act out his/her impulses without regard or respect for others if it was not for an external force, law. It is argued that a person's appetite has to be controlled. Durkheim has even argued that absent an external force, a person left to him/herself would not develop his/her two sides (duality) — egoism and altruism — in a balanced way. That is, s/he would not regulate his/her conduct, or synchronize it with social requirements. In this framework, whether we talk about a "superego," "leviathan," or the "collective conscience," an external force is needed to coerce individuals to abide by the law.

There are those who argue that some coercion is necessary, but beyond this, "surplus repression" exists (Marcuse, 1962:32-34, 80). This arises because of the existence of political elites and their interest in dominating and maintaining their ruling position. An excess amount of force is generated to maintain a political economic system advantageous to them. A full-blown version of this idea is' the instrumental Marxist position (Quinney, 1974, 2002). These theorists argue that an illegitimate ruling group dominates at the expense of the laboring classes. Weber, too, argues that even though we have formal equality in law, because of vast economic differences of exchangers (contractors) entering a contract, coercion can still exist. That is, the propertied class can simply use its leverage to maintain control (i.e., dictating the terms of the contract), while giving the formal appearance that the worker, for example, is free to enter the contract or not. Thus, the *form* can appear as assuring liberties, whereas the *content* may produce domination.

Certain questions still remain. Pure coercive definitions of law do not adequately answer the questions of: (1) why people conform to legal norms outside of the particular threats of punishment; (2) the significance of the prevailing belief in the "correctness" or "legitimacy" of law and how it correlates with actual behavior (i.e., belief in legitimacy and the actual behavior do not necessarily correlate: an individual might see law as generally "just" but still violate it: yet law may be seen as "unjust" but the individual might still conform); (3) what other functions are served by law (i.e., facilitative); and, (4) the ideological dimension of law, that is, how the "rule of law" ideology is constructed and maintained and what purpose is served by it. In sum, the issue of the repressive functions of law cannot be entirely separated from the issue of its facilitative and ideological functions.

The *facilitative function* in law can be defined as the degree to which law aids in assuring predictability and certainty in behavioral expectations. Whether we read Durkheim, Weber, Marx, Maine, Unger, or Selznick, we find the notion presented that there has been an evolution of law from *status to contract*. Durkheim, for example, shows that a primitive society is marked by "mechanical" bonds of solidarity (attraction based on similarity, sameness). Thus, similar encounters among the members of a society and the consequently similarly developed lifestyles and outlooks lead to a highly predictable order. The evolution to a more complex, differentiated type of society, however, produces bonds of solidarity he calls "organic" (the bond being attraction of opposites). In modern societies, involvements are more diverse and more transitory. But the range of behaviors existing, both normal and "pathological," have increased tremendously. As a consequence, less predictability and certainty in everyday behavior is the norm. Satisfaction of needs cannot be assured by interacting within small circles. The contract, for Durkheim, resolves some of the dilemmas: it assures certainty in behavior (see further, chapter 1).

Weber's notion of the "rationalization" of society (see chapter 2 below) also states that society evolved from the primitive *status contract* (agreements made affected the whole personality of the transactor and her/his standing in the community) to the *purposive contract* (characterized by temporary relationships in which agreements were freely made). This coincided with the coming of commerce and the competitive marketplace marked by money transactions. Here the contract, reflecting mutually and freely agreed upon terms, assured subjects in the social formation that their expectation of results would be supported by an external force, the state and its laws. Hence, economic calculation could now be made more predictable because the many variables in society could now be quantified. Profit motives, then, can find expression in a stable framework in which expectations and obligations are calculable.

Marx, too, argued that the breakup of feudalism, as a *mode of production* (a specific means of producing and distributing goods in a society), and its replacement by capitalism, entailed a movement away from barter (exchange for direct personal use) to commodity-exchange (exchange for profit) in the competitive marketplace and money economy. But in the capitalist mode of production, Marx argued, predictability and certainty in transactions needed to be assured if capitalism was to continue. What was needed, then, was a centralized state with machinery of enforcement to facilitate egocentrically-driven subjects pursuing profits.

A contemporary writer who has stated the facilitative functions of law quite precisely is Luhmann (1985). In this view, law is the "generalization of expectations" and is not primarily repressive (1985:78). His rather cumbersome definition of law is that it is a "structure of a social system which depends upon the congruent generalization of normative behavioral expectations" (1985:82). Put simply, Luhmann argues that within changing societies people need some reference point that becomes the basis of structuring expectations and obligations; absent this, people will witness endless disappointments and hardships. Law acts as that reference point. We shall have more to say about his approach in chapter 5, but here we merely wish to stress that for Luhmann law reflects the requirement that participants in a social formation need to be able to structure their expectations — or, said in another way, to be able to orient their behavior toward predictable responses and expectations.

Law, in its facilitative function allows coordination, planning, and the expectation that certain behaviors will normally follow other behaviors. So long as there is congruency between us concerning our expectations, we both can plan, participate, respond and carry projects forward with a minimum of difficulty. Luhmann argues that as society evolves to greater complexity, however, there is even a greater necessity for structuring expectations of expectations. Law is said to respond to this necessity. To this degree, Luhmann argues, law must always exist in every society (1985:83).

Many dilemmas exist when interactions cannot be planned nor outcomes predicted. Consider, for example, Laing's point of two people in interaction who cannot pinpoint a common background understanding or reference point (1970:22). Jill: "You think I am stupid." Jack: "I don't think you're stupid." Jill: "I must be stupid to think you think I'm stupid if you don't..." This guessing what the other is thinking, can go on to no end (infinite regress). If the other party is also trying to anticipate what I am thinking, then establishing meaning or coming up with a common understanding can be rather a precarious situation. At a minimum, many disappointments will occur and much remedial work would need to be done (see, especially, Goffman, 1971:95-187).

The contract is the instrument that is the purest expression of the need to assure predictability and fulfillment of obligations. Maine (1861), Renner (1949), Selznick (1969), Klare (1979) and Weber (1978) have all argued that a movement from status to contract has characterized society's progress. In brief, they argue that in primitive society one's status in the community (who you are, what position you occupy in the hierarchy or society, what specific role you play) is central in determining rights, obligations and duties. One's identity is intimately connected to a web of social relationships. This "web," in itself, assures that the contracting parties abide by their agreements. In more advanced societies this state of affairs is replaced by the contract, which assumes free agreements of individuals. Each contractor is assumed to be capable of freely exchanging what s/he possesses. And each is assumed to be able to meet the other on an equal footing, with equal rights. It is but a temporary bond touching on a very small part of the whole identity of the interacting parties. Here, fulfillment of the contract terms is assured by the state. The contract, as well as the notions of individual responsibility and liability, private property rights, the juridic subject and the state are recent inventions. We need not go far back in history for their origins. We will have more to say about this throughout the book.

In sum, the facilitative function of law concerns the question of how certain legal instruments — the contract for example — develop, why they do so, and how they answer the call for predictability and certainty in economic transactions and social interactions.

The third function of law is *ideological.* Ideology as a belief system is always present in law. In other words, law systematically embodies the values of some people, but disregards some values of others. Accordingly, the question of gender, race, class, sexual preference, etc., becomes a central issue in discussions of ideology (for an excellent critical analysis of ideology in law, see Kerruish, 1991). A particular form of discourse transmits ideology, what we will refer to as a linguistic coordinate system (chapter 6). Words attain their legal meaning only by way of struggle in which one definition comes to prevail (Milovanovic, 1987, 2002). For example, consider the Fourteenth Amendment to the U.S. Constitution, which reads, in part, "no person shall be deprived of life, liberty or property without due process of law." The words "person," "life," "liberty," "property," and the notion "due process" have been the subject of much litigation.[5]

Ideological and repressive functions in law often appear together, with the former often disguising the latter. For example, for over 200 years in Australian law the notion of *terra nullius* prevailed. This doctrine had it that Australia, when first discovered by Britain, was "uninhabited" and was thus settled as a colony. This doctrine denied the indigenous peoples the lands they had traditionally held for over 40,000 years. In 1992, the High Court of Australia in *Eddie Mabo and Others v. The State of Queensland* overturned this doctrine, recognizing "native title." Currently, much internal resistance exists within different sectors of Australia as to transforming "native title" into government practice.[6]

Several critical concepts are central when examining the ideological function of law: domination, legitimation, hegemony, and reification. We shall have more to say about each throughout the book. As to the issue of *domination*, Max Weber has informed us that subjects in a social formation orient their behavior to an order. But why do they do so? When they do, do they in fact accept it as just? This question of *legitimation* is central. Weber, for example, has shown three forms of domination: charismatic, traditional and legal (see chapter 2). Subjects predictably abide by the order because it is seen as right, or just. The question of why they do see it as so will be examined in subsequent sections of this book.

Subjects, too, advertently and inadvertently contribute to the maintenance of the socio-political-legal and ideological order, be it one that is more democratic or, ironically as it may sound, one that is totalitarian. Would-be revolutionaries or reformers often reconstruct the dominant legal order (and its ideologies) by making use of the categories, procedures, and language that are part of the dominant order in their very efforts to redress their grievances (see, for example, the case of jailhouse lawyers in Thomas and Milovanovic, 1999). This is the idea of *hegemony*. Said in yet another way, it is the active participation by subjects in the mechanism of their own oppression. Oppositional groups will often find themselves faced with the *dialectics of struggle* — struggles, on the one hand, can contribute to emancipatory practices, but on the other, also contribute, be it inadvertently, to the establishment of new forms of hierarchy and repression (see, for example, Cornell, 1998).

The continuous process of reconstructing structures that attain a relatively independent existence is known as *reification*. In other words, subjects collectively construct a social order, and this order comes to take on an "objective" appearance, now dominating subjects.

The flip side of the notion of hegemony is the question of *legitimation*. Why and how, it might be asked, do subjects inadvertently and advertently participate in the mechanism of their own oppression? Marxist analysis of law places this question in the center of its investigation of law (see chapter 3). The ideological role of law, then, is said by some, particularly Marxists, to help "persuade the dominated elements in American society that their domination is justified — or that their material conditions of existence are justified or, equivalently, that they are not dominated at all" (Tushnet, 1977:100). This legitimating function addresses the question of why subjects may follow the law, seeing it as just, where in fact the very distribution of resources might be highly skewed.

> People believe that a practice which is legal is, by that fact alone, a practice which is just. Thus, if one criticizes the distribution of wealth in the society, the ideology of the legal order answers that the distribution is just simply because it arose from transactions that were legal; property, that is, is not theft because the acquisition of property does not meet the legal definition of theft [Tushnet, 1977:100].

In other words, the power bloc's position requires that it articulate justifications for its privileged status (see chapter 2); otherwise, subjects may question the gross disparity in wealth and privilege. Looking toward the law, subjects will see what appears as an autonomous legal system that rests on such principles as formal "equality before the law." The citizen perceives the existence of a democratic society governed by the "rule of law." Hence, the perception created is that it is not the law that aids in maintaining inequality; rather, the discrepancy must be found in the lack of initiative, lack of hard work and so forth. The ideological function of law, then, includes the idea that law may legitimate domination by the power bloc.

In the forthcoming pages we shall also focus on the specialized discourse in use by the staff of enforcers (Tiersma, 1999). Whether one uses the oath or the invocation of a divine being as the guarantor of the promise made, or whether as in contemporary society one makes use of trained specialists (lawyers), a particular specialized discourse is used in resolving conflicts (see chapter 6). Law-finding — by which we mean the application of specific rules of evidence and reasoning to "factual" situations in order to construct "what happened" — entails the use of a specific linguistic coordinate system (discourse). One must situate oneself in the appropriate linguistic coordinate system in order to be able to do the "correct" reasoning to attain a legal result. Thus, in doing law in the existing form under contemporary capitalism, lawyers bring with them linguistic skills that are obtained by training in law school. The discourse available for use in decision making, in constructing "what happened," is not random; rather a particular method of legal thought must be brought to bear on the "facts" for a legal resolution (see chapters 4 and 6). Durkheim, Weber and Marx all imply that the members of a staff that engages in law-finding situate themselves within this legal discourse, which often has a sacred character to it. Only the staff knows of its complex use; the layman, the common citizen, is said to be incapable of mastering it. Consider, for example, my recent encounter with a real estate lawyer. Faced with my continuous critical questions, he finally emphatically and authoritatively blurted: "give me your thoughts and I'll find the [legal] words."

In sum, the ideological function of law focuses on how certain ideals are systematized in law and how these ideals are conveyed by the rule of law. All three functions of law — repressive, facilitative and ideological — become central in the sociology of law. Some theorists, we will note in subsequent chapters, focus more on one dimension than another. The author's position here is that all three functions must be addressed in a bona fide examination of the sociology of law.

Law and Fulfillment of Social Values

A final core issue needs to be addressed. In studying law we need to ask: What is the relationship of law and a legal order to the fulfillment of social values (see Trubek, 1977:545-555)? After all, law and its contributions must be judged by some standard. Law's legitimacy rests, according to many theorists, on the promise that law promotes certain values in a social formation. The first step in this examination then entails "understanding the nature of social ideals which law is thought to foster,... [and in examining] ...empirically and theoretically, the purported relationship between legal institutions and these ideals" (Trubek, 1977:546). To this end, Trubek has given us a conceptual model in examining the relationship of a legal order to the fulfillment of social values (see Figure 1).

This model includes two dimensions: the degree of autonomy and generality of the legal order, and the degree to which the legal order contributes to the realization of certain social values. This figure helps us pinpoint *ideal types*, or conceptually pure models. It is a heuristic model in the sense that it gives us a snapshot view of complex, ongoing dynamic systems. It provides us with a beginning point in further critical analysis. Here, in Figure 1, two degrees of freedom are incorporated. Of course we could develop more complicated models with more than two dimensions, or degrees of freedom. And the two concepts may not even go together in some occasion. For example, autonomy and generality may on occasion be mutually exclusive concepts; that is, they may not be positively correlated. Here there is a tradeoff; simplifying a model gives us a quick starting point for further refined analysis but at a cost of over simplification; a more complex model incorporating more degrees of freedom would provide us with increasingly more accurate models but at the cost of easy and useful initial understanding that sensitize us to the issues. We add that Figure 1 offers not only a descriptive snapshot of a legal order but can also provide a prescriptive dimension, offering suggestions for social change.

Let's examine the first dimension. A legal order can be operationally defined by its "autonomy" (the degree of independence of a legal order from any particular individual or interest group) and by its "generality" (the degree to which decisions and rules are made according to previous rules, and applied to all without favorable treatment to any). We can specify a range within this dimension or scale, from highly autonomous/general to not at all. A legal order that is "low" on this dimension would be one where some powerful group controls the legal apparatus and law is discriminatorily applied.

The second dimension, social values, Trubek identifies as incorporating *equality* (equal treatment by the state), *individuality* (degree of self-actualization that is realizable) and *community* (degree to which participating and sharing in a greater group is possible).[7] In other words, social values can be operationally defined in terms of these three. All three will be collapsed so that we can speak of this dimension as ranging from "high" to "low." (With some reflection on this collapsing operation we could point out that some contradictions may appear — the inherent dangers of over-simplification!) This conceptual model is portrayed in Figure 1.

Contemporary perspectives in the sociology of law can be placed at the intersections of these two dimensions. In other words, as we begin to examine different approaches in the sociology of law we need to be able to make use of some type of organizing framework, which sensitizes us to key issues. Fruitful investigation of the relationship between law and the fulfillment of social values then can take place. It is but the starting point for more refined scholarly analysis. We merely offer this conceptual model as a way of putting in perspective the many examinations of law, which follow. We shall identify four models as examples.

The upper right hand corner represents the orientation referred to as *liberal legalism*. It is also called formalism, legal formalism, formal rationality or logical formal rationality; at other times, it is simply referred to as the "rule of law." This orientation in the sociology of law states that the legal order is highly autonomous and general; that is, it is independent from the influence of some power bloc, and it is also seen as offering, at the same time, the potential for maximal fulfillment of social values (i.e., equality, individuality, community). Law is seen as being independent of some power group or individual; it stands above the interests of any one interest group or individual, and thus deals with conflicts in a neutral manner so that maximal realization of social values is achieved. In other words, the rule of law is said to allow maximal freedom and minimal coercion in law.

Figure 1. Legal Order and Fulfillment of Social Values under Western Capitalism

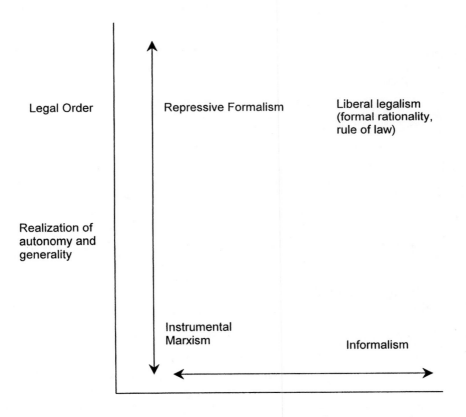

(Adapted from Trubek, 1977:551.)

The assumption in this perspective is that under present day self-proclaimed democracies, an ideal order identified as legal formalism provides the best solution to the question of how to handle ongoing conflicting interests and values for the good of all. Law schools and their curricula teach the fundamentals of correct legal reasoning in preparation for carrying out this ideal legal system. Assumed, too, in this model is that if we fine-tuned the machinery of legal formalism, eradicating *extra-legal factors* such as race, class, and gender biases in decision making, replacing them by adherence to the formal rules, logic and rationality, society would be the better for it, since maximal realization of values could then be attained. The rule of law is said to be the ideal toward which we should strive. Such a principle as the "equal protection clause" of the Fourteenth Amendment to the U.S. Constitution, a central element of the rule of law, expresses it best: equally situated should be equally treated.

Let us provide an example in the use of this model as it deals with liberal legalism's solution to racism or sexism in the legal order. We begin by identifying biases of the legal order toward certain segments of the population. The realization of social values for this segment is significantly less than others similarly situated. Thus, in this example, the ongoing workings of this biased system can be depicted somewhere in the center of Figure 1: here we have a legal order that is *not* highly autonomous or general (some segment of the population is subject to discrimination), and as a consequence this group does not completely realize social values. Law students are taught to apply an "equal protection" argument to this case in order to move the functioning of the legal order toward the upper right hand corner as an ideal, hence eradicating biases and prejudices and also providing the way for the greater realization of social values. Here, of course, in the spirit of the jurisprudential method, the analysis of the wherewithal of the "equal protection clause" does not exist; the clause is taken as a given and applied to problematic situations. Thus we can appropriately identify this legal work as primarily technical in nature. This is, in other words, the domain of those who identify with jurisprudence rather than with the sociology of law.

Since the break up of totalitarian forms of "communism" in Eastern Europe, two more radical philosophical positions have gained notoriety within the "rule of law" tradition. Roberto Unger (1986) has advocated a "superliberalism," arguing for the empowerment of the State but with the institutionalization of new forms of civil rights and protections that may pave the way to an "empowered democracy." In his analysis, he wants the proclaimed virtues of Western democracies to become reality. Jeffrey Reiman (1990) has offered a redistributive principle whereby the worse-off members as well as the better-off within society can *both* benefit. In other words, he argues for a rule of law, but also acknowledges vast structured inequities in the system. He finds that a redistributive principle based on a substantive ideal can lead to the greater realization of social values for all members of a society. For both theorists, the rule of law itself incorporates humanistic dimensions that promise to lead to the greater realization of individuality, equality and community.

Liberal legalism has most often been the focal point of those in the jurisprudential tradition. Members of the practicing legal profession as well as academic law professors most often work within this intersection. Sociologists of law, on the other hand, most often focus on trying to understand the other three ideal types in Figure 1. Hence, what we find is that different questions and solutions are offered because of these particular foci.

Instrumental Marxism appears in Figure 1 at the intersection of low autonomy and generality and low fulfillment of social values. For theorists of this persuasion, law is seen as being dependent on some dominant individual or group (i.e., the ruling class). Here the majority of the population is seen as being denied genuine opportunity in the fulfillment of equality, individuality and community. The ruling class is said to use the system of law and legal order as an instrument (hence "instrumental Marxism") to maximize its own interest in making profits ("surplus value"). Exploitation of the worker, alienation, fragmentation, excessive competition, racism, sexism, class exploitation, the rewarding of egoistic behavior at the expense of altruism — all, according to the instrumental Marxist position, are part and parcel of the workings of the capitalist mode of production. Law, then, is primarily repressive, favoring the powerful group in control. The less powerful are held in check by the legal order (for a precise statement, see Quinney, 1974, 2002). The instrumental Marxists would argue that the very ideology that develops — advocating the necessity of coercive law because of the existence of predatory individuals — is convoluted and mystifying. The system, it is said, produces these individuals ("crippled monstrosities") in the first instance and then creates an ideology for the necessity of controlling this end product.

Repressive formalism is an orientation that poses a paradox. The legal order can be highly autonomous and general, but at the same time this condition may: (1) still further the interests of the capitalist "class" *as a whole*; and (2) contribute very little to the overall realization of social values. In other words, this orientation has it that the legal order, on a formal level, may indeed reflect the ideals of autonomy and generality, and the ideals specified in the Bill of Rights. It will not be under the *direct* control of the capitalist "class," and will render the principle of formal equality a central place in society. Yet, genuine equality, individuality and community will be denied. As Trubek has argued (1977:553), "the capitalist mode of production leads to increasing inequality of income and power, to domination and destruction of genuine individuality, and to the rupture of communal ties and thus alienation." But these effects, according to those within this tradition, are obscured and mystified by a legal order that, on its face, appears as autonomous and general. Capitalists as well as workers, in other words, are both subject to the legal system and receive "equal" treatment before the law; but what is overlooked by the operations of the legal system is the vast economic disparities and how these are transformed into privileges for the powerful.

For example, consider Anatole France's quip that the rich and poor are equally prohibited from sleeping under the bridges of the Seine in France. Both are being treated (formally) on an equal footing. However, with a little reflection it becomes quite apparent that formal equality may hide and perpetuate substantive inequality. Consider the situation of two individuals, one making $100,000 the other $10,000 per year. They both are given tickets for traveling 15 miles per hour over the speed limit (thus they are equally situated vis-à-vis the infraction). Assume they both get equivalent legal services (equally treated). And they both are fined $50 dollars per person (again, equally treated). Conclusion: since equally situated were equally treated, this is constitutionally permissible; in this case it is the ideal. Those from the liberal legalist position spend much time and energy identifying the circumstances in which and by which equally situated are not equally treated (i.e., biases due to racism, sexism, etc.), and attempt to fine-tune the machinery in order that formal equality reigns.

But a close examination of this example leads us to question whether *substantive justice* results in light of the initial difference in wealth. Surely a $50 fine has a different significance for a person making $10,000 per year than it does for a person making $100,000 per year. In sum, this orientation indicates that the legal ideals of equality, individuality and community brought about after the demise of feudalism and with the development of capitalism, are both an affirmation and a negation, a dialectic (see also Balbus, 1977a; we will also return to this in the chapter on Karl Marx). Proclaimed ideals such as "equality for all" may, at a deeper level of analysis, indicate hidden repressive dimensions. Ironically, then, activists who advocate some commonly accepted ideals might at times be unintentionally reinforcing a more hidden form of repression. This is the notion of *hegemony* that we shall return to on several occasions throughout this book. It is also the basis of the *dialectics of struggle* whereby disenfranchised groups, for example, do in fact benefit from "rights discourse"; they do receive some alleviation from suffering, but inadvertently their efforts contribute to the legitimation of the rule-of-law ideology. See, for example, the ambiguous relationship people of color and women have with this: on the one hand, the are provided with a voice in law, but, on the other, by this very practice, inadvertently or not, further the legitimacy of the rule of law.

Of course, the example provided in the previous paragraph can lead to many intriguing questions and analyses. It offers, in a snapshot form, the tension between formal principles in law (i.e., the equal protection clause: equally situated should be equally treated) and substantive principles in law (i.e., Marx's notion: "from each according to his [her] abilities, to each according to his [her] needs"). Marxists, therefore, would probably have to argue for different treatments for different people (a principle of inequality?): the person who makes $100,000 per year in our example above would need to pay a fine that is proportionally greater, here ten times, that of a person who makes $10,000 per year, or $500. Consider, for a moment, the ramifications of this example for an entire legal order!

The final orientation, *informalism*, indicates a legal order that is "low" on generality and autonomy but "high" on the realization of social values (see lower right hand corner of Figure 1). We can depict a range of possible types extending from romantic informalism, to a benevolent dictatorship, to the "stateless" societies advocated by Marxists and anarchists.

One variant of informalism, romantic informalism, argues that if informal dispute settlement mechanisms increasingly replace the formal structures, more fulfillment of social values will result. Such programs as diversion, neighborhood justice centers, mediation and arbitration bodies, community "moots" and so forth, focusing on informal proceedings, would maximize the fulfillment of social values, it is said, *within* the framework of the capitalist mode of production. One historical example is Khadi justice (see chapter 2), which considers a wide range of factors to assure substantive justice (as opposed to formal justice). The law-finder's decision is based on the unique circumstances of each case. The remedy is tailored to fit such factors as personality, need, and so forth. Trubek, for example, has argued that we can keep the given mode of production as is and merely move toward more informal methods of conflict management, and by doing so, maximal realization of values could occur. This nostalgic position found many adherents in the 1960s. In the contemporary critical criminology scene, the peacemaking approach to criminology and law resurrects this approach (Pepinsky and Quinney, 1991; MacLean and Milovanovic, 1997; Quinney, 2002).

Another version of informalism, a position shared by anarchists and Marxists, advocates the "withering away" of the state and law. Only with the removal of the capitalist mode of production, it is argued, will the state, law, lawyers, and the "juridic subject" disappear. In its place, informal community "moots" would develop in the "higher forms" of communism. These would render substantive justice by considering each individual case as unique. The first line of defense against the development of troublesome behavior is, however, the establishment of a society focused on altruism, cooperation, collective development, mutual aid, and the social ideal of the Renaissance person. Here Marx's guide would be "from each according to his [her] abilities, to each according to his [her] needs."

A position midway between the previous two, theoretically derived, may be the benevolent dictator who distributes resources as they are needed. To those who need the most, so they shall receive. But a formal system of laws would not be in existence. The benevolent dictator would be guided by an extremely acute sense of justice. Weber, of course, as we shall see, would argue that the possibility of this in modern society is pure fantasy and that with the rise of the bureaucracy and forces of rationalization, formal rational laws are here to stay. But the tension, the "insoluble conflict," between the principles of formal and substantive justice would always be felt.

In sum, Trubek's conceptual model allows much fruitful conceptualization of the relationship of laws to the fulfillment of social values. It is a convenient tool in the sociology of law. It can be read descriptively as a convenient, summary snapshot of a legal order, and prescriptively, as a tool for envisioning social change. We will return to it several times throughout this book as a guide to our presentations and analyses.

This book will be divided into two parts. In Part 1 we will present the classic theorists — Durkheim, Weber and Marx. We will provide an overview of the key elements within their approaches.

In Part 2 we will focus on contemporary perspectives in the sociology of law. Four chapters will present some of the most provocative analysis that has appeared in the contemporary literature. In chapter 4 we have chosen early twentieth-century sociological jurisprudence and American legal realist approaches, the critical legal studies movement, feminist jurisprudence and critical race theory. We have indicated that these approaches can be located between jurisprudential analysis and sociology of law. In chapter

5, we offer the structural-functional approach, the autopoietic perspective, and a behavioristic approach. Here we have moved into the domain of the sociology of law (recall our earlier definition). In chapter 6, semiotics and its relationship to law will be presented. This chapter will focus on legal semiotics (Peirce, Greimas) and a Marxist semiotic perspective (e.g., structural interpellation view) in the' sociology of law. In chapter 7 we examine the postmodernist use of semiotics and more fully developed sociology of law perspectives. Here Jacques Lacan's work will be central. We will provide two examples of research taking place in this area: one will focus on a Lacanian-informed feminist analysis in the sociology of law; the other, on a constitutive approach.

Our goal in our exposition is to be primarily descriptive and expository in focus. Critical comparisons will be only done in passing and they are therefore of secondary concern. This would certainly be the next stage after the student has acquainted her/himself somewhat with the literature. The book is an introduction for getting into the sociology of law; as such, it provides overviews of some of the most compelling theoretical works on the subject. And, as a primer, it should provide some familiarization of the contours of the discipline. We turn now to the classic thinkers.

Notes

1. For a succinct overview and critique, see Kerruish, 1991:43-107; Douzinas et al., 1991:21-28, 55-91.

2. Several other theorist-specific approaches have recently developed that are making a claim for an autonomous body of semiotic inquiry, most particularly, Peircian and Greimasian (perhaps even Lacanian — although their main exponents, Drucilla Cornell, Peter Goodrich, David Caudill, Bruce Arrigo, and Dragan Milovanovic would not call themselves by the title, Lacanian). Arguably we could develop a semiotic approach based on other important theorists' work, such as Gottlob Frege (Rudmin, 1992) and the Polish theoretician, Kazimierz Twardowski with his disciples Tadeusz Kotarbinski, Stanislaw Lesniewski and Kazimierz Ajdukiewicz (Rooney, 1993). There is also the "Prague Linguistic Circle" (Winner, 1992; Kevelson, 1993a) that could become the basis of a semiotic approach in law. And an "Italian analytic school" exists (Jackson, 1991:32; Pintore, 1991; see also the special issue, edited by Pintore and Jori in the *International Journal for the Semiotics of Law*, volume 14, number 3, 2001). And more recently, the "Tartu-Moscow" school of cultural semiotics.

3. Elsewhere, for example, I have developed the outlines of a critically informed psychoanalytic semiotic approach rooted in Jacques Lacan (Milovanovic, 1992a,

2002) and critical theory. It might be the case that for those who advocate a legal semiotics as the umbrella term that some meta-narrative or meta-theory (i.e., an unstated and/or unexamined theory and collection of basic assumptions; or, if you prefer, a more hidden paradigm) is still being employed to ground the more openly semiotic analysis being done. And, implicitly, much of jurisprudes's legal analysis relies on some unsystematized semiotic analysis.

4. My current position as to whether legal semiotics can stand on its own as opposed to being an integral component in a sociology of law is that outside of the few prestigious and prolific writers in the Peircian and Greimasian approaches — Kevelson, Jackson, Landowski — most of the materials published or presented at the key annual law and semiotics conferences are mostly of the jurisprudence variety. My own inclination is that semiotics is most usefully subsumed under the sociology of law (see last chapter), and perhaps even, arguably, under jurisprudence. In other words, the conceptual tools semiotics provides may be usefully integrated within a jurisprudential or a sociology of law approach.

5. In the Canadian context see Asch's analysis of how the notion of "wildlife" was legally defined in such a way as to deny indigenous peoples access to their land and resources, 1992.

6. See, also, Flood, 1993; Kerruish, 1991:14-15, 82; Sarre, 1994; Heilpern, 1993; Cunneen, 1992; for the Canadian context, see Asch, 1992; Evan, 2002; Strelein, 2001).

7. Of course, the notion of "individuality" is problematic. It is ideologically packed. Durkheim, Weber, and Marx, as we will show below, explain how the notion of the individual — the self- directing, fully aware and consciously determining subject — was a relatively late historical development. This notion of the "centered subject" can be opposed by one developed by postmodernist thinkers (chapter 7): the "de-centered subject." The latter indicates that the subject is more determined than determining, less in control, and more the subject of semiotic forces, both idiosyncratic as well as those arising from manipulative ideological forces. Accordingly, Trubek's incorporation of the centered subject could be qualified. We could have used the notion of the decentered subject. Thus, on the second dimension of Trubek's diagram, realization of social values, we could include the Lacanian idea that self-actualization is to be measured by the degree to which the subject assumes her/his idiosyncratic desire. Lacanian ethics would operationalize the realization of this term as: "the extent to which he [she] has given ground relative to his [her] desire" (1992:314, 319; see also Rajchman, 1991:42; Lee, 1990). Accordingly, a legal order that systematically forces subjects to give ground to their desires would be one where a "low" score would be registered on the realization of social values dimension of Trubek's diagram.

PART 1:

THE CLASSIC THEORISTS — FOUNDATIONS OF A SOCIOLOGY OF LAW

1. EMILE DURKHEIM: TOWARD A SYSTEMATIC SOCIOLOGY OF LAW

Introduction. Emile Durkheim (1858-1917) was born in Epinal near Strasbourg, France. His early interest was in philosophy, but he always had a strong sociological focus. His first academic positions were minor appointments in provincial high schools. In 1885-1886, he took a year's leave of absence to study in Germany. In 1887, he received a professorship of sociology and education at Bordeaux. Later, in 1902 he attained the distinction of being appointed to the famous Sorbonne in Paris, France. There he founded an influential journal, *L'annee sociologique*. It was also at Bordeaux that Durkheim wrote three of his four most important books: *The Division of Labor in Society* (1893), *Rules of Sociological Method* (1895), and *Suicide* (1897). There was a gap of 15 years before he wrote *Elementary Forms of the Religious Life* (1912). In 1917, at the age of only 59, Durkheim died of a heart attack.[1]

Durkheim's main concern throughout his writings related to the question of social solidarity, social integration and what held society together. His approach was against focusing on the individual, suggesting that pure psychological explanations of social phenomena were sure to be incorrect (1964a:104). Pure sociology was his main concern. Take for example his classic statements: "Man is man only because he lives in society," and "collective life is not born from individual life, but it is, on the contrary, the second which is born of the first" (1958:60; 1964b:279). Many of his subsequent critics have said that this obsession for purely social or interpersonal factors led him to overlook political and economic determinants of social phenomena.

He insisted on the possibility of studying society scientifically. His very first rule was to "consider social facts as things" (1964a:14). Social facts can be characterized by their ability to resist change. They have a coercive quality, and their violation is met with some type of sanction, or at least some resistance. Law is the exemplary "social fact." But, to Durkheim, law is also a "visible symbol," an "external" index that reflects the nature of social solidarity. Since many sociological phenomena and a person's state of mind are inaccessible to an outsider, the best way to study society, according to Durkheim, is by studying law, which is the "objective" indicator of solidarity.

Much debate exists as to the importance of law in Durkheim's writing. There are those who argue that it was "indirect," "tangential," or a secondary concern (Hunt, 1978:65). To this extent, it might be argued that he did not really develop, nor was he interested in developing a sociology of law. He did not, for example, try to develop an overall framework or a particular methodology for a sociology of law. Others have argued that law indeed was his main concern (Lukes and Scull, 1983:1-2). For he has said "instead of treating sociology in *genere*... we have always been occupied only with legal or moral rules, studied in terms of their genesis and development" (Durkheim, cited in Lukes and Scull, 1983:2). A careful reading of Durkheim indicates that he was always preoccupied with the development of rules. It is a moot point whether in fact he actually wanted to develop a sociology of law. The evidence clearly indicates that in many of his writings he connected law to the whole ensemble of social existence.

EVOLUTION OF SOCIETY AND SOCIAL SOLIDARITY

The question of the evolution of society from the "simple" to the "more complex" forms played an important part in Durkheim's first major work, *The Division of Labor in Society* (1964b). By "simple" he meant a society marked by little division of labor; by "complex," or "more advanced," he meant a society characterized by an extensive division of labor. He sets out to analyze the different forms of solidarity, or the bonds, within these two types of societies. Bonds based on sameness reflected the idea that similar experiences and outlooks would find a natural attraction. "Difference," he tells us, "as likeness, can be a cause of mutual attraction" (ibid., 55). The basis of this attraction through difference rests on the idea that because of some incompleteness, the other who fulfills this lack, or who provides some resources, which make for more completeness, provides in the process a strong bonding force. Durkheim is quite direct here: "Only certain kinds of differences attract each other. They are those which, instead of opposing and excluding, compliment each other" (ibid., 55). It is in this book, too, that he advances the idea that society produces two forms of solidarity, "mechanical" and "organic." In fact, he argues that society develops from a primitive (mechanical) form to a higher (organic) form, the latter characterized by an extensive division of labor.

Mechanical solidarity was seen as the normal type of social bonds in primitive societies, where very little division of labor existed. The "glue" or the bond was sameness or similarity between members of society. Uniformity was central in this type of society. In other words, the range of personality types was not extensive. All were said to participate intimately in each others' lives. Standing above all the members of this type of society was the *conscience collective* (nowadays usually referred to as the collective conscience). It represents the collective identities, sentiments, and thoughts of the group. Its source was the same conditions and adaptations that all were said to share. All individual experiences, impressions and beliefs, then, were similar. The *conscience collective* was beyond the ability of the individual to change. It was a social fact. It was internalized by each member of society and became the background standard by which the person would judge him/herself and others. It was a conservative force in so much as those who dared to test its borders were subject to harsh reactions by the rest of the community. Individualism was almost nonexistent. It could not be tolerated because it implied that the person strayed some distance from the common bond. The morally good person was the one who participated entirely within the terms of the *conscience collective*.

Organic solidarity, on the other hand, exists in advanced, differentiated societies. In other words, it is prevalent in a society that has an extensive division of labor. In this highly specialized society, with an abundance of specialized functions and roles, mutual dependence is the glue. Organic solidarity is, Durkheim argued, much more binding than mechanical solidarity since it is based on people's need for each other because each complements the other for her/his inadequacies. In this society the *conscience collective* weakens. It does not have the same force. Collectivism is now replaced by individualism.

Durkheim argues that societies evolve from the condition of mechanical solidarity to organic solidarity. The decisive factor, the determinate cause, is *social density*.[2] With greater social density — that is, the higher concentration of the population — the formation of cities, and in the increasing development of transportation and communication, a greater division of labor is needed. The "struggle for existence is more acute" (Durkheim, 1964b:266). The result is an extended division of labor. With this increasing differentiation, the *conscience collective* loses its control. It too becomes more differentiated. And this leads to further differentiation because women/men are released from the bonds of a common morality.

But, Durkheim asks, how could all this be measured? How can we examine these phenomena scientifically? The answer for Durkheim was to look at the nature of the most prevalent type of law in existence. Knowing what type of law is most prevalent would then tell us something about the kinds of bonds of solidarity in existence. "[W]herever social solidarity exists, it resides not in a state of pure potentiality, but manifests its presence by sensible indices" (1964b:64).

The question, then, must be asked: what form of law would indicate one type of solidarity as opposed to the other? What were these "sensible indices?" Durkheim specifies the procedure to be followed. "Since law reproduces the principal forms of social solidarity, we have only to classify the different types of law to find therefrom the different types of social solidarity which correspond to it" (1964b:68). To this end, he identifies two types of sanctions or laws. One he calls "repressive," the other "restitutive."

Repressive law is characterized by punishment, by suffering, by some loss applied to the individual. This loss could include liberty, life, honor or fortune. Penal laws are its most clear type. This type of reaction arises spontaneously when acts go against the *conscience collective*. Crime, then, can be defined as acts that shock the common, or collective sentiments prevalent in most people's consciences. In primitive societies, it is the collective that reacts to acts that go against the common sentiment. Because of this, it is not necessary to have written obligatory rules. The rule is well understood by all. Punishment then is retributive. The offended collective sentiments that reside within all cannot accept contradictions or challenges. To allow such challenges is to have the very fabric of society undermined. The existence of crime can then be traced to the existence of strong collective reactions by the community.

Restitutive law can be characterized as *"the return of things as they were, in the re-establishment of troubled relations to their normal state..."* (1964b:69; emphasis in the original). He gives the example of civil laws, commercial law, administrative and constitutional law and all types of procedural laws.[3] The system of restitutive law has a non-punitive emphasis. The goal is simply to return relations to their previous state, whereas for repressive laws, it is not necessary, on a theoretical level, to have a central enforcement machinery.

For restitutive laws, special "organs" were required. Durkheim cites examples of administrative tribunals, councils of arbitration, and industrial tribunals. These, he argues, become increasingly specialized. Legislators, in codifying restitutive laws, must be especially concerned with specifying with great clarity what the obligations and the appropriate reaction to their infractions entail. Magistrates and lawyers, because of their special skills in interpreting and applying law, become necessary in resolving conflicts (law-finding). Also implied with restitutive laws is the need for a central state and the formal machinery for law-making and law enforcement.[4]

Where restitutive laws are highly developed an "occupational morality" develops with it (1964b:227). That is, within fields of specialization a certain obedience to norms and rules of behavior are required. For example, the American Bar Association and' the American Medical Association have codes of ethics. To go against these norms is to invoke censure or reprimand. These associations, then, because they have more permanence than transactions with transient clients, also develop a particular common ideological outlook. In many ways the *conscience collective* of primitive societies is now replaced by a multiplicity of smaller *conscience collectives*. Each of these binds its members.

Restitutive laws, then, are not rooted in the *conscience collective*, and thus are not marked by strong punitive reactions. Rather, they focus on re-establishing relations that have gone wrong.

A little more than seven years after the publication of *Division of Labor in Society*, Durkheim expanded his analysis in an article entitled "Two Laws of Penal Evolution" (1901; see 1983c). (Actually, the title could be clearer if we were to use "Principles" rather than "Laws.") Here he spelled out in greater detail the evolution of society, the forms of solidarity, and the form of punishment for law violation. He offered two principles, one "quantitative," the other "qualitative."

The first principle, the "quantitative" form, states that "the intensity of punishment is the greater the more closely societies approximate to a less developed type — and the more the central power assumes an absolute character" (Durkheim, 1983c:102). In primitive societies, he argues, punishments were severe. In explaining this he first notes, "it is in the evolution of crime that one must seek the cause determining the evolution of punishment" (ibid., 121). His argument, then, is circular. He already noted that primitive societies are characterized by a strong *conscience collective*. Acts going against the *conscience collective* arouse similar and focused energies. The evolution of the type of punishment, then, simply follows the evolution of the type of society. In complex societies marked by an extensive division of labor, the *conscience collective* loses its hold, and becomes more differentiated, allowing even further differentiation. Here the form of punishment is restitutive, revolving around the need to mend relations that have gone wrong. Harsh sanctions here are not necessary.

His second principle, "qualitative" law, states that "deprivation of liberty, and of liberty alone, varying in time according to the seriousness of the crime, tends to become more and more the normal means of social control" (1983c:114). In primitive societies, he argues, imprisonment serves no need. Here responsibility is collective. All take part in inflicting the punishment. In many ways, all are police, prosecutors, judges, jurors and punishers. If the violator absconds, a kinsman can be substituted. After all, it has been the collective sentiment that has been violated and the aroused sentiment must be relieved.

In primitive societies the conditions do not exist for the notion of a prison. These societies did not need separate buildings to punish, since the whole group participated in punishing any wayward group member. In primitive societies houses are built exclusively for private purposes. With the development of "city states," he notes, special houses were built to serve particular functions. Temples, for example, appear at a relatively late period. The subsequent specialization of buildings led to the logic of buildings that function as prisons. The early prisons had a philosophy of punishment consistent with repressive law. But this gradually gave way to the present-day form where deprivation of liberty itself was seen as punishment. As individualism developed in more complex societies, it was only natural that the liberty associated with it was now to be the focus of punishment. This, too, necessitated the use of prison to assure that the violator did not try to prematurely regain his liberty against the wishes of the state.

In sum, for Durkheim, to understand crime, punishment and the nature of social solidarity, one should analyze an external index which is its expression. The most prevalent form of law in existence, then, tells us much about the nature of society.[5]

The Abnormal Forms

Durkheim spends most of his analysis in the *Division of Labor in Society* on the normal, spontaneous forms of societal development. He spells out the ideal progression or evolution of a society. In the last short three chapters, however, he presents the "abnormal forms," of which there are three types.

Durkheim assumes that society, left to itself, will evolve from the primitive to the complex form. The key is spontaneous development. As society evolves, all parts and all subjects, adjust themselves to the overall structure of society. To this extent, society runs smoothly. It is in a state of "equilibrium." It is only through groping and mutual adjustments that the elements of society become adjusted. However, there are also instances (the "abnormal forms") where these adjustments do not take place, producing a state Durkheim calls "anomie."

People's desire and needs, for Durkheim, have diverse sources; they require some satisfaction, but yet also some externally imposed limitation.[6] As Durkheim (1961:39-40) says: "A need, a desire, freed of all restraints, and all rules, no longer geared to some determinate objective, and through this some connection, limited and contained, can be nothing but a source of constant anguish, for the person experiencing it." But sometimes regulation or adjustment is not brought about. The elements (the "organs") have not adjusted themselves in a rapidly advancing society. Such societies experienced a state of *anomie* (Durkheim, 1964b:368). This is one of the abnormal forms. Commentators have often translated "anomie" as a state of normlessness, at other times as a state of deregulation.

The second abnormal form focuses on the rules themselves as the cause of evil. This is the "forced" division of labor. According to Durkheim, "for the division of labor to produce solidarity, it is not sufficient... that each have his task; it is still necessary that this task be fitting to him" (1964b:375). If some "external force" coerces subjects, or constrains them in a function or a role, then a gap remains between "individual natures and social functions" (ibid., 376). "Happiness" is realized when a person's "needs are in relation to his means" (ibid.). Said in another way, equilibrium exists when a person's "nature" is in accord with the social function s/he performs. Spontaneously divided labor is where "natural" inequalities (i.e., in abilities, temperament, dexterity, potentials, and so forth) are exactly reflected or expressed in the relations that have evolved. Those, for example, who have excelled by their own talent, should be rewarded in kind. But in the forced division of labor, relations are being held together by force and constraint: individual nature and social function are not in accord. Thus it may very well be the case that on a formal level, two individuals "freely" consent to a contract; that is, there is a verbal or a written agreement. But the objective consequences may favor one over the other because one may have entered the terms with more resources at her/his disposal. The other contractor may simply have accepted what was offered.[7]

The third abnormal form is where different functions of members of society are distributed in such a way that people are deprived of fulfilling activity (1964b:389). This lack of coordination produces waste. "Where functions languish," Durkheim tells us, "they are not well specialized, they are badly co-ordinated, and incompletely feel their mutual dependence" (ibid., 390). An example here could be a rigidly bureaucratized society where functions of members no longer are in accord with changes in society, but nevertheless the person carries them out routinely and monotonously.

In sum, the abnormal forms of division of labor are pathological cases. That is, they go against the movement toward cooperation, mutual fulfillment and happiness that inheres in the spontaneous forms. If there were any convergence among the three classic thinkers in sociology — Durkheim, Weber and Marx — one of its closest examples would be with the notion of the "free" contract. We now turn to its examination by Durkheim.

FORM OF LAW, CONTRACT AND LEGAL THOUGHT

Given a form of law, the questions to be asked are: What is the appropriate form of legal thought to be used to arrive at agreements? To assure promises made are met? And if they are not, what remedies or means of enforcement can be mobilized?

Contracts, in the majority of cases, imply reciprocal obligation. Two people, in other words, orient their behavior to each other, regardless of how brief, in order to exchange something. Some agreement is reached in the process. For Durkheim, the contract "is, *par excellence*, the juridical expression of co-operation" (1964b:123, emphasis in the original). Thus "the contract is the symbol of exchange" (ibid., 125). We may safely say, with Durkheim, that the form of contract, therefore, can again be seen as an index of the type of solidarity in existence. He returns to the whole question later in his career in the form of lecture notes, which were subsequently published after his death in *Professional Ethics and Civic Morals*.

The development of the contract is connected with the development of the division of labor. Here he develops a similar notion as Maine (1861) in *Ancient Law*. Maine argued that the progression of law could be characterized by its movement from status to contract. Durkheim notes a similar development.

Durkheim's analysis once again begins with primitive societies. True contracts, he argued, did not appear until a late age. Primitive societies depended on various forms to assure that agreements were fulfilled. So, for example, the *blood covenant* was such that if people needed to create ties outside of the immediate family, the form used duplicated what they knew well. They shared blood in some manner (i.e., each placed a few drops into a jar and both dipped their hands into it and hence created blood ties), they duplicated the primary bond of kinship, namely the blood ties of the family. Similarly, one could also share common food, or drink from the same cup. Symbolically, then, these served the same function.

Real contracts are those where one thing is immediately exchanged for another. Here the relation ends. One product is exchanged directly for another and each goes her/his separate way.

Then, Durkheim argued, there is a form of exchange and the bond, however temporary, that goes with it, in which some declaration is made in words (Durkheim, 1983b:199). This he called the *solemn contract*. The oath or the invocation of a divine being is an integral part of the bond, which created a third party to the contract. This third party, a divine being, became the guarantor of the declaration made. "Each contracting party," Durkheim continued, "pronounces some phrase that binds him and a formula by which he calls down upon his head certain divine curses if he should fail in his undertaking" (ibid., 199). Thus one exchanger could pronounce: "I promise you the delivery of 20 lbs of tomatoes in two weeks, and let God be my witness." Sometimes this was even followed by sacrifices and magical rites. That is, the words themselves in the promise made became sacred. They no longer belonged to the individual transactor alone (even to this day we have such expressions as "you have my word on it"). Words became things that could be possessed. But these words had to be uttered in a precise way. There was a particular formula for their use and only this assured fulfillment of promise. Here "if the solemn ritual is lacking, there is no contract" (ibid., 200). If one does not fulfill the promise made s/he has offended the divine authority, the third party. S/he would be exposed to vengeance by the Gods. The words uttered, then, could not be changed. They were no longer hers/his to change. They could only be carried out. The solemn ritual committed the two parties to the contract. Unlike the blood covenant, it could be used for many everyday transactions.

This type of contract was to give way to a modern type, the *consensual contract*. The causes of this change were numerous. An extensive increase in trade made solemn contracts hindering formalities. The need for flexibility, particularly in a vastly increased pace of life, too, made the old types obsolete. And generally, the demands of the new economic order were too much to allow the more primitive form of contract to exist. Exchanges and transfers of property were all too frequent. But here Durkheim cautions us: just because there is a need for a particular institution does not mean that it will materialize by itself out of a vacuum. The way the new form, the consensual contract, came into being was as follows. The previous solemn contract had two major elements: promises expressed in words and guaranteed by divine authority, and promises expressed to others in words that s/he now possesses as a thing. Thus breaking a promise now means offending the Gods as well as the other. The bond was two-fold: to the Gods and to the other. It is the second that eventually detached itself from the first and became the consensual contract (Durkheim, 1983b:210). Divine authority, too, in an advancing society, was becoming generally weaker. And this, in combination with the needs generated by a complex, busier life, further necessitated this split. For Durkheim, the contract based on solemn ritual was, however, the stronger bond. And to this day the more important transactions often have some characteristics of the earlier forms. Think, for example, the various "swearing in" ceremonies during trial court proceedings and in the appointment of high government officials.

The consensual contract, or the "contract by mutual consent" (1983b:212), was for Durkheim "a revolutionary innovation in the law" (ibid., 219). Its most important feature was that it invoked the will. Only if I willingly enter into an agreement can you demand that I fulfill the promise. If the agreement was imposed on me, if my will was not responsible for the promise, the contract is not binding (ibid., 221).

This led Durkheim to offer his ideal contract, the highest form, the *just contract*, or the *contract of equity*. For Durkheim,

> the coming on the scene of the contract by mutual consent, together with an increase in human sympathies, inclined the minds of men to the idea that the contract was only moral and only to be recognized and given sanction by society, provided it was not merely a means of exploiting one of the contracting parties, in a word, provided it was just [1983b:223].

Here Durkheim recognized that a "freely" entered contract, in itself, does not necessarily mean that the contract is "just." Put in another way, consensual contracts, by focusing on a subjective dimension (free will) do not assure objective consequences that are fair and just. There are times, Durkheim argued, where the individual was compelled to "yield what he did not wish to, and it takes from him by force something that he owned... a case of extortion" (1983b:225). Thus fairness of the contract should not only turn on the question of consent.

"Equality in the external conditions of conflict" is necessary to assure that: (1) functions are linked to one another spontaneously; and (2) that individuals will attach themselves to their functions (Durkheim, 1964b:381). For example, inheritance makes the "external" conditions unbalanced and hence the contract can favor one over the other. In the forced division of labor this imbalance is at its maximum.

The key element in defining fairness, or what constitutes being *just*, for Durkheim, is "social value." He argues that objects of exchange can be measured by the amount of useful labor, which they reflect (1964b:382). Three elements (or what social scientists refer to as variables), according to Durkheim, define social value: (1) "the sum of efforts necessary to produce the object"; (2) "the intensity of the needs which it satisfies"; and (3) "the extent of the satisfaction it brings" (ibid.). Notice that a range exists for each of the elements (in the chapter below on Karl Marx we shall see that certain useful comparisons can be made with the idea of "use value.")

Genuine consent, for Durkheim, occurs only where "the services exchanged have an equivalent social value" (1964b:383). If, for example, we take two exchangers, A and B, and look at the three elements defining social value, giving each element a range from 1-10, and note that if person A and B each receives a combined score of 24 after the transaction, then the exchange or contract is "just." We are of course assuming for the sake of this example that we could provide quantitative scores reflecting these three aspects rather accurately. This notwithstanding, if person A receives a 24, person B a 12, there would be a basis to conclude that the exchange may, perhaps, have been agreed to (as in the consensual contract), but remains unjust (we shall see that there is much here that can be usefully compared with Marx's idea of the appropriation of "surplus value").

In other words, contracts are balanced and fair (an "equilibrium of wills") if inherent inequalities ("internal inequalities," ibid., 384) are the sole bases of exchange. "Internal inequalities" may reflect natural differences in, say, muscular dexterity, thereby allowing person A to pick one bushel of apples in two hours; with person B it may take two and a half hours. One subject may receive an additional advantage, say, by way of inheritance, but that does not reflect inherent difference (i.e., unequal abilities, hereditary constraints and so forth), or differences arrived at by way of self-development. "Mere verbal consent," for Durkheim, is not the determinant of a fair contract (ibid., 383). Here, one contractor is forced to accept the terms of the contract. In other words, the latter may have to accept any price for her/his services. This, for Durkheim, produces a disequilibrium in the conditions of exchange. Durkheim is quite direct:

> If one class of society is obliged, in order to live, to take any price for its services, while another can abstain from such action thanks to resources at its disposal which, however, are not neces-

sarily due to any social superiority, the second has an unjust advantage over the first at law [1964b:384].

Both Max Weber and Karl Marx, we shall show below, also describe the often hidden repressive dimensions of the contract.

For Durkheim, the contract, in the normal division of labor, is a temporary "truce" in the competition among individuals. Subjects in a complex society seek things that they need, that fulfill them. Ideally, for a just contract to exist, each should give free consent. The contract arrived at should not have forced one or the other to unwillingly agree to the terms. And this coercive consent arises where some external factor (i.e., inheritance) has placed one in a more advantageous position. An imbalance has been created.

Thus Durkheim's prediction states that the just contract arises because of an enlightened public wishing to weigh the objective outcomes of the contract in terms of fairness or equity. Society, then, intervenes to assure that the objective consequences are just. We have this in present law in such stipulations as "good faith dealings." The nemesis of the just contract, for Durkheim, again, is inheritance.

Inheritance creates inequality directly from birth. This received wealth is unrelated to a person's merits. "There cannot be rich and poor at birth," he tells us, "without there being unjust contracts" (1964b:384). Thus, to ensure a just contract, the available resources of each must be equal. Only then will things be exchanged fairly; that is, according to their true value. Indeed, for Durkheim, inheritance goes against the whole spirit of individualism that inheres in a society marked by an extensive division of labor. It was Marx and Weber, we shall see in the following chapters, who extended this notion of external inequality when analyzing the vast differences in wealth induced by capitalism.

Property

Where did private property rights come from? How has the right to private property been established? In answering these questions Durkheim turns to religious beliefs. "The origins of property are to be found in the nature of certain religious beliefs" (1983a:165).

The right to property, according to Durkheim, can be characterized by its "right of exclusion." I can use a particular thing from which I can exclude others. To understand how this right of exclusion came about one must look at how, the world over, the sacred exists separately and distinctly from the profane. Sacred entities can only be touched by priests or others who have a sacred character. In other words, they are removed from general circulation. And everything that touches the sacred also becomes sacred. Special individuals, priests, have the power to make objects they touch sacred.

Durkheim, examining primitive property markers of land of clans or families, notes that they too were permeated with the sacred. Subjects who were not members of the family or the clan were excluded from this landed property's use. Boundaries to cultivated fields were surrounded by marker stones. These stones represented the sacred. Customs assured that they would be respected. Thus, the fields had sacred qualities. Elaborate rituals established these grounds as sacred. These rituals, often combined with a sacrifice, established a moral bond between the clan or family members and the gods. Henceforth "the land has ...become attached to men by a sacred bond" (1983a:179). Thus the right to property had its origins here: "Man's right of property is only a substitute for the right of property of the gods" (ibid.). The respect we have for property, then, is respect that we once had for the sacred now transferred to property. The rights of gods now are the rights of women/men. Disrespect for property became equated with disrespect for the sacred. Both brought the wrath of god.

Initially, the clan owned the sacred land in common. The fishing and hunting grounds, too, were sacred and collectively owned. But how did individual ownership come about? How did the individual come to develop private property rights?

Durkheim offers two "causes." First, a member of the family is elevated in status "in some way — by a chain of circumstances" (1983a:186). This person becomes endowed with prestige beyond the rest of the group. Now the things that were bound to the group are directly bonded to this superior individual. Since the person was invested with this status, property belonging to the group now belongs more so to this person. With the coming of patriarchal and paternal power this process was complete (ibid.). Authority now rested with the head of the family. He became the supreme owner of property. The sacred character of the land was now invested in the head of the family.

The second cause, which "ran parallel" and "reinforced" the first, was the development of movable property. In pre-industrial societies, primarily agricultural societies, property was land, which had a sacred character and was owned by the community. All property was characterized by its immovable nature. Hence, all things of the clan were connected within this narrow sphere. But with the development of industry and trade, property became movable. The individual could now dispose of things outside of real estate more freely. Property had loosened itself from the moral and sacred binds of the community. Once cast adrift, nothing made them immovable. This property now depended only on the person who had acquired it. As opposed to real estate, this property had a much freer quality about it. The individual who possessed it had flexibility in its use. Henceforth, according to Durkheim,

> it is man who stands above *things*, and it is a certain individual in particular who occupies this position, that is, who owns or possesses. Whole categories of profane things take shape independently of the family estate, free themselves of it and thus become the subject of the new right of property, one that is in its essence individual [1983a:189; emphasis in the original].

Property, originally communal and sacred, thus becomes divided into the landed (real estate) and movable forms. Different kinds of law develop to stipulate the use of each. Movable property is the more flexible and freer. And the communal property is increasingly replaced by rights of private property. The weakening of the *conscience collective* finds its counterpart in the ascendance of individual rights to private property. This is in combination with the diminution of the sacred. The individual is released from the bonds of the collectivity and absorbs the divine qualities originally attached to communal property in the form of private property.

Summary

Law, Durkheim showed us, was intimately connected with the nature of solidarity. Knowing the most prevalent form of law would tell us much about the nature of society. Law was an external indicator of social bonds. In primitive society, the *conscience collective* was supreme. The bonds of solidarity were mechanical. What held society together, the attractive force, the "glue," was the sameness of its individual members. Those who went against the collective sentiments would be met with a uniform hostile reaction. Crime, then, could be defined as an act that offended the *conscience collective*. The stronger the collective reaction, the more serious was the crime. Laws were repressive. They were characterized by their punitiveness. Since the whole community was offended, no need existed for a professional staff of enforcers. All were police, prosecutors, judges, jurors and punishers.

As society evolved and as it became more complex, more differentiated, a new bond appeared. This bond's characteristic was the attraction of opposites. A society marked by an extensive division of labor — that is, with many specializations that were interdependent — demanded restitutive laws. It was no longer punishment that was the most prevalent form of reaction, but rather the emphasis was to reestablish an equilibrium. The *conscience collective*, too, became weaker, allowing subjects to further differentiate. The individual was born.

Whereas in primitive societies, *status* — one's overall standing in the community (the clan, the family) — was intimately implicated in transactions, in the more evolved societies the exemplary instrument, the form for exchange, was the *contract*. The state with its functionaries and machinery now assured the fulfillment of the contract. It established the external conditions for its use. A special class arose to litigate. Lawyers, with their special training and skills, were now needed to handle the numerous and complex contracts that were negotiated.

Law, in a society with an extensive division of labor (spontaneously divided), was not primarily repressive. It was primarily facilitative. In fact, in these societies the division of labor served the function that was previously fulfilled by the *conscience collective*. In the abnormal forms, however, undue constraint produced unjust contracts. Even where an agreement has been signed, where each consented to the terms of the contract "willingly," coercion could still underlie the contract. Here, repressive formalism militated against individuals realizing their full value of services or commodities in exchange. The ideal for Durkheim was that all external forces be equal. Social inequalities should match *natural* inequalities. This is the state of a spontaneously divided labor. The ideal is not anarchy, but rather a carefully regulated society where each specialized role is intimately connected in the spirit of cooperation with a multitude of others. The clearest expression of these cooperative relationships is the *just contract* where things or services exchanged realize their exact social value.

In sum, law in a spontaneous division of labor is autonomous and general. It does not reflect the interests of a particular class. At the same time liberty is found *in* law. The formally just contract, by controlling external force, assured the maximum fulfillment of social values — liberty, equality and community (cooperative development).

Notes

1. For an informative and general background about Durkheim, see Parsons, 1974. A number of works by Durkheim have been collected and published posthumously: in 1924, *Sociology and Philosophy* (1974); in 1925, *Moral Education: A Study in the Theory and Application of the Sociology of Education* (1961); in 1928, *Socialism* (1962); in 1937, *Montesquieu and Rousseau: Forerunners of Sociology* (1960); in 1938, *The Evolution of Educational Thought* (1977); in 1950, the *Professional Ethics and Civic Morals* (1958); in 1955, *Pragmatism and Sociology* (1983d).

2. Ironically, even though Durkheim wished to distance himself from Darwinism and the Social Darwinism of Herbert Spencer, he nevertheless uses this notion to explain the evolution of society.

3. Criminal law, the repressive form, can be distinguished from procedural criminal law. The question in the latter revolves around fair play, fundamental fairness, or fair process to be used in arriving at a decision.

4. Durkheim makes a further distinction. Restitutive law can be separated into two types (1964b:115-122). Relations that he calls *negative* revolve around the relationship between the individual and things. Property and tort law are primary examples. These simply dictate that the subject not harm another. On the other hand, *positive* relations are rooted in cooperation itself, which develops out of the division of labor. Here we find contract law, constitutional law, and, generally, procedural law.

5. For a critique of Durkheim's view of law, see Hunt, 1978; and Lukes and Scull, 1983. For a Marxist read of Durkheim, see Pearce, 1989. For an economic explanation of punishment, see Rusche and Kirchheimer, 1968; also see Foucault, 1977a.

6. Pearce (1989:87) has argued that Durkheim and Jacques Lacan's notion of desire "complement each other." He also notes that Lacan's notion of "the name of the father" resonates with Durkheim. Indeed, Lacan in 1950 (co-authored with Michel Cenac) presented a paper entitled "A Theoretical Introduction to the Functions of Psychoanalysis in Criminology" that very much echoes Durkheimian themes (Lacan, 1996; see also my comments on this article, Milovanovic, 1997).

7. This idea of *repressive formalism* can be extended. For example, recall, from our introductory chapter, our two speeders appearing before the court for driving 15 miles an hour over the speed limit. One makes $100,000, the other $5,000. Both are treated fairly; that is, they are formally equal before the court. At the end of the law-finding phase they are both given a $50 fine. Here, equally situated are equally treated. But the objective consequences are different. Surely, $50 for the lower income person is a greater felt punishment than it is for the higher income person.

2. MAX WEBER: LAW IN ECONOMY AND SOCIETY

Introduction. Max Weber, with little dispute, stands out as one of the foremost scholars in the sociological tradition. Even one of his staunchest critics has said "one could describe [his work]...as almost superhuman: it is astonishing that anyone could know so much about so many legal systems" (Andreski, 1984:86). Only recently have scholars turned to his thoughts on law.

Weber was born in 1864 in an upper middle class German family. He had said, "I am a member of the bourgeois classes, I feel myself as such and I am educated in its views and ideals" (cited in Hunt, 1978:94). He later chose to study law. His doctoral dissertation of 1889 was entitled "A Contribution to the History of Medieval Business Organizations." Here his studies of the early beginnings of capitalism signaled his later concerns with the rise of capitalism. While training to become a member of the legal bar in 1891, he wrote "Roman Agrarian History and Its Significance in Public and Private Law." This allowed him to become an instructor in law at the University of Berlin in 1893. In this book, he studied the early legal institutions of Roman agriculture. At the University of Berlin he taught commercial law and legal history. In 1894, he accepted a chair in economics at the University of Freiburg. Weber was to suffer a major nervous breakdown a short time later. For over four and a half years he wrote not a word.

When he recovered (late 1902 and early 1903) he began to write at an incredible rate. Three major essays came forth in 1903 alone. He had an insatiable desire to explain as many phenomena as he could. A short time later he wrote the classic *The Protestant Ethic and the Spirit of Capitalism* (1904-1905). Weber examined the relatively independent influence of ideas on the development of capitalism. Here his "debate with the ghost of Marx" was at full throttle.[1] He rejected the idea that the materialist, economic factor alone, was the cause of social phenomena.

It was in his two-volume monumental work, *Economy and Society*, first published in 1921 after his death, that we find Weber's fully developed sociology of law. The scope of the subject material, covered in incredible detail, is breathtaking. His work can truly be called encyclopedic. Marianne Weber noted in her biography of Max Weber that the book unintentionally grew into his major work. During 1918 and 1920, Weber concentrated on fine-tuning definitions and concepts, especially in part one of his work. He spent much time with the categories that he had developed, trying to clarify each. He died a short time later, in 1920, from pneumonia at the age of 56, his work incomplete. His two-volume work was, at best, his first draft.[2]

Parsons has stated that "the core of Weber's substantive sociology lies neither in his treatment of economic and political problems nor in his sociology of religion, but in his sociology of law" (cited in Hunt, 1978:102). Ironically, it is only recently that much of his analysis has been subject to careful examination.

CAPITALISM AND LAW

One of Weber's primary concerns was the rise of capitalism. He wanted to know what forces had allowed its development (Weber, 1958). He was also interested in explaining how, with the rise of capitalism, certain institutions developed. The central issues revolved around cause, the form of law and legal thought, rationality, domination, and the development of the contract and the legal subject in law (the juridic subject). Why is it, he would often ask, that subjects orient their behavior to some order? And, did the development of the contract necessarily assure greater freedom *in* law?

Part one of his *Economy and Society*, as we noted, was heavily oriented to definitions and concepts. Here he offers us a formal definition of law:

> an order will be called *law* if it is externally guaranteed by the probability that coercion (physical or psychological), to bring about conformity or avenge violation, will be applied by a *staff* of people holding themselves specially ready for that purpose [1978:34, emphasis in the original].

One can immediately note that on the surface of it, the critical element in his definition is the existence of some staff ready to apply coercion for enforcement. But further reading of Weber indicates that he had an even deeper meaning. Law was really a subcategory of his notion of legitimate order (Trubek, 1972:726). An "order" for Weber existed when "conduct is, approximately or on the average, oriented toward determinable 'maxims'" (1978:31). By "maxims," he means rules of conduct. In other words, Weber tells us that people consciously or unconsciously take into consideration some stable set of commonly accepted assumptions and rules of behavior (that is, they orient themselves to an order). Consider, for example, why mass collisions don't occur on a busy sidewalk or at a major street intersection. Furthermore, an order is *valid* (i.e., legitimate) if members not only orient their behavior to this normative order but also see it as obligatory, as binding. Externally measured, an order can be defined as valid to the degree that action has a high probability of being oriented to it.

But law was just one form of a legitimate order. He also identified other orientations: "affectual," where subjects surrender themselves emotionally to an order; "value-rational," where subjects comply because they see the order as a statement of "ultimate" values such as an ethical type; or "religious," where orientation to the order is due to the belief that salvation will occur if the order is obeyed (1978:33).

Hence, Weber's definition of law more accurately includes coercion as an *added* element. Subjects may, for example, orient their behavior to an order because of coercive sanctions. They may also do so because they feel the law is legitimate; that is, it is seen as being right. In this case, then, coercion is not necessary. The whole question of law turns on why subjects orient themselves to law.

The question of cause, for Weber, was critical. He rejected, in contrast to some variants of Marxism, the view that economic factors were necessarily the prime cause in the development of law. Consider his classic statement:

> I would like to protest the statement...that some one factor, be it technology or economy, can be the 'ultimate' or 'true' cause of another. If we look at the causal lines, we see them run, at one time, from technical to economic and political matters, at another from political to religious and economic ones, etc... [T]he view...that the economic is in some sense the ultimate point in the chain of causes is completely finished as a scientific proposition [cited in Bendix and Roth, 1971:242-243].

Weber argues that the economy is one factor, but that many factors are simultaneously at work in producing social phenomena. In this multi-causal approach, the researcher must examine many factors and determine how much weight is to be placed on each *cause*. Weber was more concerned with constellations, or the interplay of several forces together exerting an influence. For Weber, looking for a unique (singular) cause was naive and counterproductive.

The method of the social scientist should be as follows. First, the social scientist must choose a particular topic, which already reflects his or her value preference. Second, s/he must select specific possible "causes" out of a whole constellation of factors on the basis of the question s/he is addressing. Third s/he must abstract possible "causal" chains (i.e., in the form of "if X then Y," "if A then B," etc.). Fourth, s/he must then eliminate one or more of these causal chains, one by one, and see if the effect (the result) is in the predicted direction. If, for example, eliminating one of the factors indicates that the result will still be the same, then this factor would not be seen as contributory and would be removed as a possible causal factor. If, on the other hand, the result would be different, then we have identified one factor in the causal chain. Finally, s/he will determine which factors are of importance in producing a particular social phenomenon. That is, s/he can now identify the decisive factor(s) that are at work (Weber, 1949:173, 182-183; Parsons, 1968:610-611; Hekman, 1979:71-74).

According to Weber, law, once developed, can have an influence on the economic sphere. This is a "recursive" model, meaning that the economic may be one of the important factors in the development of law, but law, once established, may then have an effect on the economic sphere of society (Weber, 1978:667). In the social sciences, some argue that this way of reasoning is sound and provides an accurate picture of reality. Others, in criticism, argue that it can lead to circular reasoning or, in other words, tautological reasoning.

Why, Weber asks, is the form of law that develops under capitalism quite in accord with it? That is, why has a form of law developed that is closely related to the internal dynamics of capitalism? For example, the dynamics of formal rational law are said to be in close accord with capitalistic dynamics, e.g., as reflected in utilitarianism, profit maximization, the ethic of individual responsibility, etc. The connection may seem self-evident, but Weber wanted to know how it came to be. The key, for Weber, lies with the needs of a capitalist economic system. For Weber, "the modern capitalist enterprise rests primarily on *calculation* and presupposes a legal and administrative system, whose functioning can be rationally predicted...by virtue of its fixed general norms, just like the expected performance of a machine" (1978:1394, emphasis in the original). In other words, this economic system needs a stable framework within which firms, as well as individuals, can calculate appropriate means to attain specific ends and within which to predict possible results with a fair amount of precision.

Actions must be predictable, at least within a knowable and calculable range, for effective planning to occur. In the rational calculation of costs and benefits, for example, one must be assured that the many variables can be quantified. Some predictability must exist. Some certainty that, given act A, act B will follow, must be assured. Stability must exist so that a subject may not only know what to expect of the other, but also what the other expects of him/her. Finally, some method for enforcement must be in place to assure that agreements are kept. And if broken, remedies must be readily available.

But just because an economic system needs a particular legal system does not in itself assure that it will be discovered. How then, asks Weber, has this discovery come about? And how is it that subjects now willingly orient themselves to this order, to this stable environment?

To this end, we first examine his forms of law and legal thought. In other words, we can identify particular types of law and particular ways of legal reasoning. We then turn to the question of how "domination" is sustained (in the West, the word domination is used more often in its pejorative sense, unlike the sense that Weber implied). Then, we address the connection between domination and forms of legal thought. We will summarize his ideas concerning the development of capitalism in connection with the emergence of bureaucracy, rationalism, and the present day form of law, "formal rationality." Finally, we turn to his explanation of the exemplary form of exchange, the contract, where he discusses the notion of freedom and coercion *in* law. We turn first to his typology of forms of law and legal thought.

FORMS OF LAW AND LEGAL THOUGHT

In order to examine social phenomena, Weber constructed what he called "ideal types." These were simply theoretical constructions that aided research. They did not necessarily reflect reality. Rather, they helped the researcher in her/his investigation to illuminate and clarify existing complex phenomena. They were, in other words, "heuristic" tools. Unlike the "hard" sciences where much technology can be applied in the investigation of physical interactions, the social scientist works with conceptual tools, which offer varying degrees of access to and understanding of complex and dynamic phenomena. Weber was a pioneer in developing these heuristic tools in the sociology of law, particularly in using them to clarify the forms of law and legal thought.

The critical question for Weber was: What are the underlying processes in law-making (formulating laws) and law-finding (applying rules and reaching decisions) at particular historical periods? Are there regularities that exist? If there are, how are they structured? And how are they connected to the needs of other institutions in society?

To this end, Weber constructed a typology, a summary diagram of types of legal systems and legal thought (see Figure 2). What this typology does is to capture different ideal types; it gives us a beginning understanding of complex legal systems. It sensitizes the researcher to important aspects of a legal system and its form of reasoning used in arriving at legal decisions. In reality, of course, we are unlikely to find these clear-cut ideal types. In the real world, we probably see mixtures. However, in examining legal system historically, we can distinguish some that resemble more one type rather than another.

Weber's typology of forms of law and legal thought can be constructed by the use of two dimensions: the degree of rationality and the degree of formality. Each dimension (or variable) can be ranged from "high" to "low"; in other words, a legal order can be placed within a continuum on each dimension. For simplification purposes, however, it can be collapsed into two categories (or to use sociological jargon, we can dichotomize the variables). And since we have two possible categories on the rationality dimension (high, low), and two possible categories on the formality dimension (high, low), we have a two-by-two diagram providing four possible ideal types. In other words, we can construct four possible pure models of forms of law and legal thought. More complex ideal types could be constructed. For example, we could construct a three-by-three, a four-by-four, etc. But notice the trade-offs: a two-by-two schema provides us with a heuristic tool with a degree of simplicity and a starting point in examining complex phenomena. However, as we add categories a very complex schema with a multitude of intersecting points would emerge that may approximate actual phenomena, but would also bring the attendant loss of a "handle," a beginning point in examining complex phenomena.

The dimension referred to as "formality" stood for the employment of criteria, standards, principles and logic that are internal, that are intrinsic to the legal system. In other words, formality stood for the application by lawmakers and law-finders of rules and procedures that are totally internal to a given legal system. Put in yet another way, the decision maker is bound by some general body of laws and a procedure for its application. S/he does not have to go outside of this. Decision making takes place entirely within this framework. "Law...is 'formal' to the extent that, in both substantive and procedural matters, only unambiguous general characteristics of the facts of the case are taken into account" (Weber, 1978:656-657).

Opposing a formal system is a "substantive" system (or one with a "low" degree of "formality"). Here, decision making takes place by the use of rules and procedures that are outside of the formal system. In other words, decision making employs external criteria. Thus some ethical, ideological and political criteria or standards may be applied. For example, some "political prisoners" in U.S. prisons may attempt to introduce United Nations' standards of human rights into U.S. court proceedings. Prosecutors, however, will insist that arguments remain within the formal framework of law.

Thus, along this first dimension, legal systems can be seen as more formal or more substantive in orientation. In Figure 2, we have specified the degree of formality as being either "high" (more formal) or "low" (more substantive).

The second dimension, "rationality," means "following some criteria of decision which is applicable to all like cases." In other words, it stands for generality; it means dealing with all similarly situated subjects in a similar way. In Weber's words, it is characterized by "the reduction of the reasons relevant in the decision of concrete individual cases to one or more 'principles,' i.e., legal propositions" (ibid., 655). On the other hand, irrationality (or low rationality) means that similar cases are dealt with differently. The same case, then, can have different outcomes. Little, if any predictability exists as to how a case will be decided. In Figure 2, we have specified the degree of rationality as being either "high" (more rational) or "low" (less rational; or, better, irrational).

From Weber's analysis (1978; see also Hunt, 1978; Trubek, 1972) we can identify four ideal types of forms of law and legal thought. Let's pause for a moment and reflect on this construction and the magnitude of Weber's assertion. Weber is claiming that if we take *any* form of law and legal thought, past or present, we can locate it at some point of intersection of these two dimensions.

"Formally irrational" law, or formal irrationality, as an ideal type, occurs where decision making rests on magic, the oracle, or revelation. It employs "means which cannot be controlled by the intellect" (Weber, 1978:656). It is formal to the extent that rules, technically, do exist concerning appropriate procedures to be applied. But the authority or decision maker alone is the knower of these rules. This system is "irrational" to the extent that the decision itself is not predictable, since even where some hidden rule supposedly does exist, it is applied differently to different people. Even though the standard for decision making is intrinsic to the system (i.e., some oracle), there is no way an outsider can understand how decisions are made. As a result, similarly situated persons will receive vastly different treatment.

Figure 2. Typology of Forms of Law and Legal Thought

	High	Low
High	Formal rationality e.g., syllogism, deductive logic	Formal irrationality e.g., magic, oracles, revelation
Low	Substantive rationality e.g., affirmative action, necessity defense	Substantive irrationality e.g., jury decisions, khadi justice

Degree of Formality (vertical axis label)

"Substantively irrational" law, or substantive irrationality occurs where each concrete situation determines the decision. It is substantive to the extent that any one of a number of external ethical, political, ideological, moral, emotional, etc., criteria is used. No *general* norm, in other words, is being applied to the situation. Rather, a number of possible standards (i.e., ethical, moral, United Nations law, etc.) could be chosen for application. It is irrational to the extent that even similarly situated individuals with the same standard applied against them will be treated differently. Weber has called this "Khadi justice" (sometimes spelled Cadi, or Kadi). The authority, in other words, is not bound by any particular system of rules. S/he may decide a case by an idiosyncratic interpretation of the external standard chosen, or by the employment of some ethical principle that is personal which lies at the base of the standard chosen. The outsider cannot predict the outcome even of like cases.

Weber tells us that the jury decision is an exemplary case. After the prosecutor and defense have presented their cases in a trial, the judge instructs the jurors as to the points of law that should be the basis of their decision (formal rationality). This is called the "charge to the jury." For example, the judge might instruct the jurors that: "you will find the defendant guilty in the first degree of homicide if premeditation existed; second degree, if premeditation did not exist but gross negligence did; third degree, if mere negligence existed," etc. Even though the judge instructs the jury on the points of law that should be the basis of the verdict (consistent with the ideal type of formal rationality), in actuality the decision may be based on some other (substantive) standard(s) invoked in the jurors' minds or by some idiosyncratic interpretation of the charge. During jury deliberation, then, it remains unclear what standard(s) and/or interpretation would be invoked as the actual working standard(s) in the determination of the verdict.

Perhaps instructive were the trials surrounding the Rodney King episode. Many around the world were baffled as to why a baton or a brick delivered with great force to a victim's head was not construed as an attempted homicide. Some commentators have argued that perhaps in the final episode — the trial of three defendants who pulled a truck driver out of his vehicle and delivered a beating — what may have accounted for the rather mild verdict (the defendants being acquitted of homicide charges) was that an "equalizing principle" was at work (an external standard). That is, this principle was applied to counter what the jurors believed was a rather mild verdict delivered against the police officers who delivered a beating to Rodney King. The jury, in other words, may have tried to "even things up." If this is true, then what we see here is an external principle, one outside the formal system of law, being applied during jury deliberations.

In the context of pretrial proceedings, one might make the argument that during jury selection, where the prosecutor and defense interview and quiz prospective jurors (*voir dire*) — ostensibly in order to "stack the deck," with jurors that are potentially favorable to each's respective side — what is being investigated by the lawyers is the underlying framework, standard or principle (substantive rationality) that might lie at the basis of the prospective juror's future decision. But even if discovered, there is no accurate way of predicting how it would be interpreted (substantive irrationality).

In sum, for the substantive irrational form of law, different external criteria invoked will assure different treatment (outcomes). And even where the same external criteria are applied to similarly situated persons, different results occur. This ideal type would be the least predictable of the four.

Law is "formally rational," or "logically formal rational," where rules are applied to all similarly situated cases in an identical manner. Here the rules themselves are clearly stated and followed. In other words, there exists a "high" degree of rationality and a "high" degree of formality. High predictability in decision making exists here. This ideal finds expression, for example, in the "equal protection clause" of the Fourteenth Amendment to the U.S. Constitution and its stipulation of "formal equality." This is the standard that is taught in most U.S. law schools. In examining case law, the question for students is why law-making and law-finding may have varied from formal rationality.

In this model, no external criteria are applied. All decision making depends on the rules themselves. The rules are abstract and general. According to Weber, "only unambiguous general characteristics of the facts of the case are taken into account" (1978:656-657). For example, the elements of a crime are written into the penal codes of the state: e.g., the elements of the crime of shoplifting might include leaving the premise with merchandise without payment. Thus, only these elements are relevant in law-finding (the question of motive, for example, would be seen as "non-justiciable"). Hence, abstract interpretations of meaning, aided by the use of given rules, are generalized in law, establishing precedents (*stare decisis*) for future cases. Legal cases, in other words, are supposed to draw from past resolutions of similar controversies.[3]

The notion of "logically formal rationality," a cumbersome term, can be broken down into its elements. Law is *rational* to the extent that decisions are based on existing, unambiguous rules. It is *formal* to the degree that the criteria, the standards used for arriving at a decision, are totally internal (intrinsic) to the legal system. And it is *logical* to the degree that rules are the product of conscious construction by specific ways of reasoning (i.e., syllogistic reasoning). This reasoning, this form of legal thought, is based on deductive logic from previously established rules or principles (see below). Weber states the purest form of this law in five postulates (1978:658):

> [F]irst, that every concrete legal decision be the "application" of an abstract legal proposition to a concrete "fact situation;" second, that it must be possible in every concrete case to derive the decision from abstract legal propositions by means of legal logic; third, that the law must actually or virtually constitute a "gapless" system of legal propositions, or must, at least, be treated as if it were such a gapless system; fourth, that whatever cannot be "construed" rationally in legal terms is also legally irrelevant; and fifth, that every social action of human beings must be visualized as either an "application" or "execution" of legal propositions, or

as an "infringement" thereof, since the "gaplessness" of the legal system must result in a gapless "legal ordering" of all social conduct.

Let us return to the form of reasoning that is at the heart of formal rationality. Here, the claim is that law-making and law-finding is accomplished by *syllogistic reasoning* and *deductive logic.* Take an Aristotelian example:

All desire is good.	(major premise)
Ambition is desire.	(minor premise)
Therefore, ambition is good.	(conclusion)

Here we begin with a major premise and then apply it to the minor premise. In law, we begin with some legal principle (the major premise), such as the "equal protection clause," and apply it to the "facts" (the "what happened?") By deductive logic, it is claimed, *one* decision will ultimately be reached. The law student learns quickly how to identify the applicable and relevant major premise (i.e., some constitutional right, some statutory rule, some state or Federal regulatory norm, etc.) and how to apply it to some "factual" situation. By syllogistic reasoning, s/he learns how to arrive at the correct decision in law. One learns, for example, how to do an "equal protection argument," a "due process argument," etc. When the student researches statutory and case law, s/he summarizes each respective case in the form of a "legal brief." Here summarized are the "facts," the "issue" and the decision/rationale. It is in the latter that the student attempts to identify the formal steps in the syllogism used by the justice(s) in arriving at the decision in law.

Let's use the "equal protection clause" of the Fourteenth Amendment as an example of the major premise. Paraphrased it states that equally situated should be equally treated (formal equality). Picture a defense attorney attempting to apply this constitutional right to an incarcerated inmate who has just been deprived of two years of her "good time" (good time is awarded and accumulated for good behavior in the prison). The defense attorney makes the following comparison (see figure 3).

Here, right A may be the right to be heard; B, the right to know the charges; C, the right to counsel; D, the right to cross-examination; E, the right to confront the accuser, etc. Now applying deductive logic and syllogistic reasoning by the defense counsel: first, she states the major premise, "equally situated should be equally treated" (the notion of formal equality embedded in the Fourteenth Amendment). Then she states that the inmate and the free citizen are equally situated vis-à-vis the potential deprivation that each faces — the loss of two years liberty. She then applies syllogistic reasoning and claims that the free citizen had rights A,B,C,D,E, whereas the inmate had only A,B. And thus the conclusion: this is a deprivation of the equal protection clause of the U.S. Constitution since rights C,D,E were not provided to the inmate. Of course, she would also have to argue that the Constitution makes use of the word "persons" and does not itself make a distinction between an inmate and a free citizen. The lawyer for the government, no doubt, would argue that the citizen and inmate are not equally situated, or that the Constitution does not apply to the prison system.

Figure 3. An Equal Protection Argument in Law

Person	Situation	Legal Rights Provided in Case	Outcome
(1) Inmate	Infraction committed that places the person at risk of losing 2 years of her good time (liberty).	A,B	2 years deprivation of liberty.
(2) Free citizen	Infraction committed that places the person at risk of losing 2 years of her liberty.	A,B,C,D,E	2 years deprivation of liberty.

We should also mention that, referring to Figure 1 in the introductory chapter, formal rationality is the basis of liberal legalism (upper right hand corner of Figure 1). Those who internalize this method of reasoning are focusing on jurisprudence, rather than on the sociology of law. For jurisprudes, rationality and formality remain celebrated terms, which themselves remain unexamined. Sociologists of law, on the other hand, are much more likely to question these global forms of rationality and formality. Jurisprudes are more likely to attempt to identify biases and prejudices in legal procedures by the appropriate syllogistic reasoning and deductive logic. Their goal is to induce a shift toward a more pure formal rational model of law, with the further understanding that doing so would contribute to the furtherance of the fulfillment of social values. And certainly much reduction of suffering takes place and some fuller realization of social values results from treating people equally before the law.

Much of the activity of the student in law school deals with how to make legal forms of arguments. Students are assigned legal cases which they must examine. They fine-tune their abilities by preparing legal briefs. Here, the student states the issue (the major premise), and the "facts" (minor premise), and then attempts to trace out the syllogistic reasoning in linear fashion that was apparently involved in coming up with a conclusion in law. Through the Socratic method, by which the law professor drills the student about the case, it is said that an understanding of legal thinking can develop. This exercise, it is said, prepares the law student in the mechanics of the law.

Finally, Weber's fourth ideal type is "substantively rational" law. Substantive rationality exists where a particular *external* principle or criterion is employed. By "external" we mean outside of the dominant and state-supported body of laws and procedures used in their enforcement. This includes "ethical imperatives, utilitarian and other expediential rules, and political maxims" (Weber, 1978:657). Once chosen and applied uniformly, decisions have a higher degree of predictability. This makes them "rational" (assuming, of course, that the logic of the ethical imperative or political maxim chosen is followed precisely; if it isn't, it becomes a case of substantive irrationality). Several examples of substantive rationality are presented in Figure 4, including Marxian notions of justice, affirmative action, comparable worth, sexual preference, humanistic definitions of crime, the necessity defense, United Nation's definition of human rights, the contract of equity, Reiman's (1990) distributive principle, and postmodern definitions of crime (see the notion of "harms of reduction" and "harms of repression," Henry and Milovanovic, 1996), etc.

When activists before the U.S. courts attempt to introduce United Nations law concerning human rights, they are summoning an external principle. Exemplary was the Sandinista regime in Nicaragua in the 1980s, which brought a legal case before the United Nations Court citing principles of international law that should have been applied against the U.S.'s clandestine policy of training, funding and directing counter-revolutionary force (*contras*). U.S. lawyers argued that the United Nation's Court and law were not applicable. As of August of 2002 the U.S. still had not signed on for the International Criminal Court (ICC) in the Hague, claiming that any U.S. soldier serving in other lands should only be liable in U.S. courts. Attempts by Yugoslavian officials to bring legal action against the U.S. bombing of Belgrade and other non-combatants (TV stations, convoys, hospitals) were dismissed by U.S. courts.

On the other hand, there have been instances where the U.S. has kidnapped foreigners and tried them in the U.S. courts. Or has extradited them to the U.S. for prosecution in ·U.S. courts. Consider, for example, the appeal by Dr. Jose Solis Jordan of his conviction of setting a pipe-bomb in Chicago to bring attention to U.S. colonialization of Puerto Rico (*U.S. v. Jose Solis Jordan*, 2000). The lawyers for Professor Jordan asked the federal appeals court "whether international law, binding upon the courts of the United States, deprives the courts of the colonial power to try citizens of the nation subjected to colonialism for the offenses alleged in the indictment?" (ibid. 4; 39-50; we will return to this in chapter 7). As expected, the appeal was denied. In short, what constitutes the appropriate substantive principle and arena are political questions.

Substantive rationality, compared to the first two ideal types (formal irrationality, substantive irrationality), is more predictable. That is, once external criteria are selected and applied (e.g., some notions of universal justice), the rules for resolution are more predictable. However, the difference between substantive rationality and formally rational law, as far as predictability of decisions in similarly situated cases is concerned, is a matter of degree.

"Insoluble Conflict": Formal versus Substantive Rationality

Clearly, much tension exists between principles of substantive rationality and formal rationality. During revolutionary changes, for example, what were previously external principles may now become the basis of the dominant order, and the vanquished will now be seen as the "radical" element. But this tension often has more subtle play. Sometimes we even find that there is a dialogue between the external substantive principles and the internal formal ones, such as is the case with the necessity defense, the insanity defense, affirmative action, comparable worth, and the contract of equity. In other words, these "external" principles are allowed a standing in court. (Note the depiction in Figure 4 that some "external" principles are connected to the dominant ones; some, however, remain unconnected — meaning that no, or very little material from the "external" principles are allowed a standing in court). Here, an uneasy tension exists between the forms of law and legal thought. Consider, for example, how debates over ways of correcting racism have often been between principles of formal equality (cries of "reverse discrimination") and substantive justice (i.e., affirmative action programs). Ultimately, the question of which ones are indeed allowed or not in litigation is a political question and revolves on the ability to mobilize political power. Some principles, therefore, remain outside the dominant domain. Let's provide some further examples. These are summarized in Figure 4.

Figure 4. Formal versus Substantive Rationality

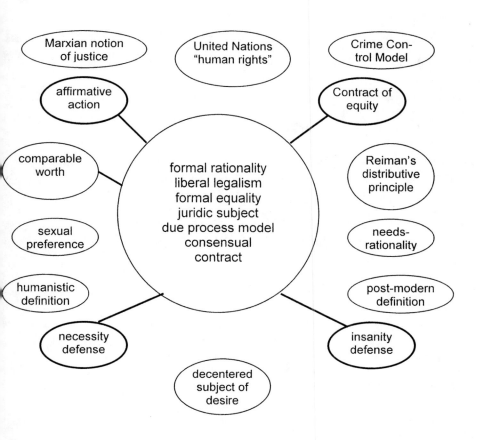

When *affirmative action* or *comparable worth* principles are introduced in law-finding and law-making, an "external" principle is being applied. Note the tension here. Ever since *Brown v. Board of Education* (1954), and subsequent governmental policies and remedies that attempted to correct for past patterned forms of racial discrimination in the U.S. through the use of affirmative action, quota systems and preferential treatment, an uneasy alliance with principles of formal rationality has existed. In fact, we may conceptualize the Supreme Court's struggles in the last six decades in terms of it first incorporating a substantive principle (suggested in *Brown v. Board of Education*); then in a series of decisions reversing this emphasis, pushing it toward the periphery of acceptable constitutional practices in the late 1960s, 70s and 80s; and finally, with a conservative U.S. Supreme Court, expelling it as outside of the acceptable ranges. Here the history has been a movement from elevating substantive rational principles as pertinent in law, to a movement to formal rational principles (e.g., formal equality).

Similarly, *comparable worth* is the idea that if two workers do similar things at the workplace, regardless of their job title, they should be paid similarly. For example, a male and a female worker might be doing similar work and exhibiting similar skills, but the male, because of his title, might be making $50,000 whereas the female worker, because of her lesser title, only $35,000. By applying the "external" standard of comparable worth, discrimination could be shown; if the principle is not allowed, the focus on the job title itself will suffice in formal rational law-finding.

Perhaps the most open-ended use of some external criterion is in the case where the "necessity defense" is permitted by a state and a presiding judge. Here, the defense attempts to show that the client broke some law to prevent some greater and imminent harm (see Bannister and Milovanovic, 1990). Note that in Figure 4 we indicate a connectedness of this principle to the general body of law, formal rationality, for, in many States, this is an available defense. If the judge allows this defense in a particular case, many external standards may be brought into the trial proceedings. Rather than merely a doctrinal legal discourse, we are much more likely to witness an oppositional discourse exercised (we shall return to this in chapter 6).

Another example of substantive rationality is Marx's ideal notion of justice (which is a substitute for bourgeois notions of formal equality): "from each according to his [her] ability, to each according to his [her] needs." Note that both "ability" and "needs" are assumed to vary for each person, a principle celebrating differences (compare this with some right wing ideological forces that claim Marx was advocating that all should be the same, automatons). Here "abilities" and "needs" evoke some standard, thus it is substantive; and by then applying this standard to all similarly situated (i.e., similar abilities and needs), it is rational. However, only in the rare case will there be pure substantive equality. The rule, being substantive, therefore, does not necessarily mean that all will be treated identically. This is because of different abilities and needs. In other words, because of the inherent uniqueness of being human, this moral principle would require that decision making should not produce similar outcomes. Human beings have varied interests, abilities, aptitudes, temperamental traits, drives, needs, desires and so forth. It is only to the extent that one treats the individual as the "reasonable man in law" — an abstraction, a general subject and bearer of universal rights — that one removes, or disregards her/his unique qualities. Only here can one talk about the logic of formally rational law. Given all the above, we are left with substantive irrationality being more dominant, with substantive rationality appearing as the rare case of equivalence in Marx's notion of justice.

Let's take another example of the tension between substantive and formal rationality. Our criminal justice system is said to be based on formal rationality as an ideal. Some years ago, Packer (1968), in "Two Models of the Criminal Process," presented the "due process model" and the "crime control model" as competing models in our criminal justice system. The former placed a premium on the possibility of error always existing; an adversary process; legal guilt; a low demand for finality; the prevention and elimination of mistakes; and a presumption of innocence. Here the most important value was "due process," or fundamental fairness. The "crime control model," however, placed a premium on repression of criminal conduct, upholding "law and order," efficiency in processing (i.e., in screening, suspects, determining guilt and sentencing), factual guilt, speed and finality, and a presumption of guilt. Here the most important value was "clearance" and conviction rates. Note that the due process model (in Figure 4) is connected with formal rationality. The crime control model is connected with substantive rationality, since some external standard is at play, focusing on the bureaucratic ideal of efficiency in dealing with large numbers of defendants. And since the vagaries of plea-bargaining come into play, perhaps we could even say that substantive irrationality is the norm. Since, in large city courts, over 90% of the cases are resolved by plea bargaining, a reasonable conclusion is that we do in fact have the crime control model as the operative model even though the due process model is the stated ideal and the one celebrated in the ideology of the rule of law. Those of the legal liberal persuasion, at best, attempt to fine-tune the criminal justice system in order that it progresses toward the stated ideal.

For another example of the tension between substantive and formal rational principles let's return to Dukheim's notion of the difference between the *consensual contract* and the *contract of equity* (see chapter 1). Consensual contracts are centrally connected with formal rationality. The contract of equity, however, is based on the idea of equality in the exchange of things possessing *equal social values*. Here the contract of equity would be "low" on the formality scale, or substantive in nature (recall his three elements defining social value), and "high" on the rationality scale, since Durkheim defines a just contract as reflecting equivalence in social values in the exchange. He did note that in the "abnormal forms" the consensual contract would invariably hide substantive inequality (repressive formalism). However, he does note the increasing incorporation of fairness standards, which correct for some of the repressive potentials inherent in consensual contract (1964b:385-386; see also how "interest balancing" has affected the delineation of rights and what constitutes fairness, chapter 2 below and Milovanovic, 1987). Present day standards of "good faith" are examples. In Figure 4 we have represented this recognition by a connectedness of this external principle with the general body of law characterized as formal rationality.

Yet other substantive principles, standards, and criteria which are in tension with formal rational principles could be mentioned (see Figure 4): Reiman, we saw in the introductory chapter, presented his distributive principle whereby gross inequities could gradually wither away (1990); the Schwendingers (1970) and Henry and Milovanovic (1996) have developed alternative definitions of harm that counter the narrowly construed legalistic definition of crime; the military has recently seen itself confronted by gay activists arguing for a sexual preference standard; the U.S. has devised separate standards and procedures for accused terrorists in the wake of "9/11"; and postmodernist theorists have challenged the individualistic philosophical underpinnings of the notion of the juridic subject (see below in the section on "the contract and the juridic subject") with their idea of the *decentered subject* (Lacan, 1977; Milovanovic, 1992; see also chapter 7). All this indicates an uneasy tension between principles of formal rationality and those of substantive rationality. And, in some cases, we see that a connectedness (conduit) does exist for substantive principles to be introduced, i.e., affirmative action, comparable worth, necessity defense, insanity defense, and the contract of equity (see Figure 4).[4]

A final word. These various tensions presented above between principles of formal and substantive rationality suggest that activists and rebels before the court need to generate creative strategies for developing a conduit for the incorporation of external standards into the formal system (i.e., human rights, sexual preference, comparable worth, alternative definitions of harm and redistributive principles, etc.). Otherwise, rebels and activists before the court will be faced with either accepting the formal system — arguing within a doctrinal legal discourse and hoping for acquittal because of a winning legal syllogism, in the process adding further legitimacy to the rule-of-law ideology — or arguing a more radical discourse replete with alternative standards which, however, will be quickly suppressed (i.e., as non-justiciable; too extensive in "scope," etc.), placing the defense team in disarray and their clients or their "cause(s)" in jeopardy. Ultimately, it remains a political question and concerns the effective mobilization of political power, as to which standard is incorporated and which is not.

Domination and Law

What motivates subjects to be obedient? Why do they orient their behavior to some order? To answer this question, Weber introduces some new terms. First, the notion of *domination*. By this he means "the probability that certain specific commands (or all commands) will be obeyed by a given group of persons" (1978:212). In addressing the question of why people comply, the answer can range from habit to purely rational calculation. For example, individuals obey because of tradition. Or they obey because of expediency; that is, because it is self-serving, it is in their best interest. In all forms of domination, Weber tells us, some minimal degree of voluntary compliance must exist. But this still does not tell us why subjects comply. The missing element, for Weber, centers on the belief in the *legitimacy* of the order. Three forms of legitimate domination are presented as ideal types.

The three "pure types" of legitimate domination are traditional, charismatic and legal. "Traditional domination" stands for obedience due to the belief in the validity of the order coming from habit, custom and tradition. Commands are seen as legitimate because they have always been followed. They are age-old rules.

"Charismatic domination" is due to commands being followed because of some exceptional qualities of the leader. Subjects abandon themselves to some person who is distinguished by holiness, exemplariness or heroism. S/he is seen to possess superhuman, supernatural, or exceptional qualities or powers. An example would be Martin Luther King, Jr.

"Legal domination," or legal authority, stems from the belief in the legitimacy of rules themselves. Obedience is due to the belief that laws are rationally constructed. These impersonal laws are perceived as standing above subjects and leaders. Leaders selected in accordance with the law are seen as legitimate authorities. The pure type of legal authority is the bureaucracy.

All three forms of domination, then, are seen as legitimate forms of domination or authority. However, in the real world, Weber tells us, these ideal types often do not come in pure forms. He merely wishes to give us conceptually pure models. These, then, are heuristic devices for further examination of complex social phenomena.

There is an important distinction to be made. In charismatic and traditional domination, law finds its legitimation outside of itself. In other words, law has no legitimation in and of itself. Rather, it is connected with either tradition or a charismatic leader. Thus claims to legitimacy are rooted in the special relationship between ruler and subject. For the charismatic type, the personal relationship is central. For the traditional type the leader also has the weight of tradition behind her/his position (see also Hunt, 1978:114). When law becomes rational law, or where legal "domination" exists, the law itself is its own legitimizing principle. In other words, the rule of law is seen in itself as worthy of being obeyed. No necessary connection exists with a particular leader or with tradition. As a matter of fact the slogan is: "the rule of law, not men."

Legal domination (authority) rests with the following ideas, 1978:217-19):

- There exist general norms established by imposition or agreement.

- The law is a consistent system, intentionally developed and made up of abstract rules.

- The "superior" is subject to the rules. S/he has to orient her/his behavior to the impersonal order.

- Obedience is directly to the rule of law itself.

- Obedience to the leader is not so much to him or her but to the impersonal order.

Weber indicates that there is a close relationship between a form of law and legal thought, and the type of domination. We can see this close connection by looking at the relationship between logically formal rationality and legal domination. In this case, abstractly derived rules are seen as legitimate in themselves. Obedience is toward the legal order because it is seen as rationally constructed. The claim to legitimacy rests "on a belief in the legality of enacted rules and the right of those elevated to authority under such rules to issue commands" (Weber, 1978:215). In fact, Weber states that the whole progress of law is toward legal authority and formal rationality (ibid., 882).

Weber refers to this process as *rationalization in law*. Obedience to individuals, over time, evolves into obedience to impersonal rules. The rule of law becomes increasingly stabilized. The impersonal, hierarchical structure of the bureaucracy and its specialized rules is increasingly duplicated in the form of law. Each becomes increasingly rationalized. Both become their own legitimating principles.

The relationship between legal thought and legitimation can be summarized. *Traditional domination* occurs where there exists an obedience owed to individuals under the guidance of traditional practices. Law is legitimated by its continuity with historical practices. It is rooted in the sanctity of tradition. The form of legal thought that would be logically connected with this form of domination is either substantive rationality or formal irrationality (see Figure 2). *Charismatic domination* is characterized by obedience owed to individuals who have some exceptional quality. Law is legitimated in "personal devotion." The form of legal thought prevalent is substantive irrationality or formal irrationality. Finally, in *legal domination*, authority is derived from law itself. Law is legitimated by the impersonal nature of the law. Law is the conscious use of logical, rational techniques by a staff which itself is subject to its law. This process lends further legitimacy to the rule of law. The form of legal thought here is formal rationality, or logically formal rationality.

In the charismatic and traditional forms of domination, the person in authority (the decision maker) has a high degree of independence in decision making. Here, too, the law is relatively unpredictable in its individual application. In legal domination, however, independence of the decision maker from law is low, and law is highly predictable in its application to individual cases. Again, these are ideal types. They are not meant to be statements exactly reflecting a desirable or even an actual state in society.

The question of domination and the rule of law focuses on political and ideological dimensions. We now, with Weber, turn to how economic factors interplay with the political and ideological institutions in producing the contemporary form of law and legal thought in capitalism.

Capitalism, Bureaucracy and Rationalization

The rule of law, as an ideology, arose in the West because of unique conditions. For Weber, attributing cause only to the economic system in explaining the evolution of a particular form of a legal system and law was a simplistic and inaccurate exercise. Instead, his multi-causal approach argued that the rise of formal rationality had its roots in a process of rationalization. Law evolved from substantive rational to formal rational systems. Political, economic, ideological as well as legal factors were influential. He stated that there was a close connection between the internal needs of the capitalist mode of production and a form of law that emphasizes logical formal rationality. But simply attributing causation of one to the other, he continued, was to overlook the complex conditions out of which each arose. And it was also to overlook the unique conditions that accounted for their mutual development.

Weber used the term *rationalization* in a number of ways (for a criticism, see Andreski, 1984:58-82; Hunt, 1978:101). At times he defined it as a systematic codification of rules. That is, it was characterized by the increasing development of internally pure logical interrelationships among elements. (This finds contemporary expression in the call for structuring judges' discretion in sentencing and in parole boards' decision making for release). At other times, he argued that the term meant the increasing differentiation and coordination of conduct, in industry and in everyday life, on the basis of an empirical knowledge of subjects' relations with each other, toward the end of greater efficiency or productivity (See, also, Freund, 1969:18). (This idea found expression in industrial "time and motion" studies of Taylorism during the early years of the 20th century particularly dealing with the assembly line form of production).

The rationalization of law, according to Weber, was due to "two forces operating side by side...on the one hand, capitalism interested in strictly formal law and legal procedure...on the other hand, the rationalism of officialdom in absolutist states led to the interest in codified systems and in homogeneous law..." (cited in Hunt, 1978:109). The development of modern law needed both these forces.

Several more specific factors are identified as critical in the development of the rule of law. First, the development of centers of commerce was decisive. This necessitated much interaction across time and space. Second, and along with the first, the development of the competitive marketplace characterized by commodity exchange (rather than barter relations), and the use of money, were of importance. Economic transactions needed to operate in an environment of stability. That is, whether it is the subject engaged in commodity exchange or a capitalist firm determining profit margins and investment potentials, the need for certainty and predictability are critical for rational planning or, in a word, calculability.

Weber's concept of rationality finds its counterpart in the economic sphere. "Rational economic action," he tells us, "requires instrumental rationality in this orientation, that is, deliberate planning" (1978:63). More primitive societies were marked by "communal" relationships (subjects orient themselves to each other because they feel a belongingness, a camaraderie). They exchanged for personal use (barter). This practice gave way, with the development of the competitive marketplace, to "associative" relationships (subjects orient themselves to each other because of rational calculation), and subjects now saw exchange as an opportunity for profit (ibid., 40-41, 63, 73). The competitive marketplace, then, is characterized as a domain where the calculation for profit motive is supreme.

But, Weber cautions us, "economic situations do not automatically give birth to new legal forms; they merely provide the opportunity for the actual spread of a legal technique if it is invented" (ibid., 687). Furthermore, "economic conditions, have...everywhere played an important role, but they have nowhere been decisive alone and by themselves" (ibid., 883). We must, then, look to additional factors.

A third factor was the rise of the monarchical powers and the nation-state, which needed a mechanism of administration. The bureaucracy supplied the ideal form of control. It was an ideal form of efficient administration. Here specialized functions guided by some centrally stated goal were combined with functionaries with specialized training who discharged their responsibilities according to some calculable rules without any reference to people as such. The late Roman Empire was to grasp this form of administration in its dealing with its vast empire.

Bureaucracies, once created, develop a life of their own. Rules tend to become more systematized; that is, more internally coordinated in a logical way. Furthermore, the more complex a society becomes, the more depersonalized the supporting structures become. That is, the former control exerted by a lord is replaced by the control by experts who administer, not on whim, but according to established rules. "[O]nly bureaucracy," Weber explains, "has established the foundation for the administration of a rational law conceptually systematized on the basis of 'statutes'..." (1978:975). In other words, apart from all else, the bureaucracy offers the ideal form of control and administration.

A bureaucracy tends to continuously expand guided by its own internal dynamics. A tendency toward more specialization of functions and roles, with the need for greater coordination and control, leads to the need for specifying clearer and more rational rules defining interrelationships. At an early stage, there is one supervisor with two workers each having four functions; with specialization of functions, we now have four workers each with two functions, with the addition of two new supervisors, each supervising two of the workers. At the next stage, we may have eight workers, each having one function with yet another layer of supervisors. The bureaucracy continues to expand, guided by the ideal of greater efficiency in production and control. Difficult tasks are broken down into their simplified component elements. Simplified tasks are coordinated into the overall plan. Rules delineate responsibilities, functional roles, and competencies. Obedience is owed to this overall impersonal machine. (We shall see in a later chapter that postmodernist theorists strongly critique this emerging impersonal machine.)

The interests of the nation-state and the capitalist firms and subjects, operating in a competitive marketplace oriented toward profit, coincided. In both spheres, the political and the economic, there was a need for calculability. This "alliance" between the needs of monarchical and bourgeois interests was "one of the major factors" leading toward the development of the rule of law (ibid., 847). We should not read "alliance" to mean a conspiratorial agreement, but rather a coincidental development of compatible interests. Nevertheless, this mutual interest, and its recognition, aided the further development of the rationalization of law. But yet other factors were at work.

Thus, a fourth factor was the relatively independent developments *within* the legal profession. The early Roman Law with its use of specialized, abstract, logical techniques was studied extensively in the universities of continental Europe. It was from these universities that specialized legal notables, trained in logic and abstract techniques of reasoning within law, arose. And they were in an opportune position to verbalize and systematize the type of law needed with the development of the "alliance" mentioned above.

Thus these four factors, or determinants, together accounted for the form of law that arose with capitalism. This is a clear reflection of Weber's multi-causal approach. A different story emerges within England, where legal training developed as a "craft." That is, the early English attorneys were recruited from the clergy. For them, lawyering was a major source of income. Gradually the clergy was replaced in about the 15th and 16th century by non-clergy lawyers. Legal guilds also developed. Many times the lawyers lived together in guild houses. It was also from them that judges were recruited. Specialized training, including apprenticeships was established. Special "guild" interests also developed. These guilds became resistant to change and attempted to maintain their own economic self-interest. This rigidness did not allow rationalization in the law to develop. During this time lawyers were only interested in the immediacy of the situation (the concrete case). The development of a body of abstract, universal, or general rules was not their central interest. They held monopoly power over the development of law. New, innovative techniques that had *general* application such as formal rational law were not encouraged.

These developments were in marked contrast to developments on mainland Europe. In Germany, for example, where there were no guild organizations, legal training was performed in universities. Here, abstract rules and logic centering on Roman law was embraced. Roman law and logic entailed reducing a lawsuit with its complex issues to the most basic issues involved. It was an exercise of a highly analytical and rational dissection of parts. No theological factors were included in the legal thought itself (Weber, 1978:793-796).

Comparing the development of law in England and mainland Europe, Weber points out that even though capitalism first appeared in England, the form of law that had close connections with it did not. Rather, it was on mainland Europe that logically formal law developed. Hence, the economic sphere itself could not be seen as the main determinant in its development (see Weber, 1978:784-802). For Weber, then, a decisive influence in the rationalization of law was exercised by legally trained specialists (ibid., 776).

In sum, the systematization or the rationalization of law (the movement toward logically formal rationality) was due to a number of unique developments. Together these forces led to the development of a form of law that was relatively autonomous, or relatively independent from the interests or influence of specific actors. Legitimate domination now rested on the rule of law itself. Subjects oriented their behavior toward the assumed impersonal rules that created predictability, stability and an environment of calculability. Put in another way, subjects and capitalist firms could operate within a framework that offered a range of predictability. They were assured, by the state, that obligations or expectations would be met by coercion if needed. The whim of an individual actor — be s/he a legislator, leader, president, capitalist, or contractor — is replaced by rules that have been consciously developed and written, thus ensuring a high probability of compliance.

Rationalization in law and the continued development of the bureaucracy go hand in hand. One supports the other. Weber saw this autonomous development in evolutionary terms. This was his "iron rule." Legitimate domination, then, is tied to the evolution and acceptance of rules that are seen as autonomously developed by legal experts who objectively and logically construct a body of laws that have general applicability. Everything falls within this "gapless" system. Everything can be litigated. New laws can be deduced from old. Previous laws now become precedents for new laws. The inherent logic of the rule of law itself determines the form of reasoning that will be respected and enforced by the state.

The Contract and the Juridic Subject

The development of the contract and juridic subject (the abstract bearer of rights, the "reasonable man" in law) finds a central place in Weber's thought. He devotes a sizable section of *Economy and Society* to this subject (1978:666-731). Here he traces the development of the contract from its primitive to its modern form. In primitive societies, it was the *status contract* that was the main form. In modern societies it was the *purposive contract*. It is in these pages that he questions whether with the development of "contractual freedom" more substantive freedom and less coercion develop.

He begins his analysis with the definition of a *right*. To him, it means "an increase of the probability that a certain expectation of the one to whom the law grants the right will not be disappointed" (ibid., 666-667). Every right, then, becomes the source of power. Freedom, for Weber, is intimately connected with the possession of rights (ibid., 668). The "reasonable man in law," can be conceived in terms of the totality of (1) contracts that s/he assumes and (2) inheritance (ibid., 669). To understand contractual freedom, he points out, we must understand the development of a legal order and the agreements that it enforces. The "decisive" factor behind the development of the kind of contracts, that are enforced, is "interest groups," particularly those from the marketplace, and their influence.

Weber describes the stages of development from the "status contract" to the "purposive contract" in some detail. Primitive societies were characterized by an organization based on the clan, kinship, and the household community. Any transactions affected the individual's entire status. That is, her/his entire standing in the community was affected. S/he became someone entirely different because of the transaction. These "fraternal" contracts with their attached magical rituals meant that the other would now become "somebody's child, father, wife, brother, master, slave, kin, comrade-in-arms, protector, client, follower, vassal, subject, friend, or, quite generally, comrade..." (ibid., 672). In other words, the person's whole personality as understood and supported by the group was profoundly affected. The oath and the calling upon a divine being for recognition and enforcement was a later variation of this type of contract.

Transactions with outsiders were marked by barter. Because no enforceability existed, these transactions were originally in the form of immediate exchange of things. Central here was the notion of possession. Enforcement revolved around the idea that vengeance was appropriate where possession was violated.

The idea of an individual "obligation" by way of a contract was alien to the primitive. Enforceability of the contract within the kinship structure revolved around arbitration by the elders. Neither vengeance nor litigation was the norm. At worst ostracism and boycott would take place. The entire community was the first line of defense against non-fulfillment of the contract. All members of the kinship were responsible for any contract made by any one of them. Hence, the notion of *collective responsibility* and liability was predominant. The notion of *individual liability* had not yet developed in primitive societies. Where a member of one group defaulted against a member of another group, collective reprisal against the other's whole group was only natural.

When the kinship group broke up, giving rise to groupings of house communities and various political associations, new notions of responsibility, liability and enforcement arose. The coming of a money economy, the competitive marketplace and centers of commerce changed the basic traditional relationships and orientations that had assured predictability and stability. Subjects became more involved, be it temporarily, in a variety of associations. The growing exchange economy placed much demand for transactions of all types. The solution: the development of the "juristic personality." All were now endowed with certain general and abstract rights respected and enforced in law. The "purposive contract" became dominant. It was but a "legal reflex" of the developed market orientation.

The juristic subject (or, juridic subject) as an abstract bearer of rights now entered many transactions without at the same time committing her/his whole personality. Here, all magical and religious elements were removed. Individual responsibility, liability and obligation were now dominant concepts. Transactions agreed to were now guaranteed by the state. (One may pause here and compare the *purposive contract* with Durkheim's idea of the *contract by mutual consent*, or the *consensual contract*.)

As can be seen, the development of the purposive contract was connected with the rationalization of law. The development of the market economy, characterized by money and commodity exchange, and the clash of egotistically driven wills, needed not only a highly formal rational system of laws, but also a new entity, the juridic subject. This abstraction, the legal subject in law, now carried with it certain rights that were general. All were formally equal in the eyes of the law. This notion allowed the legal sphere to merely plug into the grand picture of the rule of law this known quantity. S/he was but an "organ" in the whole scheme of things. Subjects and legal firms, then, were provided with a predictable and calculable order. Predicting what the other will or should do was no longer guesswork that involved judging excessive individual variations. Rather, all were required to respect certain general rights. Mutual expectations now became enforced in law.

The overall political economic order became legitimated by the rule of law itself. Legitimate domination exists because law was seen as rationally enacted and because all were endowed with formally equal rights. The legal system, then, was perceived as autonomous from political and economic manipulation. That is, the legal system was now assumed to be independent, or autonomous. It was guided by pure rational, logical thought. A body of lawyers would, through the promulgation of laws and in litigation, decide what the laws were and what they meant, but consistent with the overall internal logic of established law.

Freedom and Coercion in Law

In a scant three pages of over 1,400 pages in *Economy and Society*, Weber turns to the subject of freedom and coercion in law. But the points made are nothing short of thunderbolts. These pages deal primarily with the "insoluble conflict," the discrepancy between formal and substantive justice.

He asks: Even though contractual freedom has increased in contemporary society, does it necessarily mean that overall freedom has increased? Conversely, does it also mean that overall coercion has decreased? His answer revolves around the question of property distribution in a society.

> The exact extent to which the total amount of 'freedom' within a
> given legal community is actually increased depends entirely upon

the concrete economic order and especially upon the property distribution [Weber, 1978:730].

He gives an example of a worker entering a contract, and notes that the worker normally has little to say about the terms of the conditions of work. S/he is offered a contract, take it or leave it.

> The result of contractual freedom, then, is in the first place the opening of the opportunity to use, by the clever utilization of property ownership in the market, these resources without legal restraints as a means for the achievement of power over others. The parties interested in power in the market thus are also interested in such a legal order [ibid., 730].

Thus, for Weber, assessing the overall freedom or coercion in law cannot be simply discerned by looking at the formal qualities of law. For example, if the formal legal system stipulates that all subjects are equal in the eyes of the law, in no way does it mean at the substantive level, given the unequal property distribution in society, that overall coercion has decreased. Formal equality, then, does not necessarily mean greater freedom and less coercion. Anatole France's ironic quip that both the rich and the poor are equally prohibited from sleeping under the bridges of the Seine in Paris is a case in point.

The connection between the form of law and legitimate domination is not necessarily a "natural" one. Weber has noted the "need of any power...to justify itself," and that "every highly privileged group develops the myth of its natural...superiority" (ibid., 953). Here we are in the domain of ideology. Normally, for Weber, a "highly privileged group" will be assured that the "negatively privileged group" (for him meaning the non-propertied group) accepts the order. But, at times, this privileged status, and the attendant legitimation principle (ideology) it has created, have become "the most passionately hated object of attack" (ibid.). As long as focused critical thought concerning an existing form of domination is lacking, legitimacy is assured. However, class struggle often followed where the created myth of superiority was openly challenged upon the observation that class position determined a person's fate, or life-chances (ibid., 953-954).

Summary

Max Weber has left us with a legacy. All theories dealing with a true sociology of law must come to terms with his writing. He has developed a systematic theory in the sociology of law, unlike Emile Durkheim or Karl Marx. Weber's emphasis on a multi-causal explanation led him to look at political, economic and ideological factors. Attributing cause to one factor alone was unthinkable. The form of law that was to develop with capitalism, logically formal rationality, even though quite compatible with its internal dynamics, was not necessarily "caused" by capitalism. For Weber, law served facilitative, repressive and ideological functions. The rule of law, or formal rationality, assured predictability, calculability and stability. The purposive contract arose in capitalism as the exemplary expression of free exchange. A facilitative framework was developed where transactions by egotistically driven wills seeking profit would be assured. Law, in capitalism, then, served facilitative functions. But it also served repressive functions.

The propertied classes because of their power, benefit from the form of law that is seen as autonomous and general. Formal equality often disguises substantive inequality. Thus, for Weber, the facilitative function sometimes cannot be separated from the repressive functions. Calculability and coercion, then, could be combined even though on the face of it, the form of law and legal thought seem independent from particular interest groups.

Law also served ideological functions. The question of legitimate domination was critical for Weber. Subjects orient their behavior to the legal order because it is seen as driven by rationally derived rules. The rule of law ideology is self-justifying. Only under certain circumstances is legitimacy withdrawn from the legal order with the possible effect of mass revolt.

The relationship of the legal order to the fulfillment of social values can be summarized as follows. (Weber's position concerning greater liberty or coercion in law as we have seen was a complex one.) A form of law and legal thought that formally offers freedom in contracts or greater formal rights (for Weber, greater "empowerments") can at the same time benefit one class, the propertied, to the detriment of another, the non-propertied. This is an example of "repressive formalism." Realization of social values such as equality, individuality and community does not necessarily follow a form of law that is logically formal rational. Comparing socialist and capitalist societies, Weber notes, "which system would possess more real coercion and which one more real personal freedom cannot be decided...by the mere analysis of the actually existing or conceivable formal legal system" (1978:731).

Notes

1. For a critical comparison of Weber and Marx on law, see Milovanovic, 1989.

2. It was chapter 8 of the second volume of *Economy and Society* that was devoted to the sociology of law (related materials also appeared in chapters 1 and 3).

3. Weber calls a subcategory of this type of law "extrinsically rational law," where the emphasis is on pure documentation or words. He never returns to the idea.

4. Weber shows how some of this tension between substantive and formal rationality is played out in societies that claim to be dominated by the rule of law, indicating, for example, that with greater contractual freedom, greater amount of freedom does not necessarily follow. Durkheim makes some similar arguments in comparing the consensual contract with the contract of equity. In the next chapter on Marx, we shall see that this tension is at the basis of *repressive formalism* (upper left hand corner of Figure 1 in the introductory chapter). Recall, in this context, our example of two speeders before the court who both were equally situated vis-à-vis the number of miles an hour over the speed limit, who were then dealt with on a formally equal basis before the court (i.e., they were provided all the constitutional rights of a defendant before the court), and who each paid a $50 fine. One conclusion is that this example is the liberal legalist's ideal: equally situated were equally treated. The key here, recall, was that if we chose their respective incomes as the basis of initial comparison of being "equally situated," the argument becomes much more problematic. At this point, however, we are more likely to shift our analysis for possible answers into the domain of the sociology of law rather than that of jurisprudence.

3. KARL MARX: LAW IN A POLITICAL ECONOMY

Introduction. Karl Marx stands with Durkheim and Weber as a giant in the analysis of society. Although he never attempted to develop a sociology of law, much in his work can be used to develop a unique perspective on law. We shall see that a number of rather diverging perspectives have been derived from Marx's writings.

Marx was the third child (of nine) born to Henriette Pressburg Marx in 1818 in the city of Trier, Germany. His father, Heinrich, was a well-to-do lawyer, public notary and the recipient of rents from land and houses he owned. He was a well-respected community member in Trier. The young Marx developed a reputation of writing satirical verses. In 1835, Karl entered the University of Bonn to study law. His family wanted him to become a lawyer like his father. But at Bonn his behavior was already rebellious. He was arrested for drunkenness and noisiness. He was also arrested for dueling with a gun.

Later, in 1836, he transferred to the University of Berlin. There, where Hegel had died a short five years earlier, the Hegelian philosophy was to have a marked influence on the young Marx. Marx studied law, history and philosophy. In 1838, after the death of his father, Karl Marx dropped any intention of studying law and concentrated instead on philosophy. In 1841, he finished his doctoral degree at the University of Jena. Soon after, he became an editor of a liberal business newspaper. In 1843, he was married. Resigning the editorship, he left for Paris where he became involved with radical literature and revolutionaries. It was there also that he met Friederich Engels, who was working as a clerk in a cotton mill. This became a life long friendship.

In 1844, he wrote his first major piece, *The Economic and Philosophical Manuscripts*. It was a polemic in political economy. He was later to be expelled from France. He then settled in Brussels. Here he continued with economic studies and with an involvement in the working class movement. In 1848, with Engels, he wrote the classic study, the *Manifesto of the Communist Party*. He was subsequently arrested under suspicion of supplying arms to the revolutionaries, and expelled from Brussels. He returned to Paris.

But, after the numerous revolutions of 1848, he was again arrested for sedition and expelled.

In 1849, he went to London where he was to spend the rest of his life. The great library, the British Museum, was to be where he spent most of his research time. Although living in poverty, he was to continue his studies in political economy. His friend Engels, whose family was well-to-do, was to give him financial support. In 1867, the first volume of his influential *Das Kapital* was published. His health started to give way a little later, and by 1873 he almost had a nervous breakdown. His research and writing were irreversibly affected. In 1881, his wife died of cancer. His eldest daughter, too, died the same year. Karl Marx died in London on March 14, 1883. Eleven people attended his funeral. Engels was to deliver the eulogy (see Eugene Kamenka's biography of Marx in *The Portable Karl Marx*, 1983, xi-xlv).

Karl Marx did not try to develop a sociology of law. Law for him was a secondary interest. He was more interested in philosophy and a political-economic analysis of the development of capitalism and its effects. But as early as 1837, Marx expressed his interest in law: "if feuds were settled by a and b, the courts would be swindled out of their fee" (Marx, cited in Cain and Hunt, 1979:2). His father was to caution him about his hostility to law. However, in a letter to his father in 1837, Karl Marx stated his approach:

> exemplified by law, the state, nature, and philosophy as a whole, the object itself must be studied in its development; arbitrary divisions must not be introduced, the rational character of the object itself must develop as something imbued with contradictions in itself and find its unity in itself [cited in Cain and Hunt, 1979:16].

This philosophical position is well worth some careful thought. It reflected his early attempts to distance himself from simply studying the independent influences of ideas in history. Rather, he was already implying that contradictions in the concrete world must be the unit of analysis (i.e., focal point of inquiry). But studying law, for him, was always subordinate to philosophy, history and economics.

MARXIST PERSPECTIVES

Rather than a Marxist perspective on the sociology of law, what has developed in contemporary scholarship is a number of perspectives that draw from his voluminous writings. Interested theorists have had to gather numerous unconnected statements on his notions of law in capitalism and then systematize these in order to claim: "this is what Marx said about law." But this exercise in systematization has produced different frameworks. Thus, in the contemporary analysis of law from a Marxist perspective two major forms appear.

The first perspective, *instrumental Marxism*, traces the development of law to the control exercised by the "ruling class." Law is simply class rule. The "ruling class" controls the formation of law. Law is an instrument used for maximizing ruling class interests in society and controlling the working classes. Thus, it is said that the definition of crime, laws, policy formation, and the every day functioning of the criminal justice system are being manipulated by some conspiratorial and like-minded ruling class. From our introductory chapter, Figure 1, we recognize this framework as appearing in the lower left hand corner.

The second major variant in a Marxist approach to law is the *structural perspective*. Inspired during the late 1970s by the resurrected works of Pashukanis (2002) of the 1920s and 1930s in Russia (see Beirne and Sharlet, 1980; Beirne, 1990), this position seeks to explain law by focusing on the overall dynamics of the capitalist system itself. Law, in this approach, is not a direct servant or instrument of a ruling class; rather, law has a degree of independence from specific elites. This notion is known as "relative autonomy." In other words, a number of historically contingent forces produce specific effects at any point in time in a society. Both "capitalists" (bourgeois) as well as the working classes (proletariat) are subject to the effects of these forces, whether these actors are conscious or unconscious of them. In Figure 1, chapter 1, we locate this approach in the upper left hand corner.

At least two variations within the structural perspective have been identified (Milovanovic, 1987, 1989, 1993a). The first we can identify as the *commodity-exchange perspective*; the second, the *structural interpellation perspective* (see Figure 5). We shall have more to say below.

In both the instrumental and structural perspectives, Marxist scholars have drawn from the original works of Marx in order to decipher "what he really meant." Thus, much controversy exists about the "right" reading of Karl Marx.

Figure 5. Marxist Perspectives in the Sociology of Law

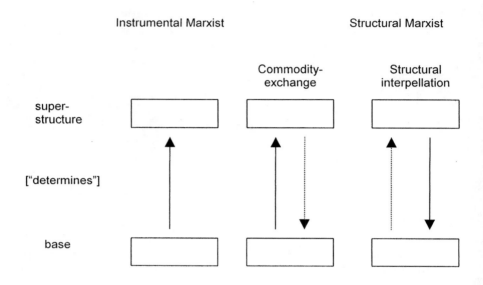

In the following sections we will separate the two major perspectives in our analysis. We will first, however, present the key concepts related to the notion of a *mode of production* and the notion of cause. We follow with an examination of some prominent themes concerning the form of this with law, the juridic subject, hegemony (domination), the contract, and property in a capitalist mode of production. We briefly consider the notion of the "dialectics of struggle." We conclude with the thesis of the withering away of the state, law and the juridic subject.[1]

Mode of Production and Law

In order to understand the development of law, it is important to come to terms with Marx's theory of general social development. This he called the "materialist conception of history." Marx notes the "guiding principle of my studies":

In the social production of their existence, people inevitably enter into definite relations, which are independent of their will, namely relations of production appropriate to a given stage in the development of their material forces of production. The totality of these relations of production constitutes the economic structure of society, the real foundations, on which arises a legal and political superstructure and to which correspond definite forms of social consciousness. The mode of production of material life conditions the general process of social, political and intellectual life. It is not the consciousness of people that determines their existence, but their social existence that determines their consciousness [1970:20-21].

In this classic statement, Marx distinguishes two general levels of society: the *base* and the *superstructure*. The economic system is the "base." The "superstructure" is the totality of beliefs, sentiments, morality, illusions, modes of thought, views of life, forms of consciousness, ideals and ideas and so forth. It also includes the political, legal and ideological spheres. The state can also be conceptualized as part of the superstructure. We should note that this base/superstructure metaphor is really more of an ideal type in the Weberian sense. It is for Marx a guiding principle. The term "social formation" will be understood to mean both base and superstructure.

The "mode of production," or the form of the economic system, may vary. In other words, every society organizes itself in some way in order to produce and distribute products or commodities. Thus, certain historical patterns do stabilize and can be conceptualized. (Weber, no doubt, would call these examples of different "orders.") Accordingly, people are offered "definite relations" that "are independent of their will." And, for Marx, one's consciousness is "determined" by one's social existence. Marx distinguishes several types of modes of production: slavery, feudalism, capitalism, and communism (yet more examples of ideal types). Socialism poses a problem as a pure type. For Marxists it is but a transitional stage to the "higher forms" (communism).

The base, in turn, can be conceptualized as having two elements. First, it includes the *productive forces*, or *forces of production*, which are characterized by available technology, general skills and knowledge, natural resources and so forth. Productive forces are the material means used by people to assure a livelihood. Second, we can identify the *relations of production* or the *socioeconomic relations*. The productive forces shape how people relate to each other in producing and exchanging goods and commodities necessary for life. Thus, there are different ways of producing and exchanging goods in societies characterized, for example, by hunting and gathering, agriculture, or industry. The productive forces are said to "determine" the socio-economic relations.

Certain *forms* of relations therefore begin to stabilize, for example, between lord and serf, master and slave, or capitalist (bourgeois) and worker (proletariat). Thus, in primitive societies, barter relationships are the ideal types. Two people exchange goods without being oriented to profit motives. They exchange product for product because of the direct personal use it has for them (*use-value*). On the other hand, in a capitalist mode of production, two people exchange commodities generally for profit motives (as *exchange-values*). That is, the commodity's inherent usefulness (its "use-value") is now transformed into a priced and exploitable entity (i.e., it takes on "exchange-value"). In sum, different modes of production produce different patterned relations. These, again, are independent of the will of those directly involved in these relations. These *definite relations* predate a newly born person. They are what s/he must subsequently negotiate.

Marx, in the long quote above, implied that the base "determines" the superstructure. In other words, the typical person in the feudal mode of production had a very different set of values, beliefs, aspirations, and needs than her/his counterpart in the capitalist society. It is also within the base that contradictions arise between the productive elements and the relations of production. That is, at a certain stage, newly developed technologies or material productive forces become incompatible with how people had normally related to each other. With the rise of commerce and trade, for example, feudal relations became obsolete. This contradiction between the new and the old sometimes led to different forms of individual resistance, at other times to revolutionary class struggle.

For Marx, "at a certain stage of development, the material productive forces of society come into conflict with existing relations of production... The changes in the economic foundation lead sooner or later to the transformation of the whole immense superstructure" (1970:21). This dynamic is referred to as "dialectical materialism." The notion of the "dialectic" states that the struggle of opposites, the new with the old, produces a new synthesis. This, in turn, eventually leads to contradictions, new struggles and yet a new need for synthesis. Thus the historical cycle: synthesis → antithesis → new synthesis → antithesis, etc.

An examination of "causes" or "determinants" must be the initial step in understanding the different Marxist perspectives on the development of law. That is, how are we to understand that the base "determines" the superstructure?

One position, we can call it the strong version of determinism, argues that a change in the base automatically produces a change in the superstructure. Given a particular economic system, specific laws, ideals and ideological systems are predicted to develop. In other words, these are reflections of the base. This position is generally referred to as economic determinism (or economic reductionism).

A second position states that the verb "determines" merely expresses the idea that the base sets limits to possible developments in the superstructure. That is, a change in the economic base will have effects in the superstructure, but other factors will come into play. These other factors could be, for example, philosophical (e.g., development of a critical consciousness), political (e.g., revolts, class struggle) and ideological (e.g., in Latin America we have seen a shift from the conventional theology of resignation to "liberation theology"; see Milovanovic, 1985). We may call the second version of "determines" the soft version. In contemporary analysis of Marxist law, it is generally referred to as "relative autonomy." The argument here is that three main spheres of influence exist, which are only relatively independent from each other: the political, economic and ideological. At times the juridic sphere has also been included. Each sphere can have an effect on each of the others and can be affected by each of the others. Understanding which sphere was the primary determinant in any period is an empirical question.

The first approach, the superstructure as reflection of the base, has its main followers in the instrumental ("determinist") Marxist perspective. They find evidence for their claim in such passages appearing in the *Manifesto of the Communist Party* as "the executive of the modern state is but a committee for managing the common affairs of the whole bourgeoisie" (1973:110). The logic of the argument is that the state appeared because of irreconcilable conflicts that developed with the appearance of the capitalist mode of production. The state was to quickly fall under the control of the more powerful class, the dominant economic class. Economic power was thus converted into political power. The "state apparatus" — police, army, judiciary — was then "bourgeois" right from the beginning. The "ruling class" influences the legislative process by financing campaigns for office, by lobbying, by corruption (bribes) and so forth. Continued selective socializing, a common education, intermarriage within the capitalist class and the development of a common outlook on life (a common ideology) assures that this "class" will continue. In other words, the "definite relations" that this group of people (bourgeois) enters assures a common way of thinking to develop. This "ruling class," then, manipulates the formation of law for its own interests (see Kolko, 1962; Domhoff, 1967; Miliband, 1969; see also Beirne's critique, 1979b).

The second approach, soft determinism, or the "relative autonomy" position, is associated with the theorists from the structural Marxist perspective. They argue that, at best, the economic sphere is determinant only in the "last instance"; in other words, when all else is said and done. Reminiscent of the Weberian multi-causal perspective, they argue that three spheres — the economic, political and ideological — have collective effects in producing social phenomena. At any one instance, the unique articulation of the three produces specific results. To understand, for example, how a particular law has come into being, one has to investigate how these three factors exerted different degrees of influence at a particular historical point in time. The structural Marxists call this process "overdetermination." Althusser (1971) and Poulantzas (1973) (but Freud before them) used this term to mean that the "cause" of something is always multiple. Many factors together produce certain results.

A social scientist has the difficult task of unraveling what combination of political, economic and ideological factors were at play in producing the specific phenomena s/he is investigating. This combination of factors is referred to as the "articulation of instances." In other words, when examining a particular law that has been introduced, perhaps the political sphere can be shown to be the most dominant "factor," and the economic and ideological as of lesser importance. At other times, perhaps all three factors are of equal importance; at yet other times, perhaps the ideological factor is the most dominant; and so forth.

In its most strict form, the notion of a subject, a person who actively confronts and attempts to change her/his environment, disappears in some versions of the structuralist approach. It is replaced by the notion that subjects are only "supports" of the socio-economic system (Althusser, 1971; Poulantzas, 1973). In its less strict form, conscious rebellion, revolutionary consciousness, and class struggle are forces that become factors in explaining such developments as substantive law and social policy (see Quinney, 1977).

Within the structuralist position we have identified two subcategories, the Commodity-Exchange perspective and the Structural Interpellation perspective (see Figure 5). The former, we shall see below, is more economistic in orientation; that is, it still assumes that the dominant factor is the economic sphere in producing superstructural effects. It is distinguishable from the instrumental Marxist perspective in that the economic sphere is said to have effects on *both* the bourgeois and proletariat, independent of their will; the instrumental Marxists, however, claim an independence in the development of consciousness of the bourgeois classes. The Structural Interpellation perspective argues that relatively independent forces within the superstructure itself — such as ideological, juridical and political factors — have effects downward; that is, they constitute economic relations and eventually forms of consciousness. In other words, here the economic sphere is a factor but not the primal determinant. (Many revolutionary leaders, or in the case of the United States, many of the early prominent radical criminologists, ironically came, and still come from the well-to-do classes. Apparently, using the structural interpellation argument, the development of a critical consciousness was relatively independent from the molding effects of the economic sphere.)

Structuralists, then, seek to examine the development of law not only by investigating economic factors (the base), but also certain relatively independent forces within the superstructure. Rather than seeing the state and laws as mere instruments of a particular "ruling class," the structural Marxists seek to examine the contradictory developments within a social formation that led to a particular state of affairs. The notion of a "ruling class" is replaced by the notion of a "hegemonic group". In other words, the structural Marxists do not assume that a conspiratorial elite exists. Rather, there is an assumed existence of a general interest amongst powerful segments to maintain the present socio-economic order. This can generally be maintained by a form of law that is relatively independent even from them. Block has said, for example, that "the state plays a critical role in maintaining the legitimacy of the social order, and this requires that the state appear to be neutral in the class struggle" (1977:8). This ironic situation will be developed below.

Domination, Form of Law, and the Juridic Subject

The instrumental and structural Marxist perspectives have diverging explanations of domination — the degree of independence between the form of law and some power elite or ruling class — and the development of rights. The instrumental Marxist perspective dominated much Western thought until the discovery of Pashukanis's work in the late 1970s.

The instrumental Marxist perspective is based on much data accumulated in the analysis of state power. Works by Domhoff (1967), Milliband (1969) and Kolko (1962) described the close relationship between those with economic and political power. Consider Friedman's point: "the [legal] system works like a blind, insensate machine. It does the bidding of those whose hands are on the controls. The laws ...reflect the goals and policies of those who call the tune..." (1973:14). In the area of law formation, Quinney (1974), Chambliss (1964), Chambliss and Seidman (1971), and Mathieson (1980) indicated the effects of the unequal distribution of power in the development of law. Quinney and Chambliss were later to develop alternative Marxist perspectives on law (see for example, Chambliss, 1988). The instrumental perspective can be best summarized by Quinney's five propositions:

(1)   The state is organized to serve the interests of the dominant economic class, the capitalist ruling class.

(2)   Criminal law is an instrument of the state and ruling class to maintain and perpetuate the existing social and economic order.

(3)   Crime control in capitalist society is accomplished through a variety of institutions and agencies established and administered by a governmental elite, representing ruling class interests, for the purpose of establishing domestic order.

(4)   The contradictions of advanced capitalism — the disjunction between existence and essence — requires that the subordinate classes remain oppressed by whatever means necessary, especially through the coercion and violence of the legal system.

(5)   Only with the collapse of capitalist society and the creation of a new society based on socialist principles, will there be a solution to the crime problem (1974:16).

Domination, in this approach, is assured by the ruling class's control of the media and educational system (sometimes also referred to as "ideological state apparatuses"). Consciousness is said to be manipulated constantly by these institutions (see, Bowles and Gintis, 1976). The family structure conveys the very values that are needed by the capitalist work place.

If these basic institutions fail to assure obedience, the legal system will provide the additional control and coercion. Law is simply an instrument to control the working classes or to curb threats made on the elite's hold on society. Formal rights given by the Constitution are said to be but mere *props* that mystify the basic repressive functions of law. In the end, formal procedure and processing in the criminal justice system itself "cool out the mark" by diverting attention from real problems. Those with power are "beyond incrimination" (Kennedy, 1976).

Those at risk of getting into trouble with the law, the instrumental Marxists tell us, are those without power. The very creation of the collective perception of crime and the need for repressive law takes place by the conspiratorial practices of elites. The concept of the "reasonable man in law," the juridic subject, serves the interests of elites in that they need predictable performances from subjects in the work force as well as citizens who are obedient to the order. In sum, the legal order, including the form of law and legal thought, are totally attributable to the ruling class's influence. No autonomy between the political and the legal order is said to exist. Law is but a reflex of changing economic conditions. The primary need of the capitalist ruling class is to maintain its position of power and to assure maximization of profits.

The structural Marxists see things differently. Although drawing from the extensive works of Marx and Engels their interpretation runs in a different direction. To begin with, the notion that the legal order is directly under the control of the "ruling class" — is not autonomous — fails to answer some deeper questions, according to the structuralist Marxists.

On the one hand we may ask: to what degree is the legal form independent from the will of some powerful group? On the other: to what degree is the legal form independent from the capitalist system itself? These are independent questions that are often handled as if they were not (Balbus, 1977a:571-572). Traditionally, it was the first question that was most often asked. Thus, some empirical studies investigating the relationship between powerful groups and a specific law have found that there are direct connections between the two. Conclusion: law is not autonomous. Other studies investigating this relationship generate data that indicate that no direct relationship exists between the will of a powerful group and particular laws and conclude: law is autonomous. But in neither case has the investigator asked the question about the relationship of the legal form to the mode of production *itself* to which the actors (powerful and powerless) belong. Thus, to simply show that the legal form did not respond directly to some powerful actors, and hence, to conclude that it is autonomous, "omits the possibility that the law is not autonomous from, but rather articulates with and must be explained by, the systemic requirements of capitalism..." (ibid., 572). This conclusion has raised a host of new critical inquiries.

The structuralists focus on a different set of questions. They are interested in the internal dynamics of capitalism, in what makes it run as a system. And how, as a consequence, certain forms develop — including the legal form — which have their basis in the needs of the mode of production itself. (Recall Marx's guiding principle that stated, in part, "people inevitably enter definite relations, which are independent of their will.") In this perspective, the capitalist "class" may not directly control the legal form but nevertheless is benefited by its continued existence. The legal form, formal rationality, then, attains a "relative autonomy." The legal form is not merely an instrument, a tool of some class. Nor does it have a totally independent development. The state, then, must be seen as a "structure to which capitalists themselves are obliged to subordinate their wills but which nevertheless — or, rather, precisely because of this subordination — functions to secure their *class interests*" (Balbus, 1977b, xxi-xxii, emphasis in the original).

The unique position of the relatively autonomous legal form, formal rationality, allows two simultaneous processes to take place: repression *and* legitimation. The core questions for the structural Marxists, then, focus on certain processes: domination (legitimation), mystification, ideology, hegemony and reification. It is to Pashukanis that we must turn for some beginning insights on these relationships.

PASHUKANIS AND COMMODITY-EXCHANGE: COMMODITY AND LEGAL FETISHISM

Pashukanis (1891-1937) is a critical figure who has stimulated much Marxist analysis in law. Specializing in law and political economy at the University of Munich prior to the Russian Revolution of 1917, Pashukanis was to become the preeminent theorist in Russia in the 1920s until his demise in the 1930s. He was identified as "an enemy of the people" and executed during the Stalin purges in 1937. His developed theory of law and the state were not in accord with Stalin's desire to intensify the "dictatorship of the proletariat." But Pashukanis was to leave us with the so-called "commodity exchange" theory of law. The core ideas can be found in his treatise of 1924 entitled *The General Theory of Law and Marxism* (we will use the reprint of 1980 for citations). The rediscovery of his works led to much Marxist analysis (Beirne, 1979; Balbus, 1977a, 1977b; Milovanovic, 1981, 1989; Fraser, 1978). The legacy of this rediscovery was that the instrumental Marxist position lost the dominance it had retained throughout the

1960s and 1970s. From early 1980 onward, the structural Marxist position became the dominant position in the Marxist sociology of law in the U.S. and Europe.

The legal form, Pashukanis argued, develops directly out of the exchange of commodities in a competitive capitalist marketplace. In other words, as commodity owners exchange their commodities something else is taking place, behind their backs. Certain "appearances" (phenomenal forms) begin to materialize. The form of law, legal thought and the juridic subject (the abstract bearer of rights), are all derived from processes taking place in the economic sphere. Thus, there exists a close relationship between the economic and the legal sphere. What eventually are expressed in law are ideas generated during commodity exchange. The form of law and legal thought, then, develop somewhat independently from any wishes by the dominant class to simply control and repress. Law, as a consequence, has relative autonomy. But we are ahead of ourselves. Let us develop Pashukanis's argument and see what impact it had on the structural Marxist perspective.

The starting point of analysis for Pashukanis was the beginning sections of the first volume of *Capital*, where Marx developed his very difficult but pivotal idea of "commodity fetishism." To understand the logic of the legal form we must understand the logic of the commodity form. In other words, we will show how the two follow a similar logical development; that is, there exists a *homology*. Let us unravel this complex process and see how the two are interconnected.

We want to first indicate how commodities start as "use-value" and get transformed into "exchange-values." A commodity initially has use-value. There are two elements here: commodities reflect unequal amounts of social labor used in their production; and they also correspond to the ability of fulfilling a concrete need, which also varies. We have, then, inherent inequalities or differences in the first instance. Producing a thing for direct use creates use-value (and here we have products, not commodities). But, in a capitalist mode of production, when an object is produced to be transferred to another for the other's use, we have commodities (Marx, 1967:40-41).

Commodities, again, are inherently unequal. They correspond to different amounts of labor used in their production. They also reflect different abilities to fulfill some concrete need. In brief, we have inherent inequality on at least two levels at this point. But when two exchangers enter the competitive marketplace, Marx tells us, the commodity takes on exchange-value. That is, it "presents itself as a quantitative relation," as a specific "proportion in which values in use of one sort are exchanged for those of another sort" (ibid., 36). And here lies a profound transformation. The initial commodity, which was characterized as having use-value and which is inherently unequal to other commodities and their use-values, during exchange takes on an equivalent form. In other words, two commodities are brought into some mathematical or quantitative relationship (e.g., two bushels of apples = one pound of butter; the equal sign is significant). This relationship of "equivalence" hides inherent inequalities. Inherent differences are now replaced by a ratio of exchange. This is also sometimes referred to as the "law of equivalence."

Let's state this complex idea in another way. What started out as a qualitative relationship — use values and inherent differences — is now transformed, behind commodity exchanger's backs so to speak, into a quantitative relationship. We have gone from quality to quantity. It's an outcome of commodity owners coming to the competitive marketplace under capitalism to seek profit for their commodities. We must remember, too, that in actuality we have thousands upon thousands of exchanges taking place.

This ratio of exchange finds further expression in money. Two bushels of apples, for example, are worth \$2. So, too, is one pound of butter. Thus: 2 bushels of apples = \$2 = 1 pound of butter. "In the marketplace, then, qualitatively distinct commodities enter a formal relationship of equivalence, in a definite ratio, facilitated by the universal equivalent — money" (Milovanovic, 1981:41). Put in another way, money, an abstract statement of a thing's worth, now replaces the inherent differences that existed prior to exchange. Here, \$2 represents the worth of 2 bushels of apples or one pound of butter.

A masking, however, has taken place. What has been removed from consciousness, what disappears from the scene, are the inherently unequal needs that existed and the differentiated labor used to produce a commodity. Money now replaces the value of all commodities. Consider, for example, the toil and suffering it actually takes in the concrete world to produce, say, a car. All this disappears from the scene for the purchaser of the car. Lost from consciousness is the alienation, the monotony, the industrial "accidents" that have been part and parcel of the production of the car. "The memory of use-value," Marx tells us, "as distinct from exchange-value, has become entirely extinguished in this incarnation of pure exchange-value" (1973:239-240).

Certain transformations have taken place. From: quality into quantity, the concrete into the abstract, content into form. This whole process Marx calls the "fetishism of commodities." All phenomena are brought under this idea. (Note that nowhere in this analysis have we blamed the conspiratorial practices of some "ruling class.")

We may note some everyday examples. We often hear of graduating students preparing to go on the job market "to see how much they are worth." Or we hear about baseball players at contract talks squabbling over a "pittance" of a $100,000 or so because they think they are worth as much as somebody else. In other words, what has happened in this process is the creation of fetishes — things are produced which we begin to worship as having sole worth, namely money. We begin to measure a person's worth in terms of money. This process extends to many diverse relations the subject now enters. Concrete human needs, differentiated labor and abilities, and genuine human value, disappear from consciousness. This whole complex process, a Marxist (and Hegelian) discovery, is duplicated in the legal form. In other words, a similar logical development occurs in the legal sphere, producing, for example, the notion of the abstraction, the "reasonable man [woman] in law." How is this possible?

It was Pashukanis who described this connection most forcefully (1980; see also, 2002). Pertinent sections concerning commodity fetishism can also be found in the following treatises by Marx: *The Critique of Hegel's Philosophy of the State*; *Capital*; *The Grundrisse*; the *Critique of the Gotha Program*; and *On the Jewish Question*.) For Pashukanis,

> People enter ... [socioeconomic] relationships not because they have consciously chosen to do so, but because the conditions of production necessitate it. Man is transformed into a legal subject in the same way that a natural product is transformed into a commodity with its mysterious quality of value [1980:51].

Legal rights and the notion of the juridic subject, for Pashukanis, develop in a similar (homologous) way as in commodity fetishism. The constant transfer of commodities in the capitalist marketplace creates certain appearances, certain notions of rights. Rights are defined as "the sum of benefits which the general will recognizes as belonging to a specific person" (ibid., 78). Let's follow the parallel development of the legal form and the commodity form.

The subject, analogous to the commodity and its use-value, is unique; s/he appears with different aptitudes, potentials, interests, wants and needs. Here we have inherent differences. But the subject who enters the marketplace to exchange finds her/himself in a definite relationship with another. At this exact moment three ideas begin to materialize. First, at the precise moment of exchange, the two commodity owners have entered a relationship of equality, of equivalence. Each recognizes the other as equal vis-à-vis the transaction. Again, there may be vast differences between the two people, but at the exact moment of the transfer of commodities we have equivalence. Second, at this precise moment, there is recognition of free will in each of the parties. Each recognizes the other as having willingly entered the transaction. Third, each recognizes the other as the rightful property owner (proprietor) of the commodity that is being exchanged.

The constant transfer of commodities — and as a logical extension, rights — in the marketplace creates the *appearance* of a bearer of rights. These appearances, these "phenomenal forms," reflect the notion of equality, free will, and proprietorship. Again, we must keep in mind thousands upon thousands of these exchanges taking place in a competitive, capitalist marketplace and certain appearances beginning to emerge. The notion of the "reasonable man in law," or the legal subject that emerges, is referred to as the juridic subject. Note that this is an abstraction. In other words, quality again has been transformed into quantity: the uniqueness of being a human being (somewhat analogous to the use-value of a commodity) has been changed into a mathematical loci of certain rights (somewhat analogous to the exchange-value of a commodity). The result of this process is the juridic subject. As Pashukanis has argued, "the legal subject... assumes the significance of a mathematical point, a centre in which a certain sum of rights is concentrated" (ibid., 78). Said in another way, the subject has now taken on the qualities of exchange-value.

This constant transfer of commodities and rights produces the idea of a general and abstract bearer of rights. Lawyers subsequently give this phenomenon an "idealized expression." That is, lawyers, unaware of this underlying process, articulate rights and what a "reasonable man" in law should look like. They verbalize what is appearing during these many exchanges of commodities. In other words, such noble ideas as "freedom, equality and property" that have found their way into many national constitutions are but reflections of the underlying process of legal fetishism. They have their roots in these transactions.

Just as money became the universal equivalent for the purposes of commodity exchange, so, too, does the juridic subject. In both instances we have created a fetish, idols that we worship. These abstractions now come to dominate our lives, even as we actively produce and reproduce them (a process referred to as *reification*). Note, for example, the emphasis placed on the "reasonable man [woman] in law." Again, this is an abstraction, but nevertheless, when a jury of peers weighs evidence during a trial, its standard is still this abstraction: what would a reasonable man [woman] in such-and-such a situation do?

In feudalism, where commodity exchange was not the norm, no conception of formal rights existed. There, one's rights, duties, and obligations were directly connected with one's standing in that particular city, town, or community. Thus status was the key.

The notion of formal equality in law, as we have seen, is but the end result of fundamental processes imperceptively taking place in the marketplace. These appearances find expression in law. For example, the Fourteenth Amendment includes the "equal protection clause." It stands for the principle that equally situated people should be equally treated. This can be shown to be an outcome of legal fetishism. But if we begin with a concrete situation of inequality, followed by an application of an equal scale (equivalence, formal equality), we end by reinforcing systemic inequalities. In other words, this is a classic case of *repressive formalism* (see the upper left hand corner of Figure 1 from the introductory chapter). For example, reconsider the speeding ticket example offered in the introductory chapter, where the initial points, income differentials, vary widely.

The whole notion of legitimate domination or, in brief, *legitimation*, is connected with the rule of law. The rule of law, in turn, finds its determinant in commodity exchange relations. The legal form gains a relative autonomy from the political sphere. Its inherent logic merely reflects the inherent logic found in the mode of production. The centrality of such historical cries and demands for "equality before the law," and for the "rule of law," reflect the persistent orientation to these abstractions that have been created "behind men's backs." Ironically, even where obvious deviations from the rule of law occur, it is but an occasion to reinforce this ideology. How often in our reform efforts do we automatically try to seek purer adherence to formal equality in our attempts to eradicate different forms of discrimination in the criminal justice system? But our ideal endpoint is still "equality for all before the law." Deviation provides the very opportunity to reinforce the dominant ideology, and hence provides legitimation. Put in another way, competitive, laissez-faire capitalism provides its own legitimation principles that can be traced back to commodity exchange's inherent logic (Habermas, 1975:25).

Pashukanis's rediscovered works provided much stimulus for further refinement in the structural Marxist perspective throughout the 1980s. Many theorists from this perspective have taken his insights as a beginning point for further analysis within the Marxist tradition. There are those who simply attribute all developments in the superstructure to the unfolding of the logic of the commodity form. At the other end are those Marxist scholars who see Pashukanis's insights as a starting point for much further analysis of additional factors. We will briefly describe some current refinements in the structural Marxist perspective. We shall see that a second variant exists, which posits primacy as to the directionality of cause, to superstructural practices.

Late Capitalism

The advanced form of capitalism, many structural Marxists argue, is no longer defined by its competitive, laissez-faire characteristics of the late 19th century. The 20th and 21st century form appears as state-regulated capitalism. Consider Klare's observation that rights are:

> increasingly being transformed from one of absolute entitlements possessed by individuals as against state power to one in which the individual has a narrow claim merely to have his or her interests 'weighed' by authoritative agencies and or represented reasonably and in good faith by large, bureaucratic corporate entities over whose direction one has no real control [1979:125].

Note, too, that:

> [t]he state sets the ground rules of most economic transactions, directly regulates many significant industries, regulates the class struggle through labor laws, through its actions determining the size of the 'social wage,' provides the infrastructure of capital accumulation, manages the tempo of business activity and economic growth, takes measures directly and indirectly to maintain effective demand, and itself participates in the market as a massive business actor and employer [ibid.].

In the more advanced form of capitalism, it is said that greater involvement by the state comes about to offset different economic crises. These economic crises can often lead to *legitimation crises* (Habermas, 1975, 1984, 1987). That is, subjects may withdraw legitimacy from the economic system and the rule of law. Also, with the state actively intervening in the economic sphere, it can no longer rely on the inherent legitimation principles developed from commodity exchange. The state must actively formulate rules toward some specific end. The form taken by the judiciary is *interest-balancing* (see Milovanovic, 1986, 1987). Particularly in the judiciary, the justices must balance the interests of the subject against some other state goal. Some ideal end point (e.g., the social good, national security, the need to run an orderly prison, crime control, etc.) guides decision making. Here, then, the form of law is changing more to a form of substantive rationality.[2]

All this, the structuralist Marxists argue, necessitates a new ideology justifying existing arrangements and the obedience to them. Maine's central thesis that law progresses from status to contract can now be restated. The progression, according to this perspective, is from status, to contract, and back to status. "Status," defined by "the set of rights and duties attendant upon membership in a particular group, rather than contract, has become the paradigmatic legal relationship of the corporate state" (Fraser, 1978:165-166; see also Reich, 1964:785; Selznick, 1969:61-62, 248-249; Renner, 1949:121). In other words, individuals increasingly gain rights by way of membership in officially recognized groups (e.g., union member, prisoner, detainee, juvenile, non-management worker, welfare recipient, incarcerated mentally ill, etc.). As Renner notes:

> Formerly based upon contract, the labour relationship has now developed into a "position," just as property has developed into a public utility. If a person occupies a "position," this means that his rights and duties are closely circumscribed, the "position" has become a legal institution in character much like the fee of feudal times. The "position" comprises the claim to adequate remuneration (settled by collective agreement or works rule), the obligation to pay certain contributions (for trade unions and insurance), the right to special benefits (sickness, accident, old age, death) and finally certain safeguards against loss of the position or in case of its loss [1949:121].

In sum, in the advanced form of capitalism one's *status* as a prisoner, welfare recipient, student, laborer, juvenile, union/non-union member, etc., becomes the key in the determination of rights honored in law. Recall that previously in a competitive, capitalist market economy, the juridic subject was more homogeneous — few distinctions, that is, were made in law. In state-regulated capitalism the notion of a global juridic subject begins to be undermined. The judiciary, then, must actively intervene in the social formation to come up with the appropriate balance in the determination of rights. But this leads to problems of legitimation. The state and its functionaries, particularly the judiciary, must increasingly create myths that justify existing exploitive socio-economic relations. *Hegemony*, the active participation of those being oppressed in their own oppression, takes on more creative and hidden forms (see Milovanovic, 1986, 2002; Bannister and Milovanovic, 1990; Henry and Milovanovic, 1991, 1996).

The notion of the state has a different significance for the instrumental Marxists than for the structural Marxists. Both base their views on Engels's classic statement that "the state arose from the need to hold class antagonisms in check" (cited in Cain and Hunt, 1979:157). The state arose as a recognition that society "has become entangled in an insoluble contradiction with itself, that it has split into irreconcilable antagonisms which it is powerless to dispel." Thus, in order to stop society from destroying itself, a process continuously fueled by "classes with conflicting economic interests," the state arose as a power "seemingly" above society (ibid., 156). Engels further states that "the... most powerful economically dominant class ...acquires new means of holding down and exploiting the oppressed class" (ibid., 157). And here lies the different interpretation. The instrumental Marxists argue that the state really is a "capitalist state": that is, the state is merely an instrument by which the dominant class rules.

The structuralists, on the other hand, argue that the state has a certain degree of autonomy. It should not be perceived simply as an empty shell to be filled at the whim of the ruling class. Nor is it immune from political struggles. Rather, the structure of the state is somewhat a product of elite interests *and* working class movements. The particular characteristics of the state therefore reflect the class struggle between workers and capitalists. The state, the structuralist Marxists continue, also attempts to resolve contradictions in the social formation. The capitalist system itself is not fundamentally altered. Rather, the state assures that key values and structures are not changed. Oppositional groups, too, are channeled into making use of procedural formalities under the rule of law rubric in the redressing of grievances (Milovanovic, 1986, 1996; Thomas and Milovanovic, 1990). Hence a dialectical struggle accounts for the particular form of the state (Esping-Anderson et al., 1979).

The "state apparatus" (police, courts, legislators, prisons, etc.), for the structuralists, has a more difficult time of maintaining legitimation in the advanced forms of capitalism. In the early laissez-faire competitive forms, we saw that legitimation is maintained in good part by the inherent "justice" found in commodity exchange. Notions of free will, equality and proprietorships arose from the subtle processes connected with commodity exchange.

In the state-regulated forms of capitalism, the state apparatus finds itself in a more active and contradictory role in an economic system that tends toward crises. The state apparatus finds itself in the difficult position of reconciling the pressures of different interest groups. At the same time, fundamental values supporting the capitalist system must be sustained. Marxists from this school of thought point out that within this contradictory situation change occurs at a gradual pace. But, they add, the central place of such ideals as property, egotism, and the pursuit of profits will not be infringed. (For an examination of how "liberty" and "property" interests developed in the Fourteenth Amendment, see Milovanovic, 1987.)

Forces within the state apparatus may have a degree of independence from the specific interests of power elites. For example, to a great degree, lawyers are committed to the ideals of the rule of law and, specifically, formal rationality as an ideal type. To this degree, the sphere of law generates its own pressure or influence on the economic, political and ideological spheres. We are left, then, with the conclusion that phenomena are "overdetermined." That is, the "cause" of things, from the structural Marxist's perspective, is always multiple. Economic, political and ideological factors can exert pressure to produce, for instance, a particular law. It is then an empirical question as to which factors in combination are the decisive ones.

The instrumental Marxists would argue that, yes, there are a number of factors, including class struggle, that force the elite to change policies, but after all is said and done it is the economically powerful actors who have the final say. In other words, "in the final analysis," class repression will be maintained.

Property and Contract

Our next point deals with the notion of contract and property. For the structuralists, the contract as "an agreement of independent wills" is central in law. In fact, for Pashukanis, it is the ultimate expression of commodity exchange (1980:82). It expresses, in concrete form, such notions as will and subjectivity. It disguises and denies, at the same time, the inherent inequalities existing between contracting parties. Contractual freedom disguises inequalities while at the same time giving the appearance of freely developed agreements. The "just" contract can only be defined in relation to the type of mode of production in existence. Marx has said it "is just whenever it corresponds, is appropriate, to the mode of production. It is unjust whenever it contradicts that mode. Slavery on the basis of capitalist production is unjust; likewise fraud in the quality of commodities" (cited in Cain and Hunt, 1979:138).

The ethical principle of equality, for example, has no standing in feudalism. Society was organized hierarchically. The serf or peasant found her/himself in a hierarchy of bondage to a lord of the manor. The notion of commodity exchange between two equal persons had no relevance. Thus, without commodity exchange, no spontaneous notions of equality, free will or proprietorship could develop. In addition, the notion of a formal legal subject, the juridic subject, had no place. That is, the notion of a formal legal status *common to all* did not exist. Subjects merely had concrete rights or privileges within each estate, city, or village. The rights were not carried with them when they left for another community.

The contract, then, arose at a unique stage in the development of society. The capitalist mode of production demanded an instrument that would facilitate exchange. It was invented. Other benefits, too, were derived from it. That is, the contract served not only a facilitative function but also a repressive and ideological one. Inequality between members was disguised. Propertied classes could dictate the terms of the contract. Workers were offered a contract, "take it or leave it." But, ideologically, the notion of contractual freedom was maintained (be it in actuality merely a myth). A society, characterized by self-centered individuals meeting in the anarchy of the marketplace, where each individual strives to maximize profits, even at the expense of the other, could be stabilized by the existence of the contract. The state would be ever-present to enforce these agreements. The result: calculability and predictability — in a word, stability.

Property rights, too, are connected with the rise of capitalism. Marx recognized that "society itself... is the root of property," and that the notion of property represents exclusion of another's will (cited in Cain and Hunt, 1979:98, 100; see also Hegel's [1955] *Philosophy of Right* which was the basis of much of Marx's analysis of property and the contract). The right to private property stems from the state's assurance for it. With the development of the idea of exchangeability, arising from stable commodity marketplaces, exchange became increasingly regulated. In addition, the notion of the right of ownership and the laws of private property developed (Pashukanis, 1980:83-84). Feudal "property" was characterized by its immobility. "[I]t is incapable of becoming an object of mutual guarantees, moving from one hand to another... Feudal or estate property violates the basic principle of bourgeois society — 'the equal possibility of obtaining inequality'" (ibid., 83).

Property in capitalism becomes "an object of mutual guarantees." I promise to give you something, which I own, and in return I receive something of which I recognize you to be the owner. This can assure a minimum of external coercion·by the state. The state, by upholding principles of formalism in law, can simply guarantee the property distributions that favor the more advantaged groups. But in times of revolt this guarantee can be dissolved.

The relationship of exchange where property is the object of mutual guarantees, once formalized, becomes a more permanent, more enduring institution. One only has to look at many challenges of the non-propertied against the powerful to find that after the revolution the former continued to meet in the marketplace to freely exchange commodities. It would be different for "proletarian" revolutions where property itself becomes the object of attack (ibid., 83-84).

Private property and rights of private property in a commodity-oriented economy, then, destroy all genuine bonds between people (ibid., 85). In a society where we find peasants and the guild crafts, where the serf is directly attached to the land, we also find in existence norms limiting private property (ibid., 87; see also, Stone, 1985:51).

On another level, with the development of the capitalist mode of production, we find a split between the owner of the means of production, the capitalist, and the worker, the seller of her/his own labor (Marx, 1967). Here the contractual terms reflect different and unequal relationships to property. The capitalist has more power to dictate the terms of the contract. Laws will often minimize some of the negative consequences of work conditions, but will not overly infringe upon such essential things as "management prerogatives." Namely, the question of the future of the organization, worker self-management, profit sharing, or generally, substantive issues, will not find a friendly ear in the court. The worker is given formal contractual and property freedoms, but the unequal distribution of property relationships will place the propertied in a more advantaged position in dictating the terms of the contract. The state stands ready and willing to support the unequal balance between the contracting parties.

But the worker is losing ground in a state-regulated capitalist society. More and more restrictions are placed on property owners. Many of these restrictions, from the worker's point of view, are welcomed, such as those that assure health and safety at the workplace; however, state restrictions extend to many other dimensions of all worker's property, including those less propertied. Since the domain of property is becoming more controlled, particularly for the worker, "zones of privacy" are becoming fewer (see Reich, 1964). A safe enclave where the worker can recover from the brutalizing conditions of the work place or the exploitive conditions in the economy is diminishing.

In sum, notions of property and the contract undergo transformations with the arrival of capitalism. They are intricately connected with the mode of production. Only with a change in the mode of production can notions of property and contract undergo a fundamental change.

The Withering Away of the State, Law and the Juridic Subject

Marxist analysis offers not only a critical description but also a direction for genuine change. Marxists see the state as repressive. At a minimum, the state maintains the relations and belief systems necessary for the continued exploitation of the worker. With the change to a different mode of production where class domination will not exist, namely to communism, it is argued that the necessity of the state will "wither away." Since law supports capitalist interests — either directly as in the instrumental perspective, or indirectly as in the structural Marxist perspective — then with the withering away of the state, and exploitive, predatory social relations based on profit and commodity exchange, so too the legal form will disappear. Furthermore, the notion of the formal abstract legal subject in law, which has meaning only in a commodity exchange competitive marketplace, will also wither away. Pashukanis is quite clear here: "the problem of the withering away of law is the cornerstone by which we measure the degree of proximity of a jurist to Marxism" (1980).

Marxists note three stages in this development. The most advanced form of capitalism is said to have so many contradictions within it that it will collapse. The next phase, socialism, will be marked by the "dictatorship of the proletariat." Here there will still be class rule and domination. But instead of the capitalist class ruling, it will now be the workers who do so. Here the "narrow horizons of bourgeois thought" would still continue. In other words, vestiges of capitalist law, ideologies and consciousness would still exist for a time. But under the control of the workers, a class law, being still coercive, would be directed toward the struggle for a classless society. This first phase of communism would be replaced by the "higher form," or communism proper.

During socialism the mode of production would still have remnants of capitalism. But, Pashukanis tells us, instead of commodity exchange, we would have a voucher system (so many hours worked can be traded in for so much produce), and the central economic policies will establish what "exchange ratios" should be. That is, these policies would establish a thing's true social value and assure that exchanged goods reflect their true value. Here, then, exchange-values will disappear. We would have a return to use-values. Products would have direct personal use. Thus, abstractions that emanate from commodity exchange, too, would gradually disappear. (We are refraining from running out all the critiques levied against this idealism due to the more expository project before us. We should mention, however, that on the point just developed, Weber would definitely have something to say about the rise of a bureaucracy that would administer this new society, which would inevitably be the basis of a new form of domination.)

Advocates of the "withering away of the state, law, and the juridic subject" would argue that people would return to appreciating the wholeness of the other. The other would be seen as someone who complements, not one who exploits. Competition and the profit motive would be replaced by such principles as mutual aid and community, and by the notions of need and ability.[3] The legal personality is no longer needed. That is, the abstraction, the juridic subject, would wither away. In the higher forms, Lenin tells us people will be:

> accustomed to observing the elementary rules of social intercourse that have been known for centuries... they will become accustomed to observing them without force, without compulsion, without subordination, without the special apparatus for compulsion which is called the state [1949:142].

Thus, habit and custom, the thesis continues, would now govern relationships. People will orient themselves to the order because they see it as consistent with time-treasured ideals such as equality and community and consistent with the potential for self and group development. "Excesses" will still exist because of individual variation. But these problems in living will be dealt with spontaneously. No special coercive apparatus is necessary. At most, community moots or mediation mechanisms will develop. But no need exists for specialists such as lawyers for mediating disputes.

In fact, the bureaucracy will be dismantled. Instead, Lenin tells us, accounting and control of the industries can be done by any literate person with the knowledge of the rules of arithmetic (1949:160-161). Thus, rather than the administration by specialized bureaucrats, Lenin assures us that the average city dweller is fully capable of learning and doing these functions. "Foremen and bookkeepers," he tells us, will coordinate industrial production (ibid., 80). "Collectivist organizations" will be the ideal forms of production. These will be based on orientations that focus on collective development (Rothschild-Whitt, 1979; see, also, Milovanovic, 1989, chapter 6).

Marxist analysis claims that each of the three stages has a particular form of justice. Under capitalism, formal equality is the ideal. In socialism, the equality principle would be more genuinely applied. But two further correlative principles would exist: (1) "he who does not work, neither shall he eat," and (2) "an equal amount of products for an equal amount of labour" (Lenin, 1949:150). And the equality principle will still exist: i.e., a formally equal scale will be applied to unequal persons. This, in the "higher forms," will be replaced by a standard that recognizes people as different in temperament, drives, abilities, potentialities, dexterity and so forth (see, for example, Lee, 1959:39-52). In other words, an alternative substantive standard of justice will prevail. Implying that people are basically the same and applying a form of law reflecting that notion, the Marxists tell us, are repressive practices. The standard of the "higher form" would be: "from each according to his[her] ability, to each according to his[her] needs" (Pashukanis, 1980:324; Lenin, 1949:152-163).[4]

Dialectics of Struggle

We want to briefly highlight an important line of theory within sociology of law that has emerged particularly since the ascendancy of the structuralist Marxist perspective. This concerns the notion of the dialectics of struggle. Our starting point of analysis is Quinney's classic statement concerning the linear development of revolutionary consciousness in *Class, State and Crime* (1977):

> Crimes of accommodation and resistance thus range from unconscious reactions to exploitation, to conscious acts of survival within the capitalist system, to politically conscious acts of rebellion. These criminal actions... evolve or progress from *unconscious reaction* to *political rebellion* [1977:59].

Some literature, however, has questioned this linear development. Studies done on jailhouse lawyers (Milovanovic, 1988; Milovanovic and Thomas, 1989; Thomas and Milovanovic, 1999), activist lawyers before the court (Bannister and Milovanovic, 1990), "rebels" being processed during mass arrests (Balbus, 1977b), and other activists (Henry and Milovanovic,

1991, 1999), indicate that ostensibly oppressed groups often *inadvertently* reconstitute the forms of domination themselves. For example, inmates who teach law themselves and practice it while imprisoned buy into legal discourse in grieving their case, and thus inadvertently give further force and legitimacy to the rule-of-law ideology. Activist lawyers before the courts find themselves in a similar position. Elsewhere, some activist movements have inadvertently further empowered the state. Environmentalists, critics of the legal system who favor a get-tough approach to the white-collar offender, and some early feminists who advocated a harsher approach to woman abusers, have all supported tougher and lengthier imprisonment. This position, ironically, solidifies the powers of the state. And some activists who advocate "reversing hierarchies" often do just that, maintaining the form of oppression itself (see Cornell, 1998).

Yet other activists, not well informed of theoretical and historical works, have often reverted to "us versus them" hate-politics (Groves, 1991; Milovanovic, 1991a, 1991b). Political correctness is one element of this form of "schmarxism" (see chapter 6). The uncritical view that some leftists embrace concerning the situation in revolutionary and post-revolutionary governments claiming to be "humanistic," "socialistic," or "communistic" has been well documented. Although some of the accomplishments of the Cuban regime, for example, are to be admired, the critical evidence certainly questions it in its totality as an example of an empowered democracy and the blueprint of a humanistic society. Some, who practice solidarity politics, would benefit from a familiarization with the critical theoretical literature, and especially with the historical literature, that has illustrated the dialectics of struggle. See, for example, Piers Beirne's book *Revolution in Law* (1990). What this does seem to indicate is that those merely practicing solidarity politics with no grounded basis in theoretical and historical analysis, or those ivory tower figures who never directly experience the barricades, are equally guilty of not developing a transpraxis, both a critique of what is and a vision of what could be (Henry and Milovanovic, 1996) as a basis of a humanistic transformative politics.

Summary

The Marxist approach to the sociology of law comes in two forms. The instrumental Marxists see law and legal thought as simply the product of class rule. The structural Marxists, on the other hand, argue that the form of law and legal thought as well as the state can be relatively autonomous from the wishes of particular capitalists, while at the same time still helping to provide an environment for the continued exploitation of the worker. Repression *and* legitimation can be combined. The structuralists focus on the notion of "overdetermination." Within the "superstructure" forces that have some degree of independence (relative autonomy) —such as ideology, the legal profession and political class struggles — can have influences in the development of laws. For Marxists the question of cause, domination (hegemony), legitimation crisis, ideology, the juridic subject, the contract and private property rights — all are central issues.

The functions of law are repressive, facilitative as well as ideological. All three, in a Marxist perspective, are interrelated. Repressive functions include violence directed toward the working class. Facilitative functions include the promotion of laws that aid commodity exchange and the maximization of personal profit. Formal rationality, the contract and contractual freedoms assure this. Self-centered, calculating individuals, seeking the maximization of profits, are given a framework within which to orient their conduct. Finally, the ideological function includes how law communicates a message to the exploited that they are free, equal and can gain unlimited property by abiding by the rule of law. That is, by endowing the order with legitimacy and by uncritically orienting their behaviors to it, all are said to be able to attain maximal fulfillment. The rule of law ideology conveys the message that if personal failure exists, it is not the law, nor the economic system that is at fault. Reasons must be sought elsewhere. "Blaming the victim" of an exploitive system is the most prevalent form.

The relationship between a legal order and fulfillment of social values of individuality, equality and community can be summarized. Instrumental Marxists argue that the genuine fulfillment of these values in a capitalist mode of production does not develop. Rather, mystification, false consciousness and hegemony are outcomes of class rule. The structuralists, too, argue that because of repressive formalism, little genuine fulfillment of social values occurs. Workers, egoists driven by economic calculation for profits in a capitalist society, become "crippled monstrosities." They do so even as they worship its majesty.

We noted that Marx did not develop a systematic sociology of law. Rather, interested researchers have had to scrutinize his voluminous writings for scattered excerpts. Out of these, a Marxist oriented sociology of law is slowly beginning to materialize.

Notes

1. We have been greatly aided by the excellent collection of passages dealing with law and ideology by Cain and Hunt in *Marx and Engels on Law* (1979), by Beirne and Quinney's *Marxism and Law* (1982), by Beirne and Sharlet's *Pashukanis: Selected Writings on Marxism and Law* (1980), Pashukanis's *Commodity Exchange Theory of Law* (2002), and by Beirne's *Revolution in Law* (1990).

2. See, also, Unger, 1976:194; Turkle, 1981; Fraser, 1978:172; Balbus, 1977a:586.

3. See, for example, Pepinsky and Quinney, 1991; Tifft and Sullivan, 1980; Kropotkin, 1902, 1913.

4. For a critical view, see Hirst, 1986:28-63, 85, 104-105.

PART 2:

CONTEMPORARY PERSPECTIVES IN THE SOCIOLOGY OF LAW

4. Between Legal Science and Sociology of Law

Introduction. In this chapter we want to survey some approaches that are focused neither purely on jurisprudence (i.e., legal science) nor on sociology of law. These are the "in-betweeners," if you will. Yet these contemporary approaches are critical in the movement toward a fully articulated theory in the sociology of law. Accordingly, in the first section we have surveyed the Sociological Jurisprudence and the Legal Realist schools of law. Roscoe Pound perhaps best epitomizes the former. American legalism realism is best represented by Karl Llewellyn and Jerome Frank. Although their analysis surely went beyond merely legal dogmatics (legal science) by the introduction of sociology, psychoanalytic, economic, philosophical and anthropological literature in their critiques, it still fell in the framework of being more jurisprudence than a sociology of law.

Our second section will concentrate on the Critical Legal Studies Movement (popularly called "crits," or "cls"), an outgrowth of the former two approaches. With formal beginnings in 1977, the CLS theorists, or "crits," have, in a heretical way, theorized *within* the formal legal institutions and have developed a formidable body of critical analysis that fundamentally questions the "neutrality" of the legal apparatus.

The third section, feminist jurisprudence ("fem-crits"), has recently emerged as a dominant position in critical legal thought. We will also return to a feminist approach in the final chapter, when we present the postmodern perspective in the sociology of law. There, we will indicate that a small but articulate and persuasive body of analysis has developed based on the works of Jacques Lacan's psychoanalytic semiotics.

Since the early 1990s, a "critical race theory" ("CRT") perspective has gained much momentum. We will cover this in the fourth section. And certainly many disenfranchised will make their voices heard in the near future as to a representative approach. In fact, this is a compelling challenge for the near future: to establish different discourses where diverse voices may genuinely be expressed in law.

SOCIOLOGICAL JURISPRUDENCE AND LEGAL REALISM

Introduction. Although not sociologies of law in the truest sense, "sociological jurisprudence" and American Legal Realism have been two major movements in law in the 20th century. Roscoe Pound, the father of the former, and Karl Llewellyn and Jerome Frank, the key thinkers of the latter, will be central in the following presentation. Both movements attacked the form of law and thought (formal rationality, or formalism) that had evolved from the 19th century. Their criticisms were levied against the model of law expressed best by Christopher Langdell, Dean of Harvard Law School in 1870 (for an poignant overview of Langdell, see Patterson, 1995).

Law, Langdell argued, was an exact science, a legal science, much like physics, zoology, botany and chemistry. The ideal jurist used the law library as her/his laboratory. Not practical experience, but knowledge gained of pure, abstract law, particularly by analyzing "case law" of appellate decisions, would assure a scientific understanding of law. Through deciphering case law, and by the use of the Socratic method of recitation and quizzing by the instructor, the principles and doctrines of law could be taught to students (Langdell, 1887; Patterson, 1995).

Realists and their predecessors from sociological jurisprudence differed with this ideal. They viewed law more as a social science. Sociology, economics, psychology and philosophy would be their guide. Their laboratory was the real world. Pragmatism was their philosophy. Their focus was on judicial decision making and its non-formal (extra-legal) aspects. The law, for them, had become stagnant. It had ossified into formal procedures that did not allow equitable justice. They challenged the stated ideal of certainty and predictability in decision making (assumedly assured by abiding by the letter of the law), the strict emphasis on precedents (*stare decisis*), and the reliance on abstract and syllogistic reasoning. Their method was a socio-legal critique. They were to apply various sociological findings to the sphere of jurisprudence. They called into question the traditional methodologies and practices of law. The gap between law in theory and law in practice was torn asunder.

Important in understanding why both movements developed were the social and historical forces at work at the turn of the 20th century in the U.S. (Hunt, 1978:13; Hunt, 1993:36-57). The first few decades of the 20th century were marked by dramatic economic growth. Along with this came concentrations of power and the centralization of the state and the bureaucratic apparatus. At the turn of the century, the legal ideology existing had, as a guiding ideal, the emphasis on the least amount of legal involvement in the economy as possible, or *laissez-faire*. Intervention by the courts in the economic and social spheres was seen as undesirable. Rather, strict adherence to legal principles and the letter of the law was seen as the ideal, a path to the maximal realization of social values. But the accelerated economic and social changes in society, with their many contradictory demands, forced the courts to confront their own internal decision-making methodologies. The assault on formalism was to be centered at the prestigious law schools of Harvard, Columbia and Yale.

Roscoe Pound: Sociological Jurisprudence

Roscoe Pound, Dean of the Harvard Law School for many years, is considered the father of sociological jurisprudence. He was a prolific writer who wrote well into his nineties. The core of his ideas was developed in the first three decades of the 20th century. It was Pound, along with the notable jurists Oliver Wendell Holmes and Benjamin Cardozo, who mounted an attack on legal formalism (formal rationality). The movement's most active period was in the years 1900 to 1920, but it continued to have some influence in the decades to come. This movement predated and in many ways set the critical groundwork for Legal Realism, which had its heyday from 1920 to 1940.

Roscoe Pound was influenced by the *social control perspective*, the prevailing school of thought in sociology at the turn of the century (see also Hunt, 1993:40). He drew heavily from the writings of sociologist Edward Ross and the philosophy of William James, a pragmatist. "Social control," Pound argued, "requires power — power to influence the behavior of men through the pressure of their fellow men" (1968:49). His notion of social control led to his definition of law as "a highly specialized form of social control, carried on in accordance with a body of authoritative precepts, applied in a judicial and an administrative process" (ibid., 41). Underlying his notions of social control was a vision of individuals pursuing diverse interests. Along with the inevitable conflict between individuals advancing claims, he was concerned with the stability and order of a society. Thus, his underlying sociological model was concerned with the maintenance of an equilibrium, or a status quo in society. He was less concerned with the causes of the development of the legal form. He was more interested in the *results* of law, that is, how its application affected people (Hunt, 1978:20-22).

From his very first article in 1903, Pound's rather eclectic style stressed practical problems rather than just the development of pure theory as in the sociology of law. There were two foci in his approach. First, a refocusing of law from analyzing legal doctrines (rules and practices) to the analysis of their social effects. That is, his approach emphasized how law affected practical, everyday life (Pound, 1907). To this end, he argued, the methods, practices and findings of the social sciences should be used. In his words, "let us look to economics and sociology and philosophy, and cease to assume that jurisprudence· is self-sufficient...let us not become legal monks" (ibid., 611-612).

His second focus dealt with the application of rules. He urged that we should get away from mechanical applications of law. We should stay clear, he argued, of simply applying the letter of the law in all cases (formal rationality). The idea that decision making should follow the letter of the law, and that mechanical deductions from previous decisions in law (*stare decisis*) should be the rule, was contrary to his law-in-action framework. Legal rules, rather, should be "general guides" for the judge. The judge should be given a degree of discretion in determining justice in individual cases. It is only with respect to property and commercial law that there should be a "mechanical application of law." The reason for this, he argued, is because these transactions were very similar and repetitive in nature. But when the question of the morality of the individual or corporate behavior was concerned, the standard should be one of "equitable application." Equity was established by the judge given individual circumstances. Formal logic, then, should be merely an "instrument" employed in arriving at a fair decision. In brief, his sociological jurisprudence was hostile to formalism. In a classic statement he said: "Legal monks who pass their lives in an atmosphere of pure law, from which every worldly and human element is excluded, cannot shape practical principles to be applied to a restless world of flesh and blood" (1907:611-612; see, also Pound, 1908).

Pound's theory of *interests* is central to his writings. Interests, he argued could be individual, social or public (arguably, public interests could be subsumed under social interests). An interest is "a demand or desire which human beings, either individually or through groups or associations or in relations, seek to satisfy..."(1968:66). Law does not create these. Conflict occurs because of competition amongst these interests in a society where no assurance exists for total satisfaction (ibid.). For Pound, "there has never been a society in which there has been such a surplus of the means of satisfying these claims..."(ibid.). A legal system gives legitimacy to certain of these interests in law (ibid., 65). That is, it recognizes some and assures their protection in law.

The law, for Pound, should act so as to assure the maximum amount of fulfillment of interests in a society. And it should do so by minimizing sacrifices, waste and senseless friction. This would occur through *interest-balancing* by the courts. They would, for example, balance a social interest, like the "general safety" or the "general health," against an individual's interest from being free from some governmental intrusion into her/his privacy and effects. Hence, he has called his model of law "social engineering."

Along with his notion of interests and social engineering, Pound stated his principle of ethics, his "jural postulates of civilized society" (1968:113-115): in the application of interest-balancing certain ethical postulates should be guiding principles. Put in another way, these postulates are the ends, the goals and objectives of substantive law. They include the more general idea that in a civilized society one should be able to depend on certain general expectations; the expectations that others will not intentionally inflict harm; that one can control what one has legally discovered, acquired or created through one's labors; that the other will act with due care and create no unreasonable risk; that the other will act with good faith in her/his contractual dealings; and that, where the other owns a potentially dangerous thing s/he will not let it get out of hand. In his later writings he added the expectations of security of a job and of compensation for injuries suffered at the work place (ibid., 115-116). As perhaps a part of the second, he also suggested a social security system in which the whole society should assume responsibility for the misfortunes of its citizens (ibid.).

Finally, Pound outlined certain stages in the development of law. His stages went from their primitive forms towards the "socialization" of the law. The goal in this latter ideal type would be the maximal fulfillment of wants and desires. Law would attempt to recognize the maximum amount of interests and allow their fulfillment *within* the framework of law. In the higher forms, greater weight would be attached to public and social over private interests (see Hunt's typology, 1978:30). One only has to look at the evolution of property rights to see how increased restrictions have developed in the name of "the public good." This, of course, has been the end result of interest-balancing.

To conclude, Pound was an important force in reconceptualizing how law should be understood. He was interested in law in practice. He did not develop a systematic sociology of law, but he did argue that the social sciences should be applied in the field of jurisprudence. It was not until after 1930, when a new movement — Legal Realism — was well under way, that the differences between sociological jurisprudence and it were brought out in some sharp debates (see, generally, Rumble, 1968).

Legal Realism: Realistic Jurisprudence

The development of Legal Realism, or "realistic jurisprudence," owes much to the groundwork set by sociological jurisprudence. In many ways it has more continuity than differences with it. The differences perhaps are more of degree.

Legal Realism must be seen more as a movement rather than as a perspective or a school. There were various positions within the movement, from the more politically centralist Karl Llewellyn, to the more leftist Jerome Frank. Frank was influenced by the sociologist William Graham Sumner and psychological theory, particularly the work of Sigmund Freud. Llewellyn was also influenced by the sociological work of Sumner. The most active period of the movement was between 1920 to 1940.

Contrary to those who argued that this was a "radical" polemic, this movement, like its predecessor, was not concerned with a critique of capitalism itself. Rather, the underlying sociological framework placed high value on the idea of pluralism. That is, it assumed a society in which individuals with varying interests compete for scarce resources. Capitalism, individualism, the Constitution, and the desirability of the existing form of the legal system (formal rationality) were taken as a given, although, at various times some elements of substantive rationality were advocated. Perhaps not sufficiently recognized was that the door which now opened for substantive rationality could both enhance and restrict the fulfillment of social values. The Realists were reformers interested in progressive change in an age of increasing social complexity and state intervention.

Given the depression of the 1930s and the increasing intensity of conflict in society, the need for change and the regulation of diverse conflicts was even more compelling than during the previous critical Sociological Jurisprudence movement in law. This had its effects on the sharpness of the Realists' attack. The Realists attacked the notion that law in practice is an exact science. The whole emphasis of "realism," generally, was to present and deal with things "as they really were." Their concern with the practical led to much direct involvement by key theorists in the New Deal Administration of Franklin Roosevelt in dealing with the great Depression of the 1930s.

The underlying philosophical assumptions of the Realists rested on Pragmatism (Rumble, 1968; Hunt, 1978:41-42; Hunt, 1993:180). In the

1920s and 1930s in the United States, Pragmatism was a dominant school in philosophy. Not abstractions, nor elaborate theories, but concrete human conditions and how humans cope with various demands of living must be understood, according to this philosophy. Theorists like William James and John Dewey were highly respected. This carried over to the legal arena. Pragmatists were hostile to formalism, the use of abstractions, and exclusive reliance on strict deductive types of reasoning. For James (1955:45), such ideals as fixed rules and principles, closed systems, dogma, and finality in truth should be discarded. For Dewey, the "problem is not to draw a conclusion from given premises; that can best be done by a piece of inanimate machinery by fingering a keyboard. The problem is to find statements of general principle and of particular fact which are worthy to serve as premises" (1931:134). Thus, rather than relying on mechanical deductive reasoning from given rules, decision makers should be result-oriented; that is, concerned with probable consequences of their decision. (Of course, recalling the discussion from chapter 3, we see here the tension between the principles of formal rationality and substantive rationality.)

The Realists attacked, even more vehemently than their predecessors, formal judicial decision making. The *classical view* in arriving at a judicial decision had it that justices merely apply specific rules in a mechanical way to the "facts" of the case. Rules structure decisions. Judges, it was felt, have little independence in interpreting these rules. The Constitution, statutes, and/or precedents (*stare decisis*) dictate decision-making processes. The manner in which a decision is reached, therefore, is formal, mechanical and predictable. Extra-legal factors — that is, factors outside of law — such as the particular feelings, or biases of a particular judge, it was argued, do not have an influence in decision-making processes.

In the *classical view*, justices engage in syllogistic reasoning. Particular (major) premises are established that are rooted in the U.S. and state constitutions, rules and precedents. Then, logical and formal reasoning is applied to the "facts" (minor premise), which leads to a conclusion. (Recall an earlier example of applying an "equal protection argument" to an inmate subject to loss of "good time" liberty, chapter 2, Figure 3.) Thus the judge has only to look at the "facts," decide on the doctrine or principle at play, search for the appropriate rule or precedent(s), and apply it, by deductive logic and syllogistic reasoning, to the case. This, then, will lead to the correct decision. Because of the assumption that uniformity, formality, value-neutrality and impersonality in the application of this method existed, predictability, certainty, and even-handedness of the decision is said to be realizable. In a word, law is an exact science. And this represents the ideal of formal rationality, the rule of law (formalism).

The Realists, in particular Llewellyn and Frank, attacked these notions of the classic view in law on two levels (Rumble, 1968). First, on the level of "rule-skepticism," and second "fact-skepticism." As to the first level, the Realists, with varying degrees of vehemence, argued that there is a difference between "paper" rules and "real" rules. That is, there is a difference between what the justices are supposed to do (and the appearance of what they are doing) and what they *actually* do. Earlier jurists such as Holmes had already argued that "I will admit any general proposition you like and decide the case either way" (cited in Rumble, 1968:40).

The assumed linearity of syllogistic reasoning was questioned. In other words, the deciding of a case is based more on hunches, feelings, intuition, flashes, instinct, conviction or unconscious processes (e.g., extra-legal factors). After the fact (*ex post facto*) justifications or rationalizations can always be provided, based on some theory, doctrine, formula, rule or precedent, which justifies the decision. This is rule-skepticism. Consider, for example, a police officer testifying before the court that s/he made an arrest based on the "plain view doctrine" — a judicially established doctrine that stipulates that a police officer in her/his normal duties, when witnessing a crime or contraband, does not have to obtain an arrest or search warrant. At times, it could be quite unclear whether, in fact, the police officer engaged within the latitude allowable by the plain view doctrine or if s/he engaged in unlawful activity and only later justified the arrest or search based on this doctrine.

Even the same "factual" situation, the Realists argued, could be interpreted in different ways. Jerome Frank has been the most forceful on this point. In *Law and the Modern Mind* (1963) he has argued:

> The process of judging, so the psychologists tell us, seldom begins with a premise from which a conclusion is subsequently worked out. Judging begins rather the other way around — with a conclusion more or less vaguely formed; a man ordinarily starts with such a conclusion and afterwards tries to find premises, which will substantiate it [1963:108].

Thus, rather than accepting the idea that the existence of formal, deductive-type syllogistic reasoning structures the decision-making process, the Realists argue that it works the other way around. Conclusions are first made based on some extra-legal factor, and then the judge works backward in providing a justification. "The court," Frank tells us, "can decide one way or the other and in either case can make it's reasoning appear equally flawless" (1963:72).

Similar attitudes and values of judges (extra-legal factors) are said to account for uniformities in decision making. Llewellyn has said that the search for certainty in law is an illusion and "you must turn, for purposes of prediction, to the reactions of the judges to the facts and to the life around them" (1960:68). Therefore, for Llewellyn, it is not the rule of law that is central but "law through men" (1962:62). Frank, much more extreme, has argued that the reasoning one finds in case opinions is more of a "window dressing," or "formal clothes in which he [the justice] dresses up his thoughts" (1963:140-141). Again, the tension between principles of formal and substantive rationality is quite apparent in these critiques. And these criticisms, it might be added, went well beyond any formulations by those from the Sociological Jurisprudence movement.

The second level of attack against the classical notions of judicial decision making revolved around "fact-skepticism" (Rumble, 1968). What, in other words, constitutes a "fact" of a case? The traditional method stated that R (a rule) x F (the "facts") = D (the decision). But establishing the "facts," the Realists argued, is the product of a multitude of factors, some of the most important of which are hidden. Frank has argued that the main source of uncertainty or unpredictability in law is "fact-uncertainty." That is, the "facts" that are established in trial proceedings are always disputable. They are constructs or the end result of definitional processes. Only through oral testimony by witnesses with vastly different capacities and motivations for describing "what happened," are the "facts" established.

A pervasive obsession for certainty, however, permeates the decision-making process according to the Realists. For example, at the higher court levels, Frank tells us, a form of "Cadi [Khadi] justice" exists. "Courts," he argues, "often decide first and then arrange their 'facts' and 'rules' so as to justify the decision previously arrived at" (1931a:29). In other words, substantive rationality, substantive irrationality, or formal irrationality could in fact have been the decisive factor in the decision-making process. Frank has stated bluntly that "our judicial system is permeated through and through with Cadi justice... Ours is a system where it [Cadi Justice] is active but concealed" (ibid., 31). Thus the formula R x F = D must be restated as S (the stimulus that is affecting the judge) x P (the personality of the particular judge) = D (the decision) (1931b:242). Again, here we are a far cry away from principles of formal rationality, even though an *ex post facto* application of linear logic (syllogistic reasoning) may make the decision appear as having been "logically" developed within the terms of law.

Frank has also criticized other Realists for simply overlooking the importance of how a "frozen record" from below gets established. By a "frozen record" it is meant that "facts" become "frozen" in trial courts and are often taken for granted by the appellate courts. Frank criticizes Pound, Cardozo, as well as Llewellyn for their emphasis on upper-court decision-making processes to the neglect of the lower trial court. It is within the trial court proceedings that "facts" are established, and it is here that much uncertainty exists.

The Realists, generally, with the major exception of Frank, argued that predictability could be reestablished if better adherence existed to the scientific method in the study of law (Rumble, 1968:140). Llewellyn, for example, presented 14 "major steadying factors in our appellate courts." These points ranged from advocating the use of experienced lawyers, to an understanding of the use of a "frozen record from below," to life tenure for the justices to, finally, a "professional judicial office" (1962:19-51). On the other hand, Frank's (1949) recommendations included:

(1) advocating the development and the institutionalization of a "constructive skepticism" concerning how courts actually operate;

(2) altering legal education so as to include more practical internships and examinations of cases in law school that included the complete record;

(3) improving the adversarial trial processes (i.e., allowing greater pretrial discovery practices where each side would know all the relevant facts of a case, and appointing an impartial government official to independently dig up facts);

(4) allowing the trial court judge to attend appeal court's review of the case;

(5) abandoning the ritualistic robes worn by judges;

(6) advocating something akin to self-analysis by judges so they could understand their own biases; and

(7) greatly improving the trial-by-jury method.

It is illuminating to briefly compare the two major theorists' views as to the desirable end in law. For Frank, judges should take as fiction the notion that rules alone make the decision. The judge should be concerned with delivering equitable justice. "The law," he tells us, "is not a machine and the judges not machine-tenders" and "there never was and there never will be a body of fixed and predetermined rules alike for all" (1949:129). In delivering justice, then, abstract rules have to be adaptable and adjustable. The sense of justice of a keen, non-biased judge will produce an equitable decision. Yet Frank also admits that law, with his proposal, could become even more unpredictable (ibid., 143-144, 169).

Llewellyn, on the other hand, first notes the distinction between the "grand" and "formal" style in decision making. The formal style represents the classical, formal method in arriving at conclusions in law. The grand style is an approach in which "every current decision is to be tested against life-wisdom." Here, "'precedent' is carefully regarded, but if it does not make sense it is ordinarily re-explored...[An] alleged 'principle' must make for wisdom as well as for order if it is to qualify as such" (cited in Rumble, 1968:201). By 1940, he informs us, the trend in law had moved away from the formal to the grand style. In Llewellyn's model, more certainty and predictability is of a greater value and is seen as more attainable, than in Frank's. Thus, for Frank, the search for predictability and certainty is illusory. These ideals can never be attained because of the uniqueness of the human condition.

Summary

The first two decades of the 20th century saw the development of a frontal attack on formalism, or formal rationality in law. The Sociological Jurisprudence movement, spearheaded by Pound, questioned the very methods that had evolved in the 19th century. The Legal Realists in the 1920s and 1930s continued the attack but in a more critical way. The emphasis in both movements was on judicial decision making. The notion that decisions by justices are formal, impersonal, value-free, and derived logically by a method of syllogistic reasoning was questioned with differing degrees of vehemence.

The appearance and sanctity of formalism in law was never the same. But Legal Realism was to disappear abruptly from its point-position by the early 1940s. No major scholar seemed to have picked up the banner during this time. It was not until some 35 years later that yet another eruption, the Critical Legal Studies movement, was once again to pick up the work that was begun by Holmes, Pound and Cardozo and sharpened by Frank and Llewellyn. But the attack was to be much more vehement and expansive in its scope. It was to be centered in one of the bastions of law — Harvard Law School.

CRITICAL LEGAL STUDIES

Introduction. Just as Legal Realism was a logical heir to Sociological Jurisprudence, Critical Legal Studies, or, more often, cls) was an outgrowth of the critical developments within the Realist initiatives (Tushnet, 1986, 1991; Freeman, 1988; Hunt, 1993:139-181, 211-226; Kennedy, 1997). CLS's formal beginnings can be traced to the First Conference on Critical Legal Studies in 1977, held at the University of Wisconsin at Madison. By 1982, its annual meeting had almost a thousand in attendance.

For over 35 years after the most active days of Legal Realism the critical perspective on law had been dormant. But things changed quickly. Due to the different social movements and struggles of the 1960s and early 1970s, and to the perception that law as it was practiced — formalism — was out of accord with the realities that existed, a group of critical lawyers surfaced to carry on the critique begun by the Realists (Gordon, 1992). Their critique was to be much more vehement and extensive. A systematic sociology of law was in the making. But those within the ivory towers responded with their own attack on CLS and its adherents (see generally, Russell, 1986).

Theoretical Orientation

The CLS movement has developed in four stages. The first stage, the initial foray, extended from the early to mid-1970s. Theorists like Duncan Kennedy led a mixed bag of criticisms against formalism and the teaching of law (1970, 1973).[1] The second stage extended from the mid-1970s to the early 1980s. This was marked by case studies and internal critiques of formalism. This period was highlighted by the publication of a collection of case studies edited by David Kairys, entitled *The Politics of Law* (1992). The third stage, from the mid-1980s to the early 1990s, can be conceptualized as a search for theory. This change has been expressed best by the publication of a special issue on the CLS in the *Stanford Law Review* in January, 1984. The CLS movement is currently, in the fourth stage, in its own "critical" phase. Although it has lost some of its appeal, as witnessed by the decline in attendance at its annual meetings, it continues to provide internal critiques of formal rationality.

Also, two new perspectives evolved from internal CLS discussions. Some critical feminists who had begun with the CLS movement are now consolidating their own distinct approach, Feminist Jurisprudence ("femcrits"). Similarly, some Critical Race Theorists ("CRT"), seeing the feminist movement as overly homogeneous (e.g., white, middle class) in its focus, raised the female African-American voice. In turn, "LatCrit" theory has emerged out of Critical Race Theory (Carrasco, 1996). Indeed, with continued internal critical discussion, and with reaching out to otherwise non-crit members, numerous voices are now raising issues of gay and lesbian rights. We will return to these approaches in the next section.

Several foci unite those within CLS. First, rule- and fact-skepticism carry over from the Realists' polemic. The traditional baggage of formalism — the reliance on "neutral" and linear syllogistic reasoning, and the belief in value-neutrality, objectivity, predictability, certainty, and the stability in law based on *stare decisis* (precedents) in law — all are said to be a Big Lie. No distinction, they argue, exists between law and politics. In fact, politics is seen as the ultimate determinant of decisions. Case opinions are but rationalizations or justifications hiding value choices (for a connection between legal reasoning and politics, see Kennedy, 1997 and comments by Klare, 2001).

Second, the notion of legitimacy is central in their critiques. One of law's functions, they argue, is to legitimize domination by power elites. People in society are led to believe that they are governed by the "rule of law, not of men." The CLS theorists are interested in how belief-systems — that is consciousness and ideologies — are shaped with the help of law. In fact, they argue, law is ideology (Kerruish, 1991; see also Litowitz, 2000). Two components of the legitimacy function are *reification* and *hegemony*. Reification stands for the process in which people together, consciously and/or unconsciously, help create the very structures and institutions that dominate them. These structures take on objective-like qualities and are, to various degrees, worshiped. Hegemony stands for the process by which ruling elites govern by the active consent of those who are oppressed (see our introductory chapter).

In a section below on critical race theory, we shall have occasion to note that some critical race theorists have argued that giving up on a "rights-discourse," even though it is understood that this discourse does have a hegemonic function, may relinquish too much and leave oppressed peoples without *any* redress (see for example, Crenshaw, 1988). Consider Crenshaw's point: "The subordinate position of Blacks in this society makes it unlikely that African-Americans will realize gains through the kind of direct challenge to the legitimacy of American liberal ideology that is now being waged by Critical scholars" (ibid., 1385; see also West, 1989).

Third, CLS theorists question the Langdellian teaching method that had been solidified in the major law schools in the last quarter of the 19th century. Law schools, they argue, prepare the lawyer for hierarchy. The good lawyer is the "cheerful robot" who functions as an automaton.

Fourth, CLS, in the late 1980s, was in search of theory. The movement appeared in the U.S. just at the time that major reexaminations of Marxian theory were taking place in social thought. CLS theorists in search of a socio-political theory to adopt in their critical examinations of law found, then, competing perspectives with unresolved contradictions. (See also Hunt, 1986b:9; Hunt, 1993:211-248). Hence, Weberian, Marxist, Anarchist, Foucaldian, Derridarian, Freudian, Lacanian, postmodern, and pluralistic theories have been variously applied (see, generally, Boyle, 1985). Central in their investigation is the work of Gramsci (1971; for a good introduction and application to law, see Litowitz, 2000) on hegemony, and the critical social theory of the Frankfurt School (Habermas, 1975). What has brought CLS into sharp relief in the 1990s and the new millennium is the extensive internal critiques by fem-crits, crit-race theorists, "global critical race feminism," and emerging perspectives from gays and lesbians. Critical legal studies has undergone qualitative internal differentiation, and has contributed profoundly to critical analysis in law.

Fifth, the CLS scholars generally discount instrumental versions of Marxism. They see law as being relatively autonomous (see Hunt, 1993:165-169). Law is neither the direct servant of a power elite, nor is it totally independent of the dynamics of capitalism. Law is an arena where contradictions are faced and struggles fought. Here interpretive processes unfold. The propertied and non-propertied classes seek to establish their view of the world and give it legitimacy.

Sixth, the CLS scholars' methodology in examining existing case law and opinions is one of "trashing." The more refined terminology is "deconstruction," which is based on Derrida (1992; see also Balkin, 1987). The approach consists of a critical examination of underlying, unstated assumptions that inhere in case opinion. These are made visible and traced to particular interest groups.

Seventh, and finally, the "crits," partially in response to criticism, particularly from "fem-crits" and "critical race theorists," are beginning to offer more comprehensive visions of a more desirable form of society and law. Roberto Unger (1987) remains the most prominent visionary for the early Critical Legal Studies movement. Ironically, however, little further systematic analysis has followed his profound visions of an "empowered democracy" and a "transformative politics." Feminist jurisprudence, which we will develop below, has taken the lead in offering not only a philosophy of deconstruction but also visions for possible reconstruction. Critical Race Theory has provided new challenges for both the "crits" and "fem-crits" (Delgado and Stefancic, 2001). They have also introduced the notion of "intersections"; that is, race, gender and class are often intersecting, and the combinations produce greater discrimination. Thus, arising from Critical Race Theory have been variants such as "critical race feminism" (Wing, 1995). More recently, a "global critical race feminism" (Wing, 2000) has emerged, which focuses on women of color in a global context. And currently, in the early days of the new millennium we see further splintering in the development of a Latina/o-critical ("LatCrit") group (Carrasco, 1996; Valdes, 1996), a queer-crit group (Stockdill, 1999), and an Asian American jurisprudence (Matsuda, 1996) (see Delgado and Stefancic, 2001:6).

Substantive Issues

In the following section we have chosen nine substantive issues that represent some of the CLS positions (for a good early overview see Kairys, 1992; see also the collection by Caudill and Stone, 1995). These have been chosen to illuminate the form of critique that has evolved. (For a useful summary of the internal and external critiques, see Boyle, 1985; Harper, 1987; Hunt, 1993:139-181, 211-226; Kramer, 1995; Kennedy, 1994, 1997, 1998.)[2]

Several theorists have argued that law school prepares the student for her/his future position in hierarchical structures (see especially Kennedy, 1970, 1992, 1994; see also a feminist critique by Menkel-Meadow, 1988; Penther, 1999). Students, it is said, are taught such topics as contracts, torts, property, criminal law and civil procedure within the time frame of late 19th-century capitalism. They are taught that legal reasoning is a distinct and an objective method in arriving at a correct decision in law. They gradually internalize the distinct language of law. Students learn doctrines, rules, principles, procedures and reasoning techniques that remove them from the real world and other possible employment or outlook (*verstehen*). Putting it another way, the "crits" claim that the ideology of the rule of law and formal rationality are internalized rather quickly by law students and become central to future practice (see especially the case studies by Granfield and Koenig, 1990a, 1990b).

In addition, a more subtle process entails disempowerment. Law school teaches "students that they are weak, lazy, incompetent, and insecure. And it also teaches them that if they are willing to accept dependency, large institutions will take care of them almost no matter what. The terms of the bargain are relatively clear" (Kennedy, 1992:52). The educational orientation itself teaches the student to be dependent, to fit into the slots, to be a team player (Alberstein, 1999; Hooks, 1994; Guinier et al., 1997). The financial rewards, particularly after the personal sacrifices and efforts made pursuing the law degree and passing the bar exam, assure this compliance.

CLS theorists have looked at labor relations law and have argued that, ever since the passage of the National Labor Relations Act (NLRA) in 1935, workers have been coopted into believing that procedural justice resolves conflicts fairly in the workplace (Klare, 1978, 1992; see also Barenberg, 1993; Kennedy, 1997:249-251). Thus, Klare has focused on three areas: how the U.S. courts have "deradicalized" the progressive intent behind the Wagner Act of 1935, how collective bargaining contracts favor management, and how grievance proceedings "cool out" the laborer.

The Wagner Act was potentially one of the most radical pieces of legislation in U.S. history. The higher courts, however, according to Klare, interpreted the act rather narrowly. Not only that, but in their interpretations (which then established precedents), the higher courts framed the acceptable ideology of worker-management interactions (acceptable labor relations) in a conservative way, heavily favoring management. The "free" labor contract, Klare claims, is but a tool for economically privileged classes to dictate the terms of work and to maintain domination. The courts' opinions had it that workers are purely sellers of labor with no interests in production. Hence, the wage was central and the structure of the workplace was seen as out of bounds for union grievances. Such things as worker self-management, profit sharing, and fulfilling work roles were defined as non-arguable, non-litigable points (i.e., they were "management prerogatives"). The courts thereby restricted the vision of workers. Finally, the courts emphasized procedural justice over substantive justice. In other words, the courts reinforced the idea that conflicts with management could be fairly resolved by arbitration, that the machinery of grievance-submission and resolution could handle conflicts. Klare argues, however, that because of power differentials between the worker and management, equitable justice is not necessarily assured. Workers, because they work within the framework established by the courts' rulings, willingly give up challenging oppressive practices at the workplace. Workers are led to believe that procedural justice translates into substantive justice.

Swidorski (1995) has also looked into U.S. Supreme Court decisions in labor law and finds that the dialectics of freedom and oppression plays itself out in this arena. He tell us: "The Court has fulfilled two principle functions since the New Deal era: (1) legitimating the transformation of property that has occurred in the modern capitalist economy; and (2) managing social conflict by ensuring formal, but limited, representation for select groups, primarily before the administrative agencies of the modern state" (ibid., 163; see also Barenberg, 1993).

Anti-discrimination law is another area that the CLS scholars have investigated (Freeman, 1992; for a different emphasis, see Crenshaw, 1988; see also Russell, 1998). Freeman, examining the court rulings on discrimination since the famous *Brown v. Board of Education* case in 1954, has concluded that law has not eradicated race discrimination but "it has served more to rationalize the continued presence of racial discrimination in our society..." (1992:97; see also Freeman, 1988). He notes that underlying a court decision, whether a judge recognizes it or not, is an emphasis on either a *victim* or *perpetrator perspective*. The victim perspective sees racial discrimination in terms of particular *conditions* — lack of adequate employment, housing, education, health facilities, etc. The perpetrator perspective, on the other hand, assumes the problem is with "bad apples." The villain is the unscrupulous, racist bigot. In the latter assumption, to effectively deal with discrimination the emphasis is in rooting out these villains. The overall political economic system is not seen as contributing to racist practices. Freeman argues that particularly since 1974, the courts have established case law, that effectively curtails the scrutiny and improvement of conditions. In other words, the "bad apples" approach has been central. Proof of intent to discriminate, not merely the showing of statistical disparities, must now be conclusively proven in law, a standard that is extremely difficult to attain. Strict standards of causation also apply. All these effectively work against the improvement of *conditions*, which contribute to racial inequities. Consider, for example, the extreme differences on the average money spent per child for schooling in poorer versus well-to-do communities. And the ideological message being created is that if failure occurs it is not because of the law or because of political economic institutions. Rather the fault lies with the individual. This has generally been referred to as the "blaming the victim" ideology.

For example, the U.S. Supreme Court, in *Johnson v. Transportation Agency* (1987), ruled that the standard to be applied in "reverse discrimination" cases is a comparison of the firm's work force with that of the general area labor market. Thus, if the firm has 99% white and 1% black in a job category, but in the area labor force the requisite skills are divided say 60% and 40% respectively between white and black, then an affirmative action program instituted to equalize the firm's labor force is not deemed equivalent to "reverse discrimination." However, if the firm employs 99% white with 1% black, and the labor force *with the requisite skills* is of the same percentage (even though the labor force *generally* is 60% white and 40% black), then no affirmative action program will be held to be constitutional. The Court says nothing about the economic *conditions* contributing to the development of these unequal skills, and merely leaves it to the "invisible hand" of capitalism to do its thing. This avoids, or glosses over the fundamental problem. Formalism again results in substantive injustice.

To counter discriminatory practice, Russell (1998:25) reviewing the 350-year history of slave codes, has offered a "fairness principle" by which our criminal justice system can be judged. This includes, at a minimum:

(1) Criminal penalties apply to everyone equally, regardless of the race of the *offender*.

(2) Criminal penalties apply to everyone equally, regardless of the race of the *victim*.

(3) The race of the offender is not relevant in determining whether his actions constitute a crime. The offender's actions would have been considered criminal, even if he were another race.

(4) The race of the victim is not relevant in determining whether the offenders' action constitutes a crime.

(5) The offender's racial pedigree (e.g., "degree of Blackness") is not used to determine punishment.

(6) There are checks and balances that mitigate against racial bias within the legal system.

Contract law has been central in the CLS scholars' critique (Gabel, 1977; Gabel and Feinman, 1992; Dalton, 1985; Ingram, 1995). In some rather dense but insightful presentations, Gabel has shown how, often, the jurist's thought is imprisoned within the functional requirements of capitalism itself. In other words, the very dynamics and structure of the economic sphere are often reproduced within the legal sphere. What underlies case decisions and opinions, particularly as they deal with the contract, is a nexus between the requirements of capitalism and the form of contract. Contract law in the 18th century society, for example, was more focused on customary and traditional practices, where a person's status within given hierarchies determined her/his standing in the community. Decision making reflected and reinforced these relations in society. Contract law, as a subdivision of property law, simply reflected individuals' exchange of things, possessions, in the immediate here and now. Thus, litigation over agreements and promises were relatively few. In disputes, the jury would apply community standards of fairness. However, in the 19th century, where laissez-faire capitalism was at its height, a person was assumed to be a calculating, profit-seeking egoist. Free competition meant that those who gained more property were in a more advantageous position in society. The moral and traditional bonds of the previous era were torn asunder. Legal decisions and opinions were but a "reflex" of the "logic" of the competitive marketplace. Citizens were seen as formally free and equal. This freedom extended to contracts made. The courts' function was to articulate an ideology that would assure that contracts made were kept. "Contractual freedom" was central. Contract law did not include the scrutiny of the substantive fairness of the transactions. (Recall, again Durkheim, Weber, and Marx on this point.)

This changed in the 20th century. With the development of monopolies, increased centralization and increased government intervention in the social order, law was concerned with balancing interests so as to assure the overall coordination of society toward some desirable end. Courts were guided by the ideals of coordination, integration, and the overall maintenance of stability in society. The state became active in intervening in the economy and society to balance various interests for the "general welfare." "Good faith" dealing in transactions was the standard that emerged. The courts decided what constitutes good faith by way of interest-balancing. Formalism was tempered by the incorporation of some standards of substantive justice. In sum, the courts reflected the changing conditions within the economic sphere. Principles, doctrines, standards, and case law — are all the product of the internal needs and the dynamics of the evolving political economic order.

Ingram's (1995:141) analysis of contract law, agreeing with other "crits," starts with the assumption that capitalism "does not resolve social conflict," but tries to "suppress and contain it." He goes on to argue that, contrary to Weber's view that rationality underlies orderly contractual relations, it is rather moral considerations that lie beneath these undertakings (ibid., 152). Following Unger, and echoing perhaps Durkheim, Ingram argues that "equity in bargaining power" (ibid., 153) is required for contractual relations to be fair. Only in this way would substantive justice become a reality.

Criminal law is yet another area the CLS scholars have "trashed" (Kelman, 1981; Reiman, 1995; Peller, 1993). Kelman has argued that underlying criminal law doctrine and decision making are "interpretive constructions" that are often unconscious. An interpretive construction is the "process by which concrete situations are reduced to substantive legal controversies: it refers both to the way we construe a factual situation and to the way we frame the possible rules to handle the situation" (ibid., 592). Thus, in deciding a case, justices often "frame" the situation outside of law. For example, in establishing the facts, a time frame can be either broad or narrow. If the time frame is narrow this means the immediate, concrete act, say assault, is the focus. A broad frame may include the relationship of the specific act to other contributing factors in society. Hence, in the broad framework, many factors in combination may be seen to have additive effects as to behavioral developments such as crime. Likewise, "intent" might be construed narrowly or broadly. So, too, in situating the defendant within the framework of society, one can use a narrow or broad frame. That is, the defendant or the act could be placed in context or taken out of an overall context.

In each of the above situations, the justice is framing time, intent, the defendant and the act either narrowly or broadly in an unconscious or semi-conscious way. The point is, if one frames these factors broadly (focusing, for a moment, on the lower-class crimes), then, more "understandability" results, and hence less legal culpability can be construed when harm has taken place. In other words, more excusability attaches as the frames expand, and less excusability as the frames narrow. It might be added that as we progress upward in the class structure (from the lower to the higher), frames applied become broader. Conversely, as we go downward, frames applied become more narrowly construed. Hence, the result: greater excusability in an upward direction; and, conversely, more culpability as we go downward. Some upper-class subjects, then, are "beyond incrimination."

Reiman's (1995) more openly Marxist critique of criminal justice explains how distinctions in law — such as civil versus criminal law — are constructs favoring the well-to-do. As he (ibid., 129) tells us, "there is considerable overlap in the content of criminal and civil law; criminal acts, such as theft or battery, can also be causes of civil action. But this overlay is largely asymmetrical: virtually any criminal act can be a cause of civil action, but only some civil causes are subject to criminal prosecution."

Along the same directions, Peller (1993) has indicated how an emphasis on procedural law, as opposed to substantive law in criminal proceedings, has undermined the effectiveness of those attempting to deal with race biases in law. We have previously seen this in chapter 2 with Weber's analysis of the difference between formal and substantive rationality. Durkheim (see chapter 1), too, had indicated this form of "repressive formalism."

The area of "tort" law has been investigated by Abel (1982) and Brion (1995). A tort can be defined as a harm done by one person to another where law gives a remedy. For Abel, the evolving notion of a tort is intimately connected with the rise of capitalism. Although formalism includes as an ideal, that individuals harmed in society, regardless of their standing in the class structure, should have available an equal remedy, in practice, substantively, gross inequality exists.

First, Abel notes that the blue-collar as opposed to the white-collar worker is subject to qualitatively and quantitatively different kinds of risks, harms and illnesses, both at the workplace and within residential areas. Inequality in the risk of harm is a function of differences in socio-economic standing. Consider, for example, the unskilled worker living next to a polluting company, as compared to the highly paid technician who lives in a well-to-do area away from the pollution. Second, race, class, and gender will affect whether and to what extent the injured party will pursue an injury claim. In other words, certain groups, perhaps based on experience with the courts, have given up the court as an avenue of redress. Third, the law discriminates as to the remedies available. Although workers' compensation pays for some of the injuries of the blue-collar worker, many other individuals — women, children, the elderly, ethnic minorities, the poor — have difficulty in successful tort recovery. Although victims of harm, including violent crime, they have great difficulty recovering for damages.

In sum, not only are there vast differences in risk, but also in the remedies available to those harmed. The law simply situates all in a position of formal equality both as to risk and as to remedy available. The majesty of formal rationality, it is claimed, hides the repressive formalistic dimensions.

Abel's recommendation to overcome this state of affairs, his "socialist approach to risk," would hinge on two guiding ideals (1982). First, he offers the ideal of the equalization of risk. That is, all should share equally in the risk of potential harm. Second, he claims, we should empower each person with the knowledge and some real control concerning the risk to which s/he will be exposed. For these two ideals to be possible, he argues, capitalism must be replaced by decentralized socialism.

Brion's (1991, 1995) analysis of tort law employs chaos theory. Brion sees decision making based on two processes: first is *heresy*, by which he means the forces of pluralism playing out their effects. The second process he calls *heritage*, by which he means the pressures of *stare decises* (decision making based on precedents set in law). Conflict takes place between these two poles in decision making. Oscillation continues until one pole gains dominance in the decision. Thus, chance plays a large factor in any particular decision. Schulman (1997) has taken this same approach in a more detailed analysis, by applying the various "attractors" that are said to exist in chaos theory. She shows how the oscillation between the two poles produces a far-from-equilibrium state within which a very slight perturbation may throw it in support of one or the other of the poles.

The role of law in women's subordination has become increasingly central in the CLS "trashing." One central argument made by the CLS scholars is that law has separated the sphere of "men's work" from "women's work" (Taub and Schneider, 1992). "[W]omen have been consigned to a private realm to carry on their primary responsibilities, i.e., bearing and rearing children, and providing men with a refuge from the pressures of the capitalist world" (ibid., 118). Male dominance has been given legitimacy in legal decisions. For example, well known statistics show that in the last 30 or 40 years females, given the same position as males, still receive only about 60-65% of the salary of the males. In the private sphere, tort law has not provided remedies for women abused, physically and/or psychologically, by their spouses. We should add that only recently has a substantial body of literature developed on a feminist jurisprudence that goes beyond the earlier critiques. We shall return to this below.

The areas of gay rights (Colker, 1995), same-sexed marriage (Hunter, 1995), and sexual freedom (Fineman, 2000; Cornell, 1998) have become central issues in Critical Legal Studies. Cornell (1998), for example, has argued that family law should be rewritten to reflect three ideas: (1) "regulation of the family should protect all lovers who choose to register in civil marriage"; (2) "the government must provide a structure for custodial responsibility for children" (see also Davis and Williams, 2000). In other words, if one partner does not wish to become a parent, s/he could still choose to stay married to the partner and choose not to have full responsibility for the child, but allow the partner to choose someone else to take the full custodial responsibility (ibid., 125); and (3) the government should provide for health care for children (ibid., 128). That is, the government should provide "some kind of publicly funded child-care as part of parental entitlement" (ibid.). According to Cornell, these provisions would provide (1) sexual freedom, and (2) stability in raising children.

Finally, crits have theorized how judges go about making their decisions. We provide a brief summary of Duncan Kennedy's (1997) much-debated book, *A Critique of Adjudication (fin de siècle)*. A special issue of *Cardozo Law Review* (volume 22, 2001) was devoted to discussion of his book. Kennedy's self-professed perspective is from a "leftist and a modernist/postmodernist point of view" (ibid., 207). In this book, Kennedy presents the role of ideology in judges' decision making. Do judges simply vote their political and ideological leanings? If they are conservative or liberal, do they blindly decide in this direction? He rejects the Marxist notion that they are merely acting in "false consciousness." He rejects the notion that judges are simply tools of elites. He rejects the idea that judges always impose their particular ideological positions in law. Rather, judges act in "bad faith" and "denial." The former concept he draws from Jean Paul Sartre's work; the latter from Anna Freud's analysis of the unconscious and its "defense mechanisms."

To begin with, a judge is faced with gaps, conflicts and ambiguities which s/he must resolve by rendering a legal decision. A number of constraints limit the judge's ability to simply act out her/his political leanings. First, the judge may find her/himself bound by the law in either of two ways. The judge could be exposed to a given set of facts and posed with two contradictory stories explaining them. If alternative interpretations of what rule to apply were not relevant, the judge might "unselfconsciously" apply the appropriate rule in the method of deductive logic. Another situation could be where the facts are known but the interpretation of the rule is in question. The judge may dislike the outcome that will result if s/he applies a particular rule, tries as hard as s/he can to develop an alternative interpretation, fails to do so, and so applies the given distasteful rule, once again in deductive fashion (ibid., 161). The duty of "fidelity" to the facts in hand constrain the judge; s/he does "what the law requires." In the second constraint, the judges "are also constrained by the reactions they anticipate from their audience" (ibid.). Judges want to look like they are following the rule-of-law. They are constrained by "internal" factors (e.g., the judge looks for legal arguments that are personally acceptable) and "external" factors (e.g., the judge looks for arguments that will appear good to the audience, her/his "interpretive community") (ibid., 161).

Given, then, ambiguities, conflicts, and gaps in a particular case, how is a judge to decide? Kennedy argues that there are three types of judges:

(1) The "constrained activist judge." This judge attempts to develop legal interpretations that fit her/his activist agenda, but has no intentions of going against the law. After numerous attempts to devise alternatives (in either the liberal or conservative direction), s/he succumbs to writing an opinion that is formalistic (deductive logic) and argues that the law requires this outcome.

(2) The "difference-splitting judge." This judge spends much time figuring out what the two opposing positions may be and chooses the middle position. Between the liberal and conservative there lies a "moderate" position towards which s/he strives.

(3) The "bipolar judge." This judge alternates between working hard in either the liberal or conservative direction. In some cases, s/he works hard to develop a liberal ruling (the "constrained activist"); in others, a conservative. However, s/he is always vigilante to be sure, that in the long run, decisions even themselves out. S/he makes a career of difference splitting; s/he alternatives between the two ideologies over her/his career.

How do the judges actually proceed? For Kennedy (ibid., 191), their activity in law finding must be described as "half-conscious." They are neither fully conscious nor fully unconscious of their decision making. They also act in "denial" and "bad faith." For Kennedy (ibid., 192), the "big secret" the judges collectively maintain is that what they do is non-ideological. But, at the more unconscious level, this contributes to quite a bit of cognitive dissonance: it is disturbing. This "secret" of seemingly abiding by the law while at the same time knowing that law finding is otherwise, can only be maintained by the unconscious defense mechanism of "denial" that Anna Freud developed. As Kennedy (ibid., 193) says, "the motive for denial is to prevent or get rid of this anxiety." And thus, in their insistence that they are non-ideological, they are acting in "bad faith." The constrained activist, difference splitter and bipolar judge who experience cognitive dissonance and role conflict make use of denial in order to maintain the appearance of neutrality in law finding and to be able to reconcile their various, often distasteful decisions to themselves. They act in bad faith because, with conscious reflection, they know exactly what is taking place.

Kennedy (ibid., 203) also argues that not all judges fall within the three types he presents. Some have nothing to deny. Apparently, they entertain the facts of the case, establish the appropriate rule, and follow deductive reasoning to its logical conclusion.

In sum, judges are neither controlled by elites, nor are they entirely independent, nor do they simply apply their political/ideological position in all cases. More often, they are in denial and act in bad faith.

CLS and Deconstruction

Earlier we had said that the "crits" offered a "trashing" technique. A more refined terminology situates it in the framework of *deconstruction,* which is based on the inspirational but rather dense (almost inaccessible) works of Jacques Derrida (1992, 1997).[3]

Balkin has probably given the most accessible rendition of the relationship of Derrida's thoughts to law. He develops this exposition in his article entitled "Deconstructive Practice and Legal Theory" (1987; see also 1998a, 1998b). There are three reasons, he tells us, to be interested in the deconstructive technique in law. First, it provides a methodology for in-depth critiquing of legal doctrines. Second, deconstruction can illuminate how legal arguments disguise ideological positions. And third, it offers a new method of interpretation of legal texts (ibid., 744).

Two particular practices are embedded in the deconstruction practice: the reversal of hierarchies and the liberation of the legal text from the original author.

The notion of *reversal of hierarchies* has been a cornerstone in the deconstructive approach (see Balkin, 1998b:2-4; for an application to prison law, see Arrigo and Williams, 1999:400-408). Any value position, it is argued, takes on its particular valuation in opposition to some other value: one becomes dominant, the other repressed. In his language, this brings out the "metaphysics of presence." What this means is that in every opposition one value dominates and is privileged as presence; the other is repressed and is rendered an absence. Consider the dominance of the male's voice, for example, over the female's. Consider, too, statements of good, which always imply the bad; sanity, which always implies insanity, etc. See also Arrigo and Williams's (1999:400) notion of receiving treatment and refusing treatment in prison. Activating one course always implies the possibility of the other. Similarly with competence to be executed and incompetence to be executed (ibid., 407-408). Each, however, implies a location in a hierarchy where one is privileged. These hierarchies are basic to all phenomena. A text, however, can always be turned on its head (reversal of hierarchies) to illuminate this opposition, and to reveal how the two are, at core, interdependent (Balkin, 1987:746-751).

This notion of a fundamental interdependence is further explained by Derrida's notion of *différance* (with an "a") (see Balkin, 1998b:4-9). This neologism implies both to differ and to defer. In any hierarchy (say of two terms where one is seemingly superior to the other), the two terms are different from each other, each defers to the other in the sense of implying the other term, and each of the two terms defers to the other in terms of its dependence on the other.

Différance also implies the *trace*. Within each term of a hierarchy, one term contains the hidden trace of the other. This is what maintains a relation between the two terms. Hence, in deconstructive strategies, one must start with the idea that any term (presence) always implies a hidden one (absence); both are essential to any meaning of each. The *trace* is that part that exists in each and maintains the relation. In many ways, it is the "glue." For those practicing deconstruction, the challenge is to identify the absent term which maintains the term that is felt as present. Thus the history of ideas can be seen as the privileging of one term over another, which nevertheless exists in relation to it. The privileging of male discourse, for example, always comes at the cost of de-privileging female discourse.

To take this argument one step further, every stage of human development has a core of privileged terms (presence) and a periphery of de-privileged terms. Thus, the strategy of deconstructive reversal attempts to make visible the hidden. As Balkin has said:

> [a]ny social theory must emphasize some human values over others. Such categorizing necessarily involves a privileging, which in turn can be deconstructed. But the goal of deconstruction is not the destruction of all possible social visions. By recalling the elements of human life relegated to the margin in a given social theory, deconstructive readings challenge us to *remake* the dominant conceptions of our society [ibid., 763; emphasis added].

The second major contribution of deconstruction is the idea of the "free play of the text." Any constructed text, including a legal decision or legal doctrine, is liberated once it is constructed. A text always says more than is "intended." In other words, once constructed, the text takes a life of its own. Consider, for example, an ongoing debate in law concerning the "founding fathers'" *intent* in the Constitution. Conservatives claim it can be clearly spelled out through consulting the original philosophical statements of its authors. Liberals and radicals, however, claim that the intent can never be reconstructed, particularly in conditions 200 years later. The meaning of the text for those making use of deconstructive strategies, is always situated historically. It means something different in different contexts. This is the idea of "iterability." The search for original meaning is a search for foundations for interpretations that in actuality do not exist.

Of course, all this leads to one of the central dilemmas that the "crits" have been facing since the turn of the 1990s. This is the dilemma of *foundational positions*. In other words, *if* indeed some truth claim can be supported by some foundational position (i.e., some ethical principle, some reliance on conclusions drawn from data, or some body of knowledge that has assumed the character of conventional wisdom), a position which can be deconstructed by some other foundational position, and this position in turn can be deconstructed by yet another position, *ad infinitum*, then there is no such thing as some cross-cultural and historical position which can substantiate for all time any claim to "truth." And this is the dilemma. Stanley Fish has been most persuasive, and a thorn in the side of the CLS Movement with this critique (see Fish, 1980, 1984; Rosenfeld, 1991:170-179). In other words, the dilemma is of profound consequence: on the one hand, one conclusion might be "why bother about anything, all is relevant," a rather conservative stance; on the other, for political activists, what possibly can an adequate support for their position be? This form of nihilism is difficult to overcome.

Feminist jurisprudence is grappling with this question, and constantly pursues ways of maintaining a deconstructive strategy without falling into the trappings of nihilism or the conservative agenda. We shall return to this in a later section, but first we want to examine Roberto Unger's reconstructive agenda.

CLS and Reconstruction

In this final section, we would like to present some key recommendations in the sociology of law made by Roberto Unger, one of the most respected members of the CLS movement. Unger has been a prolific writer (Unger, 1975, 1976, 1984, 1986, 1987). Recently, a substantial critique of his analysis has evolved.[4] Here we will focus on his books, *The Critical Legal Studies Movement* (1986) and *False Necessity* (1987), where he lays out his reconstructive agenda that includes a call for an "empowered democracy" and develops a "transformative politics."

But first a few words on *Passion* (1984), where he offers us an ethical theory that underlies his reconstructive strategies. By passion he means all "non-instrumental" dealings with other people. He situates the individual in society as a person with strivings, despairs, weaknesses, faith, hope, love and desires. The basic contradiction that s/he faces is twofold. First, the recognition that one needs the other while at the same time fearing the other. Second, the constraints of conformity and the longing for transcendence. The development of the self and the potential for solidarity revolves around this double dialectic.

In *The Critical Legal Studies Movement*, first presented at the Sixth Annual Conference of Critical Legal Studies in 1982, and in his more developed *False Necessity* (1987), Unger presents several change strategies for a transformative politics. He characterizes his philosophy as "super liberalism." He advocates the development of an "empowered democracy." As far back as 1975, Unger was attempting to develop a non-Marxist alternative in the sociology of law.

His change strategy, what he calls "transformative activity," would entail a "deviationist doctrine." Since society tends toward stagnant, non-responsive hierarchies (i.e., insensitive bureaucracies), the solution, for Unger, is to prevent their ossification. That is to say, he is concerned with ways of preventing a social order from becoming resistant to change. This can come about, he claims, if certain "destabilizing rights" are granted which, taken together, will disrupt any ossifying tendencies while assuring the protection of the individual's rights in society. These rights both support deconstructive challenges as well as provide economic and political resources for well-being and reconstructive practices. Stability, in other words, will be constantly established anew, taking into consideration new factors or conditions as they develop in a society.

To this end, he offers us four core rights. First, "immunity rights" would assure the individual zones of privacy much like existing civil liberties. Second, "destabilization rights" would give the individuals the right to challenge developing hierarchies. These rights would be guaranteed by (a) the present form of the judiciary and (b) a separate broadly based public agency established for their protection. Third, "market rights" would be derived from his two economic principles: (a) A "rotating capital fund" would be made available to teams of workers for temporary use; and (b) The interest charged would be used for governmental administration and for encouraging "risk-oriented or socially responsive investment" (ibid., 35). And fourth, "solidarity rights" would develop out of a two-stage career. Standards such as "good faith loyalty or responsibility" would be established with a degree of openness. Subsequent refinements would come about when individuals themselves in practice resolve conflicts in society (ibid., 40). Unger does not give us substantial details on how this is to occur.

Ideally, his deviationist doctrine and his transformative activity would undermine hierarchical, non-responsive structures in society. A gradual movement toward a democratic and humane society would result. The state, in this view, is necessary and inevitable. It must, however, be made responsive and held accountable.

Summary. The CLS movement, picking up from, but going beyond the Legal Realists in scope, emphasis and vehemence of attack, is in the center of a storm in the development of a sociology of law. Although some of the theorists seek guidance from Marx, others do not. Scholars are rather eclectic in their current approach. The fourth stage of the CLS movement, one in which the search for theory and more differentiated perspectives has become dominant, is a creative period for the development of a sociology of law. By the mid-1980s, much external and internal critique had already taken place.

In the 1990s CLS scholars began to develop a unified approach in the sociology of law by drawing primarily from the critical thoughts of the Frankfurt School, especially focusing on the whole question of legitimation. The work of Gramsci and his notion of hegemony are critical. The works of Max Weber and Karl Marx continue to exert an influence on the critical thought being developed. A foray into linguistics and semiotics has also led to some valuable insights. And most notably, "crits" have turned their attention specifically to the question of race and gender and their intersections with class, sexual preference, and legal repression.

CLS scholars have concentrated on the facilitative, repressive and ideological functions of law. The relationship between the legal order and fulfillment of social values is central in their critique of what is and in their projection of what could be. Although most CLS scholars agree that the current legal form is repressive (*repressive formalism*), there is disagreement as to the purpose, scope and desirable form of law in a more humane society. Even the vision of the "good" society is unclear. Nevertheless, although quite controversial, the CLS movement is on the cutting edge in the development of the sociology of law in the United States.

FEMINIST JURISPRUDENCE

Introduction. Feminist legal theory, or alternatively, feminist jurisprudence, having sources in the 1960s, took considerable shape in the late 1980s in the U.S.[5] Some of this movement had its basis in the Critical Legal Studies movement, but much lies outside of this tradition, and in fact developed as a critical response to it.[6] "Feminists believe that history was written from a male point of view and does not reflect women's role in making history and society. Male-written history has created a bias in the concepts of human nature, gender potential, and social arrangements. The language, logic, and structure of the law are male created and reinforce male values" (see note 5).

This movement fundamentally challenged some key assumptions in conventional legal theory, as well as some conventional wisdom within Critical Legal Studies. Consider, for example, Goldfarb's point: "Many feminists have identified patriarchy as an ideology more threatening to their lives than legal ideology, and have directed their efforts at undermining the former even through the use of the latter" (1992:704). The "fem-crits" are heavily influenced by feminist work in philosophy, psychoanalysis, semiotics, history, anthropology, postmodernism, literary criticism, and political theory (see Menkel-Meadow, 1988). But, more basically, they draw heavily from experiences of women.

Three key years for establishing a critical mass within the CLS movement were 1985, 1987, and 1992. In 1985 the Annual Meeting of Critical Legal Studies had as its theme feminism and law. In 1987, the theme was racism and law. And in the 1992 Annual Conference, the CLS constituency was made up of several sponsors (other sponsors being race theorists and feminist theorists). The movement's further development in the 1990s has led to far ranging challenges to contemporary law and legal institutions (see also Goldfarb, 1992). In a later chapter on the postmodern perspective, we shall have further occasion to develop yet another feminist approach in law, one based on the works of Jacques Lacan. There are currently several feminist perspectives: traditional, liberal, cultural, radical, Marxist, socialist, and postmodernist.

Women's Rights Movements

Five overlapping stages can be distinguished in the women's rights movement in the U.S. First, during the 19th century a number of efforts were organized in order to gain the right to vote, to gain access to private property in marriage, and to legal rights to birth control. The second movement began in the 1960s and was characterized by a greater number of women entering law schools and legal practice. Here a number of legal victories resulted from the greater access to power. The third movement took place in the 1970s, when the focal point was a critical analysis of employment, family law and legal definitions of rape. A number of successful litigated cases resulted. The fourth movement that began, perhaps, in the late 1980s and was carried over to the 1990s, has witnessed a number of setbacks in its early stages (e.g., the defeat of the Equal Rights Amendment, restrictions placed on abortion rights). We see in the late 1990s, however, a renewed drive that is informed by critical findings in other fields — political theory, literary criticism, philosophy, and psychoanalysis. The fifth movement, beginning with the new millennium, not only has seen further diversification in perspectives, but extensive intra- and interperspective dialogue and ever more sophisticated and keen critique amongst the various perspectives.

Law, critical feminist theorists have discovered, presents a number of limitations to the realization of social values (Bartlett and Kennedy, 1991:2-5). First, due to the reliance on precedents (*stare decisis*), feminists have noted that the established body of law is overly phallocentric (male dominated), so that any issue brought before the court that substantially deviates from this body of knowledge is less likely to attain a hearing and a favorable resolution. Thus, the status quo is more likely to predominate.

Second, the very work-context for activist feminist lawyers within the legal structure poses problems for feminists attempting to defend clients and to simultaneously contribute to larger feminist movements. Consider Bartlett and Kennedy's point (1991:3) that mounting a successful defense of "battered woman's syndrome" (Hoeffer, 2001; Coker, 2001) is difficult, and hence a legal defense is often instituted claiming "diminished capacity." The latter is a more "acceptable" defense in law, and consequently has a greater chance for a successful resolution for the defense. But consider, too, the disempowering that has taken place, not only in the particular instance but also in the sense of a larger understanding of the motive that was involved.

A third limitation concerns the court's focus on the rational and coherent. Feminists' claims often arise from a multitude of sources, and these claims may appear to be contradictory at times. Consider a woman objecting to work conditions, whose claims is opposed with the ideology of contractual freedom. She is left with the "choice" of taking it (the job), or leaving it; but, given unemployment rates and the inability to counter power inequality inherent in worker contractual relations, "choice" becomes an illusory conception. In sum, feminist analysis has shown that even where women work within the legal discursive categories themselves, they often inadvertently reinforce the legal structures that they wish to change (ibid.).

Case Material: Landmark Decisions Concerning Gender

Several major U.S. Supreme Court decisions have stipulated increased rights for women. *Roe v. Wade* (1973) was a class action sought challenging the constitutionality of Texas law on abortion. The statute had made abortion illegal except for the purpose of saving the mother's life. The U.S. Supreme Court held that up to the first trimester of pregnancy, the decision was up to the mother in consultation with her physician. Many have argued that this decision and its underlying logic spelled out a statement on the right to privacy. This could also be understood dialectically. Although a victory, it becomes a loss in terms of the further subjecting the body to the "disciplinary mechanisms" of political-economic determinants and standards of usefulness. In other words, the legal apparatus as a disciplinary mechanism furthers the development of a body of "docility" and "utility" (Foucault, 1997a; see also Milovanovic, 2002:chapter 9).

There have been several other landmark decisions. The workplace in particular has seen important litigation. Let us summarize a few.

An especially illuminating legal case concerning the ideological and repressive functions of law involved female workers in a much-discussed case, *EEOC v. Sears, Roebuck and Co.* (1988). According to Williams's analysis (1991), Sears won this suit because it was successful with its argument that women were disproportionately underrepresented in the higher paying sales positions at Sears not because they were discriminated against, but rather because they lacked "interest" in working in commission sales. The women bringing the suit had to prove not only statistical disparities, but also that women and men had "equal interest." Sears, in its defense, presented an essentialist case, arguing that men were historically competitive and self-interested, whereas women were "humane and nurturing." Accordingly, the court ruled that the sex segregation that did exist was an expression of women's own choice. The court was unwilling to entertain the view that locates women's work aspirations in the historical context of labor market discrimination (Schultz, 1991:126).

In *Burlington Industries, Inc. v. Ellerth* (1998), the issue revolved around allegations of sexual harassment by petitioner's (Ellerth's) supervisor

(Slowik). In spite of this, the "facts" showed that the petitioner was not subject to any retaliation for challenging, and even was promoted one time. However, Ellerth also argued that this forced her subsequent "constructive discharge." The larger question of a "hostile work environment" was also suggested. In other words, to what degree does a "vicarious liability" exist when the employer (Burlington industries) does not take corrective action against his/her supervisors (here Slowik)? In another related landmark decision (actually delivered the same date as the present case) — *Faragher v. City of Boca Raton* (1998) — the Court stipulated that "an employer is subject to vicarious liability to a victimized employee for an actionable hostile environment created by a supervisor with immediate (or successive higher) authority over the employee." (In *Faragher* the "sexually hostile atmosphere" involved "uninvited and offensive touching," lewd remarks, and by offensive terms directed toward women.) When no "tangible employment action" results (e.g., when no negative actions follow the sexual harassment), the Court stipulated, the employer may raise an "affirmative defense." In other words, the employer is given an opportunity to counter the claim that his/her inaction created a hostile work environment. The employer is subject to the standard of "preponderance of the evidence" (one must show more evidence for than against).

The Court stipulated two necessary elements that would clear the employer from vicarious liability: (1) "that the employer exercised reasonable care to prevent and correct promptly any sexually harassing behavior," and (2) "that the plaintiff employee unreasonably failed to take advantage of any preventive or corrective opportunities provided by the employer or to avoid harm otherwise." Again, where there exists a "tangible employment action" (i.e., demotion, firing, etc.) this defense would not be allowed in law. The Court decided that Burlington (the employer) should be given an opportunity to prove the affirmative defense concerning his supervisor, Slowik.

In an earlier U.S. Supreme Court case, *Oncale v. Sundower Offshore Services, Inc.* (1998), the Court stated that workplace harassment can violate the law (Title V11 of the Civil Rights Act of 1964) even when the harasser and the harassed employees are of the same sex. The Court, of course, defined "work environment" narrowly, focusing on individual action; however, "hostile work environments" may be difficult to attribute to the creation of one person, and in fact sexual harassment may be much more subtle and pervasive (see for example our application of the notion of "petit apartheid" in various settings, Milovanovic and Russell, 2001).

Court cases such as these have placed feminist jurisprudence front stage, and particularly require dilemmas to be addressed. On the one hand, law contributes to empowerment — having access to law to combat various instances of abuse and restrictions on the realization of social values does produce some change (see for example, Williams, 1987; Cook, 1990; Crenshaw, 1988; Delgado, 1987). On the other, working within the legal categories often reinforces the legitimacy of the legal apparatus, the rule-of-law ideology, and, in the end, the rule of men (phallocentricism, or androcentricism).

Many African-American "fem-crits" have rejected the CLS's critique of rights litigation as repressive ideology, noting that this "project...relinquishes too much, since appeals to legal ideology represents one of the only strategies that has effectively elicited a response to the desperate needs of subordinate people" (Goldfarb, 1992:696). As Crenshaw has poignantly stated: "The most troubling aspect of the Critical program, therefore, is that 'trashing' rights consciousness may have the unintended consequence of disempowering the racially oppressed while leaving white supremacy basically untouched..." (1988:1357-1358). In other words, the recognition of this dialectics of struggle has necessitated a more comprehensive approach for a feminist jurisprudence where both the concrete experiences of women as well as more comprehensive theorizing in law need to be integrated.

Equality Theory and Sexual Difference

One of the pillars of Western democracy has been the notion of formal equality, or "equal rights" (see our discussion of formal rationality, chapter 2). But this has serious implications in the feminist movement. Consider Bartlett and Kennedy's comment: "Equality doctrine requires comparisons, and the standard for comparison tends strongly to reflect existing societal norms. Thus, equality for women has come to mean equality with men — usually white, middle-class men" (1991:5; Frug, 1992:665-682; Naffine, 1990; Roach-Anleu, 1992). Accordingly, should women want to be like men? Or are there other comparisons to make to indicate "essential" differences? An affirmative answer to the former question can find an ally in the "equal protection" clause of the Fourteenth Amendment of the U.S. Constitution. If, on the other hand, the first question is rendered essentially counterproductive and the second question is taken seriously, what existing legal doctrine could be applied in situations of existing restraints on the realization of various social values? Is substantive rationality being invoked here? And doesn't it go against the "equal rights" doctrine? The tension between formal and substantive rationality (see chapter two) is quite apparent.

But this only begins the questioning. What, as Crenshaw argues (1991:57-73; see also Milovanovic and Schwartz, 1999), does one then do with the issue of the intersection of sex and race? Of class, gender and race? In other words, does an African-American woman use the standard of white women in arguing her defense? Some, such as MacKinnon (1991b:81-91) have argued that this debate is misinformed, and the issue boils down to *dominance*: how do males gain institutionalized domination and how, as a consequence, are females rendered subordinate?

These questions have led to one of the most debated issues in feminist jurisprudence concerning the underlying basis of the legal subject. This concerns the issue of "essentialism." Are women essentially different from men or should they be considered the same in law? Harris, for example, in critiquing MacKinnon for being an essentialist has argued that she

> assumes, as does the dominant culture, that there is an essential 'woman' beneath the realities of differences between women — that in describing the experiences of 'women' issues of race, class, and sexual orientation can therefore be safely ignored, or relegated to footnotes [1991:242].

For Harris, black women offer a "post-essentialist" alternative for feminist jurisprudence that includes: the assumption of a self that is multifaceted, not unitary; the idea that "differences are always relational rather than inherent"; and the belief in "the recognition that wholeness and commonality are acts of will and creativity, rather than passive discovery" (Harris, 1991:250; see also Collins, 1991; Matsuda, 1987). Minorities' experiences of oppression can be the basis of the development of a distinct political consciousness, which could, in turn, be the basis of a deconstructive practice and a transformative political agenda (Matsuda, 1987; Cook, 1990; Goldfarb, 1991, 1992; Cornell, 1991, 1998).

An outgrowth of this analysis has been the development of a feminist "standpoint epistemology" (Harding, 1991; Bartlett, 1991; Currie, 1993; Smith, 1981, 1987; Arrigo, 1993). (We shall return to a feminist postmodernist view of standpoint epistemology in chapter 7.) This view has it that:

> Feminist standpoint epistemology identifies woman's status as that of victim, and then privileges that status by claiming that it

gives access to understanding about oppression that others cannot have [Bartlett, 1991:385].

Hence, this approach sees knowledge as based upon experience of the oppressed (Matsuda, 1987; Cook, 1990), but it rejects objectivity and any possibility of an essential truth. Rather, truth is always situated, contingent and partial (Bartlett, 1991:389). Thus, while some basis can be established for concrete political action (i.e., some historically situated "truth" is established based on empirical evidence), commitments are always provisional and are always subject to further critique and revision (ibid., Cook, 1990; Schneider, 1986).

Feminist Legal Methods

What is to be done? Needed within feminist jurisprudence is a feminist legal method. Bartlett perhaps has presented one agenda rooted in a *standpoint epistemology* (1991; more recently, see Bartlett, 2000). Feminists doing law, she argues, should focus on at least three factors. First, "asking the woman question." That is, what needs to be articulated is the often-silenced voice, the voice of the excluded (see also Coombe, 1989, 1991a, 1991b, 1992; Howe, 1994). According to Bartlett, this entails "looking beneath the surface of law to identify the gender implications of rules and assumptions underlying them and insisting upon applications of rules that do not perpetuate women's subordination" (1991:373-374).

Second, this method privileges a "feminist practical reasoning," which may encompass some aspects of deductive logic, but takes into consideration the experiential — the unique, concrete experiences of the repressed. This approach does not assume a one-dimensional picture of phenomena, but sees them "as dilemmas with multiple perspectives, contradictions, and inconsistencies." This approach opposes the dichotomizations imposed by the court, e.g., yes-no answers in court proceedings. It is contextual in orientation: new situations pose yet more opportunities for understanding, and "imaginative integrations and reconciliations."

The third aspect is consciousness-raising. The goal is for individual and collective empowerment, not for personal vendettas, nor for the celebration of "hate politics," "revenge politics," or political correctness (see Cornell, 1999, on this point). Again, it is gained by the integration of concrete experiences of the oppressed, self-reflection and theorizing (see also Schneider, 1986; Cook, 1990; Cornell, 1998, 1999). It is always sensitive to the multiple forms of consciousness in existence. In sum, Bartlett's offering

of a feminist legal method is focused both on deconstruction and reconstruction.

The literature on feminist legal method has presented, among other
strategies, three distinct forms. First, reversal of hierarchies, a derivation
from Derrida, that argues that action must be directed toward liberating
women from their subordination by reversing their position in various hierarchies (see particularly MacKinnon, 1987, 1989). Second, standpoint epistemology, a position that argues that we must privilege the position
("standpoint") of the disenfranchised and help create an understanding
("epistemology") from these concrete occurrences of repression or domination (see Barlett, 1991; Howe, 1994; see also Foucault, 1977b). And third,
"contingent universalities," a position that argues that neither the search for
objective nor relative "truths" can contribute to the ideal foundations for
building political agendas, but rather a mid-course position. This position
argues that at historical moments certain positions that are "contingent"
can be temporarily forged, which become, for a time, "universalities" by
which action can follow. Perhaps Harris's "post-essentialist" alternative can
be assimilable here; or, perhaps with more, could be developed into a clear-
standing alternative. These contingent universalities, however, are always
subject to reflection, debate, qualification, redefinition and deletion as historical contingencies emerge (see Butler, 1991; see also Laclau's notion of
"historical dislocations," "structural undecidability," and "historical articulations," 1996:87-104; 2000). Critical race theory would find itself situated
between the latter two strategies: from standpoint epistemology stressing
the idea of repressed voices and pragmatism in legal challenges, and from
contingent universalities indicating the plurality of overlapping and intersecting forms of consciousness and identifications that change over time.

Each of the three strategies have been debated: the first may easily
turn into "revenge politics" (Cornell, 1999); the second, some argue, overlooks how the existing discourse (i.e., legal discourse, dominant discourse,
academic discourse, even some oppositional discourses) itself limits what
can be said in narrative constructions; and the third, dissenters say, may
quickly slip back into either of the first two.

Summary. Feminist jurisprudence has begun to make a difference in
law. Many key insights concerning the repressive and ideological functions
of law have been, and continue to be articulated. Feminist jurisprudence is
not only a quest for dismantling repressive legal institutions and their legitimizing ideological structures, but is an approach that is offering tangible

results in its reconstructive agenda. We shall return to develop a postmodernist feminist perspective in law in chapter 7.

CRITICAL RACE THEORY

Introduction. Critical Race Theory (CRT) had its beginnings in the 1960s. It "questions the very foundations of the liberal order, including equality theory, legal reasoning, Enlightenment rationalism, and neutral principles of constitutional law" (Delgado and Stefancic, 2001). Three particularly clear and concise books are foundational to understanding the perspective: Richard Delgado and Jean Stefancic's *Critical Race Theory* (2001); Kimberle Crenshaw, Neil Gotanda, Gary Peller and Kendall Thomas (eds.), *Critical Race Theory: The Key Writings That Formed the Movement* (1995); and Mari Matsuda, Charles Lawrence 111, Richard Delgado and Kimberle Crenshaw's *Words That Wound* (1993). Other introductory contributions are by Mari Matsuda, *Where is Your Body?* (1996), Katheryn Russell's *The Color of Crime* (1998), and Dragan Milovanovic and Katheryn Russell's *Petit Apartheid in the U.S. Criminal Justice System* (2001). (See also two special issues of journals: *International Journal of Qualitative Studies* [1998], and *California Law Review* [1994].)

Historical Development

Critical race theory[7] underwent an evolutionary development. The first stage of its development can be traced to various civil rights movements of the 1960s. The second stage, the 1970s, could be seen as a time of retrenchment by the legal apparatus, when many rights gained during the 1960s were being undermined. *Brown v. the Board of Education* (1954), which can be read as attacking "conditions" behind the creation of discrimination, was now being undermined in law by the reliance on standards that focused on "intent" of a particular individual to engage in racist practices. This "bad apples" approach effectively undermined the broad perspective that looked at political economy as a contributing factor to injustices suffered by African-Americans. Nevertheless, the 1970s saw the rise of activists, legal scholars and a number of lawyers, who actively engaged these rollbacks. The early 1980s saw some significant activist practices in prestigious law schools. In 1981, for example, students organized protests against Harvard Law School to increase the number of faculty of color (Matsuda et al., 1993:3-4). When the administration was not responsive, the students organized their own course. Practitioners and leading scholars were invited for weekly discussions on chapters from Derrick Bell's works (Bell had just left Harvard Law School). Kimberle Crenshaw, Mari Matsuda, Richard Delgado, and Charles Lawrence were all participants in this new course. Some in this group were also connected with the Critical Legal Studies group, although with some reservations about its predominantly white makeup. Nevertheless, by the mid 1980s a new identity was being forged.

The third stage could be envisioned as beginning in the late 1980s. Several formal conferences emerged. In 1988, at the Yale Law School, the First Annual Women of Color and Law Conference took place. In 1989, the CRTs organized their official first conference at Madison, Wisconsin. From 1987 on, the Annual Critical Legal Studies conference saw significant presentations by women of color. The CRTs encouraged the predominantly white activist of the Critical Legal Studies to reflect on their own relations and possible racism, be it at more unconscious levels.

The fourth stage, perhaps beginning in the middle of the 1990s to the turn of the new millennium, can be characterized as a time for additional differentiation and splintering. Thus, we saw the development of: global critical race feminism, Latcrit feminism, critical Asian writers, and queer-crit studies (see also the "multiracial category movement," Robinson [2000]). The internal dialogue amongst the various perspectives brought into sharp relief the various forms of racism at play and often its intersectional nature.[8]

Basic Tenets

Critical race theorists have drawn from a broad body of literature: critical legal studies, pragmatism, Marxism, literature, poetry, fiction, law and society movement, personal histories, revisionist history, feminism, and postmodernism. People of color writers were central (W.E.B Du Bois, Martin Luther King, Jr., Frederick Douglas). The Black Power movement and Chicano movements during the 1960s and 1970s were also inspirational (Delgado and Stefancic, 2001:4). Theorists that were central included Gramsci and Derrida (Matsuda et al, 1993:5). "Our work presented racism not as isolated instances of conscious bigoted decision making or prejudiced practice, but as larger, systemic, structural, and cultural, as deeply psychological and socially ingrained" (ibid., 5).

Critical Race Theory (see Matsuda et al., 1993:6):

(1) recognizes that racism is endemic to American life...

(2) expresses skepticism toward dominant legal claims of neutrality, objectivity, color blindness and meritocracy...

(3) challenges ahistoricism and insists on a contextual/historical analysis of the law...

(4) insists on recognition of the experiential knowledge of people of color and our communities of origin in analyzing law and society...

(5) is interdisciplinary and eclectic...

(6) works toward the end of eliminating racial oppression as part of the broader goal of ending all forms of oppression...This recognition of intersecting forms of subordination requires multiple consciousness and political practices that address the varied ways in which people experience subordination.

More recently, Delgado and Stefancic (2001:6-9) have provided additional themes:

(1) that racism is ordinary, not aberrational...the usual way society does its business...

(2) our system of white-over-color...serves important purposes [functions], both psychical and material...

(3) race and races are products of social thought and relations...races are categories that society invents, manipulates, or retires when convenient.

Yet another theme is the notion of "petit apartheid" (Georges-Abeyie, 1990; Milovanovic and Russell, 2001) or "microaggressions" (Russell, 1998). This represents the more hidden and subtle dimension of racism in the criminal justice system, at the moments just prior to its formal mobilization. It can range from the more covert/informal, such as in the nonverbal form (gestures, postures, other mannerisms, non-person status, etc.), to more verbal but unofficial action (put downs, fighting words, expletives, hate/race speech, etc.), to informal action (informal racial profiling such as DWB [driving while black], RWB [running while black], and SWB [standing while black]; race as a proxy for dangerousness; etc.), to official verbal behavior (invocation of selective discourse of law, *ex post facto* discursive constructions, etc.), to, finally, overt/formal verbal action (formal racial profiling, open-ended loitering laws, gang profiles, etc.) (Milovanovic and Russell, 2001:xx).

CRTs, borrowing from "crits" and legal realists before them, accept the idea of rule- and fact-skepticism. Rule-skepticism, we have previously shown in our section on the legal realists, means that "not every legal case has one outcome...[i]nstead, one can decide most cases either way" (Delgado and Stefanic, 2001:5). It often involves *ex post facto* constructions that clothe racist practices in acceptable constitutional language. As to fact-skepticism, we mean "interpreting one fact differently from the way one's adversary does" (ibid.). Thus, the "facts" are always social constructs. It is in the exercise of unequal power that determines why one version is dominant over another version.

Method: Jurisprudence of (in) Color

CRTs often refer to their method as "outsider jurisprudence," or jurisprudence of/in color" (Matsuda et al, 1993:18-20). At the outset, law is said to be inescapably political. Law should be used pragmatically, as a tool for social change. "Legalism," they argue, "is a tool of necessity" (Masuda, 1996:6). Along with this, CRT recognizes contradictions, ambiguity, and duality (ibid., 18), which lead CRTs to an uneasy alliance with some forms of postmodern analysis. This alliance is uneasy because Postmodernists, it is said by CRTs, argue for the "disutility of law as a tool of progressive social change" (Matsuda, 1996:48), while "people of color cannot afford to indulge in deconstruction for its own sake" (ibid., 24). Although CRTs also recognize some merits in postmodern analysis,[9] critical race theorists, rather, focus on pragmatism: i.e., law as a tool, a resource, even an available weapon for social change. (In the final chapter of this book, we will indicate that some in the postmodernist perspective see pragmatism and postmodern insights as reconcilable, even a very useful direction for future research, but bathed in the notion of the dialectics of struggle.)

A key component of the jurdisprudence of/in color is story telling and narrative. To this we now turn.

Narratives and Story-telling

"Language can construct understanding, language can assault, and language can exclude. Words have power...words are part of the struggle" (Matsuda, 1996:xiii).

CRTs see story telling and narrative analysis as a key component in their critical methodology (Delgado and Stefancic, 2001:chapter 7; Ross, 1996). CRTs make use of "everyday experiences with perspective, viewpoint, and the power of stories and persuasion to come to a better understanding of how Americans see race" (ibid., 38). Story telling elevates some voices and experiences, and represses others. CRTs see alternative stories as being deconstructive as well as having components of reconstruction. "Stories can name a type of discrimination; once named, it can be combated" (ibid., 39; see also Matsuda et al, 1993:13). "When ideology is deconstructed and injury is named, subordinated victims find their voices" (Matsuda et al., 1993:13). Thus story telling by such theorists as Derrick Bell and Patricia Williams has resurrected denied voices.

However, story telling in the genre of music can have contradictory effects and can come under sharp internal criticism. See, for example, Crenshaw's (1993:120-132) critique of "2 Live Crew." 2 Live Crew's lyrics, particularly their subordinate depiction of women, appeared quite controversial within the African-American community. Crenshaw takes issue with the idea that 2 Live Crew were merely trying to "explode" various stereotypes (images of sexual subordination); rather than "exploding" these stereotypes, she argues, they more often "reinforce and entrench the image" (ibid., 128). Racist humor, too, become problematic. Matsuda (1996:124-129) provides one way to deal with this issue in her suggestion of consciousness raising and "learning to talk." For Matsuda, a constructive strategy can be one in which space is opened up for people "to talk nonconfrontationally about race, gender, and sexuality," which can turn the learners into teachers (ibid., 125). She mentions how students were encouraged to present both funny and damaging stories of mistaken identities (ibid.). This "space" provides moments for new narratives to develop and for new understandings. It is a space, which encourages not political correctness, but the development of narratives more in the form of Paulo Freire's (1973, 1985) dialogical pedagogy.

Consider the recent rendition of *Gone with the Wind* by Alice Randall, in her book *The Wind Done Gone*, which was subject to much litigation (Reardon, 2001:9). Randall's book was a retelling of the classic book but from an African-American perspective. The issue was whether the new book was a "sequel" to the original, and thus covered by copyright laws, or whether it was a parody. In the book, many of the roles of whites as superordinate and African-Americans as subordinate figures are reversed. As Randall says, "In my parody the black characters are multidimensional, and the white characters are stereotypes — flat would be the word" (ibid.). She continues: "I wanted to ridicule *Gone With the Wind*. I wanted to ridicule it forcefully. I intended…to ridicule the racism in that book. I intended my book to give solace to African-American men and women, especially women, who have been injured by the stereotypes in [Mitchel's] book" (ibid.). Thus, retelling stories from an African-American perspective, particularly a women's perspective, frontally confronted an entrenched establishment, which was willing to battle long and hard with the weapons of law to maintain hegemony.

Intersectionality

CRTs look at how race, gender, class, sexual orientation, and national origins often appear in combination and, in that state, how more insidious and ubiquitous discriminatory practices take place (Delgado and Stefancic, 2001:chapter 4; Crenshaw, 1993; Milovanovic and Schwartz, 1999). Not only are these separate categories often sources of discrimination, but in various combination they can have even greater damaging effects. Intersectionality is a recognition of multiple consciousnesses, of multiple identifications and outlooks in life.

"Intersectional individuals" (Delgado and Stefancic, 2001:55) may experience diverse forms of identity constructions applied to them. Delgado and Stefancic provide the example of black responses to black criminality. Two possible responses are the "politics of distinction," and the "politics of identification." In the former, the black law-breaker is seen as evil and the black community reverts to a get-tough approach — more police, harsher punishments, tougher gang laws, etc. In the latter, the black community sees the criminal as a "race rebel," and thus he receives some support by the community. Here, the black community wants the police to stay out of the business of their neighborhood so that they can respond to it in their own way.

A variant of this has been analyzed by Russell (1998) in her notion of "black protectionism" (ibid., 56-65). "The Black community builds a fortress around its fallen hero and begins to offer explanations and defenses" (ibid., 57). Thus, "whenever colorless [e.g., "crossover status" had been achieved] Blacks fall into national disgrace and scandal, they are picked up and brushed off by the Black community. Like a good wife, Black people 'stand by their man'" (ibid.). Russell presents the example of O.J. Simpson. Russell also presents the example of U.S. Supreme Court nominee Clarence Thomas in 1991, who, attacked by an-all white Senate Judiciary Committee, invoked the symbols and metaphor of a disgraceful period in American history by referencing the hearings as a "high tech lynching." At that point he became black. However, Russell continues, black protectionism does not extend to women of color (ibid., 63). She provides two examples. In the nomination of Lani Guinier, a professor of law, to become the assistant attorney general, President Clinton dropped his support after a large conservative opposition was mounted. But there was a low black protest. Similarly, with former Surgeon General Dr. Joycelyn Elders. After coming under attack for statements about sex education, she was fired by President Clinton. But again, no large protest followed in the Black community (ibid., 64-65). Both women were denied black protectionism.

For Delgado and Stefancic (2001), by the notion of "perspectivism," intersectional individuals are likely to have their identities framed in various ways. The key, for the authors, is how to frame in such a way as to respect human complexity and minimize oversimplifying the human condition. This leads to the dilemmas of essentialism. Is there a common element for people in struggle, or does perspectivism doom social movements to being incapable of providing a common position from which to launch focused change strategies? Should, therefore, various disenfranchised compromise their uniqueness for the sake of developing a united front? (ibid., 58).

A related question here is the question of assimilation (ibid., 59-63). The authors present the example of two African Americans, William and Jamal, both successful and graduates of top universities. Whereas Jamal lives in a black community and consciously does as much business as possible with other African Americans, Williams assimilates into a white business community and integrated suburb with 90% white, but occasionally does *pro bono* work on behalf of prison inmates. Williams believes that he can break down various racial barriers. There are three middle positions that are discussed also. The question, then, revolves around "nationalism" versus "assimilation." Which could offer a better direction for social change? Although the authors go no further than posing the question and suggesting robust discussion, they have provided some key contrasts that demand devising clear-headed directions for social change.

Summary. In this section we have developed the critical feminist race theory in jurisprudence, a jurisprudence of/in color. Doing law is much connected with greater societal conditions and practices. They are interconnected. CRTs offer insightful analysis as to how law is politically mobilized and sustained. They go further than other critical legal theorists in so much as theirs is a much more encompassing methodology, from how people form identifications to how societal structures sustain racist practices in law. Although they reside at the intersections of jurisprudence and the sociology of law, their program tends towards a fully developed and comprehensive sociology of law.

Notes

1. Among the most prominent early crits were Roberto Unger, Robert Gordon, Morton Horwitz, Duncan Kennedy, Katharine MacKinnon, and Peter Gabel. Perhaps Duncan Kennedy was the early guru of the group. For an insight in Kennedy's current practice, see Goodrich, 2001.

2. Matthew Kramer, in *Critical Theory and the Challenge of Feminism* (1995), perhaps offers one of the more clearheaded critiques of Critical Legal Theory. He organizes his critique around five issues: contradictions, contingency, patterning, perspective, and ideology. He points out the various paradoxes at play in Critical Legal Theory, and thus paves the way for constructive change.

3. See, also, Cornell et al., 1992; Balkin, 1987, 1998a, 1998b; Landau, 1993; Arrigo, 2000; Goodrich, 2001; see also the special issue of the *Cardozo Law Review* devoted to deconstruction and law, December, 1991; for a general introduction to Derrida, see Culler, 1981; for an illuminating example of an application to legally defined rape, see Scheppele, 1987.

4. See, particularly, Cornell, 1985; Boyle, 1985; Milovanovic, 1988c, 1992a:243-256; 1997:195-209; Henry and Milovanovic, 1996:235-241.

5. For an excellent overview of feminist jurisprudence, see: (http://www.law.cornell.edu/topics/feminist_jurisprudence.html).

6. See Goldfarb, 1992; Bartlett and Kennedy, 1991; see also the two-volume special issue of the *New England Law Review* (vol. 26, nos. 3 and 4, 1992) devoted to feminist critical legal studies, and also Kramer, 1995.

7. Some of the key figures in the development of Critical Race Theory have been Derrick Bell, Alan Freeman, Kimberle Crenshaw, Angela Harris, Charles Lawrence, Mari Matsuda, and Patricia Williams. Latinos/as include Richard Delgado, Kevin Johnson, Margaret Montoya, Juan Perea, and Francisco Valdes. Asian scholars include Eric Yamamoto, Mari Matsuda, and Neil Gotanda (see Delgado and Stefancic, 2001:5-6).

8. One notes that during this stage that not only two special issues of journals on critical race theory were published — "Special Issue on Critical Race Theory" (1998) and "Symposium: Critical Race Theory" (1994) — but also a growing number of differentiated positions — Asian, Latino/a, queer theory (Oquendo, 1995; Delgado and Stefancic, 1998; Chang, 1999; Hutchinson, 1997; Valdes, 1995).

9. See Lawrence's (1987) oft-cited notion of "unconscious racism"; see also Crenshaw's favorable nod to postmodern analysis as contributing to an understanding of the notion of "intersectionality" (1993:114).

5. STRUCTURAL FUNCTIONALISM, AUTOPOIESIS, AND THE BEHAVIOR OF LAW

Introduction. A number of perspectives in the sociology of law have concentrated on the overall dynamics of a socio-political system and have asked how law is related to it; that is, how law functions in relation to the core structures of a particular society. In this approach, the question of agency, or, in other words, the question of the subject, is directly connected with system-created needs. Another perspective has taken the view that law "behaves" in patterned ways and is related to various structural aspects of a society such as differences in income levels and degrees of integration of two people in dispute.

This chapter is divided into three sections. The first section will provide an overview of Structural Functionalism. Talcott Parsons is the key sociological figure to have laid out the groundwork for this sociological view. Niklas Luhmann is perhaps one of the most recognized theorists in the sociology of law in this tradition. We will pay particular attention to his views.

In the second section, we shall develop the autopoiesis perspective in law. A derivative of structural functionalism, the key theorists here are Guenther Teubner and Niklas Luhmann. Its main concern is with a self-regulating legal system. That is, law is seen as developing a relatively independent existence that then provides the elements out of which it continuously reconstructs itself with the willing help of subjects. Put another way, there is a circularity that produces regularity, predictability and homeostasis in law and society.

In the third section, we will focus on a behavioristic theory of law as developed by Donald Black. Black argues that law "behaves" in predictable ways. In other words, it is patterned in its everyday functioning. He identifies these patterns in a number of summary propositions, provides some implications of these findings, and then argues for a new approach in the sociology of law — the *sociology of the case.*

STRUCTURAL FUNCTIONALISM AND THE SOCIOLOGY OF LAW

Introduction. Structural Functionalism is one of the main schools of thought in sociology. Theorists from this approach generally look at the overall functioning of a social system and ask what purpose a particular institution, including law, serves within the overall scheme of things. We will briefly present the key themes of this approach and then point out their impact on a sociology of law.

The structural-functional approach places much emphasis on the socialization process by which shared values and outlooks are acquired. It assumes a certain conception of the human subject. Human nature is connected with the idea of *tabula rasa* (a person is assumed to be born a clean slate and society writes its program on it). The notion of *homo duplex* is also closely connected with this approach. Woman/man, by nature, is assumed to be half egoistic (self-oriented) and half altruistic (social). Durkheim's position, too, reflects this view. External forces such as the family, school, religion, media, and the legal and political structures are said to produce a particular balance between the two.

According to this approach, people perform many *social roles* (i.e., mother, father, police officer, teacher, lawyer and so forth). These roles are learned in early childhood experiences and are subsequently reinforced in everyday behavior. A social role has two components. Occupiers of a role are expected to behave in certain ways. And the person within the role feels a sense of obligation to perform certain acts that are consistent with the role assumed. Roles, in turn, are always situated in some context which provides background relevancies. That is, certain community standards provide the relevant background within which social roles are performed. Thus roles in combination with some community standard structure everyday behavior. Roles and different institutions within a society must be coordinated by some mechanism to assure that smooth interactions take place.

A smooth running, well-oiled machine is the ideal society for the Structural Functionalists. In other words, to make use of an analogy with a biological organism, different organs have to be integrated in one whole for smooth functioning of the organism. Any malfunctioning in one organ will have effects on others. Deviance and pathology in this framework mean anything that disturbs the overall balance or equilibrium. Excessive strain or inadequate socialization are said to be the prime determinants of deviance. The deviant is seen as out of adjustment and harmony, or in a state of *ano-*

mie (Durkheim). Well-adjusted individuals are those who have been socialized into accepting the obligatory character of roles in society. This ideal is also referred to as homeostasis. Talcott Parsons, the key theorist, has noted that "health may be defined as the state of optimum capacity of an individual for the effective performance of the roles and tasks for which he has been socialized" (1963:176). The family, educational institutions and the media are said to be the main forces for socialization. Internal (psychological) and external (societal) constraints assure that deviation will be minimal. Norms (recurring behavior) and the normative order (generally accepted behavioral norms, particularly dealing with expectations and obligations) are established and stabilized over time.

The central purpose or function of law in this framework is to integrate various roles and institutions for the smooth functioning of the whole society. Parsons, for example, has stated that the "primary function of a legal system is integrative" (1962:58).

Laws are not necessarily written. For example, Malinowski, an anthropologist, has shown how rules stand out because they are felt to be obligatory. Sanctioning forces — those forces that assure compliance to norms (i.e., claims made on another and readily respected by the other as obligatory) — are rooted in "mutual dependence" and "reciprocal services" in a society where one finds oneself in many interconnected relationships (Malinowski, 1976:55). Put in another way, the glue, the bondage of each to the other in primitive society, was based on a web of relationships that were sustained over time (see also Durkheim). Each person depended on the other. Each found her/himself in many reciprocal relationships, which further cemented solidarity and the normative order in the group.

Niklas Luhmann: Structural Functionalism and the Sociology of Law

Niklas Luhmann is a central figure in the contemporary structural-functional approach in the sociology of law. He was born in Luneburg, Germany in 1929. His early training was in law, which he practiced for a short while. In 1960-61, he taught at Harvard, where he was influenced by the noted structural functionalist Talcott Parsons. Luhmann has authored over 30 books and numerous articles. Luhmann's clearest rendition of sociology of law was developed in *A Sociological Theory of Law* (1985). It is extremely dense in its analysis. Little disagreement, if any, exists that his approach is one of the best examples of a Structural-Functional analysis in the sociology of law (see also Luhmann, 1988, 1990).

For Luhmann, the function of law is not primarily repressive. It is facilitative. Its function is that of providing a predictable environment in which subjects can plan and carry out their everyday activities and be assured that disappointments will be few; and if they do occur, that remedies will be readily available to put things back into order.

The essence of law is "congruently generalized normative behavioural expectations." This rather cumbersome phrase, central to an understanding of Luhmann, can be clarified. "Behavioral expectations" stands for the idea that each person in interaction with others has certain expectations of the other as to what might take place. People in society find themselves orienting themselves to each other. I expect that the other will act predictably, according to the role s/he is occupying in a certain context. On the other hand, once I find myself in a social role, I feel a sense of obligation to conform to it, or at a minimum, a necessity to orient myself to it, even if only to the extent of using it to sensitize myself to what is commonly done. As long as the other and I mutually orient ourselves in this way, smooth interactions can be assured. By "normative," he means the extent to which a *pattern* of expectations develops and becomes stabilized over time. It is "congruently generalized" to the extent that both the self and the other acquire and assume *similar* expectations of each other (and understand that each understands this) in interactions. This expectational structure, social philosophers tell us, is often taken for granted and becomes a set of background relevancies in social encounters.

These normative behavioral expectations may be conscious. But many times they are unconscious. Subjects are not always aware of the structural influences on their decision making and behavior. Consider the following test. You are in a general conversation with somebody and deliberately begin to move closer to her/him during the conversation. You will note at some point that a reaction of confusion and some anxiety by the other will be forthcoming. Sometimes the other will simply back off to an appropriate distance, sometimes s/he will begin to question your motives. What has occurred is that you have offended an unstated or unwritten rule (behavioral expectations) as far as the appropriate distance (normative) two interactors should stand from each other. Normally, both understand the given rule or norm (= congruently generalized). And each understands the other as understanding this. One need not state what the rule is; this is unnecessary. Both assume that each is planning in accordance with the accepted, taken-for-granted rule. It is only in its infraction that the rule becomes clear by the reaction that it generates. (We may recall Durkheim's notion of the "social fact.")

Take a more complicated example, which brings out the central problem for Luhmann. In R.D. Laing's remarkable book entitled *Knots*, there are many examples of the potential problems in interaction (1970:21). Consider the following:

> Jill: "I'm upset you are upset."
> Jack: "I'm not upset."
> Jill: "I'm upset that you're not upset that I'm upset you're upset."
> Jack: "I'm upset that you're upset that I'm not upset that you're upset that I'm upset, when I'm not."

And so on.

This guessing what the other is thinking and vice-versa, then, can continue to no end (an infinite regress) creating problems in interactions. At what point can I be assured that I am "in sync" (congruence) with the other? And at what point can the other be assured that s/he is "in sync" with me? At what point, in other words, are we communicating at the same level (congruent generalizations)? If we are not at the same level, are we even communicating? These are not trivial questions. Law, for Luhmann, helps to stabilize mutual expectations. It produces order. That is, it establishes a rule that both interactors take as a given, as a premise for further action. Having established a rule, the interaction can continue coherently with minimal friction. Laing's potentially destabilizing infinite spiral will be minimized.

At times, we are performers who attempt to assure the smooth flow of events, even when we occasionally glimpse the role-playing that is taking place. Consider, for a moment, how on an informal level, the strength of unwritten rules assure that roles are performed correctly. Laing: "They are playing a game. They are playing at not playing a game. If I show them I see they are, I shall break the rule and they will punish me. I must play their game, of not seeing I see the game" (ibid., 1).

Differences exist in expectational structures (expectations that become general in a society) in primitive and modern societies (recall Durkheim). In primitive societies, marked by relatively low complexity, predictability is high. Tradition assures that a set of behavioral expectations is internalized by all. In other words, a "normative order" has gained stability. All understand the rule. They need not be written. In more complex societies, however, establishing common premises for action becomes a problem. Because of "contingencies" (unplanned, chance happenings), and hence the ever-present potential for conflict in interaction, subjects need some relatively stable order and a degree of predictability for their orientation. This poses the fundamental problem. Is the stranger first to ask the other for an inventory of the core assumptions upon which s/he relies on before the interaction can continue? Clearly not. Law, however, fulfills this function according to Luhmann.

Thus, the social system needs a specific form of law that reflects its degree of complexity. Rigid, concrete norms rooted in traditional practices of primitive societies would not serve a function in a relatively highly complex society, where much flexibility is demanded. Norms, in a more complex society, become separated from their original, concrete context and become applicable to many contexts. They become more abstract and less contextual (i.e., less tied to concrete situations). Law has to be more elastic, and hence more abstract, to be able to cover diverse possibilities. Thus, in a society marked by kinship structures or by the feudal order, rights and duties are concretely defined. For example, law states who "may marry whom, who may hunt, who may start a business, who must serve on foot or on horseback, etc." (Luhmann, 1985:12).

In a more complex society, particularly those that developed after the dissolution of the feudal society, an individual becomes an abstraction in law, the so-called "reasonable man" or juridic subject. An individual becomes the bearer of general abstract rights (recall Pashukanis). After the 18th century, it is the abstraction that is infused with rights and duties. Even though people vary, psychologically and in terms of social class, gender, ethnicity, etc., the law subsumes all within this category, giving all universal rights. In primitive societies as well as in feudalism this would be unheard of. One's rights, duties and obligations attach to one's position in a hierarchy, or one's status in a particular village, clan, kinship or household community.

Sir Henry Sumner Maine's evolutionary thesis of the development of law from "status to contract" is given support in Luhmann's analysis. In primitive societies, contingencies — and hence uncertainties — were fewer. Or at least, stable patterns emerged as a response to commonly faced situations over time. The normative order was stable and predictable. All knew what to expect of the other. All knew the obligations and duties, that existed. All participated very concretely and intimately with each other in society. In a more complex society, contingency increases. Hence, certainty in expectations decreases. Stability is more precarious. Disappointments are greater. There is, to use Luhmann's phrase, "an overproduction of possi-bilities." This is twofold. First, expectations of the other's behavior become more problematic. And, second, knowing what one's own behavior means to the other is also unclear. In other words, in both situations an accurate judgment, and hence planning and smooth interactions, become much more difficult. Law, here, serves to reestablish predictability. It assures that each person in an interaction orients her/his behavior to the same prem-ises. The risk of error, therefore, decreases. As Luhmann tells us,

> the orientation toward the rule makes the orientation toward ex-pectations unnecessary. It further absorbs the risk of error arising from expectation or at least reduces it... rules thus unload com-plexity and contingency from consciousness [1985:30].

The individual is relieved of testing the other. Thus potential anxieties or disappointments are reduced. Law functions so as to secure these ex-pectations. It produces a stable framework (normative order) within which planning and decision making can occur.

Evolution of Law

Luhmann has an evolutionary theory of law. The "motor" of this evolutionary process is the increasing complexity of society (ibid., 106). With increasing complexity, and with it contingency, more demands are placed on law to be more effective in establishing "congruent generaliza-tions" (ibid., 83). Put in another way, as society evolves toward greater complexity, particularly due to the development of more differentiated roles, and with the prevalence of greater stress because of greater unpre-dictability, something is needed to coordinate these roles so that constant disappointments are not faced. This "something," again, is law.

Luhmann notes three stages in the development of law. The first stage is characterized by "archaic laws." Society is based on kinship; that is, the family is of central importance. Complexity is low. Alternatives are few. The degree of abstraction, too, is low. Rather, the concrete world, the here and now, is the relevant world in which people orient their behavior. Ex-pectations of the other are stable. Where major disappointments do arise, they are often handled by "violent self-help" (ibid., 117). In other words, when someone intentionally or unintentionally goes beyond the acceptable understandings, s/he is met by anger, sometimes in a collective form. Blood revenge, the curse, and the oath are all mechanisms for restoring the expectations that had existed. Since all participate in a similar environment, and all internalize the normative order, there is no need to develop relatively sophisticated, abstract rules that exist separate from the immediate context of life in the kinship group or clan. Finally, the time perception of archaic society is in the present. A future time orientation is of less value. Laws are not constituted in such a way as to promote a future good. Rather, they are simply reactive. Their main focus is on the attempt to right a wrong, here and now.

"Pre-modern high culture" is the second stage. Here, differentiation has begun. "Economic developments," particularly the change from an agricultural to a trading society, are said to be the critical determinants (ibid., 125). A rigid hierarchy characterized the early stage of this period. That is, there was a specific rank ordering of individuals in society. And here, too, society was very stable and lacked many alternatives. But procedures began to develop to take the place of blood revenge for violation of expectations. The judge is now vested with the power to decide the correct expectations that exist or should have existed. Law becomes more complex. It is now made up of an increasing body of procedural rules. Law, too, becomes more independent of the immediate, concrete context. Decision making becomes more and more dependent on the legal procedure itself. It is as if a critical mass had been reached and law took on a life of its own. But law also became more and more abstract in order to take into consideration more situations separated out of their concrete contexts. Decision making itself becomes more predictable as it is based on procedural rules. Little choice is left for the judge but to abide by the previously created law.

The final stage is the "positivisation of law." In the most complex societies where many differentiated roles exist and where new ones continue to develop due to the demands of the economic, law must be consciously developed. Decision-making processes demand the application of consciously examined and determined laws. Technical and economic arguments now determine the law's make-up (ibid., 157). The vastly increased "overproduction of possibilities" demands deliberate law-making to offset destabilizing conflicts. Laws are more and more selectively made (positive law). In other words, many kinds of laws could develop. But certain laws are selected out of the many possible. The goal is to reduce uncertainty in interactions. The ideal end is homeostasis.

Underlying the development of law is a changing conception of time. In primitive society, one marked by archaic law, the here and now or the concrete situation was of most importance. In other words, law was not focused on some future good, or some conception of a desirable future state. The present was just a continuation of the past. The past, or tradition, reinforced the present. The person who deviated from accepted norms called into question the group's whole way of life. S/he brought confusion to the group. And her/his entire status or standing in the community was called into question. The immediate focused response — that of revenge — restored traditionally accepted practices, and thus expectations.

But a problem always existed, or its potential was always there, that the person punished might have her/his kin retaliate in turn. For Luhmann, only in society marked by the Judeo-Christian tradition, with its notion of individual guilt, can one effectively isolate these disappointments and thus their correction (ibid., 93). As he argues, "guilt permits *absolution* — i.e., it provides for an end in the temporal dimension to the consequences arising from deviant behavior" (ibid., emphasis in the original). Thus, when society has developed to the point where the ethic of individual guilt exists, it can then isolate particular deviants and punish them without having continuous challenges to the "correction" inflicted (i.e., by the punished person's supporters). Guilt implies that some feelings have been aroused and can be reduced by some action. Equilibrium is seen as restorable.

In modern society, the past loses its hold; it no longer dictates the formation of law. Rather, law is based more on future possibilities, future consequences. It is consciously made with an eye toward future effects (ibid., 268). Thus, subjects orient their behavior within a system of law in which their consequences must be thought through. Luhmann is poignant: "The central concern of law is what may happen in the future" (ibid., 264).

An important problem in law is to determine how far in the future one should contemplate and what expectations should be stabilized as normative expectations. For Luhmann, for social stability to exist, law must function to stabilize, by selecting certain expectations that should be entertained. The task for justices, then, would be to consciously select certain expectations that generally should be considered as appropriate in planning. These become the basis of evaluating the behavior of defendants, for example, before the court. The jury would decide if a "reasonable man [woman]" had relied on these expectations in doing or reacting the way s/he did. The task for this *positive law* is to create "expectancy structures" which, most of the time, would lead to desirable results for society as a whole. Luhmann does not give us a blueprint as to how this actually takes place.

In sum, modern law focuses more upon future consequences. The orientation of subjects is to these expected results. The past is said only to provide the basis for change to an open future. According to Luhmann, law's orientation to the open future should leave us "prepared for surprises" (ibid., 101). Even deviant behavior of the past, Luhmann tells us, is an opportunity for discovering new and more adaptive mechanisms to be used in the future.

Law and Its Functions

For the Structural Functionalist, law serves certain purposes (functions). Luhmann's central integrative function of law states that law stabilizes expectations and it establishes expectational structures, a framework within which subjects can work in a predictable manner.

Other functions have been specified. Aubert (1983), while cautioning us about developing classifications, nevertheless offers us five functions of law. In the real world, these overlap. The functions of law include:

- *Governance*: law shapes, influences or steers behavior into desirable directions by way of negative or positive sanctions.

- *Distribution*: law helps in the distribution of resources such as retirement pensions, social security, employment compensation and so forth. Resources are distributed to reduce burdens in society.

- *Safeguarding expectations*: law promotes predictability between subjects by securing expectations.

- *Conflict regulation*: law helps to resolve disputes between subjects.

- *Expression of values and ideals*: law functions so as to promote certain ideals in a society. Tax exemptions, for example, can be a positive incentive for subjects to contribute to some overall ideal.

Even though Aubert recognizes the repressive (coercive) function of law (ibid., 30-31), he argues that this has now "receded into the background" (ibid., 161). In the modern state, he argues, the emphasis has been more on the "promotional functions" of law; that is, law is primarily a mechanism by which the modern state promotes certain ideals by positive incentives.

Adam Podgorecki, a noted Polish authority on the sociology of law, has offered five functions of law, which he calls the "tetrad" (1974:274-278). The functions of law include:

- *Integration*: law stabilizes mutual expectations. That is, duties and rights are specified and brought into accord with the overall values of a given social system.

- *Petrification*: law selects, through trial and error, those patterns of behavior that are functional in satisfying social needs. Those behaviors that have been tested and found useful, acceptable and just between parties are given legal recognition. Non-adaptive patterns are not given force in law.

- *Reduction*: law selects out of the many diverse behaviors in a complex society those that are acceptable. Thus, law simplifies. It reduces complexity. It makes decision making manageable. It provides a framework within a complex society in which subjects may plan within a predictable, stable order.

- *Motivation*: law regulates individual's attitudes so that they will select behaviors that are in accord with the values of a society.

- *Educational*: law not only punishes and motivates but also educates and socializes. This is done by rewards, which reinforce desirable performances. The goal is to instill habitual performance.

Podgorecki (1974) also informs us that the actual practice of law — that is, living law — should not be seen as a simple communication process. He suggests a "three-step hypothesis" that explains the actual communication and functioning of law. In other words, different prisms refract the laws established by lawmakers.

First, the letter of the law can be interpreted differently over time even though the actual law does not change. The social and economic system, then, will determine the meaning of law in practice. Second, different subcultures — groups that are part of the greater society and share its general cultural ideals, yet have distinctive values, ideals and a way of life — will interpret the same law differently. In other words, students, soldiers, artists, scholars, "base-jumpers," lawyers, activists, and the homeless interpret the law differently. The law (or the legal message), is filtered through the particular culture of the group. The law, as it moves from the lawmaker to the targeted group, is refracted through subcultural prisms. These cultural forces influence its "correct" reading. The third prism consists of personality differences. Since different psycho-social, political and economic forces produce different types of personalities, various attitudes toward the law will develop. For example, older folks more than younger folks are likely to respect the law. The civil rights workers of the 1960s, the anti-war demonstrators of the late 60s and early 70s, conscientious objectors, draft resisters as well as individuals in the Puerto Rican revolutionary group, the FALN, have different interpretations of the law than the conventional law-abider. The point is that the personality prism produces different readings of the meaning of the law.

Podgorecki tells us that if we apply a "social engineering" perspective, laws made will be effective and efficient to the degree that all three of the above factors are in accord (congruent). The least efficient law would be one operating in an unpopular social and economic system, opposed by subcultures and by rebellious personalities (ibid., 236). He adds two caveats. First, additional factors to the three mentioned above are formal procedures and semantic frameworks (i.e., structures such as those conveyed by a particular discourse such as "legalize"). These can have an influence on the transmission of the content of laws. For example, formal contractual freedom may produce substantive injustices when power differentials of the parties come into play (as we saw with Max Weber's analysis in chapter 2); the propertied are in a better position to dictate the terms of the contract. But these are, for Podgorecki, of "minor importance" (ibid., 235).

Second, he cautions us that even if the social system is in a state of equilibrium where these three factors are functioning smoothly, it does not necessarily mean that the "law resembles the just distribution of rewards and punishments" (ibid., 276). He notes only in passing the effects of power, pointing out that it should be considered in the determination of what constitutes just laws.

Summary. For Luhmann, and for Structural Functionalists, law is primarily facilitative. Repressive and ideological dimensions are secondary. The relationship of the legal order to the fulfillment of social values is such that law functions to provide an optimal framework within which people can accurately plan their activities. With increased complexity in society, increased contingencies develop. It is the law that provides security and assurance in expectational structures. In this waltz, societal development leads and the form of law follows.

In modern societies, however, a greater demand is placed on consciously selecting laws, which contribute positively to system stability. Law tends to become more abstract and more removed from the immediate context. It becomes general in its application. The structural functionalists emphasize the *form* of law over its *content*. That is, such things as procedural or substantive injustice (due, for example, to power differences), although recognized, are less important than specifying how the form of law is functional for the society as a whole.

AUTOPOIESIS AND LAW

Introduction. Niklas Luhmann (1988, 1990, 1992, 1995) and Guenther Teubner (1983, 1989, 1992, 1993) have been the central figures in developing the autopoiesis perspective in law. A special issue of *Cardozo Law Review* (vol. 13, no 5, March 1992) was devoted to the subject (see also Sinclair, 1992; Jacobson, 1989; Baxter, 1998; Lempert, 1998).

The autopoietic perspective in law has been developed from drawing on an analogy to living biological systems. The work of Humberto Maturana (1970, 1987) has been a key (Luhmann, 1985, 1992). Biological systems, it is argued, are always controlled by the properties of previous generations. Systems, too, tend toward closure. An autopoietic system is therefore one in which self-reproduction continues by the use of given elements within the system. Similarly with law: as Teubner puts it, "Law is defined as an autopoietic social system, that is, a network of elementary operations that recursively reproduces elementary operations" (1989:739).

The autopoietic view has it that the legal system is a closed system (Luhmann, 1985:282), or in Luhmann's precise words it is a "normatively closed system." Thus, any element within it has a distinct life and unity only within that system. This includes forms of consciousness and communication (for a useful comparison, see Bourdieu's notion of the *legal habitus*, 1987). Consider, for example, the notion of the "reasonable man in law," "intent," "insanity," "negligent," "entrapment," etc., as well as the form of law talk.

Paradoxically, the legal system is also a "cognitively open system" (ibid., 283). It remains oriented to its particular environment; it is precisely this that allows the legal system to have a learning capacity. In other words, law attains a degree of relative autonomy. It takes on qualities of being objective, and thus retains a resistance to direct manipulation. The immediate environment is but a factor, which further fuels the relatively independent factors within the legal system itself. A form of self-justifying circularity thus reigns. As Luhmann would have it, "all hierarchies are circular structures: legal decisions are valid on the basis of legal rules, although (even because!) rules are valid on the basis of decisions" (ibid., 285).

This rather abstract analysis produces a different line of inquiry into the status of law. Consider Luhmann's point about legal theorizing by practitioners (as opposed to a sociological examination):

> legal theory for its part participates in the autopoietic process and has to reflect on its contribution to the normative qualification of rules and decisions; thus far it goes beyond the sociological analysis of law. This at the same time restricts its radius of insight and the formulations, which can be propounded in that analysis [ibid., 287].

We read this quote as meaning that legal practitioners who engage in theorizing in law, or those who are law makers and decision makers in legal proceedings, find themselves imprisoned within the categories that are of the legal system's own (self) making. In other words, legal practitioners or academics from law schools, because of their training and immersion in the categories of law, will necessarily reconstruct these same categories by their use, and consequently further support and help sustain the legal system as is.

Structural Coupling

But how is a legal system both normatively closed and cognitively open? In other words, how does a legal system respond to the environment within which it is situated? Is there a causal direction? Is there an identifiable causal priority?

In Luhmann's lead article in the 1992 special issue of *Cardozo Law Review* on autopoietic law, the answer is given in the idea of structural coupling."[1] "He tells us: "It [structural coupling] removes the idea of an overarching causality (admitting it, of course, as a construct of an observer interested in causal attribution), but retains the idea of highly selective connections between systems and environments" (Luhmann, 1992:1432). This is the process by which the extra-legal environment (i.e., factors outside of the direct legal sphere) is channeled into the legal environment and, in turn, back into the extra-legal environment.

For Luhmann, "structural couplings provide a continuous influx of disorder against which the system maintains or changes its structure" (ibid.). In other words, ideas, formulations, conceptualizations, and other data from the non-legal environment will undergo translation within the machinery of the legal order, and this translated material, in turn, will have an effect on the non-legal environment. Luhmann makes problematic the question of causality: "[s]tructural couplings are forms of simultaneous (and therefore, not causal) relations" (Luhmann cited in Cornell, 1992:77). Consider Jessop's explanation of structural coupling (1990:358). According to him, it consists of four "features":

> first, the structures... are neither hierarchically controlled nor functionally subordinate to other structures; secondly, they are not autarkic or self-sufficient but depend on inputs from their environment for their own operation; thirdly, they are not hermetically sealed off from their environments but experience changes therein as perturbations or disturbances which affect their own operation; and, fourthly, in reacting to changes in their environment, they do so in terms of their own rules for reducing the complexity of that environment and thus environmental influences are always mediated through the system's own procedures.

Examples of "structural coupling" are provided by: Jessop (1990:358-359) in his integration of this idea with Marxian analysis of relative autonomy in explaining how the State operates; Hunt (1993:296-297) in his analysis of how information moves between the courts and the police; Cornell (1992:77) in her explanation of how a dualistic gender system and hierarchy is maintained and remains a dominant point of reference for subjects; and, in a more critical way, by Sinclair (1992:88-98) in his application of the autopoietic theory to the development of statutory law.

The vehicle for the autopoietic theory and structural coupling, Luhmann tells us, is communication (1992; see also Teubner, 1992; and the critiques by Fletcher, 1992; Haverkamp, 1992; Munch, 1992). Thus, the causative arrow, from say the legal to non-legal order, goes both ways simultaneously. Law, therefore, becomes somewhat autonomous from general social communication. It has its own existence, and outside data is continuously reformulated within its categories. Structural coupling is, then, offered as the dynamic by which relatively autonomous structures such as law nevertheless have effects on other structures and are affected by them.

Teubner (1989) has examined the communicative aspects in some detail. His point is that human actors have several identities; each is located within particular domains of society. Within law, one identity will be at the forefront, or if you prefer, one mask (*persona*) will be worn. But by donning the mask, one is then subject to the discourse that is attached to it. The subject is, according to Teubner, "decentered" (ibid., 741). Cognition, or thought processes as well as forms of consciousness, are specific to a particular communicative network (i.e., particular discourses such as the legal, scientific, revolutionary, etc.). In fact, "society is seen as fragmented into a multiplicity of closed communicative networks" or, borrowing from Foucault, into *epistemes* (ibid., 738-741). Thus, law represents a sphere or an arena where a certain form of consciousness is at play subject to the discursive elements that are unique to law (i.e., legal discourse and categories).

Summary. Luhmann's theory of autopoiesis is biologically based. Much of its persuasiveness stands and falls with this basic analogy. But this biological analogy is very consistent with Structural Functionalism generally, and continues to have a strong persuasive force in theorizing in law in the Western world.

THE BEHAVIOR OF LAW AND THE SOCIOLOGY OF THE CASE

Introduction. Donald Black's sociology of law (1976, 1989, 1993, 1995) has initiated much debate. Some works have expanded on his analysis (Horwitz, 1990). Other works have attempted to subject it to empirical investigation (to name a few: Doyle and Luckenbill, 1991; Gottfredson and Hindelang, 1979a; Braithwaite and Biles, 1980; Hembroff, 1987; Meyers, 1980; Stables, 1987; Borg, 1998, 1999, 2001; Cooney, 1994, 1997, 1998). Empirical investigations have indicated both support and contrary findings. Some have even questioned its standing as a theory (Greenberg, 1983). Be that as it may, Black has offered us a conceptualization of law as patterned behavior. Law behaves in a predictable manner, he tells us. In other words, if we were to take the hundreds of thousands of interactions over the course of the year at various levels of criminal justice processing, the pattern that would emerge would take the direction of the propositions that Black provides. He also draws out his implications and tells us that law is not primarily concerned with rules and that discriminatory practices are not merely aberrations, but rather that bias is inherent in the very way law behaves. One implication of his study is that the "sociology of the case" better explains law and offers various strategies, then, for lawyers to improve their practice and for reformers to become more aware of how to minimize biases within the courtroom.

The Behavior of Law

To understand his propositions of how law behaves, Black first provides some definitions. First he defines law as "governmental social control" (1976:2; 1989:8). Then he tells us law is a quantitative variable. The amount of law mobilized can increase or decrease even in a similar situation. In other words, law is measured in terms of how much mobilization of social control takes place in a particular instance. In his words, "the quantity of law is known by the number and scope of prohibitions, obligations, and other standards to which people are subject, and by the rate of legislation, litigation, and adjudication" (ibid., 3). The more response that is mobilized, the more law that has taken place.

The peculiar thing about this is that law can vary in time and space. That is, different amounts of law can be mobilized given a similar harm at different times and at different locations. Law therefore varies "across the centuries, decades and years, months and days, even the hours of the day" (ibid.). Consider for example, the amount of law that would probably be mobilized against a 14-year-old youth if the infraction took place at 2 o'clock in the afternoon as opposed to 2 o'clock in the morning.

Apart from the law having a quantitative dimension, there also exist different *styles of law* (a qualitative dimension). Black identifies four specific styles of social control (1976:5; see Figure 6).

Figure 6. Four Styles of Social Control

	Penal	Compensatory	Therapeutic	Conciliatory
Standard	prohibition	obligation	normality	harmony
Problem	guilt	debt	need	conflict
Initiation of case	group	victim	deviant	disputants
Identity of deviant	offender	debtor	victim	disputant
Solution	punishment	payment	help	resolution

Briefly, the *penal style* is the criminal model. The standard is a prohibition of certain behavior; the problem, to determine guilt or innocence; the initiator of the case is the group (e.g., "The People of the State of Illinois vs. John Doe"); the identity of the deviant is that of an offender; and the solution to the case is punishment. Note that for each style, or ideal type, language differs with consequence (e.g., how we perceive social reality and the deviant). The *compensatory style* is somewhat analogous to the civil model. Here the standard is some obligation; the problem is some debt owed; the initiator of the case, the victim; the identity of the deviant, the debtor; and the solution, payment. The *therapeutic style* is similar to the rehabilitation model. The standard is some notion of normality; the problem is need; the initiator of the case the deviant; the identity of the deviant, the victim; and the solution, help. In the *conciliatory style,* the standard is harmony; the problem is identified as conflict; the initiator of the case is the disputant(s); the identity of the deviant, a disputant; and the solution of the problem is identified as resolution (the notion of "conflict management" is also consistent with "solution.")

A particular conflict in society may have any of the four styles of social control applied to it, but with profound difference as to how problematic situations are conceptualized and handled. Consider, for example, how at the turn of the 20th century, labor activists were dealt with by way of the penal model. Since the late 1930s in Western societies, the conciliatory model has been seen as the appropriate model (e.g., binding arbitration, mediation, etc.). In the late 1990s, the "restorative justice model" has become more prevalent (Van Ness and Strong, 2002).

Black also tells us that the penal and compensatory model can be placed together in the category of *accusatory styles* in so much as "both have contestants, a complainant and a defendant, a winner and a loser" (ibid., 4). In this combined model, there is a "zero-sum" game at work: "it is all or nothing — punishment or nothing, payment or nothing" (ibid.). In contrast, the therapeutic model and the conciliatory model can be categorized together as *remedial styles*: they are "methods of social repair and maintenance, assistance for people in trouble...[i]t is not a question of winning or losing, all or nothing. Rather, ... the question is what is necessary to ameliorate a bad situation" (ibid.). In other words, the remedial style is a "variable-sum" game.[2]

Black goes on to tell us that just as law varies quantitatively, so too the styles of law vary across time and space. In other words, even in the same situation of conflict a different style of social control could be mobilized.[3] Consider for example, the discretion police officers normally have to invoke one style of social control over another. And these have consequences as to how the situation is defined and handled. In fact, the history of the criminal justice system's response to the law-breaker can be seen in terms of the dominant model employed.

The theory of the behavior of law, according to Black, predicts how law will behave without any consideration whatsoever as to any assumption of human nature (ibid., 7): "[i]t neither assumes nor implies that he[she] is, for instance, rational, goal directed, pleasure seeking, or pain avoiding" (ibid.). In this model, deviant behavior is defined as "conduct that is subject to social control" (ibid., 9). Thus the seriousness of a crime is defined in terms of how much social control is mobilized against some behavior. The greater the quantity of social control mobilized, the more serious is the behavior perceived. Thus, as we shall see shortly, Black's propositions of the behavior of law predict: (1) the definition of crime, (2) the crime rate, (3) who the offenders are, and (4) the seriousness of the crime.[4]

Black offers us two possible dimensions in viewing a society: the vertical dimension, which stands for inequality of wealth he calls "stratification"; and the horizontal dimension, which stands for the relation of people to each other, including the degree of intimacy and integration, which he calls "morphology." Given these two dimensions, he presents his propositions that predict how law will behave. These are probabilistic statements: they predict the likelihood that law will behave in a particular manner. Of course, with prediction comes deviation from the norm. We will have occasion to choose only some of his propositions to exemplify how his theory predicts the behavior of law and to draw out some consequences.

We should point out some further definitions here. By "varies directly," sociologists mean that two variables increase or decrease at similar rates (e.g.., the more one studies for an exam, the higher the grade one expects); by "varies inversely" they mean the situation where one variable increases while the other decreases at a similar rate (e.g., the warmer the weather, the fewer the clothes one wears; and the colder the weather, the more the clothes one wears). In each of his propositions, there are two people (dyad) in a conflict situation. Black also assumes "all else constant" for each variable: here he means the harm inflicted in each of the dyads is similar, either by the way it is formally constructed in law, or by a more abstract analysis of equivalent harm. (For example, Henry and Milovanovic, 1996, have developed an alternative notion of crime/harm as "harms of reduction" — a reduction from a position one has — and "harms of repression" — a denial from a position one seeks.) In each proposition, he tells us "how" law behaves, not "why." To answer the "why" we need to do some additional application of relevant theories.

His first proposition states: "law varies directly with stratification." Here the two variables are "stratification" and "quantity of law." The more stratified a society, the greater the quantity of law that is mobilized. As he explains, "as traditional modes of production and distribution disappear, inequality proliferates across the world and law increases in every way" (ibid., 14-15). If, in fact, the movement of society is toward greater stratification, and if more law is proportionally mobilized, then it would seem to follow that more "crime" will be discovered. Note that he does not explain "why" this is so (i.e., law proliferating). In answering the "why" question, we must integrate additional theoretical models. We may, for example, draw from Durkheim, Weber, Marx and others.

The second proposition states: "law varies directly with rank." In other words, the higher the rank, the more likelihood of law employed. With "all else constant" (meaning, two situations are similar without any undue variation in external force), "if a poor man commits a crime against another poor man, for example, this is less serious than if both are wealthy. Less happens." (ibid., 17). Lower ranks are less likely to invoke law.

The third proposition is: "downward law is greater than upward law." This can be pictured for clarification (see Figure 7). Here: "all else is constant"; meaning, situation A = situation B as to the harm inflicted and income differences. What varies is the direction of the deviance and law.

Figure 7. Downward Law Is Greater Than Upward Law

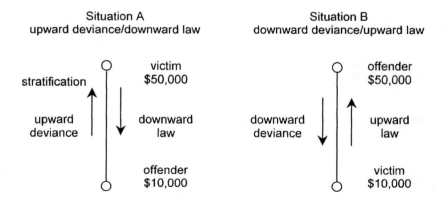

Notice that the only difference in the two situations is with which direction the harm is inflicted. Thus, in situation A there is "upward" deviance (i.e., harm inflicted by a lower income person against a higher income person) and, as a consequence, downward law (i.e., law being applied against the lower ranking person). In situation B, this is reversed. The prediction in the model is that there exists greater overall downward law than upward law. More law is likely to be applied (mobilized) downward than upward. Notice that if this is indeed the case, and if we multiply this schema several hundred thousand times in the course of the year in the U.S., the model is then predicting who the most likely offenders are, the seriousness of their offenses, the crime rate, and the very definition of crime. And these predictions are supported by *official* (governmental) crime statistics (the Uniform Crime Reports), which indicate the lower classes commit disproportionally more crime than the upper classes.

But this may be a perception created by the behavior of law. The model is not arguing that the lower class is necessarily committing more crimes; rather, it is predicting who will *more likely be the recipients of law*. If law is indeed mobilized at a greater rate against the lower end of the stratification schema, then these people as a group will be perceived as the dangerous class. If the penal style is more likely to applied in a downward direction, the net societal perception is that the lower classes are committing more serious crimes. Self-report studies — a random sample is asked to anonymously confess to crimes they have committed — have often shown that the middle and lower class rates of self-reported crimes are not that far apart; if this so, then, what accounts for the official crime rates that indicate as we move downward in the income scale that the crime rates increase? Black would respond that it is an artifact of how law behaves. Lower classes are more likely to be recipients of the penal style of social control, and the social perceptions of the criminal class are molded accordingly.

A fourth proposition is: "downward law varies directly with vertical distance"; and the converse, "upward law varies inversely with vertical distance" (see Figure 8). The two variables are: "law" and "vertical distance." Again, all else is constant (situation A=B=C). The former part can be illustrated. Note that the "vertical distance" — the difference in income levels — increases, respectively, from A to B to C. For situation A, the difference is $15,000; for B, $40,000; for C, $490,000. In each situation, the lower income person inflicts some harm against a higher income person ("upward deviance"), and, as a consequence, law is mobilized "downward," against the offender.

What the model is predicting is that in situation A less law will be mobilized than in situation B, and even less than in C. A poor offender who commits a harm against victims who are progressively more well-to-do would be subject to progressively more law. More happens, more law is mobilized. Conversely, a harm inflicted by the well-to-do against the very poor (diagram not included) is likely to see less happening: less law will be mobilized, or the quantity of law will be less ("upward law varies inversely with vertical distance").

Figure 8. Downward Law Varies Directly With Vertical Distance

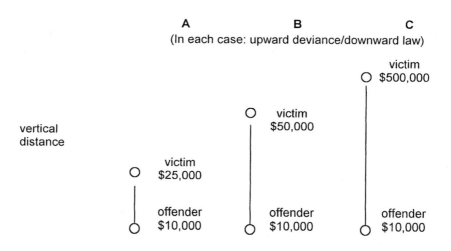

Black's propositions also explain the behavior of the *styles* of law (see Figure 6). For example, our fifth selected proposition is that: "downward law is more penal than upward law." And the sixth proposition: "upward law is more compensatory [or more therapeutic] than downward law." This is pictured in Figure 9. The fifth proposition considers a situation where the less wealthy person commits harm against the more wealthy person. Here, law is mobilized in a "downward" direction. Here, too, we are not looking at how much law is mobilized (the quantitative variable), but the type (style) of law mobilized (qualitative aspect).

The proposition predicts that in a downward direction, law, when it is mobilized, is more likely to be the penal style (the criminal model); in an upward direction, all else constant, it is likely to be the compensatory (the civil model) or therapeutic style (the rehabilitation model). In fact, it is proportionally so (seventh proposition): "in a downward direction, penal law varies directly with vertical distance, and in an upward direction it varies inversely with vertical distance." (Recall, here "inversely" means the greater the vertical distance, the less the imposition of law.) What this means is that, with all else constant, and the only differentiating factor being the direction of the harm committed and vertical distance, the style of social control will be qualitatively different (i.e., different styles will be more likely to be mobilized). The higher income person, having committed a harm against a lower, will less likely have penal law inflicted against him/her. In fact, as the differences in wealth increase, this becomes increasingly the more likely event. More likely, too, in an upward direction, non-penal styles of law will be inflicted.

Figure 9. Upward Law Is More Compensatory [or More Therapeutic] Than Downward Law

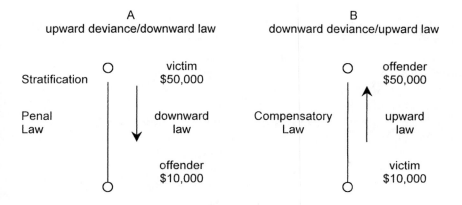

If, over hundreds of thousands of interactions between agents of social control and the law-breaker, this pattern appears, then the societal *perception* that will develop is that the lower classes are disproportionally committing crimes, and more serious ones at that. Said in another way, if the penal style is consistently more likely to be applied against lower income persons, and the compensatory and therapeutic styles against higher income persons — with lower income persons put behind bars, higher income persons paying fines or doing some non-institutionalized treatment — the perception created is that the lower classes are doing more serious crimes. In other words, by observing how law behaves in a predictable way, we predict the seriousness of the event, who the offenders are, the crime rate, and the definition of the crime. For example, a person behind bars (penal model) is *perceived* as a more dangerous offender than one who is at liberty and is paying a fine (compensatory model). We are implying something about how "harms" are categorized by looking at what "style" of law is being mobilized. Black does not engage the political dimensions that possibly interface with the economic. He explains "how" the law behaves, not "why?" To explain the "why?", again, we would need to integrate or consult some other theorist or theory (i.e., Durkheim, Weber, Marx, CLS, CRT, etc.)

Black also tells us that (eighth proposition): "conciliatory law varies inversely with stratification." In other words, the greater the stratification in a society, the less the use of the conciliatory style. Or to approach it from the other direction, the less the stratification, the greater the use of the conciliatory style. That is, for the latter, crime begins to "disappear." Conflicts are handled by way of mediation, arbitration, community moots, and other informal proceedings.

With more stratification, more penal law and more crime results as we previously stated. In answering the "why," we would need to consult various relevant theorists. For example, we could draw from Durkheim and Weber and note the significance of greater social density, the rise of individualism, the development of contrasting styles of life, increased amounts of conflict and alienation, depersonalization and growing power differentials — all could be offered as possible explanatory theories or hypotheses as to why crimes increase as stratification increases.

We now move briefly to some propositions that exemplify the relationship between *morphology* (the horizontal aspects of social life) and the behavior of law. Before continuing, we offer further clarification on terminology. In Black's conceptualization, there are two forms of deviance: one is committed by a more socially integrated person against a more marginal person — this is *centrifugal deviance* (and consequently, we have *centripetal law*); the second is where the marginal member commits a harm against a well-integrated member — this is *centripetal deviance* (and consequently, we have *centrifugal law*).

The ninth proposition is: "centrifugal law is greater than centripetal law." The proposition, then, predicts that "all else constant," more law will be mobilized against those who commit centripetal deviance (i.e., a marginal person who commits a harm against a well-integrated person) than against those who commit centrifugal deviance. And there are degrees of this (tenth proposition): "centrifugal law varies directly with radial distance" and "centripetal law varies inversely with radial distance."

In this model, Black assumes a social organization where there are different degrees of social involvement among people. "Every kind of social life," he tells us, "has a center, periphery, and rings of participation... Each [person] is more or less integrated" (ibid., 48). Thus, based on one's integration, there exist degrees of vulnerability to law. As Black states: "At every stage of the legal process, a marginal person is more vulnerable to law" (ibid., 55). In fact, he continues,

> Since law varies inversely with the integration of the offender...
> so do criminality and delinquency... a person without work, a
> family, or other involvements is more likely to get into trouble
> with the law. Indeed the authorities may even justify their severity
> by invoking the marginality theory of deviant behavior [ibid.].

Let's briefly provide two related examples of this invocation of a "marginality theory of deviant behavior." Take bail decisions as well as pre-sentence investigations (PSIs). The former, ostensibly justified to assure the appearance of the defendant for trial, is based to a considerable extent on the status of the defendant (i.e., community ties/roots; employment, residential stability). The PSI takes place after conviction and before sentencing, and leads eventually to a recommendation (presentence report, PSR) to the judge concerning probation or prison. And once again, it too relies heavily on community ties/roots. It should be noted that structural factors that may be at the base of the defendant's situation are not being entertained to any considerable degree. In other words, the "conditions" behind different degrees of attaining stability are not scrutinized (recall the focus on "conditions" behind racism in *Brown v. Board of Education*, 1954; recall, also, the critique by "crits" of how excusability in criminal law can expand or contract as a function of class location.)

Certainly, then, some segments of the population (the poor, minorities, marginal, disenfranchised, etc.) are at risk as to: (1) being denied bail, i.e., poor employment history, residential instability, history of continuous family problems. And there exists much evidence for a positive correlation between being denied bail and the likelihood of conviction, even holding constant the seriousness of the crime. And (2) being deemed, after conviction, a "poor risk" for probation, with the consequence that this person is more likely to be committed to prison by the judge. Marginal people (the less integrated) are at greater risk before the law. The "marginality theory of law" predicts, once again, the particular "social reality of crime" (Quinney, 1970, 2000) constructed.

In sum, Black's "behavior of law" has offered us an entirely novel conceptualization in the sociology of law. Whether it is in fact a full-blown theory is still subject to some debate. But nevertheless, there exist some profound consequences to his sociology of law. It should also be remembered that his theory does not explain *why* law behaves as it does. It is simply descriptive, explaining *how* it behaves. In other words, Black settles for informing us how certain patterns exist, not why they have *emerged*. The latter question would entail the application of a more holistic theory to account for these emergent patterns. Interested theorists must be willing to integrate his findings with some larger schema to explain the *why*. For example, Weberian and Marxian theories might be applied in generating answers to *why* law is patterned the way it is.

THE SOCIOLOGY OF THE CASE

We now turn to some of the implications of Black's theory. He offers the notion of the "sociology of the case." He tells us that it is rooted in the tradition of legal realism (1989:5). It is offered as a direct challenge to legal formalism, which sees law primarily as an affair of formal rules and their application. Consider, for example, the importance attached to the notion of precedents (*stare decisis*) in the legal ideal type of formal rationality. In Black's approach, a lawyer searching for precedents should go beyond cases that are similar in legal technicalities; s/he should also search for cases in which similarity exists as to their "social structure," even if the cases themselves are *technically* dissimilar (ibid., 30). Black argues that the lawyer should also investigate such things as differences in stratification and morphology — vertical distance, direction of deviance, integration, etc. (see Borg, 1998,

2001). In fact, Black goes so far as to say that a lawyer who does not take into consideration legal sociology is incompetent (ibid., 39).

Black contrasts the *jurisprudential model* (formal rationality, or the classical view of law) with the *sociological model* (ibid., 19-22). The former "regards law as a logical process. The facts of each case are assessed in light of the applicable rules, and logic determines the result." For the latter, on the other hand, "law is not assumed to be logical. Law is how people actually behave, and that is all" (ibid., 20). In the sociological model, the emphasis is on the social structure of the case, whereas in the jurisprudential model social characteristics are supposed to be irrelevant, they are extra-legal. Of course, law school emphasizes the jurisprudential. The sociological model is seen as an extra-legal affair.

Recall, from the previous chapter, the "classical view," following the principles of formal rationality, claims to make use of syllogistic reasoning and deductive logic and follows the dictates of the "rule of law," not men.

Black argues that the outcome of any litigation is based not so much on formal rationality but rather on the sociology of the case. What he means is that the social status of the parties, the degree of intimacy, speech organization between conflictual parties, as well as the perceived authoritativeness of actors before the court, and other factors will all influence: (1) whether a complaint will be filed in court, (2) who will win, who will lose, and (3) what the outcome will be (punishment, fine, etc.). Let's summarize some of his examples.

Let's take the example of social status. Conventional and everyday wisdom has it that social status (usually defined in terms of such things as wealth, education, etc.) has a direct effect on how a case will be handled before the courts. For Black, however, "we must consider simultaneously each adversary's social status in relation to the other's" (ibid., 9).

The degree of intimacy, or relational distance is also a factor. Black tells us that "the closer people's relationships are, the less law enters into their affairs" (ibid., 11). Thus, in handling a case involving intimates, "the police are less likely to regard it as a crime or to make an arrest. If an arrest is made, the prosecutor will be less likely to bring formal charges; and if the case goes to court, a conviction and a prison sentence will be less likely" (ibid., 12). We may note, however, that "spouse abuse" has undergone a change in social perception, and, in fact, police departments now often require their officers, faced with evidence that assault has taken place between spouses, make use of the penal code, not the conciliatory model as was often the previous case. Here, all else is not constant; rather, a political and ideological dimension has been introduced affecting how law currently "behaves."

Black goes on to tell us that his sociology of the case also predicts how "third-parties" to the case affect it. Lawyers, for example, can produce diverging effects on litigants who are strangers as opposed to litigants who are more intimate. In the first case, lawyers, because of their continued involvement and sharing of a bond, may make the litigants much closer than they were at the outset of the case. In other words, the lawyers, perhaps inadvertently, narrow the social distance. On the other hand, in cases where the litigants are more intimate, the entrance of lawyers could produce greater social distance, as witnessed in conflicts in marriage, within family and business operations, or within the same organization.

The authoritativeness of third parties (i.e., judges, jurors) also affects how the case will be handled. More authoritative judges (and jurors), for example, are more likely to see a winner and loser (i.e., zero-sum games) without prospects for a compromise, whereas less authoritative judges (and jurors) are likely to be more lenient and more likely to seek some variable-sum resolution (ibid., 15).

Speech forms also have an effect on the outcome of the case, Black tells us. Two forms of speech can be distinguished: "powerful" and "powerless." "Powerful speech," Black informs us, "involves fewer hedges such as 'sort of' and 'kind of'... fewer fillers such as 'uh,' 'um,' and 'let's see,' fewer questions directed at the examiner by the witness, fewer deferential expressions such as 'sir,' and fewer intensifiers such as 'very' and 'surely'" (ibid., 18). Those testifying in a court in the "powerful speech" mode are seen as more credible. Thus, since higher status people are more likely to speak in this mode, they are seen as more believable and competent. On the other hand, manual laborers more than professionals, blacks more than whites, and other disenfranchised and marginalized people generally, are more likely to employ "powerless speech," and hence are more at risk in court proceedings (ibid., 18-19).

In addition, those who give short answers are more at risk as to believability and credibility than are those who present longer narratives or verbose styles (ibid.). Higher status people are more prone to talk at will and at some length, and lawyers are more likely to yield to their interjections and lengthy prose. Thus, again, higher status people before the court are more likely to be seen as credible. Conversely, lower status people are at risk before the court. We recall in earlier chapters how legal discourse is a form of story telling, and how some voices are denied expression in law (for example, see Jackson's narrative coherence model and CRTs' critique of dominant story forms).

All this suggests some profound reconsideration of what law-finding is in fact about. Black tells us that doing "sociological litigation" (ibid., 25) — that is, taking into consideration all these extra-legal factors — should be a central component of the legal practice. Therefore, sociological analysis should be brought to bear on: screening cases; scheduling fees; choosing particular participants in the proceedings; deciding whether to settle out of court; preparing a case for trial; selecting judges, jurors, etc.; devising trial tactics; and, choosing whether to appeal. (For his specific suggestions see 1989:25-38.) Black, in other words, is arguing that lawyers should familiarize themselves with what are often seen as extra-legal factors so as to fully understand their consequences.

Law professors, it needs to be added, most often present these factors to their students only in anecdotal form, even while acknowledging their importance in particular cases. But no systematic "sociological litigation" is taught in law school. Black, in passing, does qualify his suggestions for sociological litigation by saying that he is not at this time questioning its social desirability (ibid., 25). He only tells us how it may be done and why it should be done given the widespread misinformed nature as to factors contributing to formal decision making in law.

For reformers, understanding the dimensions of sociological litigation better prepares them to fight different forms of biases entering court proceedings. Discrimination can enter law-finding practices, as Black has indicated, in many subtle ways that formal rationality and conventional wisdom have overlooked.

Summary. Black's thesis of the behavior of law and the sociology of the case provides, once again, an understanding of the tension between formal rationality and substantive rationality (or, for that matter, even substantive irrationality and formal irrationality). The notion that law is preoccupied exclusively with rules must be abandoned as incomplete, Black has argued. Sociological litigation, the sociology of the case, and the behavior of law — all indicate that formal rationality exists in an uneasy alliance with other forms of decision making.

Notes

1. This term has also been used by critical legal theorists; see Cornell, 1992:76-78, 81-83; Hunt, 1993:295-297; Jessop, 1990:331-35, 358-360; see also Sinclair's critique, 1992; see also Baxter, 1998; Lempert, 1998.

2. See also the excellent overview of restorative justice programs oriented on this model in Van Ness and Strong, 2002.

3. For example, during the middle of a "shift" or "tour," a police officer might invoke the "penal style" to an infraction; however, a few minutes before his/her shift is over, in haste to "punch out," s/he might invoke the "conciliatory style" for the very same type of infraction. A number of years ago, the New York City Police Department was plagued with "courtesy arrests." With upcoming holidays such as Christmas, a number of police were invoking the "penal style" near the end of their shift in hopes of collecting overtime pay for the 3 to 5 hours extra time needed to "book" a suspect in the crowded New York City courts.

4. For a quantitative critique of the behavior of law thesis, a response by Black, and a counter, see Gottfredson and Hindelang, 1979a, 1979b; Black, 1979.

6. LEGAL SEMIOTICS AND A MARXIST SEMIOTIC PERSPECTIVE IN LAW

Introduction

Since the middle to late 1980s, a growing body of theory has been developing on a semiotic perspective in law. Semiotics is "the science of signs" (Morris, 1938; for a concise and accessible introduction, see Chandler, 2002; see also his website, 1994). Legal Semiotics is currently in the process of defining the contours of its terrain (for an accessible introduction, see Tiersma, 1999; for comments on a Saussurean and Derridarian semiotics of law, see Kennedy, 2001). Accordingly, many new and complex terms are being introduced with, at times, conflicting definitions and usages. Various perspectives have emerged and continue to emerge that are Saussurean, Peircian, Greimasian, Lacanian, etc. There are also perspectives that derive from Jacques Derrida, Ludwig Wittgenstein, and C.W. Morris. We are witnessing integrations of semiotics with law by the jurisprudence school of thought (legal science) as well by those who are attempting to integrate it into a fuller sociology of law. Accordingly, in this chapter, we will offer two more dominant approaches in "legal semiotics" and one Marxist semiotic perspective in the sociology of law.

In chapter 4 we had occasion to present story-telling and narrative analysis in law. This is distinguished from a semiotic perspective in terms of emphasis. Whereas the former takes stories and narratives at face value, the latter delves deeper into the very structure of stories themselves. This is not to dismiss story-telling and narrative analysis; these approaches are sensitive to diverse groups and their unique representational styles in narratives. They are informative as to what they tell us about various subcultures and indigenous groups in a society. A semiotics emphasis, however, focuses on how in fact reality is being codified by the linguistic forms at hand and how certain stories can be readily presented within the prevalent discourse available (be it an indigenous or dominant discourse). Discourse is not taken as a given, but is seen as placing limitations on what can and cannot be said. Below, for example, we will distinguish the Hopis' grammatical structures from standard English to show how world-views fundamentally differ as a consequence.

The use of semiotics comes in various concentrations in legal analysis. Jurisprudential forms of analysis in law (see the five points that are its elements, in the introductory chapter) often make use of semiotics implicitly. An author might make use of various perspectives in semiotics and also a more everyday understanding. S/he usually makes a minimal use of a coherent theory of semiotics. In fact, jurisprudes often argue against its abstractness. Most of the legal analysis we find in university law school journals is more jurisprudential in form.

In legal semiotics the author makes explicit use of a particular perspective (Peirce, Greimas, Lacan, Derrida, Wittgenstein, Eco, Barthes, etc). S/he makes a priority of being true to the semiotic perspective that is in use. S/he often crosses the boundary of doing jurisprudence versus doing a sociology of law. This work often finds a home in law school journals, but occasionally appears in social science-type journals.

In the sociology of law perspective (see the eight points that are its elements in our introductory chapter), a particular semiotic perspective (or perspectives) is (are) integrated with a more sociological, political-economic and sometimes historical analysis in understanding law in society. Here, coherent integration is the key. Semiotics becomes a key element in the overall perspective of the author. Usually these studies are published in social science journals as opposed to law journals. Examples of a more "sociology of law" focus with heavy integration of semiotics are the Marxist structural interpellation, postmodern feminist, and constitutive perspectives. We will present the first in this chapter and the latter two in chapter 7.

In the first two sections of this chapter we will briefly introduce the ideas of two non-legal thinkers who have strongly influenced the American and European traditions of legal semiotics, respectively: (1) the 19th Century American philosopher Charles S. Peirce (pronounced like "purse"; 1931); and (2) the French philosopher and semiotician Algirdas Greimas (1987, 1990). We will also survey some of the applications of Peirce's and Greimas's ideas in law.

In the third section, we will describe one recent attempt in developing a Marxist semiotic view, the *Structural Interpellation* approach (see chapter 3). The work of the Italian philosopher Ferruccio Rossi-Landi (1977, 1983) will be critical. Of course, other Marxist perspectives in the semiotics of law could also be developed, based on, for example, the instrumental Marxist variant.

We can safely say that approaches that employ semiotic analysis in law vary in the degree of its incorporation: at one extreme making the claim for its autonomous existence as a paradigm; or, alternatively, integrating elements of semiotic analysis with other theoretical perspectives in the analysis of law. A more fully developed sociology of law would incorporate a particular semiotic perspective (or perspectives).

LEGAL SEMIOTICS

Introduction. Although a number of semiotic perspectives in law have recently emerged, we have chosen the Peircian and Greimasian perspectives as the more dominant in the Western world. A Peircian Legal Semiotics has been centered on Roberta Kevelson, whose incredible amount of sheer energy, commitment and precise scholarly work had thrust her into the center stage of Legal Semiotics. The Greimasian approach has been developed primarily by Bernard Jackson. Eric Landowski has also been a key figure. Although neither approach would claim to be doing a sociology of law, we do think that, at a minimum, legal semiotics finds a home as an "in-betweener" (between jurisprudence and sociology of law); and, at best, it may even make a claim to being a third force beyond jurisprudence, but something short of a pure "sociology of law."

A Legal Semiotics will find itself based on one of two main directions of semiotic thought: European or American (Jackson, 1985; Corrington, 1993:117). The European tradition is more concerned with:

- Structural and semantic analysis: some "deep" structural level is said to exist which is coordinated by the paradigmatic and syntagmatic axes. Paradigm stands for the totality of dictionary meanings of words; syntagm the proper method of arranging them in linear form in order to make sense. In law, for example, a legal concept which is chosen must be placed in a particular linear narrative; in cross-examination and in deductive logic, there is a very particular way of choosing only relevant legal terms and arranging them in particular sequences in narratives (consider also, for example: the allowable form in the introduction of testimony or expert witness information; the injunction against "leading the witness"; or consider the allowable "scope" for a particular line of questioning that constitutes the boundaries of discursive exchanges during the trial court proceedings);

- The binary nature of the sign: A sign, that is, a word is composed of two parts, the signifier and the signified. The former stands for the acoustic-image, the psychic imprint; the latter, to what it refers (e.g., the concept, or mental image). Say the word "tree," for example, and the image of a tree appears (see Figure 13, chapter 7); in law, signifiers such as "person," "life," "liberty" and "property" have specific meanings, specific signifieds attached to them; and

- Non-referentiality: meaning is *internal* to some linguistic system, such as legal discourse. One word refers for it's meaning to another, which, in turn, refers to another, etc. Consider, for example, looking up a word in a standard dictionary. In law, one does not make use of the everyday dictionary, but *Black's Law Dictionary*, which provides very particular meanings of signifiers in law.

In this tradition of semiotics, exemplary are the works of Ferdinand de Saussure (1966), Greimas (1987, 1990), and R. Jakobson (1971). Application to law emphasizing the European tradition in semiotics has been pioneered by Algirdas Greimas, Bernard Jackson and Eric Landowski.

The American tradition is more rooted in:

- Pragmatism: this favors the contextual and situated nature of meaning;

- Referentiality: ultimately, sign systems and meaning refer to something outside of themselves for meaning. In other words, unlike the European tradition of non-referentiality, words refer to some particular object itself ; and

- The triadic nature of meaning: the sign (or the word), interpretant (or referant), and the object.

Exemplary in the development of this American style of semiotics are the works of Charles S. Peirce and C.W. Morris. The key theorist who has pioneered a Peircian approach to law is Roberta Kevelson.

It should be noted that some variations of the Peircian approach have recently developed in the American tradition, such as those of "speech act theory." This variation looks at the intentions of the users of a discourse. Here, "'to mean something' is grammatically equivalent to the expression 'to intend something', and this intention 'imparts a purpose or point to language use'" (Jackson, 1985:15 and Brown, 1974:118). So "referring" is equated with goal-oriented behavior; put in another way, "'action' in this tradition is firmly identified with 'intensionality'" (Jackson, 1985:15).[1]

Similarly, in the European tradition, some variations have developed that focus on unconscious motivations and forces as a basis of social action (e.g., Lacan, Kristeva, Foucault, Derrida). Eco, for example, tells us that "the subject is spoken by language" (1984:45; Kennedy, 1997:134). Lacan defines the subject as a *parlêtre*, or *l'être parlant* (the "speaking," or the speaking-being). Peirce, himself, is opposed to the Cartesian notion of a centered ego in control and has been identified with arguing for a subject immersed in sign usages, a "sign-using self," or "semiotic self" (Corrington, 1993:76-115). Perhaps the most enigmatic of the definitions of the signifier has been offered by Lacan: "a signifier is that which represents the subject for another signifier" (1977:316; for some similarities between Peirce and Lacan, see Milovanovic, 1998). Here the subject disappears in the signifier, which then comes to represent it for other signifiers within the unconscious realm. Again, meaning is non-referential; here it refers to a psychic (unconscious) reality, which has a semi-autonomous existence. Some of Lacan's work has been clearly guided by Peircian semiotics. We will return to this in chapter 7.

In Lacan's formulation, the deep structure includes the unconscious; the binary nature of the sign, signifier and signified, always implies a third element, perhaps Peirce's interpretant (referant), which is the "*objet petit a*," the object of desire; and meaning (Lacan's "truth") is more idiosyncratic and internal to the subject. Or, alternatively, the interpretant could be conceptualized as the unconscious chain of signifiers to which the consciously applied signifier in narrative constructions is connected. In "political" trials, the state prosecutor attempts to surface the "true" meanings of the ideology professed by the defendant, attempting to show its "subversive" and "violent" intent. In Lacan's "four discourses," for example, it is connected with the effects that consciously stated signifiers have in the production of unconscious associations. Consider, for example, jury selection. The prosecutor and the defense counselor attempt to surface the prospective juror's hidden biases. We will have more to say about Lacan below.

Elsewhere we have developed a position that draws from both traditions in positing five elements of meaning, the "quintrivium." It consists of the deep structure of desire, discursive structure of paradigm and syntagm, referential structure of metaphor and metonymy, extra-verbal context or pragmatics, and linguistic coordinate systems with their embedded discursive subject-positions (see Milovanovic, 1992a; see also Caudill's review, 1993).

Regardless of whether the European or American semiotic tradition is concerned, two semiotic axes are generally recognized as the basic starting point in meaning production: the paradigmatic and the syntagmatic axes. The paradigmatic axis stands for word choices; it is the vertical structure, if you will. It is connected with semantics or word meanings. The syntagmatic axes stands for grammatical rules for correct linear positioning of the words chosen from the paradigmatic axis (for an accessible explanation see Chandler, 2002 and his website, 1994, chapter 6). It is the horizontal structure. Morphology has to do with the rules that govern word placements and their meaning generated in context.

Jakobson's (1971) study of speech disorders was a concise statement as to how the two axes interact in narrative constructions. Given a particular word-association test, for example, some subjects respond to the word by using synonyms or antonyms (paradigm axis); say the word hut, for example, and the subject says house. Others connect the word directly to some activity (syntagm); say the word horse for example, and the subject says jumps. For the subject who is more predisposed toward the paradigm axis, the subject would respond to the word horse by saying pony. There existed a range of responses from those who favored the paradigmatic to those who favored the syntagmatic axis. Thus, these two axes work together in producing meaning in a narrative.

Each discourse (i.e., legal, scientific, philosophic, religious, etc.) is structured by particular paradigmatic and syntagmatic structures. Constructing a narrative in law, therefore, is a confined exercise, and thus the construction of "reality" in law is also limited. (In chapter 7 we will extend the two basic semiotic axes to two additional ones operating at more unconscious levels in semiotic production.)

Peircian Legal Semiotics

The Peircian approach has been spearheaded by Roberta Kevelson, or "Bobbie" as we affectionately called her (1987, 1988, 1990, 1991, 1992, 1993a, 1993b, 1996, 1998). She coordinated, up until her death (November 28, 1998), the Center for Semiotics Research in Law, Government and Economics at the University of Pennsylvania; organized an annual conference ("roundtable") on semiotics and law (a conference of some of the most intense discussions on semiotics and law one possibly could find); was an active contributor to the literature in the semiotics of law; and edited a yearly publication on legal semiotics, currently in its eleventh volume, "Semiotics and the Human Sciences." Kevelson was at the center of much activity by numerous theorists debating the value of a Peircian legal semiotics.[2]

Kevelson provides a definition of her enterprise:

Semiotics, a method of inquiry into the process of inquiry ... assumes that inquiry, always dialogic, is a process of communication or message exchange by means of signs and sign systems. Law is one such sign system, as are other social institutions, e.g., language, economics, politics, the family, and so on [1988:3].

Kevelson's view is that for Charles S. Peirce "law served ... as the prototypical system for his entire theory of signs" (1991:3). Kevelson has also argued that Peirce influenced the legal realists (1988:50; 1991b) and Durkheim (1992). Some lively debate does exist as to the influence that Peirce supposedly has had on the legal realists and, at the minimum, it seems that an indirect influence did exist.[3] And he has had an influence on Lacan (Samuels, 1993). We are unable to discuss all the complex ideas of Peirce due to space limitations, but would like to present some of his key points and then show the applicability to law.

Peirce (1839-1914) was an American scientist and philosopher. Central to Peirce was the question of semiotics. We shall review two of his critical triadic structures (Pierce, 1956:98-119). The first trichotomy includes the *sign, interpretant,* and *object.* The *sign* (or *sign-vehicle,* or even *representamen*) "stands to somebody for something in some respect or capacity" (the sign might be a word). This creates an *interpretant* — that is, "creates in the mind of that person an equivalent sign, or perhaps a more developed sign." The interpretant is the effect created in an interpreter. A sign, too, must come to stand for something, its *object* (Pierce, 1956:99, 275). (A later version makes use of the idea of the *referent* of the object.) Consider, for example, in law the "insanity defense." It is a sign which communicates to another a particular legalistically defined situation, and also refers to its object, a particular person said to be facing a particular state of being. In Arrigo's (1997a) study of the abolition of the insanity defense in Montana, the sign, "abolition," stood for the need to eliminate the insanity defense in criminal cases; the interpretant stood for "what the appropriate relationship between the law and psychology ought to be when confronting matters of forensic decision making" (ibid., 196); and the object, stood for the Montana Reform Act of 1979.

Peirce's second trichotomy focuses on the sign, and defines it as an *icon*, *index* or a *symbol*. In other words, he points out three ways in which the sign can refer to its object. An *icon* "is a sign which refers to the Object that it denotes merely by virtue of characters of its own, and which it possesses" (ibid., 102). An icon, then, relates to an object in terms of likeness. An algebraic formula, for example, is an icon. An *index* resembles an icon but has additional qualities; that is, the object also modifies the icon. For example, seeing a person dressed in blue with a firearm in public leads me to believe that s/he is a police officer. Similarly, smoke is an index, a sign of fire. Here the sign relates to the object in terms of some factual link. Finally, the *symbol* resembles an index, but has the additional quality of being a sign "which refers to the Object that it denotes by virtue of a law, usually an association of general ideas" (ibid.). For example, words, sentences, books and all conventional signs are in the category of symbols (ibid., 112). Here the relation between the sign and the object is due to some convention rather than to nature. In law, legal concepts have particular meanings that are defined in *Black's Law Dictionary.* We will show below, for example, in a Marxist perspective, how particular signifieds are attached to particular signifiers during the stage of higher court linguistic production (e.g., how the meaning of "person," "life," "liberty," and "property" are constructed in law).

For Peirce, the subject is a semiotic self immersed in the sea of signs (Corrington, 1993). Kevelson extends this to indicate how different legal actors, too, work within a specialized system of signs (1988). But the subject is more than a sign user; s/he is constituted by the signs being used. Doing law, is being a lawyer; being a lawyer is the act by which one immerses oneself in legalistic discourse, bounded by its terms (paradigm/syntagm), in the construction of narratives; being a philosopher, an activist, or a revolutionary and engaging in those particular discourses while doing law will bring an avalanche of "objections" by the prosecutor, which will be sustained by the judge.

All thought is *in* signs. All understanding of self is through given sign systems. In fact, man/woman is a sign. All this goes against the traditional conception of man/woman as centered, in control, determining, self-aware and the initiator of action that Cartesian philosophy celebrates. Consider Peirce's classic statement:

> the word or sign which man uses is the man himself. For, as the
> fact that every thought is a sign, taken in conjunction with the
> fact that life is a train of thought, proves that man is a sign; so,
> that every thought is an external sign, proves that man is an ex-

ternal sign. That is to say, the man and the external sign are identical, in the same sense in which the words homo and man are identical. Thus my language is the sum total of myself; for the man is the thought [Peirce in Corrington, 1993:91].

Peirce's semiotics, in turn, can be placed in relation to three primal categories: *firstness, secondness, and thirdness. Firstness* has to do with primordial sense data: it is composed of "no necessary structures, only pure heterogeneous momentum" (Corrington, 1993:127). It remains the domain of the possible. It is in a state of pure flux and potentiality. It is pure existence.[4] Everyday activity has much to do with firstness; not all is given a conscious meaning.

Secondness comes into play when two elements interact. It is the sphere of "things and facts." "[T]heir being," Peirce tells us, "consists of reactions against Brute forces..." (cited in Corrington, 1993:69). It emerges from firstness. (It has similarities with Lacan's notion of the Imaginary Order and with Freud's notion of the ego [Samuels, 1993:9].) Consider, for example, an altercation that developed during some street-corner encounter; things took place, but the legal narrative explaining it is a construction that comes after the event.

Thirdness brings firstness and secondness together in some relation. Here the qualitative dimension of firstness is changed into a different form: "conscious, purposive and funded with intelligence" (Corrington, 1993:133). It is the sphere where active and conscious connections are established between different objects. It is also the sphere of the ethical and moral. (Kevelson, on the other hand, argues that Peircian ethics is better situated in secondness [1991b:117].) A sign can only take form if purpose exists; hence, it is in the domain of thirdness (ibid., 142). Only with thirdness can a sign become a symbol (ibid., 144).[5]

Thus various, often diverging narrative constructions in law explaining the "what happened?" are in the domain of thirdness. These are *ex post facto* constructions, and, as we saw from the Realist school, are often motivated in a particular direction by various actors in the criminal justice system. Arrigo (1997a:197) provides another example of thirdness in his study of the abolition of the insanity defense: "Montana's sign of abolition, as symbolized through its object, the Reform Act of 1979, constituted Pericean thirdness in that a dominant understanding of insanity defense...was codified, enacted, and legitimized."

Gordon Whitney has applied the notion of thirdness to legal reasoning (1991). The legal order is the sphere of thirdness, of subject-produced law.

(Kevelson also includes customs, promises, trusts, public opinion, etc. [1993:59]). Implied here, of course, is a certain degree of arbitrariness of what will in fact be constituted as a body of law. It would seem that at the level of secondness many codifications of reality are at the beginning (incipient) stages of taking form, and only after the clash of alternative and budding positions will a more dominant understanding of "reality" be established at the level of thirdness, in law, for example, and in prevailing conventional wisdom. Consider, for example, trial court proceedings where there is a clash of alternative views of the "what happened?" Although a plurality of opposing positions may seek expression in signs, it would seem that Peirce is arguing that only some become part of the dominant system of signs. At the end of a trial court proceeding, for example, a "frozen record" often results, which then becomes the basis of a possible appellate review (see the section on the Legal Realists, above, on this point). Crits, fem-crits, CRTs, and Lacanians would argue that understanding the connection between secondness and thirdness must be placed in the context of power differentials (i.e., power derived from class, gender and race differences; the "law-of-the-father") and how certain voices are denied expression. At the level of "thirdness," some understandings are more likely to be codified in law; others, those of the disenfranchised, often remain in the domain of "secondness."

Peirce also tells us there is a state of mind in which one occasionally enters, one of "Pure Play," where boundaries are routinely traversed. "[I]t involves no purpose save that of casting aside all serious purpose...[it] is a lively exercise of one's powers. Pure Play has no rules, except this very law of liberty" (Peirce, 1965:313; see also Corringston, 1993:70; Kevelson, 1988:122-123; 1991a:108). This "musement," or "interpretive musement", 1965:313-314; see also Corrington, 1993:70) allows the freedom to search out possible alternative connections among the three spheres; it allows for creative connections between the sign and that which it designates. Cornell's (1998) advocacy of expanding the "imaginary domain" as a basis of alternative visions of society and being human can find its basis in this dynamic. It is here, too, that active *abduction*, as a form of inferential reasoning, unfolds (see below). It would seem that musement is what militates against entropy (ibid., 70-72), stagnation, and closure.[6] Kevelson tells us this notion of "Pure Play" is what is at the core of the indeterminacy of law advocated by legal realisms as opposed to the rigidity (determinism) of legal positivism (1991b:108-109). Contrary to legal positivists,

[t]he main objective in Peirce's thought is for more quests, which is to say for more indeterminate situations, more problems, more chaos. The movement is not from chaos to order, but rather is from each level of a definitive and orderly arrangement of meaning thus far to a new level of disorder and meaning not yet ascertained but still vague [ibid.; see also Brion, 1991; Schulman, 1997].

Finally, the question of pragmatism (*pragmaticism*) and *abduction* (sometimes translated as "retroduction") is important to a Peircian semiotic inquiry in law (see Brion, 1997). For him, subjects draw from both conceptual experimentation and practical experiences in formulating maxims for orientating their conduct. A number of methods exist in formulating these maxims whether done for scientific explorations or for everyday behavior. Peirce outlines the two better-understood and more conventional methods of inquiry: *induction*, by which we start with a case and infer some rule; and *deduction*, where we start with some rule and through syllogistic reasoning conclude in some way. Peirce argued against the unquestioned belief in a purely Cartesian syllogistic reasoning operating in law, opting for a pragmatically-based thought process in law-finding practices (Valauri, 1991). (Previously we had provided an example of deductive logic in a lawyer doing an "equal protection" argument in law.) Peirce offers a third method: *abduction* (1956:152). For him, *pragmaticism* is the study of the logic of abduction.

Let's take a simple example of abduction provided by Peirce. A clock on the wall that strikes every half hour goes afoul and mis-strikes. Normally the strikes are not given conscious attention. With the error noticed, conscious attention must be given to correct the problem. New adjustments are made. Thereafter a minimal conscious level of attention once again is needed to keep track of time.

Abduction, then, is the active process of developing a hypothesis explaining some problematic event. It is a creative act, and accordingly may be connected in the most active way to "Pure Play." According to Peirce, "[i]f one's observations and reflections are allowed to specialize themselves too much, the Play will be converted into scientific study..." (1965:314). Explanatory hypotheses may simply come "in a flash," or through some process of fantasizing. Once formulated they compete with other hypotheses to explain the case at hand. Peirce then argues that a simplicity rule should prevail. Thus a dialectic remains between concrete experiences and the abductive process (Corrington, 1993:67-68). The three forms of inferences —

inductive, deductive, abductive — are brought to bear on problematic situations, resulting in a more parsimonious hypothesis that explains things, including decision making in law. A newly emergent hypothesis then becomes operative in the everyday activity of the subject until, once again, s/he is confronted with an anomaly.

The notion of abduction has been applied to legal semiotics (Summers, 1991; Brion, 1991; Milovanovic, 1993d; Schum, 1994). David Schum's (1994) book, *The Evidential Foundations of Probabilistic Reasoning*, includes extensive analysis of the importance of Peirce's semiotic ideas, especially the idea of abduction as it is applied to "discovery" in law. "Discovery" is associated with the attorney's "various legally sanctioned coercive measures by which he can obtain evidence from his opponent" (ibid., 452) in law. But what is important data? Once received, how useful is it for the prosecutor's or defense's case? How does it fit into a "story" being presented as to guilt or innocence of the defendant?

Evidence is presented by lawyers for the purpose of indicating why there is only one conclusion in law. Much like a scientist, police officer, software engineer, auditor, physician and historian, the person must collect data and reach a conclusion based on this evidence (ibid.). During various stages of a court trial, these conclusions become the basis of further decision making. Schum argues, following Peirce's notion of abduction, that this process is neither entirely deductive nor inductive, but rather makes use of both until some "flash" of insight develops. As the noted philosopher Wesley Salmon argues, "our minds wander, we daydream, reveries intrude, irrelevant free associations occur, and blind alleys are followed" (cited in Schum, 1994:453). Salmon suggests three stages: first, we generate a hypothesis; second, we entertain its plausibility; and third, we test the hypothesis (ibid., 454). This is an imaginative type of reasoning leading up to some conclusion. "In some cases," Schum (ibid., 491) tells us, "we may be fortunate in having a datum that immediately suggests a plausible hypothesis (e.g., finding a fingerprint at the scene of a crime). In other cases extensive inquiry and the gathering of information may be required before we can even begin to generate hypotheses." Following Peirce, this is not purely a deductive, nor inductive process. Rather, the investigator goes back and forth, creating hypotheses, checking them out, developing new ones, checking those out, drawing conclusions, making decisions at various stages of litigation, and pushing ahead in further investigation.

It matters, too, what "standpoint" one is coming from (ibid., 459). Thus, a prosecutor and a defense counselor have very different motivations in constructing story elements leading to some type of conclusion. And even within defense counseling there are many frameworks or standpoints from which investigation flows.

Another noted author, Denis Brion, looking at indeterminacy in law-making practices, notes that the law of tort in particular and common law in general can be better understood by abduction, whereby "the doctrinal major premises never achieve stability" (1991:68). He also draws from chaos theory and indicates that the "strange attractor" — a figure that appears very much like butterfly wings indicating that a system perpetually oscillates between two possible outcome basins (e.g., the "wings," representing various possible and opposing resolutions) — has some affinity with this notion (see particularly, Schulman, 1997; see also Schum, 1994:473-476).[7] Schum (ibid., 474), similarly, argues that it is often a "flash of insight" that develops in this state which becomes the basis of some stable meaning or a particular hypothesis. It often takes place at the intersection of two different frames of reference. Up to this point, there had been oscillation as to possible conclusions one could reach given some evidence; but, with the addition of one more small piece of information, even something appearing quite trivial, amplification in thought results, which then makes thought jump to a very different frame of reference which may bring the solution to the problem (ibid., 476).

A number of applications of a Peircian semiotics to law have appeared in the literature, mostly spearheaded by the efforts of Roberta Kevelson. See for example, applications to contract and property (Kevelson, 1988; 1993b; 1998; Brion, 1999), the idea of community (Kevelson, 1991b), legal reasoning (Valauri, 1991; Uusitalo, 1991; Whitney, 1991; 1993; Kevelson, 1998), the law of tort (Brion, 1991, 1995), legal classification schemas (Kellog, 1991), expression of feelings in law (Lachs, 1991), economic justice and economic theory (Kevelson, 1988; Whitney, 1992), law and market economy (Malloy, 1999, 2000; Ahonen, 1995), money (Klinck, 1993), international law (Kevelson, 1998; Werner, 1999), and an esthetics of freedom (Kevelson, 1993c; Brigham, 1999).

Summary. We have covered, albeit in a brief way, a Peircian legal semiotics. As was seen, many novel concepts of semiotics developed by Peirce have become key tools for the more critical examination of law. We introduced Peirce's notion of the sign, the notion of abduction, the three orders (firstness, secondness, thirdness), musement or Pure Play, and pragmatism. Peircian semiotics has more often appeared in legal science (e.g., jurisprudence, legal dogmatic) approaches; an emphasis on a more sociological approach to law employing Peirce's thought has been slowly emerging, and offers many scholarly conceptual tools for integration and application.

Greimasian Legal Semiotics

This approach has focused on the works of the Russian-born and French-educated theorist, Algirdas Greimas (1917-1992). He has developed his ideas in several works (1987, 1990; for a biographical sketch, see Katilius-Boydstun, 1990). The most prominent legal semioticians from this perspective are Bernard Jackson (1985, 1991, 1993, 1995, 1998) and Eric Landowski (1988, 1989, 1992; see also Greimas and Landowski, 1990:102-138). Many of their works appear in the *International Journal for the Semiotics of Law* and are presented at the Annual Meeting of the International Association for the Semiotics of Law, held mostly in Europe. (Recently this organization has been consolidated with Kevelson's Roundtables for the Semiotics for Law. This new organization of Peircian, Greimasian, Lacanian, and other scholars is now called the International Roundtables for the Semiotics of Law. The First Annual Conference was held in Onati, Spain, in May, 2002.)

Greimas's semiotics is rooted in a structuralist tradition. He draws from a number of European semioticians: Saussure, Jakobson, Levi-Straus, Hjemlslev. His central concern is to account for the underlying structures of semiotic production; that is, how meaning is generated from these hidden (deep) structures. The conscious subject (the so-called "wide awake self") simply assumes these; they are rarely the bases of understanding or analysis, but they form a more unconscious sphere within which paradigmatic structures reside. In his semiotic perspective, language does not refer to an outside reality, but has its referent totally within language itself (e.g., it is non-referential). As Conklin (1998:18) states, "Signs alone (the juncture of a signifier and a signified) constitute existence for Greimas." Thus, to draw from Peirce for a moment, the referent or mental image, (or here called the interpretant) which the signifier (the word) conveys is part of a discoverable underlying structure of language itself.

A lawyer's task is therefore to first give objects and lived-experiences legal representations, signifiers (ibid.). "An event does not exist until it is recognized through legal nomenclature and grammar" (ibid.). Subsequent legal discussions, then, are situated within the totality of these representative forms; real existence recedes into the background. Legal representations remain interconnected with others within a jargonistic legal discourse. Lawyers are trained in its interpretation and use.

It is the "Greimasian Square" or "semiotic square" that will uncover the meaning of words (its semantic variations) as they exist within a particular discourse. It is a conceptual device used in discovering hidden connections between signs. Applied to law, Greimasian semiotics has been integrated into a narrative coherence model by Jackson (1985, 1991; Roermund, 1990; see also comments by Conklin, 1998:18-19). We will return to this below. Let's develop these points.

The Semiotic Square

The most elementary structure of Greimasian semiotics is the "semiotic square" (Greimas, 1987:49; Greimas and Landowski, 1990:108-114; see also Jackson, 1985:75-110, 117; Jackson, 1988:137; 1998; Jameson, 1987:xiv-xxii; Arrigo, 1997a, 1998a, 1999a). The semiotic square, a "discovery instrument," tells us about the process taking place in the creation of meaning; it tells us about how the paradigmatic axis operates in producing semantic variations (for a concise introduction, see Chandler, 1994, chapter 6; 2002). It tells us all this by assuming a closed system of signification. In other words, each person retains a more hidden, more unconscious storehouse of signifiers and their relatively stabilized inter-relationships. These "deep" structures provide the basis of more conscious narrative constructions, and provide a relative stability and coherence to verbalized narratives. The semiotic square is useful because it is a discovery principle allowing us to map our thoughts and different possible interpretations. Thus it is a pedagogical tool. It has heuristic value in experimentation and creative theorizing (Jameson, 1987:xv).

Narrative constructions (e.g., legal texts) for Greimas involve an interaction between a "deep structure," characterized by "a definable logical status," and the "superficial structure, which arranges, through a grammar, semiotic materials from the deep structure into discursive forms" (Greimas, 1987:48; Jackson, 1985:53-57; Landowski, 1988). The "deep structure" is essentially constituted by the paradigmatic axis, is quite logical, and is understood by the operation of the "semiotic square." The deep structure is self-referring; it has no "outside" (Conklin, 1998:18). Each discourse, such as law, has its own deep structure. The "superficial structure" is connected with the syntagmatic axis. It is the more conscious, more deliberate organization of signifiers in particular narratives. For example, a lawyer must draw from a storehouse of acceptable legal signifiers (paradigm) — such as "intent," "duress," "responsibility," "cause," etc. — and place these signifiers in a particular ordering (syntagm) in narratives to be acceptable in a court of law.

Figure 10. Greimasian Semiotic Square

Basic Model

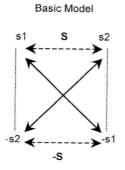

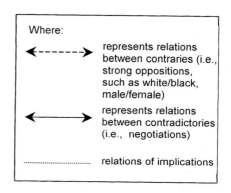

Where:

← - - - - - → represents relations between contraries (i.e., strong oppositions, such as white/black, male/female)

← - - - - - → represents relations between contradictories (i.e., negotiations)

···················· relations of implications

Example 1

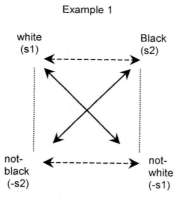

Example 2

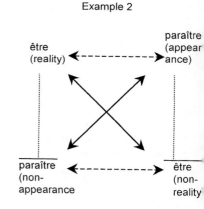

(Adapted from Greimas, 1987:49; Jackson, 1985:77, 102; Jameson, 1987:xiv.)

The semiotic square (see Figure 10) is composed of binary oppositions: s1 versus s2; s1 versus -s2; -s2 versus s2; etc. These symbols represent positions within the semiotic square which may be creatively occupied
by various concepts, signifiers, and abstract notions. Once making the initial operative decision to arrange the words "black" versus "white" (or "reality" versus "appearance") as the dominant terms in oppositions, immediately implied are the negatives (negations) of the two dominant terms,
"not-black," "not-white." Notice, too, that in this logical exercise, which is
said to reveal the play of semantics, "not-black" includes more than
"white," and "non-appearance" more than "reality."[8] This logical model's
claim is that if we start from any corner we can logically derive the other
three by making use of the operations of contraries and contradictories.
Said in another way, given one of the corners, the other three exist in a
state of potentiality (Jackson, 1985:77).

The diagonals represent the tensions that are distinct from the primary
ones. S and -S (capital letters), which unite the two sides of the square, represent "synthesis," or new conceptual possibilities. Thus -S may represent:
"non-black" plus "non-white" = "colorless." Whereas S may represent:
"black" plus "white" = "mestizo" (Jameson, 1987:xiv). If we started with s1
= day; s2 = night; -s1 = not day; -s2 = not night; then, -S would represent
twilight.

The "relations of implications" (in Figure 10, the vertical dotted lines)
are also suggestive. Arrigo's (1997a) study of the abolition of the insanity
defense is instructive. The Montana legislative reform act doing away with
the insanity defense can be semantically studied by the semiotic square to
identify the various tensions and implications. Thus: s1 = insanity defense;
s2 = abolition; -s2 = non—abolition; -s1 = non-insanity defense. The relations of implications could include: between "abolition" and "non-insanity
defense," the defense of "guilty-but-mentally-ill" (note, we could also see
this as an example of "synthesis," -S); between "insanity defense" and
"non-abolition" there is suggested the presence of mental illness and the
use of the "insanity defense."

Jameson points out two qualifications: (1) the placement of the initial
terms affects the logical possibilities, and (2) each primary term must be
conceived as a site of a number of possible synonyms (1987:xv-xvi; see also
Jackson, 1985:102). Jackson, in the example above, argues that the binary
opposition, "reality" versus "appearance," might conceivably take the form
of "reality" versus "possibility" (Jackson, 1985:102). It would seem that
Greimas's position is that the binary terms are derived from a concerted

study and developed understanding of actual concrete discourses (e.g., legal discourse, religious discourse, philosophical discourse, etc.) wherein these oppositions are modal types (ibid.).

Jameson also points out that the lower left hand corner, -s2, the fourth term, or the "negation of the negation," is the "place of novelty and of paradoxical emergence." He continues:

> It is always the most critical position and the one that remains open or empty for the longest time, for its identification completes the process and in that sense constitutes the most creative act of the construction...the fourth one [term] is the place of the great leap, the great deduction, the intuition that falls from the ceiling, or from heaven [ibid.].[9]

Let's briefly look at Jackson's analysis of Greimas's French word, "être" (here translated as "reality"). Here it assumes the s1 position. It is opposed to "appearance" (s2). The other corners, then, would be "non-reality" (-s1) and the fourth term would be "non-appearance" (-s2). Using the semiotic square as a means of discovery, we see that it generates a structure of meaning in the relationships offered. For example, the relationship between "reality" and "non-reality" could be defined as "immanence"; between "appearance" and "non-appearance" as "manifestation"; between "reality" and "appearance" as "truth"; between "non-appearance" and "non-reality" as "falsity"; between "appearance" and "non-reality" as "lie"; and between "reality" and "non-appearance" as "secret" (Jackson, 1985:102). Thus the words immanence, manifestation, truth, falsity, lie, and secret all arise logically from these relationships that appear in binary opposition. These are discoveries made possible by the semiotic square. According to Greimas, these words are not randomly chosen or based on personal whim, or derived from any particular ideological persuasion; they are logically derived from the semiotic square.[10]

The semiotic square has been employed to analyze the right to refuse treatment and to competency to be executed proceedings (Arrigo and Williams, 1999:391-400). First, as to the right to refuse treatment, they define: s1 as "receive treatment"; s2, "refuse treatment"; -s2, "not refuse treatment"; and -s1, "not receive treatment." The implications of the semiotic square are noted: between s1 and -s2, "intervention"; between s2 and -s1, isolation for criminally insane. As to synthesis: S represents "coerced treatment"; and -S, "negotiated treatment." The second semiotic square deals with competency to be executed, where the values are: s1, "competent to be executed"; s2, "incompetent to be executed"; -s2, "not incompetent to be executed"; and -s1, "not competent to be executed." The implications: be-tween s2 and -s1, "confinement for criminally insane"; between -s2 and s1, "psychological assessment ordered."

The semiotic square has been applied by others to the study of law (Greimas and Landowski, 1990:104-114; Jackson, 1985:80-86, 11-22; 1995; 1998; Arrigo, 1997a). By placing legal discourse and non-legal discourse on the semiotic square, Greimas and Landowski (1990) have shown how trans-formations from the latter to the former take place. In other words, his model demonstrates how the "what happened?" is translated into legal dis-course. Jackson has also reviewed how syllogistic reasoning in law could be conceptualized on the semiotic square (1985:86-99) and how the dialectics between true and false, and guilty and not guilty in criminal trials can be fruitfully studied by the semiotic square (1998). Jackson (1998:243) shows how the implications of one of his semiotic squares dealing with jury ver-dicts, where s1 = "found guilty," could lead to -S being "not proven." In other words, if -s2 is "not found not guilty" and -s1 is "not found guilty," the implication is not that the person is "innocent," but rather that the case was unproven in law. This gets to the issue of legal versus factual guilt.

Narrative Coherence Model of Law (Bernard Jackson)

Derived from Greimas's work is the narrative coherence model of Bernard S. Jackson (1988; Landowski, 1988). Lawyers and judges, it is said, share a common nomenclature and grammar (Conklin, 1998:19). "[L]awyers and judges apply the nomenclature and grammar through little stories which share narrative structures with other legal stories, thereby re-inforcing the importance of the specialized nomenclature and grammar of lawyers" (ibid.). Going beyond an early attempt in explaining how "reality" is semiotically constructed in the courtroom (Bennet and Feldman, 1981), Jackson indicates that decision making does not follow a purely syllogistic logic. In fact, it rests on an underlying, unverbalized narrative (deep) struc-ture. Thus, the major premise in the syllogism hides narrative structures. The major premise of a syllogism "is informed by subconscious narrative models, of typifications of action, and our reaction to them" (Jackson, 1988:58). The minor premise should be seen as the end result of competing narratives that claim an explanation of the event.

In other words, syllogistic reasoning in law entails the guiding use of hidden structures (deep structure) in combination with the superficial structure (legal discourse) in arriving at a decision in law. It is within the "deep" structure, for example, that biases, prejudices, and "unconscious racism" (Lawrence, 1987) may reside. These extra-legal influences, nevertheless, end up guiding decision making, producing, for example, prejudicial effects.

The jury, then, is more concerned with comparing the narratives being offered in trial proceedings with the background of conventional social knowledge that they carry with them (i.e., background assumptions, the deep structure). Thus, narrative coherence is said to account for the disposition of cases. Narratives that go against the given conventional body of knowledge are more likely to be seen as suspect by the jury.

The source of the jurors' decision, according to Jackson, "draws upon notions of unconscious rationality derived largely from structuralism — an unconscious rationality which transmits cultural values and which *is* expressed in cultural products, albeit in an often transformed manner" (1988:93). This "subconscious" or "unconscious rationality" in law is manifested by, or can be seen as teased out by the logical workings of the semiotic square (ibid., 110-111). Greimas' deep structure, in other words, is materialized in the *superficial structure* of legal discourse and decision making. Thus, we see a play of the paradigmatic semiotic axis with the syntagmatic semiotic axis: the former provides semantic variation, the latter the appropriate linear narrative constructions. Both are constrained, to various degrees, by the pragmatics of the legal sphere. In other words, meaning construction is aided by internalized legal structures, legal rationality, discursive forms, and legally defined signifiers. But ultimately, juries decide on the basis of narrative coherence models. It is the creative strategy and tactics of lawyers, who tap into the possible deep structures in existence of the jury and make use of this knowledge, that will carry the day.

During jury selection (*voir dire*), opposing lawyers attempt to discover the "deep structure" of the respective jurors to gain insights as to how they might decide in a case. Lawyers, by consulting jury experts, may gain an advantage by the use of the semiotic square in jury selecting proceedings.

Responding to criticism that his model overlooks how political factors come into play, privileging some narratives and repressing other voices, Jackson responds that the player must consider the given pragmatics of power structures and consider them in making strategic decisions (1988:171). Ultimately, Jackson tells us, the best solution is to commit ourselves to the values of "telling the truth," "integrity," "honesty," and that "we commit ourselves to honest communication of the force or importance of that which we seek to say" (ibid., 173, 189). He adds that better critical self-reflection should lead to the "demystification of the grounds of one's own thought," which, in turn, "is undoubtedly a necessary condition for demystification of the thought of others" (ibid., 189). This would lead to a person characterized by "integrity." Since "truth" is embedded in narrative constructions, and is essentially illusive, then the best one can do, according to Jackson is to depend on integrity (ibid., 193). This is not far from a Lacanian position.

Jackson ends his analysis by stating that semiotics is not in itself a transformative discourse (ibid., 190); that is, it is not a discourse that will necessarily produce social change. Semiotics is "purely descriptive." It can be either radical or conservative — all is dependent upon its use (ibid., 191). In chapter 7 we will see others in the semiotic tradition who argue that discourse is an arena of struggle, and the task of revolutionaries is to develop replacement discourses. For these theorists, in other words, we see a prescriptive dimension in studying semiotics and its relation to law and political economy.

Summary. This section was devoted to Legal Semiotics. We chose the Greimasian and Peircian perspectives as exemplary. Key contemporary legal thinkers for the former include Landowski and Jackson. For the latter, Kevelson is the catalyst. Whereas the Greimasian structuralist approach assumes a finite (closed) universe and a play of signification that is already embedded in deep structures, the Peircian perspective celebrates openness, the rule of chance, change, and ongoing transformation.

TOWARD A MARXIST SEMIOTIC PERSPECTIVE IN THE SOCIOLOGY OF LAW: A STRUCTURAL INTERPELLATION VIEW

Introduction. A critical semiotic approach to law is in its infancy in the U.S. For many years it has been recognized that the language of law and lawyers is unique and has effects, yet until the 1990s little in the way of a systematic analysis had taken place. This emerging perspective was more likely to be situated in an overly legal analysis and critique (e.g., jurisprudence/legal science), which drew from various perspectives without any motivation for developing a coherent theory. Here we want to develop the outlines of a possible Marxist-informed semiotics of law. We shall focus on the *Structural Interpellation* variant (see also Chandler's [1994] introduction to semiotics as it relates to Marxist cultural analysis).

Here, the *superstructure* (i.e., juridico-ideological and political practices) is seen as the overdetermining force in the constitution of subjectivity, the legal subject, legitimation principles, and the establishment of a dominant discourse (linguistic coordinate system), including legal discourse. Once stabilized, a discourse offers a medium within which subjects must situate themselves in order to construct texts and narratives. Invariably, some voices will be heard, some will not.

The key semioticians from whom we may begin to develop the basis of a critically (Marxist) semiotically informed sociology of law are Volosinov (1983), Whorf (1956), Rossi-Landi (1977) and Bakhtin (1981). Some of the most provocative analyses in a semiotic approach have also integrated the critical ideas of Habermas (1984), Gramsci (1971), Althusser (1971) and Poulantzas (1973). Our overall thrust here will be to outline the beginnings of a Marxist-informed semiotics of law. (For background reading for this section it will be helpful to first read chapter 3.)

To put in perspective what follows, consider the following situations and linguistic usages:

- A U.S. infantryman in Vietnam: "We have to hump five clicks today and I've got point. Yesterday five grunts got sent home in body bags after a firefight. We had puff-the-magic Dragon rolling hot, 155s, foo gas, quad-fifties and a cobra around but the VC were able to over-run the perimeter. Wish I was on the freedom bird for the states."

- Skydivers preparing for a jump: "Okay, let's figure out who are in the base and who are going to be floaters and stingers. We'll exit at fifteen thousand on the second pass of the DC, do a slot-perfect round, an opposed diamond, then fly wedges, then a cat, then a horny gorilla. We'll first do a dirt-dive and a door-jam. At three five we break off, track away, big wave off and dump. We don't want any one to go in, and no mals. Do a good throw out; we don't want a pilot-in-tow, or a line-over. If you do have a mal, cut away and go for the reserve. Make sure you flair high today and no low hook turns."

- Police officer: "I caught the perpetrator on the premises who was in plain view. It was a B-and-E. Since I had probable cause, I arrested him and conducted a search incidental to the arrest. He had a concealed weapon and resisted arrest. I gave him the Miranda, but he willingly confessed. I took him into custody and booked him."

- Member of the FALN, the Puerto Rican Nationalist group: "The fascist, exploitive, imperialist U.S. is subjecting the peoples of the free world to its domination. We must rid ourselves of this enslavement by taking up arms against colonialism and exploitation."

- Prosecuting attorney in court: "And is it not true that on the 13th you were at the Shopwell supermarket at two o' clock?" Defendant: "Yes." Prosecutor: "And isn't it true that when you were there you took several steaks, placed them under your clothing and then walked out of the store without paying for them?" Defendant: "Yes, but I can't get a job, my family is starving, they closed down my plant after I worked there for twenty years..." Prosecutor: "Objection, your honor, the witness wasn't asked to explain why he did it." Judge: "Sustained, the witness will answer the question asked. The jury will disregard those answers. They have nothing to do with the commission of the crime."

In each of the above situations a unique linguistic form is being used. To understand the full meaning of what is taking place, one must situate oneself within the respective linguistic coordinate systems. To be a skydiver is to not only do the activity, but to internalize the verbal constructions of the activity and to frame activity in terms of it. To do law is to internalize legal language and to construct "reality" according to its linguistic forms.

A critical semiotic perspective in law (Marxist, of the Structural Interpellation variety) can be summed up in several tentative propositions (these will be explored in the following pages):

(1) Language is not neutral. It is value-laden. Notions of space, time, and subjectivity are embedded within linguistic forms and grammatical structures.

(2) Language structures thought. The world "out there" does not appear in a random flux. The users of a language and its grammar are, to a considerable degree, predisposed to making certain observations.

(3) Language can be more usefully conceptualized as a linguistic coordinate system. Several prominent ones can be identified: dominant, juridic, pluralistic and oppositional. A political economy can be seen as composed of various linguistic coordinate systems that often pose alternative ways of "seeing the world."

Accordingly, some become more dominant, some subservient, and yet others are denied the opportunity for development.

(4) Rationality, logic and meaning are unique to a particular language in use. Reality construction is circumscribed by the language in use.

(5) Language may be analyzed at two levels. First, at the level of *linguistic production*. This level includes the political process by which new linguistic forms (i.e., words and utterances) develop and how they are given content (meaning). Second, once words are established and given meaning, they circulate within a particular linguistic coordinate system. This is the sphere of *linguistic circulation*. Subjects situate themselves within these coordinates to construct conceptions of reality. For example, once a person situates her/himself in the legal arena, s/he also must make use of the signifiers (paradigm) and grammatical structures (syntagm) that are an integral part of legal discourse.

(6) A linguistic coordinate system can be evaluated by the ease with which things and ideas can be expressed and communicated in it. Thus, we can speak of fulfillment, ease, difficulty, or alienation in language.

(7) Linguistic coordinate systems are relatively autonomous. On one level, the form of language can be neutral. Put in another way, there is equal opportunity in the use of language: all are said to have "equal" access to language. However, the acquisition of language forms and the skill in their usage varies as a function of socio-economic class. On another level, the content of linguistic forms (that which is established through a political process) is selectively established, often supporting dominant understandings of the world (reification).

(8) Hegemony exists to a considerable degree by the aid of the dominant and juridic linguistic coordinate systems. Hegemony is maintained by the transformation or by the channeling of oppositional language forms into dominant linguistic coordinate systems (i.e., by psychiatrists, lawyers, teachers, politicians and the judiciary, to name a few). One understanding of the world is often replaced by another supportive of the status quo. Defendants before the court contribute to their own continued

oppression by the unquestioned use of the juridic language form.

(9) Lawyers can be better conceptualized as the sellers of juridic linguistic skills. These linguistic skills are learned. They are learned in specialized institutions, law schools, which more often reflect and support the dominant political and economic system.

(10) Authentic and open communication (non-alienating communication) can only take place within a mode of production where hierarchy, exploitation, and repression are eliminated.

Linguistic Coordinate Systems

Key statements in semiotics have come from Benjamin Whorf (1956) and Ferruccio Rossi-Landi (1977). The so called Sapir-Whorf linguistic relativity principle states that "users of markedly different grammars are pointed by their grammars toward different types of observations and different evaluations of externally similar acts of observation, and hence are not equivalent as observers but must arrive at somewhat different views of the world" (Whorf, 1956:221). Whorf's comparison of the "Standard Average European" (SAE) languages with the Hopi Indian of Southwest United States indicated that there were vast differences in the way each language allowed its user to perceive. He uses SAE to refer to the many European languages, such as English, French and German, which are similarly structured (ibid., 138).

The Hopi language, he argued, has no verb forms expressing the clean separations of past, present and future (see also Lee, 1959:105-20). Rather, things are expressed as *ever becoming*. Furthermore, for the Hopi, the idea found in SAE, that a sentence must have a substantive and a verb, is unnecessary. We, for example, attribute an action to a subject whom we see as its author (see also Lee, 1959:94-95, 134, 137; Benveniste, 1971:195-204, 223-224). Take, for example, the statement: She is roller-blading. Consider the implications: we have a subject that is responsible for some action (roller-blading). (Consider, too, for a moment, how in trial proceedings the court is totally preoccupied with establishing individual responsibility — an individual connected to some willed act. Generally, the effects of larger socio-political and economic factors, for example, are pushed to the side.) The Hopi, on the other hand, see action states. A particular author is unnecessary. If the Hopi were asked what the woman was doing, it would be simply described in terms of some action word such as roller-blading. For the Hopi, action is connected intimately and holistically with the surrounding environment.

Abstracting an entity — such as a self-contained subject (the self) — from the social formation, and attributing causal primacy to it, is inconsistent with the world-view of the Hopi. Compare this to the Western courts, where there is a heavy reliance in proving *mens rea* (criminal intent). The model we employ is one of individual responsibility. Compare, for example, the focus on the individual author in Western copyright laws with the notion of collective authorship and ownership of aboriginal people in their art production (Puri, 1992).

The user of SAE also splits up phenomena by the use of "form + formless." That is, we are accustomed to saying "glass of water," "piece of cake," etc. The Hopi are quite comfortable expressing these amorphous forms without the aid of a quantity term. No boundaries need exist. Note again how our language, including legal discourse, imposes bounded terms. We operate as if the world is divided into rigid categories, that at best are only partly connected. For the Hopi, a trace of each part of existence appears in various other sites, *all at once.*

Finally, we make heavy use of metaphors. We place phenomena in an imaginary space in our mind when communicating or thinking. We say, for example, "spring into action," "coiled for action," "she's a real dynamo," etc. It's as if we have to create an image in our minds that duplicates some concrete technology in order to express ourselves. According to Whorf, the Hopi live *in* their expressions as they live in their experiences. They use neither the notion of "form + formless" nor an imaginary space. They are not removed but are connected to the thing they talk about. Whorf suggests that much of this in the industrialized world can be attributed to the coming of commerce and industrialization and its needs of precise measurement and its technologies. Here, then, the "form + formless" and the use of metaphor became more prevalent.

There are two forms of linguistic relativity. The "soft" version of linguistic relativity has it that language has a minor degree of independent influence in structuring thought. The "strong" version (linguistic determinism) implies that we are prisoners of the linguistic coordinate system within which we locate ourselves.

Several noted authorities have commented on the notion of *linguistic relativity*. Sapir has said that "we see and hear and otherwise experience very largely as we do because the language habits of our community predispose certain choices of interpretation" (cited in Fishman, 1960:324). Vygotsky has noted that the development of "grammar precedes logic" (1962:127). A child might use such words as "because," "if," "when," and so forth before s/he grasps their meaning. Whorf is even more direct: "every language is a vast pattern system, different from others, in which are culturally ordained the forms and categories by which the personality not only communicates, but also analyzes nature, notices or neglects types of relationships and phenomena, channels his reasoning, and builds the house of his consciousness" (1956:252). In sum, the linguistic relativity principle points out the independent effects of language on thought processes.

The Italian philosopher Ferruccio Rossi-Landi offers the idea that we can apply the notion of "commodity fetishism" (see chapter 3) to the sphere of language. He notes a similar development of commodity and linguistic forms. Marxists have argued that a commodity has both a use-value and an exchange-value. The use-value stands for the ability of a thing to fulfill some concrete need. It also stands for a quantity of labor used in its production. When commodity owners enter the marketplace and exchange their commodities, the use-value is replaced by the abstraction, exchange-value. This represents a ratio of exchange. Money is the universal form. Five dollars can buy either three pounds of butter or two bushels of corn. This, the Marxists tell us, is the principle of fetishism of commodities. We create the abstraction, money, which we worship. We reduce everything to a money value. The inherent use-value of a thing loses importance.

Rossi-Landi argues that linguistic forms undergo the same process. Words and utterances have initial use-value, they correspond to the ability to express. But when used in interactions they take on exchange-value. In other words, they take on more universal meaning. Their nuances, their subtle shadings of meaning, become smoothed over and are given a generally understood meaning. Thus, we can now identify three forms of fetishisms (and the homologies, or similarities in development, that tie the three together; see Figure 11).

Furthermore, Rossi-Landi argues, just as the commodity is produced in the sphere of production and circulates in the marketplace, the same applies to the linguistic form. In other words, there exists a homology. A sphere of *linguistic production* exists in which linguistic forms and their content are established. Consider, for example, how linguistic forms such as particular words — mens rea, duress, intent, willingly, etc. — are given precise content, and then how they must be used accordingly for anyone claiming to be doing law. Once established, in other words, they enter the *sphere of circulation.* These linguistic forms are then used in narrative constructions.

Figure 11. Fetishism of Commodity, Juridic and Linguistic Forms

Commodity Sphere	Juridic Sphere	Linguistic Sphere
Use-value	Desiring subject; unique being	Signifiers embodied with unique desires of the socio-historically situated subjects. Contextual meanings of signifiers (words).
Exchange-value	Juridic subject; the "reasonable man" in law	Signifiers with abstract, dictionary meanings. Words with common meaning.

Thus, the higher courts (state appeal and supreme courts as well as the U.S. appeals and Supreme Court) can be envisioned as the sphere of juridic linguistic production. Here particular legal concepts are created and given precise meaning. To use the language of semiotics, new legal terms (the signifier) are given precise content or meaning (the signified); (see, for example, Milovanovic, 1986:294-296). Consider how "life," "liberty," and "property," as signifiers, have been connected with particular content (signified). Drawing together the ideas of Whorf and Rossi-Landi, we may say that several linguistic coordinate systems exist.[11]

Generally, in modern society, one discourse is dominant. It becomes the main medium through and by which we communicate. We shall refer to it as the *dominant linguistic coordinate system.* We also have the juridic discourse, or as we characterize it, the juridic linguistic coordinate system. Training in law schools indoctrinates the developing lawyer with particular linguistic skills. A specialized vocabulary and syntax is learned. A form of deductive reasoning is internalized. The juridic linguistic coordinate system that the student learns is abstract, general and removed from concrete contexts. Here, previously established doctrines, premises, and principles (by way of precedents or *stare decisis*) guide legal reasoning. The lawyer, in litigating some "factual" situation, has only to seek the legal principle that is applicable, select the premises of her/his argument that are relevant, and then through logical syllogistic reasoning, draw the appropriate conclusion. (See also chapter 2 concerning the ideal-type of formal rational law.) The lawyer, through her/his training and everyday practice, finds her/himself immersed in this language system. To do law is to situate oneself within this framework. Anything outside of this is not good law. It is likely to be judged as non-justiciable.

The *pluralistic linguistic coordinate system* consists of the language styles of the many subcultures within a society. Each has a particular way of expressing and communicating. Each communicates different relevancies of the world. In other words, each accents the world differently. Bernstein (1975), for example, has shown that working classes more often use a "restrictive code" that binds its user to concrete reality. Here, gestures, intonation and the use of verbal metaphor are rooted in concrete, everyday life. The use of many nonverbal signs is the norm. The middle class, however, operates with an "elaborate code," which roots its user in the more abstract and less context-bound terminology. It focuses on verbalizations directed toward more general audiences removed from the concrete here-and-now.[12]

The *oppositional linguistic coordinate system* stands for critical and politically motivated discourses. The users of this discourse will find many categories by which to challenge a particular state of affairs. Revolutionary groups have the most systematized framework within which the rebel thinks and conceptualizes the world. Take for example, the Black Panthers, The Weathermen, the Puerto Rican Nationalist group (the FALN), and others. With each, a well-developed language exists (or existed) which opposes (or opposed) the given status quo. Users of this language view the world in oppositional terms.

To give a more concrete example, *liberation theology* in Central and South America developed in the mid-1960s. Its basic tenets are in marked contrast to those readings of the Bible by traditional priests. For the faithful, one resigns oneself to the way things are and looks toward being judged in her/his afterlife. In comparison, for those immersed in liberation theology, the here and now must be confronted. If oppressive structures exist, they must be challenged *now*. Thus, the linguistic coordinate systems convey vastly different ideologies of what is to be done. Liberation theology has been a key element for many successful revolutions in Central and South America. Note, too, that liberation theology may be appropriated for a diversity of political agendas.

Meaning and rationality are specific to the linguistic coordinate system in use. Pitkin (1971), drawing from Winch's examination (1964) of rationality in primitive societies, has concluded that "looking for experimental proof in the realm of religion is as irrational as looking for revelation in the realm of science." For example, "in science or mathematics, the rationality of an argument depends upon its leading from premises all parties accept, in steps all can follow, to an agreement upon a conclusion which all must accept." And "anyone who fails to accept the conclusion is regarded as either incompetent *in that mode or reasoning*, or irrational" (1971:153; my emphasis).

Linguistics, Hegemony and Reality Construction

We now turn our attention to reality construction in the courtroom. The typical defendant from the lower classes must present information to a middle class lawyer schooled well in a qualitatively different discursive framework. There is conflict between two world-views. This is resolved by the defense lawyer translating "what happened" into "legalese," or to be more precise, into the juridic linguistic coordinate system (see, for example, Milovanovic, 1988; Milovanovic and Thomas, 1989; Bannister and Milovanovic, 1990; Henry and Milovanovic, 1996). But meaning is lost in the translation. One worldview, the one supported by the language structure of the courts, is reinforced, another is denied.

The courts have even excluded whole spheres from being argued. For example, the trial court proceedings focus on establishing *mens rea* (criminal intent) and *actus reus* (the criminal act). If both are shown, a conviction results. The defendant, however, may not present his motive. If the defendant insists, the opposing lawyer will simply "object" and the judge will sustain, even telling the jury to disregard what was said. The point is, certain factors that are part of why people act the way they do are not given codification, are not entertained in a court of law (see also Goodrich, 1990:193-201; Bourdieu, 1987:831-832). They are non-justiciable. Thus, another reality is never made visible. "Relevant" factors for decision making are reduced to a narrow frame. "Facts" are cleansed and sterilized. They are abstracted and removed from their overall concrete context.

Consider, on the other hand, a corporate offender before the court. Here the traditional proceedings consist of the use of the injunction. The corporation is asked why it should not be stopped from doing what it is doing. In other words, corporations are permitted to offer articulations revolving around capitalist business practices, such as maintaining profit margins and providing "contributions" such as jobs and taxes to their community — all "safe," system-maintaining codifications. Even when a "consent decree" is arranged, the guilty party simply accepts the penalty without admitting responsibility. The reality that is reinforced is the dominant one, supportive of the status quo. What develops is a rather rich, complex understanding concerning the necessity of capitalism, all of which is rooted in and reflected by the dominant discourse. On the other hand, for the disenfranchised and marginalized, what is minimally developed is a deep understanding of their struggles for survival in a mode of production where economic survival is never assured. Some voices, in short, are denied meaningful expression.

In sum, one discourse is enriched, another impoverished. In this framework the defense lawyer can better be seen as a "social tranquilizer." The lawyer buys into the relevance of the linguistic coordinate system and is thus bounded by the effects of this language (Arrigo, 1993b, 1994). During this process, the potential development of an oppositional discourse is arrested. The disenfranchised, and those victimized by the political-economic system, are denied the very tools for critical thought, expression and communication. No stabilized linguistic coordinate system is established that reflects a critical reading of "reality."

Thus, those brutalized, exploited, and alienated, and the victims of injustices, must attempt to express themselves within the narrow framework of the dominant or juridic discourse, with its value-laden linguistic forms. Their feelings of being exploited, then, find no genuine means of expression. (For an application to the mentally ill, see Arrigo [1993b, 1994]). For example, until a 1992 high court ruling in Australia, aboriginal people were denied any legal claims to their land by the policy of *terra nullius*, Heilpern (1993; Sarre, 1994). We may define this as linguistic alienation. Through this process, then, reality is constructed anew, but in the direction supportive of the status quo (Marxists call this process "reification"). Those most brutalized, as well as those aiding them are often, inadvertently, their own gravediggers. The notion of hegemony, a Gramsci insight (1971), by which we mean the willing participation by those most oppressed in their own oppression, is one of the most subtle forms of maintaining oppression.

Applications of the Semiotic Approach in the Sociology of Law: A Structural Interpellation View

Linguistic production, we have said, stands for the process by which new linguistic terms (signifiers) are created and their content is given expression or meaning (signified). The two elements of the sign are thus the signifier and the signified. Legal terms and expressions (signs) such as mens rea (criminal intent), duress, product, proximate cause, reckless, willful, good faith, plain view, custodial arrest, reasonable cause, probable cause, expectations of privacy, conspiracy, attempt, voluntary, and so forth, are given precise meaning predominantly in the higher courts. It is here that we find linguistic production. Lower courts and their lawyers must litigate within this framework — the linguistic coordinate system (the sphere of linguistic circulation) established by the higher courts. Let us present some examples. These exemplifications can be seen as supporting a Structural Interpellationist view in the sociology of law.

The Fourteenth Amendment to the Constitution includes the "equal protection clause," which reads, in part, that no state may "deprive any person of life, liberty, or property without due process of law." In litigation, two questions must be addressed. First, what constitutes a constitutionally accepted life, liberty or property interest? Second, and only if the threshold point has been reached, what is the appropriate process due before their infringement? We shall focus on the first question here, particularly the question concerning what constitutes a liberty and property interest recognized by the Constitution.

The courts in advanced, state-regulated, corporate capitalism have had to actively intervene in the economic and political spheres to offset crisis tendencies (see chapter 3). As a means to this end, the higher courts have embraced the mechanism of interest-balancing in determining the rights of a particular group. Notions of a "liberty" or a "property" interest require the courts to balance: (1) a particular government interest (such as national security, the general welfare, the need to run an orderly prison, etc.), and (2) the interests of the particular person or group affected by the governmental policy. In the process of arriving at a liberty interest — say the liberty interest to privacy, or an inmate's interest in not being placed in solitary confinement — the courts fill in the content of the term "liberty interest" with precise meaning. This is *linguistic production*. Once the sign is given meaning, it enters the sphere of *linguistic circulation*. Lawyers, to do acceptable lawyering, must now use the precise meaning established by the higher courts.

Much critical analysis, however, indicates that many uncodified practices or phenomena (primordial sense data) are selectively given signification (codification). Offe, for example, has shown how the state and state apparatuses such as the courts must be seen as filtering mechanisms (Milovanovic, 1987). Only those interests that are organizable and capable of conflict have a chance of being articulated and hence entertained in the courts (see also Laclau and Mouffe's analysis of new forms of interests that have developed beyond those of mere class interests, 1985; Laclau, 1996). In other words, unless inmates (or welfare recipients, the homeless, "illegal" aliens from Central America and other disenfranchised), for example, can form a class *for itself* (rather than just a class *in itself*), producing the capability of a united and conscious challenge to the dominant class, the former's interests will be amorphous, unarticulated and non-challenging. During interest-balancing by the courts, an inequality exists in the inputs: social protest movements, and oppositional groups generally, while they do have an influence in the development of law, are, however, a poor match for the entrenched forces wishing to sustain things as they are. Thus, giving meaning — that is, giving content to the signifier, "liberty interest" — is a political process, which favors groups with power.[13]

The second illustrative example concerns jailhouse lawyers (JHLs) and their practice (Milovanovic, 1988; see also Thomas, 1988; Milovanovic and Thomas, 1989; Thomas and Milovanovic, 1999). This brings out the notion of the *dialectics of struggle* (see also chapter 3). JHLs — inmates who have taught themselves law and practice it (most often against their keepers) — find themselves in a dialectical struggle that often resolves itself in the direction of reifying legal discourse and the form of law. The JHL finds her/himself within two linguistic coordinate systems. First, most inmates are from the lower class — disenfranchised, exploited, and subject to the worst living conditions. JHLs initially situate themselves within the linguistic coordinate system of the streets. Notions of identity, cause, responsibility, assault, etc., on the one hand, and a particular relatively coherent world view on the other, are established and stabilized, revolving around much of the indignities and exploitive practices inflicted on them. Not all of these perceived exploitive practices are given precise articulation. Some escape expression but can be communicated outside of, or in combination with, the linguistic coordinate system (i.e., by way of gestures, facial expressions, statements like "you know what I mean").

But JHLs, in learning the law, and in situating themselves within its linguistic coordinate system, come to see the world in different terms. In other words, a different world-view develops. To do law, they quickly find out, is to situate arguments and to construct "what happened" within this linguistic coordinate system. Otherwise what is argued is judged nonjusticiable. Thus, the JHL, in helping a fellow inmate prepare for trial or appeal, or in filing a petition against oppressive practices by the keepers, finds her/himself in two worlds, two linguistic coordinate systems.

At the trial stage, the defendant must attempt to convincingly explain "what happened." Prior to the trial, the JHL listens to the story of the client. But what the JHL does is to re-situate "what happened" into the language of law. Thus, there is a shift in linguistic coordinate systems. What is denied in the process is the articulation, the codification of the oppressive conditions under which the defendant lives. These are not codified; but even if they are, they are not allowed in court. They are seen as non-justiciable. The court is only interested in knowing whether intent existed and a crime occurred; never mind the motive. And here lies the dilemma for the JHL: s/he knows only too well how these conditions result in crime, but s/he also knows that the court will not allow this articulation to be expressed in court. The JHL opts for the practical (pragmatism): s/he takes the story of the defendant and re-situates bits and pieces of it within the juridic linguistic communicative market and builds a legally acceptable, and hopefully a believable story of "what happened." Reification is the result. One understanding of the world is denied, another upheld as the legitimate version. A cleansing, a sterilizing of any potential oppositional reading has taken place. The JHL becomes implicated, becomes a conspirator of sorts in this hegemonic process.

A third illustrative example deals with activist lawyers defending rebels before the court (Bannister and Milovanovic, 1990). This example, much like the second above, brings out the notion of the *dialectics of struggle*. Consider the following: activists in the mid-1980s protesting against the U.S. involvement in Central America — claiming that the U.S. government had organized, trained, financed, and directed the *contras* (ex-national guardsmen under the dictator Somoza) in their killings of thousands of innocent women, children, and the elderly — were arrested and charged with crimes ranging from criminal trespass, to destruction of government property, to resisting arrest, to assault on a police officer. These are formidable charges, and, in some cases, potentially adding up to many years spent in prison. The politically motivated activist lawyer was approached to defend these rebels. Both the defendant and the activist lawyer wished to mount a political defense, pointing out the broader picture behind their "crime." In other words, they would want to situate themselves within an oppositional linguistic coordinate system, making use of its vocabulary. But then there was the judiciary and its linguistic coordinate system that finds all these readings non-justiciable, having nothing to do with a legally acceptable defense.

(One of the few allowable, but only at the discretion of the judge, is the "necessity defense." See also chapter 2 where Weber indicated the tension between formal and substantive rationality.)

What is to be done? The sensitive lawyer finds her/himself in two discourses. Does the defense situate itself within the juridic sphere and run out a traditional defense, citing different technical points of law? That is, does s/he explain "what happened" within the categories of the juridic discourse, and in the process leave aside the political issues that were behind the "crime?" Or does the defense try to mount a political trial, situating the "what happened" within the context of an oppositional discourse, knowing full well that it will not be accepted by the court and will antagonize the judge (the result particularly made clear at sentencing time)? More often than not, the defense mounts a traditional defense. Any political arguments that surface will be objected to by the prosecutor and sustained by the judge. Whether the defense "wins" or loses, the movement loses. That is, the broader issues are not codified, they are not given a day in court. The case has been depoliticized. A stabilized oppositional discourse, then, is denied development.

Consider the following transcripts of a recent trial of Professor Jose Solis Jordon, accused of a pipe-bombing in Chicago, to bring attention to the U.S. colonization of Puerto Rico (*U.S. vs. Jose Solis Jordan*, March 9, 1999:1487-1486).

> Question [Prosecutor's recross-examination; hereafter, Q]: You said on direct examination, though, ma'am, that your husband believes in armed struggle, right?
>
> Answer [hereafter, A]: He believes in the right of Puerto Ricans to armed struggle according to the international law.
>
> Q: Okay. But according to U.S. law, that would include illegal acts of terrorism, right, ma'am?
>
> A: I don't want to call it "terrorism." Isn't international law U.S. law, also?
>
> Q: So that would include acts of violence against the United States Government, for example?
>
> A: Okay. Yes.
>
> Q: Acts of violence in support of Puerto Rican independence?
>
> A: We have to define it, because I understand that the international law protects people against colonialism.
>
> Q: Your honor, I'm going to object and ask that the answer be stricken.

The Court [presiding judge]: The answer will be stricken as unresponsive. Listen carefully, ma'am, to the question and try to answer. If you can't answer it, let us know.

Or consider the following objections by the prosecutor to the sworn testimony being introduced by the defendant, Dr. Jose Solis Jordan, in his response to his defense counsel's questions (ibid., 1503-1504):

> Q: And, Dr. Solis, I guess at this point who are the political prisoners?
> A: Puerto Rico's political prisoners are persons who have been incarcerated for their engagement or alleged engagement in armed struggle recognized under the United Nations Resolution 15, 4, United Nations Resolutions 26, 21, the Geneva Convention ...
> [Prosecutor]: Objection, irrelevant.
> A: ...the Algier's Declaration, and other international conventions.
> [The Court]: All right. Just a moment. Just a moment , sir.
> [Prosecutor]: Objection to the narrative, the relevance, and move to strike the last part of that answer.
> [Defense counsel]: Judge, the answer was responsive and not narrative. The relevance is that we're putting a context on the discussion of political prisoners who everybody here has been talking about for the last couple of weeks, and the jury is certainly entitled to know who they are...
> [The Court]: Knowing who they are and hearing narration from Dr. Solis about the legality of their activities are two different things. So I will sustain the Government's objection with respect to the latter portion of the answer that went into the sections of international law that supposedly covered this area.
> [Prosecutor]: And I move to strike.
> [The Court]: It will be stricken, and the jury is instructed to disregard that portion of the answer.

By arguing within the categories of the juridic linguistic coordinate system, one reifies dominant understandings of the world. Other worldviews, particularly of the oppositional variety, are denied articulation. And again, even politically motivated lawyers contribute to the very system that exploits.

Summary. A critical, semiotic approach is just beginning to have an impact in the sociology of law. Some key concepts are beginning to emerge. We have argued that several linguistic coordinate systems exist. To meaningfully communicate, one must situate oneself within the relevant discourse. However, these discourses are not neutral. Words are value-laden. They convey an embedded ideology. Thus, users of a particular discourse are somewhat bound by the structuring properties of linguistic forms. We have also argued that to better understand linguistic processes we can conceptualize a domain in which they are produced, the sphere of linguistic production, and a domain in which they circulate, the sphere of linguistic circulation. We noted the tension between the pluralist and oppositional discourses on the one hand, and the juridic linguistic coordinate system on the other. We indicated that hegemony and reification could occur by the continued use of the latter discourse. Finally, we noted the dialectical quality of oppositional praxis.

The critical semiotic approach argues that repressive formalism (see chapter 1) is the nature of law in a capitalist mode of production. Higher courts are active in developing an ideology supportive of the given economic system. During juridic linguistic production, one accenting (codifying) of the world takes place at the expense of another, the oppositional variety. We noted that the judiciary is not an instrument of an elite group; rather, it is relatively autonomous. That is, it has some degree of independence in development. However, the juridico-ideological structures within the capitalist superstructure are the more dominant forces in the construction of socio-economic relations. Thus, causal directionality in this semiotic approach is said to move from the superstructure to the base. Hence, we have explained the Structural Interpellation view of law.

Fulfillment of social values — individuality, equality and community — in this model will be minimal. Law mystifies the prevailing exploitive conditions. Subjects are alienated, separated from each other, captured within ideological structures. At the same time, subjects are given false assurances in law that they are equal, and that neither the law nor the political economic system, are to blame when failures occur. On the contrary, the fault is said to be of their own making.

Future directions in a semiotically informed Marxist sociology of law would point to the need for the transformation of the given mode of production in the direction of re-establishing woman/man's well-being as the measure of the progress of civilization, not artificial abstractions such as the Gross National Product. Hierarchies must be removed and replaced by collectivist organizations that rely on forms of interaction that lead to fulfillment by way of discourses that approach what Habermas has called the "ideal speech situations" where greater equality exists. Bakhtin, with the same thrust, has called for an "internally persuasive discourse" whereby interactions would unfold with each participant genuinely contributing to their outcomes.

Notes

1. See also Searle 1971:7; Searle, 1983; Lepore and Gulick, 1993; Brown, 1974:118; Strawson, 1950; Schauer, 1982; see also Kevelson's critique, 1988:chapter 8.

2. See the special issue of the *International Journal for the Semiotics of Law* posthumously devoted to Roberta Kevelson, volume 12, no. 3, 1999.

3. See Whitney, 1993; Summers, 1991; Benson, 1991; Sanders, 1991; Valauri, 1991; see also Malloy's review on theorists influenced by Peirce, 2000:23-29. See also Peirce's influence on "crits" (Malloy, 2000:24).

4. This notion shares some similarities with Lacan's "Real Order," Sartre's "being-in-itself," and Freud's idea of the unconscious and the "id" (see Samuels, 1993:9).

5. This notion has similarities with Lacan's notion of the Symbolic Order and Freud's notion of the superego (Samuels, 1993:9); see also Milovanovic, 1998; we shall return to Lacanian psychoanalytic semiotics in chapter 7.

6. Chaos theory would see this as the inducing of far-from-equilibrium conditions within which alternative forms arise, such as novel ideas, vistas, insights, formulations, etc., and even the basis of legal decision making (see Brion, 1991, 1995; Schulman, 1997). A fully developed semiotics of law based on chaos theory waits for creative development.

7. Elsewhere (Milovanovic, 1993d:330-334), I have indicated that abduction in a socio-political system characterized as being in far-from-equilibrium conditions — a term chaos theorists offer to indicate a social system that remains in flux, resisting closure, and in a perpetual state of change — certainly could be a celebrated mechanism for humanistic practices (we shall return to this in the last section of chapter 7). Here the interpretant of the sign would consistently shift; it would be a site where a number of competing voices attempt asserting their dominance. It would be a condition in which diverse voices that have normally been denied expression now find a means of embodiment and receptive structures for their message.

Yet other variants in the use of abduction in law, not necessarily by name (e.g., "reflexive law"), have recently developed (Summers, 1991; Teubner, 1983, 1989; Eco, 1984; Wilhemsson, 1989; Unger, 1987). Wilhemsson, for example, argues for a standard in law he defines as "need-rationality," a form of substantive rationality (see Weber's ideal-types of forms of law and legal thought, chapter 2) as a replacement for formal rationality. Here abduction would be the underlying principle in developing the distributive principle for the consideration of "needs" of members of a society.

8. In Arrigo's (1997) application to the insanity defense and its possible abolition, he has s1 as insanity defense, s2 as abolition, -s2 as non-abolition, and -s1 as non-insanity defense. In Jackson's (1998) analysis of the criminal verdict, he has s1 as true, s2 as false, -s2 as not false, and -s1 as not true. Another variation he analyzes is: s1 as found guilty, s2 as found not guilty, -s2 as not found not guilty, and -s1 as not found guilty. Yet another is: s1 as guilty, s2 as innocent, -s2 as not innocent, and —s1 as not guilty. Each of these can be placed on the semiotic square and be analyzed for the logical implications. Again, this is a discovery tool.

For an application of the semiotic square to media analysis, see Fleming, 1996; Floch, 2000; see also Chandler, 1994:chapter 6. Chandler's website (1994) provides a "message board" and "chartroom" where the interested student can pursue her/his understanding of these concepts.

9. From note 8, -s2 can represent non-abolition, not false, not found not guilty, or not innocent. Consider the implications of each -s2s. Of course, we are looking at the particular deep structure of law. Thus, a verdict of "not guilty" in law does not mean the same thing for a layperson, in the popular view, or even in the factual sense (Jackson, 1998:241).

10. For other examples, see Jameson, 1987:xvii-xxii, where he examines Hayden White's book *Metahistory*; for application of the semiotic square to various novels, see Jameson, 1981:166-167, 253-280; for situating Nietzsche, Hegel and Marx, see Jameson, 1987:xx-xxii.

11. Alternatively, Wittgenstein has used the term "language games," (1958); Pitken, the term "language regions," or forms of discourse, i.e., moral, scientific, political discourse (1971); to name a few.

12. See also our previous presentation of Black's sociology of the case, chapter 5. For an application of semiotics to delinquency theorizing, see Schwendinger and Schwendinger, 1985:128-159. The authors argue that different "moral rhetorics" exist, one of which justifies committing crime.

13. In fact, many critical theorists argue that the "reasonable man in law" is being actively created ("interpellated," Althusser, 1971) by the higher courts. A stable set of rights in the advanced capitalist mode of production has given way to rights that change over time because of interest-balancing. Status, one's standing in a particular recognized group (i.e., union, student, civil service, welfare recipient, prisoner, juvenile, etc.), rather than the contract, is now the more important factor as to what rights one possesses. The courts in the advanced state will increasingly use principles of substantive rationality (see chapter 2) in establishing liberty and property interests and in heading off crisis tendencies (see chapter 3).

7. SEMIOTICS AND POSTMODERN PERSPECTIVES IN LAW

Introduction

A semiotic perspective in law is in its adolescent stages. Taking off in the late 1980s and gaining a foothold in the social sciences and the sociology of law, this focus on discourse analysis has taken on a variety of forms. In the previous chapter we provided an overview of two modernist theorists who have been inspirational for developments in the legal semiotic perspective. We also provided an example of a more fully developed sociology of law incorporating semiotics by focusing on the Structural Interpellation perspective. This, too, was from the modernist perspective. In this chapter we want to provide further examples of perspectives that are more rooted in a sociology of law, and, in particular, approaches that are postmodern in their framework. The notion of a "postmodern" perspective will be developed below.

Semiotics will be defined as the study of: linguistic codes (the particular grammar in use); the codification of primordial sense data (i.e., how lived experiences are given symbolic representation); the constitution of subjectivity (i.e., how the subject is given more coherent and stable forms of representation); the construction of conceptions of reality (i.e., how "reality" is given various form) in discourse; and the constitutive effects of specific linguistic coordinate systems (i.e., how discourse affects the subject and social interactions). A critical semiotic perspective illuminates the facilitative, repressive, and ideological functions of law. We shall see that a semiotic analysis can be integrated in various critical perspectives in constructing a more holistic approach in the sociology of law. The two perspectives included in the following sections have also noted the potential for the development of replacement discourses (i.e., an alternative discourse which allows for a more genuine codification of "reality").

In our next section, we first provide a brief overview of the development of postmodernist thought (as compared to "modernist" thought). We then move to Jacques Lacan and briefly explain some salient points in his psychoanalytic semiotics. For Lacan, there exists no possibility of separating the desiring subject from the discourse within which s/he embodies her/his desire in textual production of various soughts (i.e., legal, textual and cinematic discourse; art, etc.). Lacan's views are arguably the core set of ideas that lie at the base of the postmodernist thrust.

For exemplification purposes, we next move to two emerging perspectives within the postmodern tradition: feminist postmodernist law, and constitutive law. The former has derived much support from the French feminists, who have undertaken an ongoing polemic against the body of theory established by Jacques Lacan (see Arrigo et al., 2000). The leading figures in applying a Lacanian-based feminist view in law are Drucilla Cornell and Judith Butler (see also Brennan's polemic and offering of an integrated approach, 1993). We shall have an opportunity to present some of Cornell's and Butler's recent insights in law.

Our second exemplification is the constitutive law perspective. Here, it is argued, subjects within social encounters construct reality jointly (codeterminously). They produce and reproduce the structures that often are the very ones that place limitations in the social construction of reality. This emerging perspective in the sociology of law integrates and synthesizes much of the literature in social constructionism, Marxist and other critical theory, feminist analysis, and semiotics. The thrust of the variation of constitutive law being offered here will be one that is Lacanian-informed. There exists no reason why other semiotic perspectives (Derrida, Foucault, Wittgenstein, etc.) shouldn't be the basis for integration (Arrigo, 1999; Barak, 1998; Barak and Henry, 1999 Einstadter and Henry, 1995:301-309; Lanier and Henry, 1998:289-292).

POSTMODERNIST PERSPECTIVES IN THE SOCIOLOGY OF LAW

Introduction

The postmodern perspective in the sociology of law began to make its presence felt in the academic community in the early 1990s. At various times it has been identified as incorporating post-structuralism, deconstruction and semiotics. It is a view that can be described only by comparing it to the modernist view.

Modernist thought developed out of the Enlightenment in 17th and 18th Century Europe. It is characterized by the celebration of: (1) economic growth and property ownership; (2) the liberating potentials for human development of the newly discovered sciences; (3) the new legal (formal) freedoms of equality, free will, proprietorship interests, and the notion of due process; (4) the discovery of the individual as an autonomous, self-directing, coherent and unified being (the idea of the *centered subject* expressed best by the idea of *cogito ergo sum* — "I think, therefore I am"); (5) global rationalism as a method in attaining self-development and the good society; and (6) the juridic subject as an abstract bearer of rights (the so-called "reasonable man in law"). This was a time period of optimism.

Postmodernist thought developed a very different picture (see also Dews, 1987; Sarup, 1989). At the end of the 19th century and carrying over into the 20th century, several (non-postmodernist) writers began to portray the negative side of the coming modernist society. To name a few: Karl Marx showed how the newly developed mode of production that replaced feudalism was essentially hierarchical, exploitive and denied the fulfillment of social values for the many. This society, it was argued, produced "crippled monstrosities." Max Weber also criticized the emerging society as offering, on the one hand, new liberties (i.e., contractual freedoms), but also the "iron cage" of capitalism and socialism wherein the loss of meaning and freedom would be prevalent, particularly because of the dominance of rationality and bureaucracy. Nietzsche, perhaps even more insightfully, showed how the new person of modernism was weak and sought idols to overcome her/his state in being. Semiotic fictions were the salvations. These fictions included the idea that persons are centered subjects (i.e., self-determining individuals). These fictions were necessary in overcoming the inner sense of loss; accordingly, they created certainty, stability, and predictability. Fictions and idols were sought and constructed to overcome our everyday meager being. And, of course, Sigmund Freud was to change the notion of the consciously, self-determining individual forever. Most of what accounts for our behavior, Freud argued, was really unconscious. The person was more determined than determining. Finally, the critical thought of the Frankfurt school, which synthesized Marxism with psychoanalysis, was to fundamentally challenge the newly emerging "sane society."

Thus, what characterized postmodernist thought was that many of the perceived virtues of the emerging post-enlightenment society must be balanced against the new forms of manipulation and control. Human emancipation was not an inevitable development, the postmodernists argued. Recognized were: (1) the manipulative powers of the media; (2) the entrenched powers of monopolies; (3) the rigid rationalism of bureaucracies and new forms of domination and disciplining mechanisms; (4) the biases and dominance of a monolithic "global knowledge"; (5) the idea that the dominant discourse often denies other hidden voices, and only provides the medium by which conventional ideologies are constructed and reconstructed anew; (6) the unexamined reliance on "foundational truths" (i.e., positing truth claims for all times and settings), which were claimed to be objective and potentially subject to verification through the "neutral" scientific method; (7) the fallacies of the linear development of history, as for example in the Hegelian model of the unfolding of an idea (i.e., the Absolute Spirit), in contrast to the "genealogical method," rooted more in Nietzsche, which celebrates chance, randomness, contingency, the unpredictable; (8) that the subject is not as centered and in control as prevalent ideology claimed, but instead the person should be seen as the *decentered subject;* and (9) that struggles against different forms of hierarchies can produce unintended consequences, and even further reinforce forms of domination (i.e., the dialectics of struggle). In a few words, consciousness was the subject of new forms of manipulation and control.

The more formal take-off period of postmodernist thought can be isolated as the late 1960s in France. Here, as student unrest and leftist politics dominated all aspects of society, the legacy of Hegel was giving way to the profound insights of Nietzsche. Key postmodernist thinkers, the founding figures, if you will, began to emerge from the French scene: these included Deleuze, Guattari, Lyotard, Derrida, Kristeva, Foucault, Barthes and Baudrillard. But the debate was further refined and brought sharply into focus by French postmodernist feminists: Irigaray, Moi, Cixous, and Kristeva, to name a few. By the late 1970s, a return to Freud's work was underway. The key figure in the fundamental reorientation to postmodernist thought was Jacques Lacan.

We shall first briefly present some important elements in Lacanian thought. Then, we shall present two exemplary approaches, which have drawn from his works, one focused on a postmodernist feminist sociology of law, the other, on constitutive law.[1] We should hasten to add that some non-Lacanian informed postmodernist analysis in law is also taking place (see for example, Douzinas, et al., 1991; Litowitz, 1997). Elsewhere, a postmodern approach has been applied in criminology (for a good overview, see Schwartz and Friedrichs, 1994; for a Lacanian view, see Salecl, 1993; Henry and Milovanovic, 1996, 1999). Unfortunately, much material appearing in the literature has found it fashionable to self-identify as being "postmodern" without a fuller understanding of its core concepts. Given the compelling insights of Lacan, and their effects on most of the key figures in the early development of postmodernist thought, it is hard to see how any material claiming to be "postmodern" could in fact be complete without coming to terms with his work, even if polemical in nature (Caudill, 1993).

Jacques Lacan and Psychoanalytic Semiotics

Jacques Lacan (1901-1981) was a revisionist Freudian. He was influenced by: Saussure's posthumously published lectures on linguistics (1966); Kojeve's lectures given in the 1930s on Hegel, especially on the nature of desire (1980); Levi-Strauss's anthropological studies on the nature of the Symbolic Order; Benveniste's examination of the nature of the personal pronouns ("I" and "you") (1971); Jakobson's analysis of the nature of aphasic (speech) disorders and how two specific axes (metaphor, metonymy) can be isolated as the determinants of semiotic production (1971); and Freud's work on the nature of the psychic apparatus, particularly the secrets of "dream work" (1965). For Lacan, Freud was doing linguistic analysis when he uncovered how desire becomes embodied in particular forms, especially verbal and imaginary. Yes, dreams were the royal road to the unconscious, as Freud said, but Lacan followed with the idea that the unconscious itself is structured like a language.

Lacan delivered a series of seminars from the early 1950s until 1980. These were attended by some of the most prominent intellectuals in the European community. Some of these figures were: Althusser, Foucault, Barthes, Guattari, Kristeva, Irigaray, Ricouer, Sartre, Levi-Strauss, Merly-Ponty. Several of these seminars have been transcribed and published in French. They are also beginning to appear in English translation. Lacan's son-in-law, Jacques-Alain Miller, has coordinated this effort. Most of his material still remains unpublished. Even the material transcribed and published has been subject to much critique. It should be added that interested readers should be forewarned: Lacan's work is difficult prose, and it is challenging reading. Secondary sources are a must. Fortunately several have appeared (Ragland-Sullivan, 1986; Lee, 1990; Borch-Jakobson, 1991; Zizek, 1989; Sarup, 1992; Marini, 1992; Clement, 1983; MacCannell, 1986; Samuels, 1993; Nasio, 1998; Dor, 1997; Haute, 2002; see also feminist readings by Grosz, 1990; Sellers, 1991; see also a Lacanian dictionary, Evans, 1996).

In the following sections we want to briefly lay out some of the key elements of Lacan's thought. Following that we shall indicate how Lacan's psychoanalytic semiotics has influenced, amongst others, two views of law: the postmodernist feminist view, and the constitutive view.

Subjectivity and Discourse

Lacan explained that the subject is inherently connected to the discourse s/he employs. There is no separating the two. He dismisses the modernist conception of "cogito, ergo sum," as idle chatter, and offers his notion of the decentered subject: "I think where I am not, therefore I am where I do not think" (1977:166).

There are two planes for the Lacanian desiring subject. One plane is the subject of speech. In other words, this is the grammatical subject (*le sujet de l'énoncé*). Put in another way, when the subject is speaking and makes use of the "I," s/he fills in this "I," giving it content. This allows vocal or written narrative constructions. The "I" of discourse is referred to as a "shifter"; it only takes on substance on the occasion when someone uses the pronoun; otherwise it is empty (Benveniste, 1971). It also stands for the presence of an absence. In other words, when I am speaking another plane is hidden which is the locus of the actual producer of the narrative or text. This other plane is the locus of the speaking subject (*le sujet de l'énonciation*). It is that sphere that is responsible for producing the statements that are being uttered. It is an area that is not directly accessible; it is unconscious. This is the area that Lacan calls the Other (capital "O"). In sum, we have two subjects: the speaking subject and the subject of speech. Lacan refers to the person as the speaking-being (*l'être parlant, or parlêtre*). Consider, for example, Lawrence's (1987) analysis of "unconscious racism" in law; here, two planes are operative, with the "deeper" often materializing in conscious discourse. That is, racism may have deeper rootings in the unconscious and it emerges in a more disguised form in legal discourse.

The subject as well as speech production, for Lacan, is an outcome of the interaction of three orders: the Symbolic, Imaginary and Real. The Symbolic Order is the sphere of language and culture. In a hierarchically organized society where the male voice is dominant, the female subordinate, the Symbolic Order is said to be phallocentric (we shall pick up on this theme in our exemplifications that follow our exposition of Lacan). The Symbolic Order is also represented by the idea of the Other, which is the sphere of the unconscious. Within the Other we have unconscious and relatively independent processes taking place. The Other is where signifiers (i.e., words) unique to the being are located. These include legal signifiers learned in law schools and practiced in doing law. The Symbolic Order predates the child; and so too, legal discourse predates the entering law student or practitioner. The child enters this order and both gains but also loses something. In other words, the child is inaugurated into the Symbolic Order and gains mastery of a discourse with which s/he can embody desire, but loses (is separated from) the *direct* experience itself. This is a fundamental loss creating an inherent lack-in-being. The person will forever try to compensate for this fundamental loss. The child, in other words, is castrated from being. Consider, too, a law student finally succumbing to constructing stories by legal signifiers and in reasoning by deductive logic and syllogistic reasoning. She may want to bring in philosophical or political economic arguments to bear on the issue, but is quickly encouraged not to do so. She both deliberately constructs legal narratives and yet remains alienated by this very construction, for it does not completely represent her.

The Imaginary Order is the sphere of imaginary constructions and imagoes. These provide illusory constructions of completeness. It is developed during the mirror stage (6 to 18 months) of child development. Prior to the mirror stage the child perceives itself only in a fragmented state, but at a certain point it glimpses itself in the mirror (not necessarily the physical mirror) and for a moment develops the illusion of completeness. This is followed with jubilation, a *jouissance*. This is the first of the imaginary constructions of self, or the *moi*. But many others will follow.

The Real Order is the domain of lived experience. This is forever foreclosed to congruent representation in signifiers. It cannot be accurately represented in the Symbolic Order. These three orders work together in the production of speech and subjectivity.

The Lacanian desiring subject, the speaking-being, is conceptualized in Schema L, see Figure 12.

Here the "je," the "I" is the personal pronoun that a subject "fills in" with content only in use. Otherwise it is a shifter referring to no one (it has no content). The "I" is the grammatical subject. (Consider the legal practitioner verbally presenting her case in court.) It stands for the presence of an absence. As words are uttered they then stand for or represent the subject. As Grosz has it, "the child acquires a position from which to speak, a place where a signifier, the I, can represent the subject (for another signifier)..." (1990:72). The Other is the domain of the unconscious, particularly the locus of a whole constellation of signifiers that, because of biography, are unique to the being. We shall see that this sphere or locus is organized in a particular manner (by metaphor and metonymy). The principle that provides constancy, or stability to the Other, is the law-of-the father (for application to law, see Voruz, 2000; Caudill, 1997).

Figure 12. Schema L

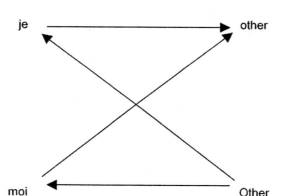

The "Other," for the law practitioner, is also the repository of legal signifiers. The "*moi*" is an imago, is an illusory construction of self; is the conception one has of oneself that is gained through the eyes of the other person. Consider a lawyer presenting her case, mindful of how the jury may be perceiving her and the story being constructed. In Lacan's words it is "that which is reflected of his form in his objects" (1977:194). In other words, it is the imaginary constructions one has of oneself. The *other* is that person or object of desire that reflects to the *moi* its sense of unity. Thus, in the Lacanian construct, we have an inter- and intra-subjective basis of being.

Within Schema L we see two axes: the je-Other represents the unconscious axis; the moi-other, the imaginary. These two axes are at work when discursive production takes place. When interactions unfold, or when narratives are being constructed, the interaction between these two axes are responsible for the particular outcome. Thus, for Lacan, the subject is drawn out over all four corners of Schema L at the same time. Put in another way, it is *decentered*. For example, think in terms of how a lawyer performs in a trial court proceeding: she must situate herself in the discourse of law, making use of allowable signifiers in law (the je-Other axis; more unconscious), and she engages in speculations as to how she and her client are being perceived (moi-other axis; more imaginary). These two axes are simultaneously at work.

What mobilizes the psychic apparatus, for Lacan, is desire. The person is essentially a *desiring subject*. Periodically, the subject experiences a lack-in-being. There can be no escape; this is the price paid for the inauguration into the Symbolic Order. The subject is forever separated (castrated) from the Real. This lack mobilizes desire.[2]

To return to the process by which desire mobilizes the psychic apparatus and by which it is given expressive form (embodied in signifiers). What happens is that the subject attempts to *suture* or stitch over, as in a surgical repair, the gaps in being. The subject must first find an appropriate object of desire, which Lacan refers to as the *objet petit(a)*. Words can be considered one possibility. For example, think in terms of lawyer's active narrative constructions in trial court proceedings. Faced with contradictions or things that are not sufficiently explained, or questions put before her, she "selects" legal signifiers from her "storehouse" of signifiers residing in the Other (paradigm), and places them in the required linear ordering (syntagm) in creating a story. Here, *objet petit (a)* consists of particular signifiers (words), which provide the vehicle for the expression of the unique desire of the practicing lawyer. Keep in mind, too, that the two axes described in Schema L are also at work during this process. Thus both the imaginary and symbolic axes are at work in the construction of legal narratives.

This suturing operation implicates the three Orders. The Imaginary Order provides certain illusions that are potential sources for filling in gaps-in-being (*manque d'être*). The Symbolic Order provides a wealth of signifiers, or words, which can embody desire. The Real Order will also have its presence felt. What actually happens is that the subject selects appropriate objects of desire and embodies them with its unique form of desire. Lacan pictures this as:

$$\$ <> a.$$

Note that the "S" has a slash that passes through it. This is Lacan's way of saying that the subject disappears in the signifiers that represent it in discourse. Again, this is the play of presence and absence. In actually uttering words, the producing entity has disappeared (absence) from the scene, replaced by a certain presence, the "I" of grammatical constructions. The <> represents a movement. The subject is disappearing into its objects of desire (a). This is a two-way process, for the objects of desire now come to reflect (mirror), be it illusory at base, the subject's being.

Semiotic Axes, Embodying Desire, and Anchoring Points

Lacan has built on the insights of Freud, particularly from *The Inter-pretation of Dreams*, in generating answers to how precisely desire is embodied in signifiers, or words, and how narratives and texts are established possessing sense. For example, for lawyers, how is it that certain narratives can be constructed and others are denied expression? How is it that certain voices do find expression, others do not? The key elements in his theory are signifiers and their coordinating mechanisms. Let's first turn to the nature of signifiers, then to the fundamental principles that lie behind discursive production. We will then provide two examples.

For Lacan, the relationship of a signifier to a signified can be depicted as follows:

Figure 13. Signifier and Signified

S	or	Signifier	or	acoustic image	example:	tree
s		Signified		concept		(image of tree is evoked)

A sign is therefore made up of two elements: the *signifier* and the *signi-fied*. The signifier is an acoustic image, a psychological imprint in the psychic apparatus. The signifier in the Lacanian project actually has many dimensions and only in its formal properties can we say that a word is equal to a signifier. The signified is the concept, that which is evoked, usually in visual form. A close parallel to this is found in Freud's notion of *word-presentation* and *thing-presentation*, where the former is more like the signifier, the latter, the signified (1965). In our example above, one only has to say the word "tree" and a particular image is evoked. Notice that one doesn't even have to audibly say "tree." Similarly, in law, particular signifiers (duress, malicious, negligently, voluntarily, intent, liberty, person, incompetent, etc.) are connected with particular signifieds (e.g., understandings in law).

In constructing a sentence, then, one really is stringing together a series of signifiers; hence in Lacan's framework these are *signifying chains* (i.e., a legal narrative). In fact, signifying chains embody knowledge; they are somewhat autonomous from the immediate user. For example, we recall from Whorf that linguistic determinism is such that words already have meaning on their own, independent of the particular desire of the subject who utters them. Recall also, from our previous section, the idea of the fetishism of linguistic forms that follow commodity fetishism. For Lacan, signifiers are what embody the idiosyncratic desires of the subject, even though these embodiments are incomplete.

Initially, the unconscious is populated with "letters" that "insist" (Lacan, 1977:147-155); that is to say, psychic material (located within the unconscious) with different degrees of intensity is forever seeking expression (it "insists"). In its most formal aspect, this "letter" is transformed into the formal properties of a signifier, a word that is uttered in some social encounter, or a legal signifier expressed in a trial court proceeding.

Each subject has a unique biography and hence embodies signifiers in an idiosyncratic way. These signifiers slumber in anticipation within the locus of the Other. The Other, for Lacan, is "the treasure of signifiers." The totality of signifiers learned in law school and practiced in law resides in the "Other." The normal state of the 11/21/02s is that they "float" within the unconscious and periodically attach themselves to certain signifieds. Lacan calls this attaching process the *point de capitonnage*. For example, the signifier "bounce" remains in an unconnected form in the unconscious — it may eventually, in context, be connected to: doing one's laundry, the image of the bouncer at a bar, a child playing with a ball, a person concerned with check writing, or, for skydivers, a person who dies on a drop zone. Some signifiers are more permanently connected to particular signifieds; this is the locus of *symptoms* (e.g., constellations of inter-connected signifiers) which produce a certain consistency in the subject's psychic apparatus and hence his speech production. A lawyer, for example, in doing law, invokes this particular sphere of her/his unconscious. Outside the context of work, she may invoke various other constellations of signifiers in particular contexts.

Lacan has built up on Freud's idea of *displacement*. Freud (1965) had shown how psychic material within the psychic apparatus flows freely within the unconscious. This quanta of psychic energy can attach itself to a variety of images or words that appear. Lacan was to call this mechanism by the name of *metonymy*, one of the axes behind semiotic production. The other Lacanian axis, *metaphor,* is strongly connected to Freud's idea of *condensation*. In explaining dreams and the underlying psychic mechanism in their construction — "dream work" — Freud had indicated that images and words are really an amalgamation (compression, or condensation) of a diversity of charged psychic material. Thus, we have the close connection of metaphor with condensation, on the one hand, and metonymy with displacement, on the other.[3]

Let's give an example of this complex analysis and draw out an implication to someone doing law (see also the perceptive commentary by Naffine, 1990:29-47; Arrigo, 1998a). What a law student actually does in law school is to internalize a number of legal signifiers that have particular content (signified). Words such as *mens rea*, intent, maliciously, negligently, and so forth, have precise meaning in law. These are internalized by the student and become the basis of understanding. Consider, for example, Asch's analysis (1992) of the word "wildlife" as it was defined in Canadian courts. The court's narrow definition stated that whereas domesticated animals are held by private individuals, wild animals are not recognized as owned until capture, leaving ownership by default to the state. This effectively denied indigenous peoples their time honored hunting rights. Apart from learning the definitions of words, the student learns how they are connected in linear form to produce acceptable legal discourse. In other words, the student has learned dictionary meanings (in conventional semiotic analysis this is usually referred to as the *paradigm* axis) and how to string these words together (conventionally defined as *syntagm*) to produce a particular text or narrative.

The available signifiers and the appropriate manner of linear construction, however, have limited the constructed text. A word such as "intent," for example, has been greatly circumscribed temporally and spatially to consider mostly the more immediate factors at play rather than including larger political economic forces that may be contributing to the event in question. Expanding the time and space dimensions included in the definition of "intent" would surely implicate a constellation of factors and certainly place a question mark to the notion of a centered subject.

Let us provide another example. Consider an incarcerated subject. She finds herself in a situation of frustration, confusion, anger, bitterness and hostility. In communicating her plight, she must avail herself of the linguistic forms derived from inmate subcultures, discourses of the numerous health professionals, discourses of the guards, legalistic jargon picked up during litigation, bureaucratic jargon as she is processed in the system, and personal biographical linguistic forms. Articulating her plight will be in terms of these linguistic forms. In other words, reality construction is a constitutive process. More often than not, an amorphous "they" or "them" is verbalized as the culprit in her situation. Note, however, that no relatively stable oppositional linguistic coordinate system exists by which to embody desire and by which to develop a more critical view of existing forms of hierarchy and oppression. Desire is merely embodied in the categories available. The dominant order may safely continue its different forms of oppression as it is faced by inarticulate and contradictory tiltings at wind-mills.

Discursive Production and Linguistic Coordinate Systems: Lacan's Four Discourses

Lacan presented the thesis of the four discourses in his 1969-1970 seminar. This seminar was published in French as *L'Envers de la Psychanalyse* (1991). These discourses — those of the *master, university, hysteric,* and *analyst* — were offered as the four main forms of discourses in existence. They accounted for how desire found, or did not find, expression in discourse. They also accounted for how in fact a body of knowledge was constituted or reconstituted. Several theorists have provided translations and commentary on Lacan's work (Bracher, 1988, 1993; Lee, 1990; Melville, 1987). These discourses have also been applied to law (Arrigo, 1994, 1998a, 1998b; Stacy, 1996; Schroeder, 2000; Shon, 2000). Let us first explain the four discourses and then provide illustrative examples of their applications in law.

Lacan identifies four main terms in these discourses — S1, S2, $, a; and four locations — agent, other, truth, and production. S1 represents *master signifiers.* These have been defined as key signifiers, which stem from childhood experiences and which have subsequently been the basis of ideologically-infused content. In other words, these are anchored signifiers (*capitonnage*). In our application to law, key signifiers in law can also be conceived of as master signifiers. *S2* represents knowledge. For Lacan, knowledge always exists within a chain of signifiers. Meaning "insists" within these chains. Thus, within the chain, a signifier represents a subject for another signifier. The producing entity has disappeared from the scene, now represented by a signifier. For example, the narratives constructed in a trial court proceeding as well as by appeal court's decisions, take on a static meaning once they have been transcribed and published. Meanings of these narratives, however, are henceforth interpreted in various ways (i.e., the free play of the text). $ represents the desiring subject. And *a* represents the *objet petit(a),* though in the context of the four discourses, Lacan defines it as *le-plus-de-jouir:* the excess in enjoyment, and what is left out. In other words, in unfolding discourse, one always says less than what one desires, and also, ironically, more (think in terms of the Freudian slip on the one hand, and, on the other, occasions of Lawrence's "unconscious racism").

Lacan has also identified four structural positions in the four discourses. These can be pictured:

<u>agent</u>   <u>other</u>
truth   production

Here, the left side represents the sender of some message; the right side, the receiver and enactor of that message. The upper left hand corner stands for the initiator of the message, the *agent*. The upper right corner, the *other*, represents the receiver and enactor of the message. These (locations above the bar) exist at the more overt, manifest or conscious levels. The lower left corner represents *truth* that is unique to the being who initiates some message for an other. In Lacan's schema it is in essence only partly knowable. Each person has her/his unique truth, which resides in the unconscious. The lower right corner represents *production*. In other words, it is what is produced as an effect in the receiver's unconscious. What appears below the bar is more covert, latent, and unconscious. Having said this we can construct the four discourses:

The discourse of the master:

$$\frac{S1}{\$} \quad \rightarrow \quad \frac{S2}{a}$$

Here, some sender of a message (who conveys master signifiers, S1), produces an enactment of knowledge by the other, S2. In other words, the other produces a body of knowledge based on the implications of S1. S/he enacts what is implicit; s/he makes it explicit. Althusser's theory of *interpellation* is one example. The cinema theory's notion of the *spoken subject* is another. Linguistic determinism could be explained by this dynamic. A marxist semiotic view from the structural interpellation framework would incorporate this formula, perhaps in combination with the discourse of the university (below). And the basis of a phallic symbolic order could be explained by this formulation.

Consider colonizers, bringing some Truth to a native population as yet another example. But note that something else is taking place: below the bar, in the lower right corner there results *le-plus-de-jouir*. In other words, something is left out and has effects in unconscious production. This is the notion of *pas-toute* (not all, incompleteness). Consider the disenfranchised who bring their grievances to the court only to have it formulated in the language of the courts (see, for example, Merry, 1985; Brigham, 1987; Salyer, 1989, 1991; Stacy, 1996; Bannister and Milovanovic, 1990). Also, note that the subject of desire finds itself below the bar, supporting the master signifiers that inhere within her/him as her/his truth.

The discourse of the university:

$$\frac{S2}{S1} \quad \rightarrow \quad \frac{a}{\$}$$

Here we see some body of knowledge, S2, being enacted by the other who produces *le-plus-de-jouir*. The other is relegated to accepting and enacting some body of information or truth claims. For example, consider the shift from Newtonian to Einsteinian physics. Or consider legal knowledge that is communicated to a law student or practitioner. Or consider some overzealous revolutionaries that appear with some dogma. Or, finally, consider propaganda campaigns and brainwashing. What remains below the bar, as unconscious production, is the desiring subject. In other words, the subject is denied a full place (discursive subject-position[4]) within which to find alternative forms of embodying desire. S/he must enact S2. In the process, the subject reconstitutes dominant understanding and master signifiers. This clearly provides one mechanism whereby even subjects that find conditions exploitive continuously reproduce dominant ideology. It therefore fits the constitutive approach in law as to the socio- psychological mechanism at play. And note that master signifiers exist as truth, acting as the support for S2. In other words, given some body of knowledge posing as legitimate or dominant knowledge (conventional wisdom), one can locate a number of truth-claims upon which it is premised. Consider a student in law school presented with a body of knowledge (S2, legal signifiers, legal discourse) from which to construct understandings of social reality (see Arrigo, 1998a).

The discourse of the hysteric:

$$\frac{\$}{a} \quad \rightarrow \quad \frac{S1}{S2}$$

Here the hysteric (we read as not only the clinical type, but those who are alienated, in revolt, or in opposition) attempts to communicate her/his suffering to the other who only offers master signifiers as answers; in law, legal concepts and signifiers from which the "issue" can be constructed. Consider the everyday poor client before the court attempting to present her/his grievance. These offered master signifiers produce S2 in the receiver, or reconstitute a body of knowledge in so much as the offered categories fit into a larger body of acceptable knowledge. Master signifiers could be clinical diagnoses, stereotypes, clichés, deviant categories, or other linguistic categories that the media or bureaucratic organizations often provide and which are incorporated as "meaningful" summary representations of social reality. Consider, for example, a lower class inarticulate client attempting to present her/his suffering or grievance to some bureaucratic official and the categories and ·discourses that will invariably be invoked (see Manning, 1988). Truth here is represented by *le-plus-de-jouir*. In other words, the subject in opposition finds her/himself facing an excess, a feeling of despair, due to not having a more complete discourse within which to embody her/his desire. S/he is denied the means of expression of truth.

The desiring subject that appears above the bar can only reflect despair, alienation, or revolt to the other without the aid of precise signifiers reflective of her/his being. S/he is incapable of assuming her/his desire. This subject often finds her/himself ultimately expressing despair in the prevailing dominant discourse in existence and hence, ironically, continuing her/his despairing state. Some might revert to a discourse of the master and attempt to impose their convoluted view of the world on others, as is the case in hate or revenge politics, political correctness, exorcism, and schmarxism. Here Nietzsche's subject of *resentiment* has emerged.

The discourse of the analyst:

$$\frac{a}{S2} \quad \rightarrow \quad \frac{\$}{S1}$$

Here the analyst provides information to the other (hysteric) whom, faced with new information about her/his being, begins to reconstitute a new body of master signifiers (S1). In other words, what are produced in the hysteric are alternative anchorings of signifiers to signifieds as the hysteric comes to realize her/his despair, or nature of revolt. These, in turn, support a body of knowledge developing in the analyst and act as the truth that supports the mirrored information reflected in turn to the hysteric. This mirrored information then becomes further information which the hysteric enacts by producing yet more master signifiers that better embody her/his unique and contextualized desire, and so forth. This dynamic could be seen at play in Paulo Freire's dialogical pedagogy (1973, 1985). The "analyst," or social change agent, or revolutionary, works with the "hysteric" (again more broadly defined than the clinical; to include people in struggle) as a catalyst, in producing a narrative that better reflects her/his unique desire (see Arrigo, 1998a).

Let us provide some examples in applying the four discourses to law:

(1) Stacy (1996) has explained how aboriginal women (the Ngar-rindjeri) were denied a voice before the Australian courts. Their stories were not allowed expression in law; their stories were translated into legal narratives. For the courts, the aboriginal women were hysterics, did not have an identity formally recognized in law, and were provided the discourse of law (S2, S1) from which to create their stories. In the discourse of the hysteric, the aboriginal women found themselves in the place of the sender of the message as $\$$ (from above, the upper left corner) and were offered only master signifiers (S1) or dominant legal signifiers with which to frame their narratives in law. This produced a body of knowledge, S2, which ultimately reflected dominant knowledges. This in turn left the aboriginal women *pas-toute* (lower left corner), incomplete, without a genuine voice. Their own unique experiences and understanding underwent transformation into the dominant linguistic coordinate system of law. The master discourse rendered them *pas-toute*, incomplete, before the law.

(2) Arrigo (1998a) described the nature of legal education by situating students in law school within the discourses of the hysteric, who succumbed, eventually, to internalizing the discourse of the university (legal discourse), which could easily be converted into a discourse of the master in dealing with clients. Consider, again, the discourse of the hysteric. The student finds her/himself as the sender of the message, $\$$, but is only provided dominant legal signifiers (S1) with which to construct various narratives and hence understandings, S2, in law. To develop a "replacement grammar" (ibid., 20) he examined the discourse of the hysteric, considered in combination with the discourse of the analyst, and how a revolutionary subject can emerge by keeping these two discourses constantly in tension. For example, the use of "dialogical pedagogy" could allow students to better embody their desires. The discourse of the analyst provided an alternative method by which new conceptualizations (e.g., S1, S2) could be developed.

(3) Shon (2000) has shown how police invoke the discourse of the master in their dealings with the everyday citizen, who is seen more as a hysteric. For the police, it is a way of structuring the event in legalistic categories. Police work proceeds more

smoothly, then, when this imposition takes place. In other words, the police officer codes "reality" in a particular way in anticipation of further legal processing. S/he must be particularly attentive to various constitutional rights ("plain view doctrine," "probable cause," etc.) in framing his/her understanding of the "what happened?" Accordingly, one rendition begins to take form rather than another. For the citizen, finding her/himself in the discourse of the hysteric, this all too often equates to being rendered *pas-toute*.

(4) Milovanovic (2002) integrates Lopez's Freire-driven analysis in his book, *Rebellious Lawyering,* with Lacan's four discourses and chaos theory to indicate how the discourse of the hysteric in combination with the discourse of the analyst could provide moments in which an alternative discourse could emerge. That is, the everyday client before the law is often relegated to the discourse of the university (legal speak) and often becomes the recipient of the discourse of the master. A Freirean-driven approach, integrated with the four discourses and chaos theory, indicates an alternative interaction between lawyer and client within which an alternative body of master signifiers could emerge. This becomes the basis of embodying desire in narratives that better reflect the unique desires of the client.

(5) Schroeder (2000) shows how a lawyer engages in the discourse of the master in writing about the law, and the discourse of the university when s/he attempts to interpret the law. The client consulting a lawyer appears in the discourse of the hysteric. For developing sensitive understanding, Schroeder advocates coming to terms with the discourse of the hysteric.

FEMINIST POSTMODERNIST PERSPECTIVES

Introduction. A Lacanian-informed, feminist postmodernist perspective in the sociology of law is unfolding within the academic community. This analysis rests on much of the work done by French feminists (see the overviews by Grosz, 1990; Sellers, 1991; see also the collection of essays by Brennan, 1989; Nicholson, 1990; Moi, 1990; Ferguson and Wicke, 1994). The leading figures in applying a Lacanian view in the sociology of law, from the feminist perspective, have been Drucilla Cornell (1993, 1998,

1999),[5] Teresa Brennan, 1992, 1993), and Judith Butler (1990, 1993, 1997a, 1997b, 1999).

The Phallic Symbolic Order and Pas-Toute

French feminists have analyzed how it is that gender roles are constructed in the Symbolic Order and how in fact women are constituted as subordinate (Irigaray, 1985, 1993; Moi, 1985, 1987; Kristeva, 1986; Cixous, 1986, 1990). Since the Symbolic Order privileges the man's voice over the woman's, it is phallocentric at its core. Let's see how a critical insight of Lacan's was the starting point of much of the subsequent analysis of how exactly women are deprivileged in the Symbolic Order (Lacan, 1985:149-161, 137-148; see also Melville, 1987; Lee, 1990:172-186; Cornell, 1998, 1999).

Lacan tells us that two different gender positions can be assumed within the Symbolic Order: man or woman. These can also be referred to as *discursive subject-positions* (implying that a particular position within society has attached to it a particular, relevant and relatively stable discourse). Arguably, certain master discursive subject-positions exist. The notion of discursive subject-positions is closely tied to the notion of "standpoint" (see Kerruish's illuminating discussion of standpoint, 1991:33-34, 167, 174, 177-193, 196-198). In Lacan's essay entitled "A Love Letter" (1985:149-161) a diagram is presented summarizing the possible gendered subject positions that may be assumed within a Symbolic Order.

Figure 14. Discursive Subject-Positions

For man: (1) $\forall X \cdot \overline{\phi X}$ For woman: (3) $\overline{\forall X \cdot \phi X}$

(2) $\exists X \cdot \overline{\phi X}$ (4) $\overline{\exists X} \cdot \phi X$

What the first formula means is that for man (or the person who assumes this discursive subject-position), all x is a function of the phallus. That is, all discursive production answers to the call of the phallus (the symbolic phallus and all that it has come to stand for: power, potency, the road to *jouissance*). Put in another way, all signifiers are colored by the function of the phallus (the symbolic phallus, not the biological organ). Man, then, has open to him the upper limit of *jouissance*, a phallic jouissance. The second formula means that there is an x, that is not a function of the phallus. Lacan makes it clear that the male *or* female can take up the phallic function. In Formula 2, what is indicated is man not taking up the phallic function. Formula 3 states that for woman (or the person who takes up this discursive subject-position), not all x is a function of the phallus. In other words, woman is not totally incorporated in the phallic symbolic order. Formula 4 means that there is not an x, which is not a function of the phallus.

A person assuming the masculine discursive subject-position may experience a phallic *jouissance*, the upper limit within the phallic symbolic order. Women, on other hand, are not imprisoned within this function; they have a privileged access to a *bodily jouissance*. However, there exists no language that embodies this form of jouissance — it is unspeakable. Hence, Lacan's seemingly outlandish statement: "woman does not exist." She essentially "lacks" within the dominant phallic symbolic order. She is *pas-toute* (not all).

She does, however, experience another *jouissance* beyond the phallic function. Lacan has referred to this as a *bodily jouissance* or the *jouissance of the Other*. Whereas phallic *jouissance* is found at the confluence of the Symbolic and Real Orders; the *jouissance* of the Other is found at the intersection of the Imaginary and Real Order. Lacan gives examples of the words of the poet or mystic (see also Lecercle's notion *délire*, 1985). At best, this sense can only be half-said (*mi-dire*). He does not go further to draw out the implications for transformative politics.

Sexual Differences, or Sexual Equality?

Much of the critical debate within the feminist postmodernist view focuses on whether women are basically different (a position referred to as "essentialism") or whether they are equal before the law. The "essentialist" view assumes the existence of "some essential aspect of "human nature"; "in something pre-given, innate, natural, biological; in something that cannot be changed" (Brennan, 1989:6; Cornell, 1999:179-183). Thus, much of the debate rests on this profound split: assuming differences or assuming equality (see also Grant, 1993; Naffine, 1990; Cornell, 1998; 1999; Butler, 1990, 1993; Lorraine, 1999:chapter 2).

There has been a historical difference in the development of these views. Early French feminists have argued for differences; early Anglo-American theorists for equality (Brennan, 1989:2; see also Grant, 1993:132-144; Naffine, 1990). Much of this debate has been carried over from the

1970s from critiques levied against some understandings of Marxism as supporting a "human essence" (Brennan, 1989:2). Structuralist critiques in particular undermined much of the support for this assumption. By the 1980s, Lacan's views were being seen more and more as non-essentialist (ibid., 6-8). As we saw above, both a man and a woman can assume a particular discursive subject-position such as a gender role. If this is compelling, the debate must then shift to the constitution of the Symbolic Order itself. Lacan's writings must be seen as *descriptive* on this issue; he is explaining the existence of a particular Symbolic Order that is based on the phallus (not, as some have posited, as providing an apology for the phallocentric order). Theoretically, a Symbolic Order may have another basis. Necessary, for a transformative politics to develop, then, is a *prescriptive* analysis (see Cornell, 1998, 1999).

Lacan's profound analysis concerning the nature of the phallic symbolic order, that gender roles are created in the Symbolic Order, and the fact that women are *pas-toute*, but yet have access to a different form of *jouissance*, supported the development of an *écriture féminine* (woman's writing). But this could lead to various strategies.

Essentialists support the development of an entirely new Symbolic Order that recognizes the uniqueness of being a woman. After all, the argument went, if one cannot establish some "foundational truth" then a transformative politics could not be carried through. It is claimed that only in the overthrow of the phallocentric symbolic order and its replacement by one that recognizes women's writings (*écriture féminine*) can emancipation take place. The non-essentialist theorists, however, argued that this could, without more, lead to a "reversal of hierarchies": the form of domination would still remain (Cornell, 1999:11, 139, 185).[6]

Accordingly, strategies for change in society and law are being developed that are sensitive to *not* reinventing hierarchy nor to fueling forms of revenge politics (as Cornell has attributed to MacKinnon, 1999:139). And here there is much agreement by the postmodern feminists with the critical race theorists that a useful strategy to pursue is a "post-essentialist" alternative (see Harris, 1991).

Standpoint Epistemology, Transformative Politics and Law

One form this has taken is "standpoint epistemology" (Bartlett, 1991:385; Jagger, 1983:369-370; see also our chapter on feminist jurisprudence above, chapter 4; for an illuminating analysis of the connection between standpoint and ideology, see Kerruish, 1991:33-34, 167, 174, 177-

193, 196-198). Bartlett's "feminist legal method" incorporating a standpoint epistemology is exemplary (1991). Jagger has made the point succinctly for a:

> special epistemological standpoint which makes possible a view of the world that is more reliable and less distorted than that available either to capitalist or to working class men [1983:370].

However, there has been much critique and debate over this issue. Contemporary critical feminists argue for the existence of multiple standpoints, i.e., based on gender, race, class, sexual preference, etc.[7] Where the postmodernist feminists go further than the *fem-crits* is in their stronger adherence to Lacanian theory as a guide to a transformative politics. In our next section we will briefly develop one such approach by Drucilla Cornell.

Based on the considerable internal debate concerning standpoint, many from this perspective have now grounded their epistemology and transpraxis on the experiential dimension of oppressive feminine experiences, but with a qualification centered on the contingent and provisional nature of political commitments, which are always subject to critical evaluation and possible revision (see, for example, Bartlett, 1991; Currie, 1993; Arrigo, 1993a). In other words, rather than arguing for the existence of some "foundational" position that is somehow objective and transhistorical and trans-cultural, or rather than arguing for relativism, this position sees, at best, provisional political commitments that are rooted in historical conditions and political economies with their attendant manifest hierarchies and exploitive practices.

Grant has well argued the position that if we merely rely on the experiential and supposed unique position that women find themselves in as the wherewithal of the development of a unified transformative politics, we have overlooked the critically important factor that a subject constructs a perspective by the use of certain, pre-given lenses (1993:107, 125; Kerruish, 1991:177-193). Indeed, this is a constitutive process (Hunt, 1993; Harrington and Yngvesson, 1990; we will also return to the constitutive approach in law below). Said in another way, subjects in a society always appear on the scene with internalized perspectives and background assumptions as guides to social activity and co-produce conceptions of social reality. And this is an important limitation in transformative politics. As Grant tells us, "without a feminist interpretive lens through which to see and reinvent gender, the idea of a standpoint of women will always be essentialist" (1990:109). Very precisely, she informs us that "the question is what possibilities are immanent in this current reality, and this cannot be based on the experiences of the oppressed woman, but on the feminist revision of what woman can be" (ibid., 116).

Accordingly, the imaginary order must also be integral to a transformative politics. Cornell (1998), for example, has suggested various strategies to expand and protect the imaginary domain. As she suggests, "the imaginary domain is the space of the 'as if' in which we imagine who we might be if we made ourselves our own end and claimed ourselves as our own person" (ibid., 8). Thus, for Cornell, metaphors are especially in need of reconceptualization, particularly those that maintain traditional forms of domination.

Further, necessary for a *bona fide* statement on an alternative transformative politics and law, therefore, is an integration of the three Lacanian Orders. Only in this way can we deconstruct oppressive legal structures and reconstruct an alternative legal and political order. Given the existence of legal abstractions such as the juridic subject, linear forms of reasoning, circumscribed codifications of signifieds, dualistic conceptualizations of social reality, and forms of hate or revenge politics historically inherent in many "humanistic" movements — all of which support hierarchy — genuine change can only take place by way of a *transpraxis*. We turn to Cornell's work, which has focused on the Imaginary Order that opens a vista as to what could be.

Cornell's (1993, 1999) extraordinary synthesis of Lacan's psychoanalysis, Luhmann's notion of autopoieses, postmodern feminist's perspectives and Derrida's deconstructive epistemology has emphasized the imaginary elements for potential change (see also Murray, 1986; Arrigo, 1992:24-27; Ricoeir, 1973:111; Brennan, 1993). Media studies have also brought out how certain images are culturally derived and sustained (Silverman, 1983; Williamson, 1987; Newman, 1993; Barak, 1993, 1994). Cornell has also partly integrated Lacan's other two Orders. She has provided a profound analysis of the wherewithal of alternative imaginary constructions.

Cornell builds particularly upon Irigaray's idea of *mimesis* (1999:147-152), by which subordination is disrupted and transformed into an affirmation, and on Cixous' idea of the "retelling of the myth" (ibid., 178), in developing the wherewithal of a "utopian thinking" (ibid., 169). As she explains it: "utopian thinking demands the continual exploration and re-exploration of the possible and yet also the unrepresentable" (ibid.). In other words, the imaginary constituted by metaphoric and metonymic always implies a slippage, an excess (what Lacan refers to as *le plus de jouir*) especially apparent in myths. "[I]deology," Grant tells us, "leaves some critical space" (1993:116). Given this "space" or "slippage," consider Cornell's view:

> Without the aesthetic evocation of utopian possibility of feminine difference, we are left with the politics of revenge... the politics of feminism needs its poetry [ibid., 185].

And consider Arrigo (1992:26):

> Precisely because the myth is a story, its beginnings are born in the imagination's capacity to conceive of and describe on-going, lived experience in intimately meaningful ways... The work of experiential feminism through myth is to render the telling of narratives that more authentically depict the experience of women and the situations in which they find themselves.

In recreating myths we are in the position of creating an "elsewhere." According to Cornell's read of Cixous, "[w]e re-collect the mythic figures of the past, but as we do so we reimagine them. It is the potential variability of myth that allows us to work within myth, and the significance it offers, so as to reimagine our world and by so doing, to begin to dream of a new one" (ibid., 178). In this way, an affirmative politics of the feminine can begin to emerge that is also utopian in trying to point to an elsewhere (ibid., 182, 200). As she states:

> consciousness-raising must involve creation, not just discovery. We need our poetry, our fantasies and our fables; we need the poetic evocation of the feminine body in Irigaray and in Cixous if we are to finally find a way beyond the muteness imposed by a gender hierarchy in which our desire is "unspeakable" [ibid., 201].

Butler (1990:145-149) has suggested a practice of subverting repetition. This entails strategies of intervention and contestation (ibid., 147; see also, Butler, 1993:187-222; 1997a:86-95, 102; 1997b:83-105). It also acknowledges the "contingent" nature of discursive formations (1990:192, 202; 2000:136-179). She argues for the development of an alternative language (2000:179): "a language between languages will have to be found....It will be the labour of transaction and translation which belongs to no single site, but is the movement between languages, and has it final destination in this movement itself." Earlier, we had indicated two other strategies: reversal of hierarchies and standpoint epistemologies. Both, for postmodernist feminists in law, fall short of a bonafide strategy for change. Thus, for Butler, contingent universalities is a position that argues for the possibilities of establishing "universalities," common platforms for political change, but also recognizes their contingent nature. They are continuously subject to reflection, revisions, and substitution as socio-historical conditions present novel moments.

Much of this notion of social change sits well with the work of Laclau and Mouffe (Laclau, 1990, 1996; Laclau and Mouffe, 1985; Smith, 1998) with their view that traditional Marxist's reliance on "class" is outdated, for, continuously new groupings are developing, each with unique standpoints and epistemologies, that vary in their ideological positions over time. The political economy, too, can be conceived of as structurally undecidable in so much as it is in continuous change. And identities in this view are constantly in states of change: "social agents are becoming more and more 'multiple selves,' with loosely integrated and unstable identities ..." (Laclau, 1996:99; see also Cornell, 1998:183). Struggles, too, are multiple in form (ibid., 101). Postmodernist feminists are beginning to look more carefully at possible integrations between the work of Irigaray and Deleuze and Guattari, particularly as to how bodies are constituted in political economy (Grosz, 1994; Lorraine, 1999).

There have been ambivalent feelings by some postmodernist feminists in embracing the work of Michel Foucault. For example, Howe (1994:170), citing his work favorably in the context of prison struggles, and echoing a weak position within standpoint epistemology, says "all we can do, apparently, is to help create the conditions which permit prisoners to speak for themselves," and, continuing, "appreciate the fact that only those directly concerned can speak in a practical way on their own behalf" (Foucault, cited in Howe, ibid.). Howe, however, counters this, in so much as since "Foucault's framework was masculinist, the strategies he had in mind privileged the men's prison struggle" (ibid., 209). Thus, the role of the cultural revolutionary becomes critical in various struggles in working together with the disenfranchised allowing the "subaltern" to speak.

One especially fascinating analysis of what could be has been provided by Haraway (1991) where she asks us to imagine a "postgender world" where the subject is constituted by "transgressed boundaries, potent fusions, and dangerous possibilities" (ibid., 150-199). It is a conceptualization of the subject as forever unfixed and contingent. Elsewhere, we have integrated some insights from chaos theory and advocated the vision of a "strange attractor," a notion that advocates an orderly disorder where change, multiplicity, contingency, chance, irony, non-linearity, and the spontaneous are celebrated.

Some integration of Lacan with Marx has taken place (Brennan, 1989:6-7; Brennan, 1992; Brennan, 1993). Recognized is the shortcoming of Lacan's work *by itself*, even if it does provide some key elements or tools for critical inquiry. It has been best said by Braidotti: "...the politico-epistemological question of achieving structural transformations of the subject cannot be dissociated from the need to effect changes in the socio-material frames of reference..."(1989:95). Future developments will surely arise in the integration and synthesis of a psychoanalytic semiotic examination grounded in a historical, materialistic critique of the given mode of production. Necessarily, the effects of the Imaginary, Symbolic and Real Orders need to be integrated into any transformative political agenda.

Summary. In sum, Lacanian informed, feminist postmodernist sociology of law directs its focus on the prevalent Symbolic Order and its inherent ideologies that sustain the subordination of women (and others). It sees the possibility of change as being directly connected with many of the insights of Lacan concerning the wherewithal of the gendered subject. Whereas non-essentialists would more likely advocate formal equality and use the Fourteenth Amendment's protection for societal change, essentialists find themselves in deep debate over the nature of differences and its implications for transformative politics. On the one hand, arguing for essentialism provides a grounded politics rooted in women's historically exploited existence. But also recognized here is that this stance may, in extreme forms, lead to simple reversal of hierarchies. On the other hand, to not argue for some form of essentialism, even of a temporary nature, may place would-be reformers without foundational positions from which to develop a sound transformative politics.

CONSTITUTIVE LAW

Introduction. The constitutive approach is a second exemplification of a postmodernist approach in the sociology of law. It has had a rather recent beginning. Nevertheless, its main point is that law should be considered neither as an autonomous nor as a dependent body of rules and that law is codetermined by subjects within historically situated social relations.

A number of theorists have been actively engaged in trying to work out the implications of this approach.[8] A number of case studies have also appeared (see Merry, 1985; Brigham, 1987; Salyer, 1989, 1991; Barak, 1993; Ewick and Silbey, 1998; Barak and Henry, 1999; Arrigo, 2001). It has developed out of the ongoing debates that had begun in the late 1970s over

Marxists' interpretations concerning the relationship of the base to the superstructure (see our chapter on Karl Marx). The elevation of the importance of the ideological function of law, especially given the work by Gramsci on hegemony, and Poulantzas's (1973, 1978) analysis of the superstructure, was also critical in the development of the constitutive approach.

Constitutive theory has built on these and other insights. Poulantzas, for example, has said that law is "a constitutive element of the socio-political field" (1978:82-83); Klare has noted: "legal discourse shapes our beliefs about the experience and capacities of the human species, our conceptions of justice, freedom and fulfillment, and our visions of the future" (1982:135); and that law making should be seen "as a form of praxis" (1979:128). Henry and Milovanovic have noted that the constitutive approach "recognizes human agent's power to undermine the structures that confront them and asserts that agents both use and are used in the generation of knowledge and truth about what they do" (1991:296; 1996). And finally, Hunt has pointed out that rather than limiting debate to law being either autonomous or dependent, we should see how

> law constitutes or participates in the constitution of a terrain or field within which social relations are generated, reproduced, disputed and struggled over, the most important implication being that within such a field... the legal discourses in play both place limits of possibility on social action and impose specific forms of discursive possibility [1993:293].

Thus for Hunt, the key orientating methodology to further developments of a constitutive theory in law is the call: "neither autonomous law, nor dependent law, but constitutive law" (1993:182-183).

Neither Autonomy nor Dependence

The constitutive approach has shifted the attribution of causal priority in the development of law from the economic sphere to the interdependent effects of political, juridic, economic and cultural relations. That is to say, rather than assuming that any one factor, alone, is accountable for the development of law, the constitutive approach recognizes co-determination. Relatively independent spheres appear historically in particular configurations with effects.

In many ways, this approach has grown out of the Structural Interpellation view developed in our chapter on Karl Marx. But it goes beyond it in underscoring the idea that the question of causality must recognize that none of the spheres are reducible to each other. Rather, "directionality and causality must always be questions of specific historical and contextual investigation" (Hunt, 1993:294; for a mild critique, see Douzinas et al., 1991:119-120). Recall that in the Structural Interpellation view, juridical, ideological and political factors were seen as the determinants in constituting socioeconomic relations.

The notion of *relative autonomy* is closely connected with constitutive theory. But neither structure nor different elements within an ongoing social system are understandable on their own: "neither is reducible to or explainable in terms of the other" (Hunt, 1993:179). This gives new meaning to the notion of multicausality.

In the Structural Interpellation view, a very strong version of linguistic determinism prevailed, and subjects were seen as passive receptacles of ideologies conveyed in particular linguistic coordinate systems, especially the juridic form. The subject was merely *interpellated*. The constitutive approach, however, recognizes subjects in struggle and the *subject-in-process* (Kristeva, 1980). Thus, rather than the call for a praxis as is the case in traditional Marxist camps, the call is for a *transpraxis* (Henry and Milovanovic, 1991:295; 1996; we shall have more to say about this below).

Constitutive theory attempts to show how law is an element in subjects' social constructions of reality; law both constitutes social relations and is constituted in turn by subjects' use of it (see also Ewick and Silbey, 1998:245-250; Kennedy, 1997:152). Consider Kennedy's (1997:152) point: "although legal discourse is in one sense driven by the underlying opposition of ideologized interests, it may also react back on the ideologies and the interests and transform them." And further (ibid.), "the modern legal discourse of civil rights is as much a cause as an effect of civil rights thinking..." This appears as somewhat circular, but this is the precise point. Law both constitutes and is constituted in everyday social encounters and social constructions of reality. It is constituted communicatively. This does, however, pose the question of the chicken and the egg: which came first? Several lines of inquiry are attempting to address this.

Hunt (1993), for example, has shown that the relationship between law and social practice is not only two-way, but that "neither term is reducible to or explainable entirely in terms of the other" (Hunt, 1993:179). With this beginning, he argues that a number of theoretical integrations can take place (ibid.).

Hunt's specific proposal is that law helps constitute *discursive formations* (our own terminology is "linguistic coordinate systems"), which then function to "both place limits of possibility on social action and impose specific forms of discursive possibility" (1993:293).[9] In other words, subjects both use and reconstitute the law "field" in their everyday activity. Consider activist lawyers who must make use of legal discourse, legal categories, and principles of formal rationality to defend rebels before the court. In the process, a case may be "won," but legal ideology, the rule of law, is given further unintentional legitimation. It is inadvertently reconstituted.

Drawing from Lacan, we could say that lawyers' continuous use of key master signifiers in trial court proceedings, and in other interactions at the courthouse, energizes these same signifiers, to the exclusion of other possible signifiers that might have been used in other contexts to construct "reality."[10]

As to how a discursive "field" (i.e., a linguistic coordinate system) is "originally" constituted, Hunt tells us that directionality and causality must be understood by investigations that consider historical and contextual developments (1993:294). In fact, a number of discourses or linguistic coordinate systems exist, sometimes competing, sometimes complimentary.[11] Hunt then provides an example of how a constitutive approach could be applied.

The example offered is the interaction between the courts and the police. If we envision the courts and the police as two relatively independent spheres, but nevertheless in a situation of mutual dependence, we can then seen how constitutive theory is pertinent. For example, Hunt tells us that courts often legitimize police practices, but courts in turn need police to legitimize their own task; that is, police practices provide an opportunity for the courts to legitimize their own existence and effectiveness (ibid., 296). Consider, for example, how such juridically established case opinion as the "plain view doctrine," the "Miranda warning," and the "exclusionary rule," came into being. Once the plain view doctrine was established it became a basis of constructing narratives by police, both in restricting law enforcement practices and in an *ex post facto* fashion.

However, crises could upset this balance, as for example, when the media exposes the police engaging in unconstitutional behavior (i.e., illegal searches, arrests, surveillance, etc.), or when some "sting operation" uncovers some unscrupulous judge. The mutual dependence between relatively autonomous spheres, therefore, is always unstable (ibid., 297). This produces change. But attributing change to one sphere or the other is misleading; rather, both spheres are implicated in change as they adjust to each other.

Let us provide our own example of the application of a constitutive approach to the interaction between the sphere of policing and the sphere of law-making/law-finding. Consider the *plain view doctrine* (police who are investigating a crime who come across other illicit activity in plain view need not return to a judge to obtain an arrest or search warrant). Police training educates the neophyte police officer as to its constitutional origins and importance in a democratic society based on the "rule of law." Much of the everyday activity of the police may be guided by this doctrine; much, however, uses it as a way of constructing narratives after the fact that fit constitutionally permissible police operations. In other words, it is a way of avoiding the dismissal of otherwise illegally obtained "evidence" during "suppression hearings" prior to trial. After-the-fact narratives are constructed by incorporating given legal principles and linguistic forms (words, concepts, principles, etc.) to obtain, on the face, a logically, coherently appearing story of the "what happened?" Thus both spheres — the police and the judiciary — are implicated in the construction of narratives and in the continuance of their form. Police constructions give continuous form, scope and energy to legally established principles, providing them with further support and legitimacy which in turn appear to be guiding police everyday behavior. Police stories are therefore carefully constructed with the discursive elements dictated by the higher courts, and provide readily available examples of their constitutional behavior. Courts, by accepting these narratives provide legitimation for these renditions of "what happened?"

Hunt also provides a thesis that perhaps law could be better understood in terms of how it combines and recombines with different relatively autonomous spheres (ibid., 299-300). Law, in modern society, he tells us, increasingly penetrates different disciplines (e.g., mental health, corrections, education, the sciences, etc.) and is penetrated by them. The significance of law, in Hunt's words, is that it acts as "a mediating mechanism — law as the bearer of the normative framework of the normalization worked on by a diversity of disciplinary practices" (ibid., 299).

Elsewhere (Henry and Milovanovic, 1991, 1996, 2002), we have shown how particular discourses — as in the case of Cohen's (1985) "control talk," Manning's (1988) "organizational talk," Thomas's (1988) and Thomas and Milovanovic's (1999) "law talk" — both constitute and are constituted by subjects in their everyday social encounters with the law. Consider Kennedy's (1997:134) point: "speech is never fully controlled by the speaker (the speaker is in some sense 'spoken' by his or her language)..."

Subjects must take everyday experiences and provide summary representations in symbolic categories. But this construction process always implies that some ongoing discourse and its categories (i.e., anchored signifiers) and some particular coordinating semiotic axes (paradigm, syntagm) provide the medium (discursive field) within which these social constructions must take place. Again, we see that subjects infuse further life into the categories being used in the process of constructing meaningful everyday narratives, which are the basis of social interactions. The legal field, or the legal linguistic coordinate system, offers an abundance of material out of which a more limited narrative construction can take place. Here, Lacan's psychoanalytic semiotics is instructive. As Henry and Milovanovic have said (1991:300): "[o]nce social structures are constituted as summary representations, their ongoing existence depends on their continued and often unwitting reconstruction in everyday discourse, a discourse replete with tacit understandings..." Subjects are offered discursive subject-positions which are always already populated with signifiers that "speak."

But constitutive theory argues that relatively stabilized discursive fields do not necessarily represent all voices; some, in other words, deny the means for easy expression by diverging or dissenting voices. Consider Harrington and Yngvesson (1990:143):

> To speak of the constitutive dimension of ideology is to examine legal ideology as a form of power that also creates a particular kind of world, specifically, a liberal-legal world constituted as separate spheres of "law" and "community," with "practice" or "process" located uneasily between the two. In such a world actors impose ideologies or persuade others to take them on as "voluntary."

COREL Sets

Elsewhere (Henry and Milovanovic, 1996), we have developed the notion of COREL sets. This stands for constitutive interrelational sets. It builds primarily on the work of autopoeises and "structural coupling" (Luhmann, 1992), Hunt's (1993) relational sets, and chaos theory's concept of iteration.[12] COREL sets is a conceptualization that sees phenomena being interconnected at different levels. There are various feedback loops and reciprocally interacting states. These "couplings" assure a degree of stability, but yet, in the constitutive view, are always subject to re-coupling in a variety of configurations. It is repetition that provides the appearance of stability (see Butler, 1993:220). The notion of iterative loop suggests that feedback loops activated produce non-linear results. Take for example a legal concept or signifier. As it is continuously interpreted by the courts it undergoes a modification (see also Balkin, 1987). Thus, establishing "original intent" in law — some foundational principle that is said to be embedded in original thought by the "founding fathers" — is illusory. An iterative loop, once perturbed, runs out its inherent logic, but returns always as more than one, as something slightly different with each iteration.

We could envision a number of intersecting, or coupling "iterative loops." We could also specify a number of these "iterative loops" being interconnected and having effects on each other. Thus, at historical junctures, we have configurations of relatively stable, interconnected iterative loops. In legal theory, as in social science literature, these are more often seen to exist in equilibrium conditions. Structural functionalism attempts to explain this. However, in chaos theory, they lie or could lie in far-from-equilibrium conditions where flux and continuous dynamic change takes place, where even a very slight perturbation can have, with iteration, disproportional effects.

For example, the emergence of legal discourse and particular couplings of signifiers to signifieds could be envisioned in one of these matrixes. We could identify the various coupled iterative loops: political economy with capital logic at play; various cultural forces; media interventions in framing stories; judicial decision making; legal practices; law school pedagogy; police practices; street usages of discourses, etc. It is in the totality of interpenetrating forces that a distinct legal discourse emerges. In other words, it is being constituted at all "levels." A subject who enters this scene is offered various discursive subject-positions within which s/he can take up residence as a grammatical "I" (*le sujet de l'énoncé*), from which to speak. Some discursive regions (linguistic coordinate systems) may become more rigid, and thus offer Lacan's discourse of the master or the discourse of the university. It is through repetition that stability is maintained; and it is in subversive repetition (Butler, 1993) that they are undermined.

Matza (1964), for example, has shown how the discourse of juvenile offenders often is replete with many of the same excuses and denials of full responsibility that we find in the courts. Arrigo's study (1997b, 2001) of "transcarceration" indicates that a sizable number of inmates find themselves circulating from one institution to another, often subject to a similar discourse of surveillance and control found in these institutions. He also argues that this discourse of surveillance and control is very similar to what Foucault (1977) spelled out in his notion of the "disciplining mechanisms" and "panopticism." And Schwendinger and Schwendinger (1985) have found that a certain "rhetoric" is developed by juveniles that allows the targeting of certain people, without feeling shame or regret. This rhetoric can be traced to economic conditions, and to unique appropriations and adaptations during the youth's development. Thus, in each case, we can see how a particular discourse develops. It is a joint production: a person is implicated in co-production — s/he actively produces a discourse, and is produced by discourse. Arrigo's (1997b:43) study "showed how enactors of this specialized discourse (e.g., clinicians, judges, hospital administrators, attorneys) simply engage in the circulation and re-validation of that language esteemed in criminal justice and mental health circles." "This," he concludes, "was understood as linguistic hegemony. Disordered defendants were also shown to contribute to their own loss of desire, their own discursive marginalization. This was understood as linguistic reification."

Karl Marx had it partly correct that dialectical materialism (thesis, antithesis, thesis, etc.) was the "motor" for social change. However, this must be tempered by the thesis of COREL sets, which suggests nonlinear and unpredictable change. Configurations of relatively stable, interconnected iterative loops, once placed in resonance, and once iteration unfolds, produce unexpected, often disproportional effects in society at all levels. In the extreme, we could see certain perturbations as *solitons*.[13] Such occurrences as "9/11," sensational crimes, moon landings, Afghanistan and Iraquian incursions, national scandals, a profound public speech or novel, street uprisings, a terrorist act, etc., may resonate more forcefully and traverse numerous configurations of interconnected iterative loops, producing some expected, but many unexpected results at all levels. Consider, for example, the increased use of security discourses after "9/11," and decreased use of privacy discourses. Consider, too, the circulation of more circumscribed signifiers with particular content (signified) that attain greater dominance in every discourse. Constitutive law thus poses a holistic vision of change. Various factors interpenetrate each other, and may develop a relative stable equilibrium. From these, particular discursive formations spring. Abstraction, taking any one factor in isolation, does a disservice to our understanding of COREL sets. Their basis lies more in orderly (dis)order dynamics. As Ewick and Silbey (1998:243) tell us, "even the most personal story relies on and invokes collective narratives — symbols, linguistic formations, structures, and vocabularies of motive — without which the personal would remain unintelligible and uninterpretable."

Prioritization of factors varies in space and time. Internal contradictions, too, play themselves out in this process. Ewick and Silbey (1998:226), in their analysis of the connection between consciousness and structure, argue, "contradictions become the bases for the invocations, reworkings, applications, and transpositions through which structures (schemas and resources) are enacted in daily life...contradictions and oppositions underwrite everyday ideological engagement, and thus ensure an ideology's vitality and potency." Thus, the ideological does not exist in some separate domain: it is constantly constructed anew by everyday interactions in life. And they (ibid., 225) conclude: "ideology can be understood to represent an intersection between structure and consciousness." Ideology, we add, is constituted by configurations of coupled signifiers. It is a particular "knowledge" (Lacan's S2).

Legal consciousness is a collective construction (ibid., 247); it is not merely "reducible to what individuals think about the law." They continue: "each person does not invent an independent and unique conception of legality...People relied on culturally available narratives of law to interpret their lives and relationships...They combined elements of different schemas with scraps of their own biographies to forge distinctive accounts of events and relationships." In short, this is a constitutive process. Arrigo's (1997b, 2001) work on transcarceration, too, is particularly illuminating in indicating how a relatively stable discourse of incarceration emerges, within which identities and socially constructed realities emerge.

Law-finding practices, too, can be investigated with the aid of one of the threads of constitutive theory, referred to as dynamic systems theory, or chaos theory (see the collection of essays in Milovanovic, 1997a; see also Williams and Arrigo, 2001). Legal reasoning and decision making has more to do with nonlinear dynamics than linear constructions to which orthodox lawyers overtly subscribe. A number of studies in the literature (Brion, 1991; Schulman, 1997; Williams and Arrigo, 2002) have indicated how chaos theory underlies law practices. In Williams and Arrigo's (2002:229) application to mental health law, they were to conclude: "all events are expressions of intricate, complex, and largely imperceptible relations between an incalculable number of variables, some exerting their influence well before the present moment." Consistent with Nietzsche, all too often, after the fact, we impose an orderly world upon this otherwise more chaotic state.

Toward a Constitutive Definition of Harm

The sociology of law literature has grappled with the question of law and crime (see Henry and Lanier, 2001). But how to more adequately define crime? Recognizing the inadequacies with the legalist definition of crime, we (Henry and Milovanovic, 1996:102-104) have developed a constitutive view. Crimes, or harms, can be seen as two broad types: "harms of reduction," whereby a person is reduced in some way from a position s/he has; and "harms of repression," whereby a person is denied (structurally, individually, circumstantially, etc.) being able to achieve a position or standing. Admittedly broad, this reconceptualization can be the basis of more refined specification, including the connection with ethical and moral issues. But, in its current form, it challenges the existing definition of crime, with its abstract categories of the criminal and which often overlooks other social injuries that are extensive. Thus, to take the example of COREL sets that have reached a rigid stabilization and that have as an outcome the systematic denial of a segment of the population the ability to self-actualize, we could, irrespective of legalist definitions of crimes, make claim that this configuration of forces itself is criminogenic. The configuration of forces could then be the basis of nomination (naming injurious forces), and the target of the subversion of repetition, as Butler (1993) has suggested.

Summary

In our last section we developed a second exemplification of a postmodern approach in the sociology of law, one based on the integration of various perspectives, including Lacan's psychoanalytic semiotics. It builds on ideas from earlier social constructionist theories, Marxist debates on the nature of the relationship between the base and superstructure, and postmodernist thinkers. The constitutive approach[14] in the sociology of law offers the idea that the directionality of causality is always subject to historical case examination. It criticizes the master-slave analysis of Hegel in favor of Nietzsche. Rather than reaction-negation dynamics — the basis of deconstruction and the oppositional subject, and generally the ideal of praxis being a guide — the Nietzschean position is advocated, one based on an affirmative action, a transpraxis. The task ahead for those interested in developing a more complete postmodernist sociology of law is to more precisely develop the linkages amongst the revolutionary subject, legal discourse, a transformative politics, and new replacement discourses which may better embody the desires of the speaking-being.

A semiotically driven sociology of law from a postmodern approach, as exemplified by postmodern feminist perspectives and constitutive theory, provide advances in sociology of law. This evolving sociology of law provides novel conceptual tools for examining complex issues of social control. It provides advances over traditional modernist perspectives in so much as it arms us with high-powered critical tools for inquiry, particular when race, class and gender discrimination and their intersectional forms are involved. Yes, the semiotic and postmodernist approaches see the dominant classes as having advantages in the legal arena, a conclusion shared with many other modernist thinkers; but specifying with great precision how this is so is aided by semiotic analysis. Postmodern feminists and constitutive theorists have provided key tools for furthering this inquiry. There is much to be done in this exciting and challenging area. Surely semiotics will be a key element in the various integrations that are emerging, all of which illuminate the necessity of comprehensive analysis in the sociology of law.

Notes

1. For other developments in applying Lacan, see Caudill (1992a, 1992b, 1992c, 1993, 1994, 1997), Goodrich (1984, 1990), Arrigo (1992, 1993a, 1993b, 1994, 1998a, 1998b, 2000a, 2001), and Brennan (1993). For explanations and applications of Lacanian topology, see Ragland and Milovanovic (2003).

2. The basis of desire can be developed from a more conservative tradition, rooted in Hegel, to a more radical tradition rooted in Nietzsche. For the former tradition, desire is essentially homeostatic in nature: the end point of desire seeking expression is some equilibrium, homeostasis, or reduction of tension. Desire finds itself being embodied during the process in which the subject reacts to and negates different tension-producing situations (i.e., hierarchical structures). In other words, this focus is on reaction-negation. For the latter model of desire rooted in Nietzsche, there is an affirmative, value-creating, forward movement (see Lecercle, 1985; Deleuze, 1983; Deleuze and Guattari, 1987; Grosz, 1994; Lorraine, 1999). Whereas the first movement is connected to the idea of *praxis*, the second is connected to *transpraxis*.

3. We have extended Lacan's analysis by indicating that the three semiotic axes interact in complex ways.

Figure 15. Semiotic Axes

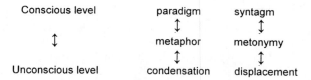

What this depicts is that at some deeper level within the psychic apparatus, desire is mobilized as a response to some periodically perceived lack-in-being. It begins a zigzag journey toward conscious expression. In other words, desire begins to be embodied. One form within which this desire is embodied is the word. Poets, of course, excel in allowing us not only to describe an apple, for example, but also to come very close to allowing us to even taste it. But the signifier as a receptacle of desire must undergo further manipulation by the metaphor-metonymy semiotic axis (see Lacan, 1977:164-167) before it is finally given expression in some particular discourse such as legal discourse (or in our terminology, within the legal linguistic coordinate system). Thus the end product of this process is a particular word being expressed in a particular discourse.

4. Discursive-subject position is a more precise way to refer to a person found in social encounters. Sociologists often use the term "role." But this is too limiting. Rather, a person often assumes a position in social encounters that already has a particular discourse attached to it. For example, think in terms of the difference between a prosecuting attorney versus a defense attorney.

5. As Cornell (1999:xxi) states: "There are a number of insights I find valuable in Lacan for feminist theory in particular... These include, amongst others, Lacan's break with all theories of sexual difference based in nature, the related analysis of the feminine and masculine as positions before the phallic that either sex can take up, the linguistic reconceptualization of the unconscious so that it is no longer rooted in one reading of Freud's theory of the sexual drive, and the move from an actual purportedly literal account of the figures in the family drama to a symbolic account of how sexual personas are perpetuated."

6. Several prominent feminists have argued that "essentialism may be a necessary strategy" (Braidotti, 1989:92, 100, 102). Grosz, recognizing the dilemma of using Lacan's insights but fearing being seduced, supports a "tactical position" in which Lacan's insights are used in attempts to make substantial societal changes (1990). Spivek, too, takes this position and calls it "strategic essentialism" (cited in Cornell, 1999:179). Cornell has also opted for some aspects of this position (1999:100, 118, 182). Those who have taken this view have insisted that transformative politics must be grounded.

7. See, for example, Cain, 1986, 1990; Harding, 1991; Aptheka, 1989; Hartsock, 1983; Collins, 1990; Collins, 1992; Smith, 1987, 1992; Wicke, 1994; for a good overall critique see Grant, 1993:91-125.

8. See, for example, Klare, 1979; Fitzpatrick, 1984; Harrington and Merry, 1988; Hunt, 1987, 1993; Henry and Milovanovic, 1991, 1993, 1994, 1996; see also the anthology devoted to applications of the constitutive approach in Henry and Milovanovic, 1999; Milovanovic and Henry, 1991, 2002; Barak, 1997; Barak and Henry, 1999; Nelken, 1986.

9. See also Bourdieu's notion of a "juridical field," or "habitus," 1987; Deleuze and Guattari's notion of "regimes of signs," (1987:111-148); see also Irigaray's call that "sexual liberation implies linguistic transformations," (1993:30-36).

10. We recall Lacan's idea that "a signifier represents [stands for] the subject for another signifier." In other words, it is in the circulation of signifiers (even more so than any conscious acknowledgement of their signifieds) that we find circumscribed reality constructions, and subjective identifications. Here, instructive was Lacan's (1988) classic "Seminar on the 'Purloined Letter,'" an analysis of Edgar Allan Poe's short story where a compromising letter is stolen and circulates among three people. We never get to know the content of the letter, but nevertheless, it "insists," it has effects by its very circulation and by the very relationships the three officials make with it. Here, a signifier represents the subject for another signifier.

11. According to Hunt, this is where Foucault's investigation stops. Foucault falls short in "providing a satisfactory account of how specific discourses arose or how they came to prevail over rival discourses" (ibid., 295). Hunt's answer is two-fold. One necessary element needed to answer this question is some aspect of Gramsci's work on hegemony (1971). Recall that by hegemony we meant that otherwise repressed subjects often actively, be it inadvertently, reconstitute repressive structures, even while trying to negate them. (For example, first wave feminists who advocated "get tough" approaches with abusers found themselves also further solidifying the power of the state, a goal they did not intend; similarly, many activist movements often advocate tougher measures against some culprits, and in the process often further solidify state power, extend state intrusions, and the legitimacy of the rule of law.) The second element Hunt borrows from Luhmann's idea of "structural coupling" developed from his autopoeitic law (see chapter 5), especially how it has been incorporated by Jessop (1990). Jessop had developed the implications of this idea in his neo-Marxist analysis and had followed the work of Althusser and Poulantzas.

12. Derrida's notion of iteration is compatible; see also Balkin's (1987) application to law and nonlinear effects (Milovanovic, 1997b).

13. E.g., waves that grow in intensity, such as in tidal waves, and which are capable of traveling large distances without dissipating; see Briggs and Peat (1989:119-33).

14. For a response to the critics of the constitutive perspective, see Henry and Milovanovic (1999:287-305).

REFERENCES

Abel, R. "A Socialist Approach to Risk," *Maryland Law Review* 41:695-754. 1982.

Ahonen, P. "Regulating, Deregulating and Reregulating Universities," in R. Malloy and C. Braun (eds.) *Law and Economics*, pp. 127-52, 1995.

Alberstein, M. "Getting to Where? On Peace Making and Law Teaching at Harvard Law School," *Law and Critique* 10:323-342, 1999.

Althusser, L. *Lenin and Philosophy*. New York: Monthly Review Press, 1971.

Alexander, J.W. "Topological Invariants of Knots and Links," *Transactions of the American Mathematical Society* 30:275-306, 1928.

Andreski, S. *Max Weber's Insight's and Errors*. Boston, MA: Routledge and Kegan Paul, 1984.

Aptheker, B. *Tapestries of Life: Women's Work, Women's Consciousness and Meaning of Daily Experience*. Amherst, MA: University of Massachusetts Press, 1989.

Archard, D. *Consciousness and the Unconscious*. London: Hutchinson, 1984.

Arrigo, B. "Deconstructing Jurisprudence: An Experiential Feminist Critique," *Journal of Human Justice* 4(1):13-30, 1992.

—— "An Experientially-Informed Feminist Jurisprudence: Rape and the Move Toward Praxis," *Humanity and Society* 17(1):28-47, 1993a.

—— *Madness, Language and the Law*. New York: Harrow and Heston, 1993b.

—— "Legal Decisions and the Disabled Criminal Defendant: Contributions from Psychoanalytic Semiotics and Chaos Theory," *Legal Studies Forum* 18(2):93-112, 1994.

—— "Insanity Defense Reform and the Sign of Abolition," *International Journal for the Semiotics of Law* 10:191-211, 1997a.

—— "Transcarceration: Notes on a Psychoanalytically-Informed Theory of Social Practice in the Criminal Justice and Mental Health System," *Crime, Law, and Social Change* 27:31-48, 1997b.

—— "Reason and Desire in Legal Education," *International Journal for the Semiotics of Law* 11:2-24, 1998a.

—— "Restoring Justice for Juveniles," *Justice Quarterly* 15(4):629-66, 1998b.

—— *Social Justice/Criminal Justice* (ed.). Belmont, CA: West/Wadsworth, 1999.

—— "Law and Social Inquiry," *International Journal for the Semiotics of Law* 13(2):127-32, 2000.

—— "Transcareration: A Constitutive Ethnography of Mentally Ill Offenders," *The Prison Journal* 81(2):162-186, 2001.

Arrigo, B. and C. Williams. "Law, Ideology, and Critical Inquiry: A Case of Treatment Refusal for Incompetent Prisoners Awaiting Execution," *New England Journal on Criminal and Civil Confinement* 25(2):367-412, 1999.

—— "The (Im)Possibility of Democratic Justice and the 'Gift' of the Majority," *Journal of Contemporary Criminal Justice* 16(3):321-343, 2000a.

—— "The Philosophy of the Gift and the Psychology of Advocacy," *International Journal for the Semiotics of Law* 13:215-242, 2000b.

Arrigo, B., D. Milovanovic and R. Schehr. "The French Connection," *Humanity and Society* 24(2):162-203, 2000.

Asch, M. "Wildlife, Domestic Animals, and the Dene Aboriginal Rights Claim," in D. Currie and B. MacLean (eds.), *Rethinking the Administration of Justice*. Vancouver, Canada: Collective Press, pp. 115-129, 1992.

Aubert, J. *Joyce Avec Lacan*. Paris: Navarin, 1987.

Aubert, V. *In Search of Law*. New Jersey: Barnes and Nobles Books, 1983.

Bakhtin, M. *The Dialogic Imagination*. M. Holquist (ed.). Austin, Texas: University of Texas Press, 1981.

—— *Speech Genres and Other Late Essays*. C. Emerson and M. Holquist (eds.). Austin, Texas: University of Texas Press, 1986.

Balbus, I. "Commodity Form and Legal Form: An Essay on the Relative Autonomy of the Law," *Law and Society Review* 11:571-87, 1977a.

—— *The Dialectics of Legal Repression*. New York: Russell Sage, 1977b.

Baldinger, K. *Semantic Theory*. Oxford: Blackwell, 1980.

Balkin, J.M. "Deconstructive Practice and Legal Theory," *Yale Law Journal* 96(4):743-86, 1987.

—— Deconstruction's Legal Career: Part 1: http://www.yale.edu/lawweb/jbalkin /articles/deccar1.htm, 1-7, 1998a.

—— Deconstruction's Legal Career: Part 2: http://www.yale.edu/lawweb/jbalkin /articles/deccar2.htm, 1-5, 1998b.

—— Deconstructive Practice and Legal Theory: http://www.yale.edu/lawweb /jbalkin/articles/decprac1.htm, 1-9, 1998c.

Bannister, S. and D. Milovanovic, "The Necessity Defense, Substantive Justice and Oppositional Linguistic Praxis," *International Journal of The Sociology of Law* 18(2):179-198, 1990.

Barak, G. "Media, Crime, and Justice: A Case for Constitutive Criminology," *Humanity and Society* 17(3):272-96, 1993.

—— *Media, Process, and the Social Construction of Crime: Studies in Newsmaking Criminology*. New York: Garland, 1994.

—— *Integrating Criminologies*. Boston, MA: Allyn and Bacon.

Barak, G. and S. Henry. "An Integrative-Constitutive Theory of Crime, Law, and Social Justice," in B. Arrigo (ed.) *Social Justice/Criminal Justice*. Boston: West/Wadsworth, pp. 150-175, 1999.

Barenberg, M. "The Political Economy of the Wagner Act: Power, Symbol, and Workplace Cooperation," *Harvard Law Review* 106:1381-1460, 1993.

Barkum, M. *Law Without Sanctions*. New Haven, CT.: Yale University Press, 1968.

Barley, S. "Semiotics and the Study of Occupational and Organizational Cultures," *Administrative Science Quarterly* 28:393-413, 1983.

Barthes, R. *Mythologies*. New York: Hill and Wang, 1972.

—— *S/Z*. New York: Hill and Wang, 1974.

Bartlett, K. "Feminist Legal Methods," in K. Bartlett and R. Kennedy (eds.), *Feminist Legal Theory*. Oxford: Westview Press, 370-403, 1991.

—— "Cracking Foundations as Feminist Method," *American University Journal of Gender, Society and Policy and Law* 8:31, 2000.

Bartlett, K. and R. Kennedy (eds.). *Feminist Legal Theory: Readings in Law and Gender*. Oxford: Westview Press, 1991.

—— "Introduction," in K. Bartlett and R. Kennedy (eds.) *Feminist Legal Theory*. Oxford: Westview Press, 1-11, 1991.

Baudrillard, J. *For a Critique of the Political Economy of the Sign*. St. Louis, MO: Telos Press, 1981.

Baxter, H. "Autopoiesis and the 'Relative Autonomy' of Law," *Cardozo Law Review* 19:1987-2050, 1998.

Beirne, P. "Ideology and Rationality in Max Weber's Sociology of Law," in S. Spitzer (ed.), *Research in Law and Sociology* 2:103-31. Greenwich, Conn.: JAI Press, 1979a.

—— "Empiricism and the Critique of Marxism on Law and Crime," *Social Problems* 26:373-85, 1979b.

—— (ed.) *Revolution in Law: Contributions to the Development of Soviet Legal Theory, 1917-1938*. New York: M.E. Sharpe, 1990.

Beirne, P and A. Hunt. "Law and the Constitution of Soviet Society: The Case of Comrade Lenin," in P. Beirne (ed.) *Revolution in Law*. New York: M.E. Sharpe, 61-98, 1990a.

—— "Lenin, Crime, and Penal Politics," in P. Beirne (ed.) *Revolution in Law*. New York: M.E. Sharpe, 99-135, 1990.

Beirne, P. and R. Quinney (eds.). *Marxism and Law*. New York: John Wiley, 1982.

Beirne, P. and R. Sharlet (eds.). *Pashukanis: Selected Writings on Marxism and Law*. New York: Academic Press, 1980.

Bell, D. *Confronting Authority*. Boston, MA: Beacon Press, 1994.

Bellah, N. (ed.). *Emile Durkheim on Morality and Society.* Chicago, IL: University of Chicago Press, 1973.

Bendix, R. *Max Weber: An Intellectual Portrait.* Berkeley, CA: University of California Press, 1977.

Bendix, R. and G. Roth. *Scholarship and Partisanship: Essays on Max Weber.* Berkeley, CA: University of California Press, 1971.

Bennet, L and M. Feldman. *Reconstructing Reality in the Courtroom.* New Brunswick, NJ: Rutgers University Press, 1981.

Benson, R.W. "Peirce and Critical Legal Studies," in R. Kevelson (ed.), *Peirce and Law.* New York: Peter Lang, 15-43, 1991.

Benveniste, E. *Problems in General Linguistics.* Coral Gables, FL: University of Miami Press, 1971.

Bergson, H. *Time and Free Will.* New York: Harper and Row, 1960.

Bernstein, B. *Class, Codes and Control.* London: Routledge and Kegan Paul, 1975.

Best, S. *Postmodern Theory.* London: MacMillan, 1991.

Black, D. *The Behavior of Law.* New York: Academic Press, 1976.

—— "Comment: Common Sense in the Sociology of Law," *American Sociological Review* 44(1):27-37, 1979.

—— "The Boundaries of Legal Sociology," in C. Reasons and R. Rich (eds.), *The Sociology of Law: A Conflict Perspective.* Toronto: Butterworths, 1978.

—— *Sociological Justice.* New York: Oxford University Press, 1989.

—— *The Social Structure of Right and Wrong.* San Diego, CA: Academic Press, 1993.

—— "The Epistemology of Pure Sociology." *Law and Social Inquiry* 20:829-70, 1995.

Block, F. "The Ruling Class Does Not Rule: Notes on the Marxist Theory of the State," *Socialist Review* 33:6-28, 1977.

Bogue, R. *Deleuze and Guattari.* New York: Routledge, 1989.

Borch-Jacobsen, M. "What is Called Subject?: A Note on Lacan's 'Linguistery,'" Paper presented to the Annual Congress of the Society for Phenomenology and Existential Philosophy, Northwestern University, Chicago, IL, October, 1988.

—— *Lacan: The Absolute Master.* Stanford, CA: Stanford University Press, 1991.

Borg, M. "Effect of Vicarious Homicide Victimization on Support for Capital Punishment: A Test of Black's Theory of Law," *Criminologist* 36:537-68, 1998.

—— "Using Violence as Social Control: Applying a Theory of Conflict Management to Juvenile Disputes," *University of Florida Journal of Law and Public Policy* 10:313-39, 1999.

—— "Mobilizing Law in Urban Areas," *Law and Society Review* 35:435-456, 2001.

Bourdieu, P. "The Force of Law: Toward a Sociology of the Juridical Field," *Hastings Law Journal* 38:814-853, 1987.

Boyle, J. "The Politics of Reason: Critical Legal Studies and Local Social Thought," *University of Pennsylvania Law Review* 133:685-780, 1985.

Bowles, S. and H. Gintis. *Schooling in Capitalist Society*. New York: Basic Books, 1976.

—— *Democracy and Capitalism*. New York: Basic Books, 1986.

Bracher, M. "Lacan's Theory of the Four Discourses," *Prose Studies* 11:32-49, 1988.

—— *Lacan, Discourse and Social Change: A Psychoanalytic Cultural Criticism*. Ithaca, NY: Cornell University Press, 1993.

Braidotti, R. "The Politics of Ontological Difference," in T. Brennan (ed.). *Between Feminism and Psychoanalysis*. New York: Routledge, 89-105, 1989.

Braithwaite, J. and D. Biles. "Empirical Verification and Black's *The Behavior of Law*," *American Sociological Review* 45:334-38, 1980.

Brennan, T. (ed.). *Between Feminism and Psychoanalysis*. New York: Routledge, 1989.

—— "Introduction," in T. Brennan (ed.) *Between Feminism and Psychoanalysis*. New York: Routledge, 1-23, 1989.

—— *The Interpretation of the Flesh*. London: Routledge, 1992.

—— *History After Lacan*. New York: Routledge, 1993.

Brigham, J. "Right, Rage, and Remedy: Forms of Law in Political Discourse," *Studies in American Political Development* 2:303-16, 1987.

—— *The Constitution of Interests*. New York: New York University Press, 1996.

—— "Millenium Reflections," *International Journal for the Semiotics of Law* 12(3):333-42, 1999.

Briggs, J. and D. Peat. *Turbulent Mirrors*. New York: Harper and Row, 1989.

Brion, D. "The Chaotic Law of Tort: Legal Formalism and the Problem of Indeterminacy," in R. Kevelson (ed.), *Peirce and Law*. New York: Peter Lang, 45-77, 1991.

—— " The Chaotic Indeterminacy of Tort Law," in D. Caudill and S. Gold (eds.), *Radical Philosophy of Law*. New Jersey: Humanities Press, 179-199, 1995.

—— "The Ethics of Property," *International Journal for the Semiotics of Law* 12(3):247-283, 1999.

Brown, C.H. *Wittgensteinian Linguistics*. The Hague: Mouton, 1974.

Brown, R. *A Poetic For Sociology*. Cambridge: Cambridge University Press, 1977.

Butler, J. *Gender Trouble*. New York: Routledge, 1990.

—— *Bodies That Matter*. New York: Routledge, 1993.

—— *Excitable Speech*. New York: Routledge, 1997a.

—— *The Psychic Life of Power*. Stanford, California: Stanford University Press, 1997b.

—— *The Subject of Desire*. New York: Columbia University Press, 1999.

Butler, J., E. Laclau and S. Zizek. *Contingency, Hegemony, Universality*. London: Verso, 2000.

Butz, M. "Systemic Family Therapy and Symbolic Chaos," *Humanity and Society* 17(2):200-22, 1993.

Caudill, D. and S. Gold (eds.). *Radical Philosophy of Law*. Atlantic Highlands, NJ: Humanities Press, 1995.

Cain, M. "Realism, Feminism, Methodology and Law," *International Journal of the Sociology of Law* 14:255-67, 1986.

—— "Realist Philosophy and Standpoint Epistemologies *or* Feminist Criminology as a Successor Science," in L. Gelsthorpe and A. Morris (eds.), *Feminist Perspectives in Criminology*. Milton Keynes: Open University Press, 1990.

Cain, P. "Feminist Jurisprudence: Grounding the Theories," in K. Bartlett and R. Kennedy (eds.), *Feminist Legal Theory*. Oxford: Westview Press, 263-80, 1991.

Cain, M. and A. Hunt. *Marx and Engels on Law*. New York: Academic Press, 1979.

Carrasco, E. "Opposition, Justice, Structuralism, and Particularity: Intersections Between LatCrit Theory and Law and Development Studies," *University of Miami Inter-American Law Review* 28:313-328, 1996.

Carrington, K. "Essentialism and Feminist Criminologies: Relevant to All — Specific to None," *The Critical Criminologist* 5(4):5-6, 14-15, 19-20, 1993.

Caudill, D. "Freud and Critical Legal Studies: Contours of a Radical-Legal Psychoanalysis," *Indiana Law Journal* 66(3):651-97, 1991.

—— "Lacan and Law: Networking with the Big O[ther]," *Studies in Psychoanalytic Theory* 1(1):25-5, 1992a.

—— "'Name-of-the-Father' and the Logic of Psychosis: Lacan's Law and Ours," *Legal Studies Forum* 16(4):23-46, 1992b.

—— "Jacques Lacan and Our State of Affairs: Preliminary Remarks on Law as Other," in R. Kevelson (ed.) *Law and the Human Sciences*. New York: Peter Lang, 95-113, 1992c.

—— "Coming to Terms With Lacan," *International Journal for the Semiotics of Law*," 17:203-220, 1993.

—— "Re-Returning to Freud: Critical Legal Studies as Cultural Psychoanalysis," in D. Caudill and S. Stone (eds.) *Radical Philosophy of Law*. Humanities Press, forthcoming, 1994.

—— *Lacan and the Subject of Law*. Atlantic Highlands, NJ: Humanities Press, 1997.

Caudill, D. and S. Stone (eds.). *Radical Philosophy of Law*. Atlantic Highlands, NJ: Humanities Press, 1995.

Chambliss, W. *On the Take*. Bloomington, In. 1988.

—— "A Sociological Analysis of Vagrancy," *Social Problems* 12:67-77, 1964.

Chambliss, W. and R. Seidman. *Law, Order and Power*. Boston, MA: Addison-Wesley, 1971.

Chandler, D. *Semiotics for Beginners* [www document, 1994] url: (http://www.aber.ac.uk/media/documents/s4b/semiotic.html).

—— *Semiotics: The Basics*. London, UK: Routledge, 2002.

Chang, R. *Disoriented: Asian Americans, Law, and the Nation-State*. New York: New York University Press, 1999.

Cheah, P., D. Fraser and J. Grbich. *Thinking Through the Body of the Law*. New York: New York University Press, 1996.

Cixous, H. "The Laugh of the Medusa," *Signs* 7(1):23-36, 1976.

—— *The Newly Born Woman*. Minneapolis, MN: University of Minnesota Press, 1986.

—— *Reading with Clarice Lispector*. Minneapolis, MN: University of Minnesota Press, 1990.

Clark, G. "A Conversation with Duncan Kennedy," *The Advocate: The Suffolk University Law School Journal* 24(2):56-71, 1994.

Clement, C. *The Lives and Legends of Jacques Lacan*. New York: Columbia University Press, 1983.

Cohen, S. *Visions of Social Control*. Oxford: Polity Press, 1985.

Coker, D. "Crime Control and Feminist Law Reform in Domestic Violence Law," *Buffalo Criminal Law Review* 4:801-840, 2001.

Cole, D. *No Equal Justice*. New York: The New Press, 1999.

Collins, H. *Marxism and Law*. New York: Oxford University Press, 1982.

Collins, P.H. *Black Feminist Thought: Knowledge, Consciousness, and the Politics of Empowerment*. Hammersmith, UK: Harper Collins Academic, 1991.

—— "Transforming the Inner Circle: Dorothy Smith's Challenge to Sociological Theory," *Sociological Theory* 78, 1992.

Committee to End the Marion Lockdown. *Can't Jail the Spirit: Political Prisoners in the U.S. A Collection of Biographies*, 1988.

Conklin, W. *The Phenomenology of Modern Legal Discourse*. Aldershot, UK: Ashgate, 1998.

Conley, J. and W. M. O'Barr. *Just Words: Law, Language and Power*. Chicago, IL: University of Chicago Press, 1998.

Cook, A. "Beyond Critical Legal Studies: The Reconstructive Theology of Dr. Martin Luther King Jr.," *Harvard Law Review* 103:985-1001, 1990.

Coombe, R. "Room for Manoeuver: Towards a Theory of Practice in Critical Legal Studies," *Law and Social Inquiry* 14:69-121, 1989.

—— "Contesting the Self: Negotiating Subjectivities in Nineteenth-Century Ontario Defamation Trials," *Studies in Legal Policy and Society* 11:3, 1991a.

—— "Beyond Modernity's Meanings: Engaging the Postmodern in Cultural Anthropology," *Culture* 11:111, 1991b.

—— "Publicity Rights and Political Aspiration: Mass, Culture, Gender Identity, and Democracy," *New England Law Review* 26(4):1221-80, 1992.

Cooney, M. *Warriors and Peacemakers*. New York: New York University Press., 1998.

—— "The Decline of Elite Homicide," *Criminology* 35:381-407, 1997.

—— "Evidence as Partisanship," *Law and Society Review* 28:833-58, 1994.

Cornell, D. "Toward a Modern/Postmodern Reconstruction of Ethics," *University of Pennsylvania Law Review* 133:291-380, 1985.

—— "The Philosophy of the Limit: System Theory and Feminist Legal Reform," in D. Cornell, M. Rosenfeld and D. Carlson (eds.), *Deconstruction and the Possibility of Justice*. New York: Routledge, 68-91, 1992.

—— *Transformations: Recollective Imagination and Sexual Difference*. New York, NY: Routledge, 1993.

—— *At the Heart of Freedom*. Princeton, NJ: Princeton University Press, 1998.

—— *Beyond Accommodation: Ethical Feminism, Deconstruction and the Law*. New York: Rowman and Littlefield Publishers, Inc., 1999.

Cornell, D., M. Rosenfeld and D. Carlson (eds.). *Deconstruction and the Possibility of Justice*. New York: Routledge, 1992.

Corrington, R. *An Introduction to C.S. Peirce*. Lanham, MD: Rowman and Littlefield, 1993.

Cotterell, R. *The Sociology of Law*. London: Butterworths, 1984.

Crawford, J. "The Recognition of Aboriginal Customary Laws: An Overview," in C. Cunneen (ed.), *Aboriginal Perspectives on Criminal Justice*. Sydney, Australia: Institute of Criminology, 53-75, 1992.

Crenshaw, K. "Race, Reform and Retrenchment: Transformation and Legitimation in Antidiscrimination," *Harvard Law Review* 101:1356-87, 1988.

—— "Beyond Racism and Misogyny," in Matsuda, M. et al., *Words That Wound*. Oxford: Westview Press, 111-132, 1993.

Crenshaw, K., N. Gotanda, G. Peller and K. Tholmas (eds.). *Critical Race Theory: The Writings That Formed the Movement*, New York: New Press, 1995.

Culler, J. *Deconstruction*. Ithaca, NY: Cornell University Press, 1981.

—— "Demarginalizing the Intersection of Race and Sex: A Black Feminist Critique of Antidiscrimination Doctrine, Feminist Theory, and Antiracist Politics," in K. Bartlett and R. Kennedy (eds.), *Feminist Legal Theory*. Oxford: Westview Press, 57-80, 1991.

Cunneen, C. *Aboriginal Perspectives on Criminal Justice*. Sydney, Australia: Institute of Criminology, 1992.

Curran, V. G. "The Legalization of Racism in a Constitutional State," *Hastings Law Journal* 50:1-45, 1998a.

―――― "Cultural Immersions, Difference and Categories in US Comparative Law," *American Journal of Comparative Law* 46:43-78, 1998b.

Currie, D. "Female Criminality: A Crisis in Feminist Theory," in B. MacLean, *The Political Economy of Crime*. Scarborough, Canada: Prentice-Hall Canada, 232-246, 1986.

―――― "Unhiding the Hidden: Race, Class, and Gender in the Construction of Knowledge," *Humanity and Society* 17(1):3-27, 1993.

Currie, D. and M. Kline. "Challenging Privilege: Women, Knowledge, and Feminist Struggles," *Journal of Human Justice* 2(2):1-36, 1991.

Currie, D., B. MacLean and D. Milovanovic. "Three Traditions of Critical Justice Inquiry: Class, Gender, and Discourse," in D. Currie and B. MacLean (eds.), *Re-Thinking the Administration of Justice*. Halifax, Nova Scotia: Fernwood Publishing, 3-44, 1992.

Daly, K. and M. Chesney-Lind. "Feminism and Criminology," *Justice Quarterly* 5:101-143, 1988.

Dalton, H. "The Clouded Prism," *Harvard Critical Law Review* 22:435, 1987.

Dalton, K. "An Essay in the Deconstruction of Contract Law," *Yale Law Journal* 94:977, 1985.

Danner, M. "Socialist Feminism: A Brief Introduction," in B. MacLean and D. Milovanovic (eds.) *New Directions in Critical Criminology*. Vancouver, Canada: Collective Press, 1991.

de Haan, W. *The Politics of Redress*. Boston, MA: Unwin Hyman, 1990.

Davis, A.D. and J.C. Williams. "Gender, Work and Family Project Inaugural Feminist Legal Theory Lecture Foreword," *American University Journal of Gender, Social Policy and Law* 8:1-12, 2000.

DeKeseredy, W.S. "Exploring the Gender, Race and Class Dimensions of Victimization: A Left Realist Critique of the Canadian Urban Victimization Survey," *International Journal of Offender Therapy and Comparative Criminology* 35:143-61, 1991.

DeKeseredy, W.S. and R. Hinch. *Woman Abuse: Sociological Perspectives*. Toronto: Thompson, 1991.

DeKeseredy, W.D. and M. Schwartz. "British Left Realism on the Abuse of Women," in H. Pepinsky and R. Quinney (eds.), *Criminology as Peacemaking*. Bloomington, IN: Indiana University Press, 1991.

Deleuze, G. *Proust and Signs*. New York: Braziller, Inc., 1972.

—— *Spinoza*. Paris: Minuit, 1981.

—— *Nietzsche and Philosophy*. New York: Columbia University Press, 1983.

—— *Foucault*. Minneapolis, MN: University of Minnesota Press, 1986a.

—— *Cinema 1: The Movement Image*. Minneapolis, MN: University of Minnesota Press, 1986b.

Deleuze, G. and F. Guattari *Anti-Oedipus*. Minneapolis, MN: University of Minnesota Press, 1977.

—— *Kafka: Toward a Minor Literature*. Minneapolis, MN: University of Minnesota Press, 1986.

—— *A Thousand Plateaus*. Minneapolis, MN: University of Minnesota Press, 1987.

Delgado, D. "The Ethereal Scholar: Does Critical Legal Studies Have What Minorities Want?" *Harvard Critical Law Review* 22:301, 1987.

Delgado, R. and J. Stefancic. *Critical Race Theory*. New York: New York University Press, 2001.

—— *The Latino/a Condition: A Critical Reader*. New York: New York University Press, 1998.

de Man, P. *Allegories of Reading: Figural Language in Rousseau, Nietzsche, Rilke, and Proust*. New Haven, CT: Yale University Press, 1979.

—— *The Resistance to Theory*. Minneapolis, MN: University of Minnesota Press, 1986.

Derrida, J. *Speech and Other Phenomena*. Evanston: Northwestern University Press, 1973.

—— *Positions*. Chicago, IL: University of Chicago Press, 1981.

—— *Writing and Difference*. Chicago: University of Chicago Press, 1978.

—— "Force of Law: The 'Mystical Foundation of Authority,'" in D. Cornell, M. Rosenfeld and D. Carlson (eds.). *Deconstruction and the Possibility of Justice*. New York: Routledge, 3-67, 1992.

—— "The Villanova Roundtable," in J. Caputo (ed.), *Deconstruction in a Nutshell: A Conversation with Jacques Derrida*. New York: Fordham University Press, 1997.

Dewey, J. *Philosophy and Civilization*. New York: Milton-Balch, 1931.

Dews, P. *Logics of Disintegration: Post-Structuralist Thought and the Claims of Critical Theory*. New York: Verso, 1987.

Diamond, A., *The Evolution of Law and Order*. Great Britain: Richard Clay and Co., 1951.

—— "The Rule of Law Versus the Order of Custom," in R.P. Wolff (ed.). *The Rule of Law*. New York: Simon and Schuster, 1971.

Dixon, R., W. Ramson and M. Thomas. *Australian Aboriginal Words in English: Their Origin and Meaning*. New York: Oxford University Press, 1990.

Domhoff, W. *Who Rules America?* New York: Prentice Hall, 1967.

Dor, J. *Introduction to the Reading of Lacan.* New Jersey: Jason Aronowitz, 1997.

Douzinas, C., R. Warrington and S. McVeigh. *Postmodern Jurisprudence: The Law of Text in the Texts of Law.* London: Routledge, 1991.

Doyle, D. and D. Luckenbill. "Mobilizing Law in Response to Collective Problems: A Test of Black's Theory of Law," *Law and Society Review* 25(1):103-16, 1991.

Durkheim, E. *Professional Ethics and Civic Morals.* Glencoe, IL: The Free Press, 1958.

—— *Montesquieu and Rousseau: Forerunners of Sociology.* Ann Arbor, MI: University of Michigan Press, 1960.

—— *Moral Education: A Study in the Theory and Application of the Sociology of Education.* New York: Free Press, 1961.

—— *Socialism.* New York: Collier Books, 1962.

—— *The Rules of Sociological Method.* New York: The Free Press, 1964a.

—— *The Division of Labor in Society.* New York: The Free Press, 1964b.

—— *Sociology and Philosophy.* New York: The Free Press, 1974.

—— *The Evolution of Educational Thought.* London: Routledge and Kegan Paul, 1977.

—— "The Nature and Origins of the Right to Property," in S. Lukes and A. Scull (eds.), *Durkheim and the Law.* New York: St. Martin's Press, 1983a.

—— "The Nature and Evolution of Contract," in S. Lukes and A. Scull (eds.), *Durkheim and the Law.* New York: St. Martin's Press, 1983b.

—— "The Evolution of Punishment," in S. Lukes and A. Scull (eds.). *Durkheim and the Law.* New York: St. Martin's Press, 1983c.

—— *Pragmatism and Sociology.* New York: Cambridge University Press, 1983d.

Dworkin, R. *Taking Rights Seriously.* London: Duckworth, 1978.

—— *A Matter of Principle.* Cambridge, MA: Harvard University Press, 1985.

—— *Law's Empire.* London, UK: Fontana Paperbacks, 1986.

Eco, U. *A Theory of Semiotics.* Bloomington, IN: University of Indiana Press, 1976.

—— *Semiotics and the Philosophy of Language.* London: MacMillan, 1984.

Edie, J. "Husserl's Conception of 'The Grammatical' and Contemporary Linguistics," in Lester Embrie (ed.). *Life-World and Consciousness.* Evanston, IL: Northwestern University Press, 1972.

Eisenstein, S. *The Film Sense.* New York: Harcourt Brace Jovanovic, 1975.

Einstadter, W. and S. Henry. *Criminological Theory.* Fort Worth, TX: Harcourt Brace College Publishers, 1995.

Ellis, J. *Against Deconstruction.* Princeton, NJ: Princeton University Press, 1989.

Esping-Anderson, G., R. Friedland and E. Ohlin. "Class Struggle and the Capitalist State," in R. Quinney (ed.), *Capitalist Society*. Homewood, IL.: The Dorsey Press, 1979.

Evans, D. *An Introductory Dictionary of Lacanian Psychoanalysis*. London: Routledge, 1996.

Evan, J. "Indigenous Australians: Language and the Law," *International Journal for the Semiotics of Law* 15(2):127-141, 2002.

Ewick, P. and S. Silbey, *The Common Place of Law: Stories from Everyday Life*. Chicago, IL: University of Chicago Press, 1998.

Feldstein, R. and H. Sussman (eds.). *Psychoanalysis and...* New York: Routledge, 1990.

Felski, R. "Feminism, Postmodernism, and the Critique of Modernity," *Cultural Critique* (Fall):33-57, 1989.

Ferguson, M. and J. Wicke (eds.). *Feminism and Postmodernism*. Durham, NC: Duke University Press, 1994.

Ferrell, J. "Anarchy Against the Discipline," *Journal of Criminal Justice and Popular Culture* 3(4):86-91, 1995.

—— "Against the Law: Anarchist Criminology," in B. MacLean and D. Milovanovic (eds.) *Thinking Critically About Crime*, 146-54, 1997.

—— "Anarchist Criminology and Social Justice," in B. Arrigo (ed.) *Social Justice/Criminal Justice: The Maturation of Critical Theory in Law, Crime, and Deviance*. Belmont, CA: West/Wasworth, pp. 93-108, 1999.

Fine, B. *Democracy and the Rule of Law*. London: Pluto, 1984.

Fineman, M.A. "Cracking the Foundational Myths: Independence, Autonomy and Self-Sufficiency," *American University Journal of Gender, Social Policy and Law* 8:13-46, 2000.

Finnis, J. *Natural Law and Natural Rights*. Oxford: Clarendon Press, 1980.

—— *Fundamentals of Ethics*. Oxford: Clarendon, 1983.

Fish, S. *Is There a Text in This Class?: The Authority of Interpretive Communities*. Cambridge, MA: Harvard University Press, 1980.

—— "With the Compliments of the Author: Reflections on Austin and Derrida," *Critical Inquiry* 4:693-722, 1982.

—— "Fish v Fiss," *Stanford Law Review* 36(6):1325-1347, 1984.

—— *Doing What Comes Naturally: Change, Rhetoric, and the Practice of Theory, in Literary and Legal Studies*. Durham, NC: Duke University Press, 1989.

Fishman, J. *The Sociology of Language*. Rawley, MA: Newbury House, 1960.

Fitzpatrick, P. "Marxism and Legal Pluralism," *Australian Journal of Law and Society* 1:45-59, 1983.

—— "Law and Societies," *Osgood Hall Law Journal* 22:115-38, 1984.

—— "The Rise and Fall of Informalism," in R. Mathews (ed.), *Informal Justice*. London: Sage, 1988.

Fitzpatrick, P. and A. Hunt (eds.). *Critical Legal Studies*. Oxford: Basil Blackwell, 1987.

Flax, J. "Postmodernism and Gender Relations in Feminist Theory," in L.J. Nicholson (ed.) *Feminism/Postmodernism*. London: Routledge, 1990.

Fleming, D. *Powerplay: Toys as Popular Culture*. Manchester, UK: Manchester University Press., 1996.

Fletcher, G. "Law as Discourse," *Cardozo Law Review* 13(5):1631-37, 1992.

Floch, J.M. *Visual Identities*. London, UK: Continuum, 2000.

Flood, S. *Mabo: A Symbol of Sharing*. Glebe, NSW, Australia: Fast Books, 1993.

Foucault, M. *The Archeology of Knowledge*. New York: Pantheon, 1972.

—— *The Order of Things*. New York: Vintage Books, 1973.

—— *Discipline and Punish*. New York: Pantheon, 1977a.

—— *Language, Counter-Memory, Practice*. New York: Cornell University Press, 1977b.

—— *The History of Sexuality: Vol. 1. An Introduction*. New York: Random House, 1978.

—— "The Juridical Apparatus," in W. Connolly (ed.), *Legitimacy and the State*. New York: New York University Press, 1984.

Frank, J. "Are Judges Human?" *University of Pennsylvania Law Review* 80:17-53, 1931a.

—— "Are Judges Human: Part Two?" *University of Pennsylvania Law Review* 80:233-67, 1931b.

—— *Courts on Trial: Myth and Reality in American Justice*. Princeton, NJ: Princeton University Press, 1949.

—— *Law and the Modern Mind*. New York: Doubleday, 1963.

Fraser, A. "The Legal Theory We Need Now," *Socialist Review* 8:164-166, 1978.

Freeman, A. "Racism, Rights and the Quest for Equality of Opportunity: A Critical Legal Essay," *Harvard Critical Law Review* 23:295, 1988.

—— "Antidiscrimination Law: A Critical Review," in D. Kairys (ed.), *The Politics of Law*. New York: Pantheon Books, 1992.

Freire, P. *Pedagogy of the Oppressed*. New York: Herder and Herder, 1973.

—— *The Politics of Education*. South Hadley, MA: Bergin and Garvey, 1985.

Freud, S. *The Psychopathology of Everyday Life*. New York: MacMillan, 1914.

—— *The Standard Edition of the Complete Psychological Works of Sigmund Freud*. J. Strachey (ed.). London: The Hogarth Press, 1956.

—— *The Interpretation of Dreams*. New York: Avon Books, 1965.

Freund, J. *The Sociology of Max Weber*. New York: Random House, 1969.

Friedman, L. *A History of American Law*. New York: Simon and Schuster, 1973.

Friedrichs, D. "The Legitimacy Crises in the United States: A Conceptual Analysis," *Social Problems* 27:540-554, 1980.

—— "Critical Legal Studies and the Critique of Criminal Justice," *Criminal Justice Review* 11:15-22, 1986.

Frug, M.J. "Sexual Equality and Sexual Difference in American Law," *New England Law Review* 26(4):665-82, 1992.

Gabel, P. "Intention and Structure in Contractual Conditions: Outline of a Method for Critical Legal Theory," *Minnesota Law Review* 61:601-43, 1977.

Gabel, P. and J. Feinman. "Contract Law as Ideology," in D. Kairys (ed.), *The Politics of Law*. New York: Pantheon Books, 1992.

Gallop, J. *The Daughter's Seduction: Feminism and Psychoanalysis*. Ithaca, New York: Cornell University Press, 1982.

Game, A. *Undoing the Social: Towards a Deconstructive Sociology*. Milton Keynes: Open University Press, 1991.

Geertz, C. *The Interpretation of Cultures*. New York: Basic Books, 1973.

—— *Local Knowledge*. New York: Basic Books, 1983.

Georges Abeyie, D. "The Myth of a Racist Criminal Justice System," in B. MacLean and D. Milovanovic (eds.), *Racism, Empiricism, and Criminal Justice*. Vancouver, Canada: Collective Press, 1990.

Gibbs, J. "Definitions of Law and Empirical Questions," *Law and Society Review* 11:429-46, 1967.

Giddens, A. (ed.). *Durkheim on Politics and the State*. Cambridge, UK: Polity Press, 1986.

Gilsinan, J. *Doing Justice*. Englewood Cliffs, NJ: Prentice-Hall, 1982.

Gluckman, M. *Politics, Law and Ritual in Tribal Society*. New York: Mentor Books, 1965.

Goffman, E. *Asylums*. New York: Anchor Books, 1961.

—— *Interaction Ritual*. New York: Anchor Books, 1967.

—— *Relations in Public*. New York: Harper and Row, 1971.

Goldfarb, P. "A Theory-Practice Spiral: The Ethics of Feminism and Clinical Education," *Minnesota Law Review* 75:1599, 1991.

—— "From the Worlds of 'Others': Minority and Feminist Responses to Critical Legal Studies," *New England Law Review* 26:683-710, 1992.

Goodrich, P. "Law and Language: An Historical and Critical Introduction," *Journal of Law and Society* 11:173-206, 1984.

—— "The Role of Linguistics in Legal Analysis," *Modern Law Review* 523-534, 1984.

—— *Legal Discourse: Studies in Linguistics, Rhetoric and Legal Analysis.* London: MacMillan, 1987.

—— *Languages of Law: From Logics of Memory to Nomadic Masks.* London: Weidenfeld and Nicolson, 1990.

—— "The Personal and the Political," *Cardozo Law Review* 22:971-999, 2001.

—— "Europe in America: Grammatology, Legal Studies and the Politics of Transmission." *Columbia Law Review* 101:2033, 2001.

Gordon, R. "New Developments in Legal Theory," in D. Kairys (ed.), *The Politics of Law.* New York: Pantheon Books, 1992.

Gottfredson, M. and M. Hindelang. "A Study of the Behavior of Law," *American Sociological Review* 44(3):3-18, 1979a.

—— "Response: Theory and Research in the Sociology of Law," *American Sociological Review* 44(1):27-37, 1979b.

Gramsci, A. *Prison Notebooks.* London: Lawrence and Wishart, 1971.

Granfield, R. and T. Koenig. "From Activisim to Pro Bono: The Redirecting of Working Class Altruism at Harvard Law School," *Critical Sociology* 17(1):57-80, 1990a.

—— "Socialization into the Power Elite: Learning Collective Eminence at Harvard Law School." Unpublished manuscript, 1990b.

Grant, J. *Fundamental Feminism: Contesting the Core Concepts of Feminist Theory.* New York: Routledge, 1993.

Greenberg, D. "Donald Black's Sociology of Law: A Critique," *Law and Society Review* 17(2):337-51, 1983.

Greimas, A. *Structural Semantics* Lincoln: University of Nebraska Press, 1983.

—— *On Meaning.* Minneapolis, MN: Minnesota University Press, 1987.

—— *The Social Sciences: A Semiotic View.* Minneapolis, MN: University of Minnesota Press, 1990.

Greimas, A. and E. Landowski, "The Semiotic Analysis of Legal Discourse: Commercial Laws That Govern Companies and Groups of Companies," in A. Greimas, *The Social Sciences: A Semiotic View.* Minneapolis: University of Minnesota Press, 102-38, 1990.

Grosz, E. "Feminist Theory and the Challenge to Knowledges," *Women's Studies International Forum* 10:475-80, 1987.

—— *Jacques Lacan: A Feminist Introduction.* New York: Routledge, 1990.

—— *Volatile Bodies.* Bloomington, IN: Indiana University Press, 1994.

Groves, C. "Us and Them: Reflections of the Dialectics of Moral Hate," in B. MacLean and D. Milovanovic (eds.), *New Directions in Critical Criminology.* Vancouver, Canada: Collective Press, 1991.

Guinier, L., M. Fine and J. Balin. *Becoming Gentleman: Women, Law School, and Institutional Change*, Boston, MA: Beacon Press, 1997.

Habermas, J. *The Theory of Communicative Action. Vol. One. Reason and the Rationalization of Society.* (Trans. T. McCarthy.) Boston, MA: Beacon Press, 1984.

—— *The Theory of Communicative Action. Vol. Two. Lifeworld and System: A Critique of Functionalist Reason.* (Trans. T. McCarthy.) Boston, MA: Beacon Press, 1987.

—— *Legitimation Crises.* Boston: Beacon Press, 1975.

Harraway, D. "Situated Knowledge," in D. Harraway, *Simians, Cyborgs and Women: The Reinvention of Nature.* New York: Routledge, 1991.

Harding, S. *Whose Science? Whose Knowledge? Thinking From Women's Lives.* Ithaca, NY: Cornell University Press, 1991.

Harper, W. "Review Essay: The Critical Legal Studies Movement," *American Philosophical Association Newsletter* November, 3-11, 1987.

Harrington, C. "Moving From Integrative to Constitutive Theories of Law," *Law and Society Review* 22:963-67, 1988.

Harrington, C. and S. Merry. "Ideological Production: The Masking of Community Mediation," *Law and Society Review* 22:709-35, 1988.

Harrington, C. and B. Yngvesson. "Interpretive Sociolegal Research," *Law and Social Inquiry* 15:135-48, 1990.

Harris, A. "Race and Essentialism in Feminist Legal Theory," in K. Bartlett and R. Kennedy (eds.), *Feminist Legal Theory.* Oxford: Westview Press, 235-62, 1991.

—— "Foreword: The Jurisprudence of Reconstruction," *California Law Review* 82:741, 1994.

Harris, J.W. "A Structuralist Theory of Law: An Agnostic View," in A. Podgorecki and C. Whelan (eds.) *Sociological Approaches to Law.* New York: St. Martin's Press, 1981.

Hart, H.L.A. "Positivism and the Separation of Law and Morals," *Harvard Law Review* 71:593-629, 1958.

—— *The Concept of Law.* Oxford: Clarendon Press, 1961.

—— *Essays in Jurisprudence and Philosophy.* Oxford: Clarendon Press, 1983.

Hartsock, N. *Money, Sex and Power.* Boston, MA: Longman, 1983.

—— "Postmodernism and Political Change: Issues for Feminist Theory," *Cultural Critique* (Winter):15-33, 1990.

Harvey, I. *Derrida and the Economy of Differance.* Bloomington, IN: Indiana University Press, 1986.

Hatty, S.E. "Narratives on Crime," *The Critical Criminologist* 5(4):3-4, 13, 1993.

Haute, P.V. *Against Adaptation: Lacan's "Subversion" of the Subject.* New York: Other Press, 2002.

Haverkamp, A. "Rhetoric, Law, and the Poetics of Memory," *Cardozo Law Review* 13(5):1639-53, 1992.

Hayman, R. "The Coor of Tradition: Critical Race Theory and Postmodern Constitutional Traditionalism." *Harvard Civil Rights-Civil Liberties Law Review* 30:57-93, 1995.

Heath, S. *Questions of Cinema.* Bloomington, IN: Indiana University Press, 1981.

Hegel, F. *Philosophy of Right.* (Trans. T.M. Knox..) New York: Oxford University Press, 1955.

Heilpern, D. "The Mabo Case — Black Law, White Order," *The Critical Criminologist* 5(4):7-8, 16-17, 1993.

Hekman, S. "Weber's Concept of Causality and the Modern Critique" *Sociological Inquiry* 49(4):67-76, 1979.

—— *Gender and Knowledge: Elements of a Postmodern Feminism.* London: Polity Press, 1990.

Hembroff, L. "The Seriousness of Acts and Social Control: A Test of Black's Theory of the Behavior of Law," *American Journal of Sociology* 93:322-47, 1987.

Hennis, W. *Max Weber: Essays on Reconstruction.* Boston, MA: Allen and Unwin, 1988.

Henry, S. *Private Justice.* London: Routledge and Kegan Paul, 1983.

—— "Private Justice, Capitalist Society and Human Agency: The Dialectics of Collective Law in the Cooperative," *Law and Society Review* 19:301-25, 1985.

—— "Can the Hidden Economy be Revolutionary? Toward a Dialectic Analysis of the Relations Between Formal and Informal Economies," *Social Justice* 15:29-60, 1988.

—— "Justice on the Margins: Can Alternative Justice Be Different?" *Howard Journal of Criminal Justice* 28:255-71, 1989.

—— "Newsmaking Criminology as Replacement Discourse," in G. Barak (ed.), *Media, Process, and the Social Construction of Crime: Studies in Newsmaking Criminology.* New York: Garland. pp. 241-72, 1994.

Henry, S. and M. Lanier. *What is Crime?* New York: Rowman and Littlefield, 2001.

Henry, S. and D. Milovanovic "Constitutive Criminology," *Criminology* 29(2):293-316, 1991.

—— "Back to Basics: A Postmodern Redefinition of Crime," *The Critical Criminologist* 5(2/3):1-2, 6, 12, 1993.

—— "The Constitution of Constitutive Criminology," in D. Nelken (ed.) *The Futures of Criminology.* London: Sage, 1994.

—— *Constitutive Criminology*. London: Sage, 1996

—— (eds.). *Constitutive Criminology at Work*. Albany, NY: SUNY Press, 1999.

Hernandez, T.K. "Multiracial Discourse: Raced Classification in an Era of Color-Blind Jurisprudence," *Maryland Law Review* 57:97, 1998.

Hirst, P. *Law, Socialism and Democracy*. London: Allen and Unwin, 1986.

Hirvonen, A. "A Postmodern Challenge or the Seducing Other: From the Politics of the Unfinished to the Politics of Undecidability," in B. MacLean and H. Pepinsky (eds.), *We Who Would Take No Prisoners*. Vancouver, Canada: Collective Press, 1993.

Hobbes, T. *Leviathan*. Oxford: Basic Blackwell, 1946.

Hobbsbawm, E. *Bandits*. London: George Weidenfeld and Nicolson, 1969.

Hoebel, A. *The Law of Primitive Man*. New York: Atheneum, 1974.

Hoeffer, J. "The Gender Gap: Revealing Inequities in Admission of Social Science Evidence in Criminal Cases," *University of Arkansas Law Review* 24:41-98, 2001.

Hogan, P. and L. Pandit (eds.). *Criticism and Lacan*. Athens, GA: University of Georgia Press, 1990.

Hooks, B. *Ain't I a Woman? Black Women and Feminism*. Boston, MA: South End, 1981.

—— *Talking Back: Thinking Feminist, Thinking Black*. Boston, MA: South End, 1988.

—— *Teaching to Transgress*. New York: Routledge, 1994.

Horwitz, A. *The Logic of Social Control*. New York: Plenum Press, 1990.

Howe, A. *Punish and Discipline*. New York: Routledge, 1994.

Hunt. A. *The Sociological Movement in Law*. Philadelphia, PA: Temple University Press, 1978.

—— "The Ideology of law: Advances and Problems in Recent Applications of the Concept of Ideology to the Analysis of law," *Law and Society Review* 19:11-37, 1985.

—— "Legal Positivism and Positivistic Semiotics: Old Wines in New Bottles," *Journal of Law and Society* 13(2):271-278, 1986a.

—— "The Theory of Critical Legal Studies," *Oxford Journal of Legal Studies* 6:1-45, 1986b.

—— "The Critique of Law: What is 'Critical' About Critical Theory?" *Journal of Law and Society* 14:5-19, 1987.

—— "The Role and Place of Theory in Legal Education: Reflections on Foundationalism," *Legal Studies* 9:146-64, 1988.

—— "Why Did Foucault Get Law So Wrong?: Reflections on Law, Power and Sovereignty," Unpublished manuscript, 1991.

—— *Explorations in Law and Society: Toward a Constitutive Theory of Law*. New York: Routledge, 1993.

Hunter, N. "Marriage, Law, and Gender," *Radical Philosophy of Law*. New Jersey: Humanities Press, pp. 221-233,1995.

Husserl, E. *Ideas*. (Trans. W.R. Gibson.) New York: Collier Books, 1975.

Hutchinson, D. "Out Yet Unseen: A Racial Critique of Gay and Lesbian Legal Theory and Political Discourse," *Connecticut Law Review* 29:561, 1997.

Ingram, D. "Legitimation Crises in Contract Law: A Test Case for Critical Legal Studies and Its Critics," In Caudill, D. and S. Gold (eds.), *Radical Philosophy of Law*. Atlantic Fields, NJ: Humanities Press, p. 140-161, 1995.

International Journal of Qualitative Studies. "Special Issue on Critical Race Theory," 1, 1998.

Irigaray, L. *Speculum of the Other Woman*, Ithaca, NY: Cornell University Press, 1985.

—— *Je, Tu, Nous: Toward a Culture of Difference*. New York: Routledge, 1993.

Jackson, B. *Semiotics and Legal Theory*. New York: Routledge and Kegan Paul, 1985.

—— *Law, Fact and Narrative Coherence*. Merseyside, UK: Deborah Charles Publications, 1991.

—— "European Convention of Human Rights Articles 6 & 12: Some Semiotic Observations," *International Journal for the Semiotics of Law* 6(16):45-69, 1993.

—— *Making Sense in Law*. Liverpool, UK: Deborah Charles Publications, 1995.

—— "Truth or Proof?: The Criminal Verdict," *International Journal for the Semiotics of Law* 33:227-273, 1998.

Jacobson, R. "Autopoietic Law: The New Science of Niklas Luhmann," *Michigan Law Review* 87:1647, 1989.

Jakobson, R., "Two Aspects of Language and Two Types of Aphasic Disorders," in R. Jakobson and M. Halle, *Fundamentals of Language*. Paris: Mouton, 1971.

Jagger, A. *Feminist Politics and Human Nature*. Totowa, NJ: Rowman and Littlefield, 1983.

James, W. *Pragmatism and Four Essays From the Meaning of Truth*. New York: Meridian Books, 1955.

Jameson, F. *The Political Unconscious*. Ithaca, New York: Cornell University Press, 1981.

—— "Foreword," in A.J. Greimas, *On Meaning*. Minneapolis, MN: University of Minnesota Press, 1987.

Janikowski, R. and D. Milovanovic (eds.). *Legality and Illegality*. New York: Peter Lang Publishing Co., 1994.

Jessop, B. *State Theory: Putting the Capitalist State in its Place*. Cambridge, UK: Polity Press, 1990.

Kairys, D. (ed.). *The Politics of Law*. New York: Pantheon, 1992.

Kamenka, E. (ed.) *The Portable Marx*. New York: Penguin Books, 1983.

Katilius-Boydstun, M. "The Semiotics of A. J. Greimas: An Introduction," (http://www.lituanus.org/1990_3/90_3_02.htm).

Kelman, M. "Interpretive Construction in the Substantive Criminal Law," *Stanford Law Review* 33:591-74, 1981.

Kelsen, H. *General Theory of Law and State*. New York: Russell and Russell, 1970.

—— *A Guide to Critical Legal Studies*. Cambridge, MA: Harvard University Press, 1987.

Kennedy, D. "How the Law School Fails: A Polemic," *Yale Review of Law and Social Action* 1:71-90, 1970.

—— "Legal Formality," *The Journal of Legal Studies* 2:351-98, 1973.

—— "Legal Education as Training for Hierarchy," in D. Kairys (ed.) *The Politics of Law*. New York: Pantheon Books, 1992.

—— *A Critique of Adjudication: Fin de Siecle*. Cambridge, MA: Harvard University Press, 1997.

—— "Afterword A Semiotics of Critique," *Cardozo Law Review* 22:1147-1186, 2001.

Kennedy, M. "Beyond Incrimination," in W. Chambliss and M. Mankoff (eds.), *Whose Law? What Order?* New York: John Wiley, 1976.

Kerruish, V. *Jurisprudence as Ideology*. New York: Routledge, 1991.

Kevelson, R. *Charles S. Peirce's Method of Methods*. Amsterdam: John Benjamins, 1987.

—— *The Law as a System of Signs*. New York: Plenum Publishers, 1988.

—— *Peirce, Praxis, Paradox*. Berlin: Mouton De Gruyter, 1990.

—— (ed.). *Peirce and Law: Issues in Pragmatism, Legal Realism and Semiotics*. New York: Peter Lang Publishing Co., 1991a.

——. "Peirce and Community: Public Opinion and the Legitimization of Value in Law," in R. Kevelson (ed.), *Peirce and Law*. New York: Peter Lang, pp. 99-119, 1991b.

—— "Pragmatism, Utopic Constructions and Legal Myth: A Glance at Durkheim's View of Peirce's *Method* of Semiotics as Related to Legal Norms," in R. Kevelson (ed.), *Law and the Human Sciences, Volume 3, Semiotics and the Human Sciences*. New York: Peter Lang, 193-218, 1992.

—— "Some Possible Meanings of the Idea of Human Rights," *International Journal for the Semiotics of Law* 6(16):71-88, 1993a.

—— "Aspects of Property in Law: The Cultural, the Incorporeal, the Intellectual, the 'New,'" in R. Kevelson (ed.) *Flux, Complexity, and Illusion*. New York: Peter Lang, 209-227, 1993b.

—— *Peirce's Esthetics of Freedom*. New York: Peter Lang, 1993c.

—— *Peirce, Science, Signs.* New York: Peter Lang, 1996.

—— "Law's Revolution: Negation, and Property as Institution," in J. Levin and R. Kevelson (eds.), *Revolution, Institutions, and Law.* New York: Peter Lang, 71-87, 1998.

—— *Peirce's Pragmatism.* New York: Peter Lang, 1998.

Klare, K. "Judicial Deradizalization of the Wagner Act and the Origins of Modern Legal Consciousness, 1937-1941," *Minnesota Law Review* 62:265-339, 1978.

—— "Law-Making as Praxis," *Telos* 40:123-35, 1979.

—— "Labor Law and the Liberal Political Imagination," *Socialist Review* 61:45-71; 1982.

—— "Power/Dressing: Regulation of Employee Appearance," *New England Law Review* 26(4):1395-1451, 1992.

—— "Critical Legal Politics: Left vs. Mpm: The Politics of Duncan Kennedy," *Cardozo Law Review* 22:1073, 2001.

Klinck, D.R. "The Semiotics of Money and Environmental Regulation," in R. Kevelson (ed.), *Flux, Complexity and Illusion.* New York: Peter Lang, 229-50, 1993.

Kline, M. "Race, Racism and Feminist Legal Theory," *Harvard Women's Law Review* 12:115-50, 1989.

Knopp, F. H. "On Radical Feminism and Abolition," in B. MacLean and H. Pepinsky (eds.), *We Who Would Take No Prisoners.* Vancouver, Canada: Collective Press, 1993.

Kojeve, A. *Introduction to the Reading of Hegel.* Ithaca, NY: Cornell University Press, 1980.

Kolko, G. *Wealth and Power in America.* New York: Praeger, 1962.

Kramer, M. *Critical Legal Theory and the Challenge of Feminism.* London, UK: Rowman and Littlefield Publishers, 1995.

Kristeva, J. *Desire in Language.* New York: Columbia University Press, 1980.

—— *Revolution in Poetic Language.* New York: Columbia University Press, 1984.

Kropotkin, P. *Mutual Aid.* Boston, MA: Extending Horizons Books, 1902.

—— *The Conquest of Bread.* New York: Benjamin Blom, 1913.

Kruttschnitt, C. "Social Status and Sentences of Female Offenders," *Law and Society Review* 15:247-65, 1981.

Lacan, J. *The Seminar of Jacques Lacan, Book 11. The Ego in Freud's Theory and in the Technique of Psychoanalysis 1954-1955.* Cambridge, UK: Cambridge University Press, 1988.

—— *The Four Fundamental Concepts of Psycho-Analysis.* New York: W.W. Norton, 1981.

—— *Ecrits: A Selection.* (Trans. A. Sheridan.) New York: Norton, 1977.

—— "Desire and the Interpretation of Desire in Hamlet," *Yale French Studies* 55/56:11-52, 1978.

—— *Feminine Sexuality.* New York: W.W. Norton and Pantheon Books, 1985.

—— "Seminar on the 'Purloined Letter,'" in J. Muller and W. Richardson (eds.) *The Purloined Poe.* Baltimore, MD: Johns Hopkins University Press, 28-53, 1988.

—— *L'Envers de La Psychanalyse.* Paris, France: Editions du Seuil, 1991.

—— *The Ethics of Psychoanalysis, 1959-1960.* New York: W.W. Norton and Company, 1992.

—— "A Theoretical Introduction to the Functions of Psychoanalysis in Criminology," *Journal for the Psychoanalysis of Culture and Society* 1(2):13-25, 1996.

Laclau, E. *New Reflections of the Revolution of Our Time.* London: Verso, 1990.

—— *Emancipations.* London: Verson, 1996.

Laclau, E. and C. Mouffe. *Hegemony and Socialist Strategy.* New York: Verso, 1985.

Laing, R.D. *Knots.* New York: Pantheon Books, 1970.

Landau, I. "Early and Later Deconstruction in the Writings of Jacques Derrida," *Cardozo Law Review* 14(6):1895-1909, 1993.

Landowski, E. "Towards a Semiotic and Narrative Approach to Law," *International Journal for the Semiotics of Law* 1/1:101-105, 1988.

—— "Truth and Veridication in Law," *International Journal for the Semiotics of Law* 2/4:29-47, 1989.

—— "A Note on Meaning, Interaction and Narrativity," *International Journal for the Semiotics of Law* 11:151-61, 1991.

—— "In Memoriam Algirdas Julien Greimas," *International Journal for the Semiotics of Law* 5(15):227-28, 1992.

Langdell, C. "Harvard Celebration Speeches," *Law Quarterly Review* 3:123-25, 1887.

Lanier, M. and S. Henry. *Essential Criminology.* Boulder, CO: Westview, 1998.

Laplanche, J. and J. Pontalis. *The Language of Psycho-Analysis.* New York: Norton, 1973.

Laplanche, J. and S. Leclaire. "The Unconscious: A Psychoanalytic Study," *Yale French Studies* 48:118-202, 1972.

Lauretis, T. de. *Alice Doesn't.* Bloomington, IN: Indiana University Press, 1984.

Lecercle, J.J. *Philosophy Through the Looking Glass: Language, Nonsense, Desire.* London: Hutchinson, 1985.

—— *The Violence of Language.* New York: Routledge, 1990.

Lee, D. *Freedom and Culture.* Englewood Cliffs, NJ: Prentice-Hall, 1959.

Lee, J.S. *Jacques Lacan.* Amherst, MA: University of Massachusetts Press, 1990.

Lempert, R. "Built on Lies: Preliminary Reflection on Evidence as an Autopoietic System," *Hasting Law Journal* 49:343, 1998.

Lenin, V. *The State and Revolution.* Moscow: Foreign Languages Publishing House, 1949.

Lemaire, A. *Jacques Lacan.* (Trans. D. Macey.) New York: Routledge and Kegan Paul, 1977.

Litowitz, D. *Postmodern Philosophy of Law.* Lawrence, KS: University Press of Kansas, 1997.

―――― "Gramsci, Hegemony and the Law," *Brigham Young University Law Review* 20:515-43, 2000.

Llewellyn, K. "A Realistic Jurisprudence ― The Next Step," *Columbia Law Review* 30:431, 1930.

―――― "Some Realism About Realism," *Harvard Law Review* 44:1222, 1931.

―――― *The Bramble Bush: On Our Law and Its Study.* New York: Oceana, 1960.

―――― *The Common Law Tradition: Deciding Appeals.* Boston: Little Brown, 1961.

―――― *Jurisprudence: Realism in Theory and Practice.* Chicago: University of Chicago Press, 1962.

Llewellyn, K. and A. Hoebel. *The Cheyenne Way: Conflict and Case Law in Primitive Jurisprudence.* Norman, OK: University of Oklahoma Press, 1941.

Lorraine, T. *Irigary and Deleuze.* Ithaca: Cornell University Press, 1999.

Love, N. *Marx, Nietzsche, and Modernity.* New York: Columbia University Press, 1986.

Luhmann, N. *A Sociological Theory of Law.* Boston, MA: Routledge and Kegan Paul, 1985.

―――― "The Third Question: The Creative Use of Paradoxes in Law and Legal History," *Journal of Law and Society* 15:153, 1988.

―――― "The Coding of a Legal System," in A. Febbrajo and G. Teubner (eds.), *State, Law, Economy as Autopoietic Systems.* Milano: Giuffre, 1990.

―――― "Operational Closure and Structural Coupling: The Differentiation of the Legal System," *Cardozo Law Review* 13(5):1419-41, 1992.

―――― *Social Systems.* 1995.

Lukes, S. and A. Scull (eds.). *Durkheim and the Law.* New York: St. Martin's Press, 1983.

Lukes, S. *Emile Durkheim, His Life and Work: A Historical and Critical Study.* Harmondsworth, Middlesex: Penguin Books, 1975.

Lynch, M., and D. Milovanovic. "Deconstruction and Radical Criminology, Contradictions and the Problem of 'The Text,'" in R. Janikowski and D.

Milovanovic (eds.) *Legality and Illegality*. New York: Peter Lang Publishing Co, 199-232, 1994.

Lynch, M. and C. Groves. *A Primer in Radical Criminology*. New York: Harrow and Heston, 1992.

Lyotard, J.F. *The Postmodern Condition: A Report on Knowledge*. Minneapolis, MN: University of Minnesota Press, 1984.

MacCabe, C. *James Joyce and the Revolution of the Word*. London: MacMillan Press, 1979.

—— *Tracking the Signifier*. Minneapolis, MN: University of Minnesota Press, 1985.

MacCannell, J. F. *Figuring Lacan*. Lincoln, NE: University of Nebraska Press, 1986.

MacKinnon, D. "Feminism, Marxism, Method, and the State: Toward Feminist Jurisprudence," in K. Bartlett and R. Kennedy (eds.), *Feminist Legal Theory*. Oxford: Westview Press, 181-200, 1991a.

—— "Difference and Dominance: On Sex Discrimination," in K. Bartlett and R. Kennedy (eds.), *Feminist Legal Theory*. Oxford: Westview Press, 81-94, 1991b.

MacLean, B. (ed.). *The Political Economy of Crime*. Scarborough, Ontario: Prentice-Hall Canada, 1986.

MacLean, B. and D. Milovanovic (eds.). *Racism, Empiricism and Criminal Justice*. Vancouver, Canada: Collective Press, 1990.

—— (eds.). *New Directions in Critical Criminology*. Vancouver, Canada: Collective Press, 1991.

—— (eds.). *Thinking Critically About Crime*. Vancouver, Canada: Collective Press, 1997.

Maine, Sir H.S. *Ancient Law*. London: J.M. Dent and Sons, 1861.

Malinowski, B. *Crime and Custom in Savage Society*. Totowa, NJ: Littlefield, Adams and Co., 1976.

Malloy, R.P. *Law and Market Economy*. Cambridge, UK: Cambridge University Press, 2000.

—— "Law and Market Economy: The Triadic Linking of Law, Economics and Semiotics," *International Journal for the Semiotics of Law* 12: 285-307, 1999.

Manning, P. "Metaphors of the Field: Varieties of Organizational Discourse," *Administrative Science Quarterly* 24:660- 671, 1979.

—— *Symbolic Communication: Signifying Calls and the Police Response*. Cambridge, MA: MIT Press, 1988.

Marcuse, H. *Eros and Civilization*. New York: Vintage Books, 1962.

Marini, M. *Jacques Lacan*. New Brunswick, NJ: Rutgers University Press, 1992.

Marx, K. *Capital*. New York: International Publishing House, 1967.

—— *A Contribution to the Critique of Political Economy.* New York: International Publishing House, 1970.

—— *Grundrisse.* New York: Random House, 1972.

—— "The Communist Manifesto," in D. Fernback (ed.), *Karl Marx.* New York: Random House, 1973.

Marx, K. and F. Engels. *The German Ideology.* Moscow: Progress Publishers, 1976.

Mathiesen, T. *Law, Society and Political Action: Toward a Strategy Under Late Capitalism.* New York: Academic Press, 1980.

Matoeisan, G. *Reproducing Rape: Domination Through Talk in the Courtroom.* Chicago, IL: University of Chicago Press, 1993.

—— *Law and the Language of Identity.* Cambridge, MA: Oxford University Press, 2001.

Matsuda, M. "Liberal Jurisprudence and Abstracted Visions of Human Nature: A Feminist Critique of Rawls' Theory of Justice," *New Mexico Law Review* 16:613, 1986.

—— "Looking to the Bottom: Critical Legal Studies and Reparation," *Harvard Critical Law Review* 22:323, 1987.

—— *Where is Your Body?* Boston, MA: Beacon Press, 1996.

Matsuda, M., C. Lawrence, R. Delgado and K. Crenshaw. *Words That Wound.* Oxford: Westview, 1993.

Maturana, H. *Biology of Cognition.* Urbana, IL: Illinois University Press, 1970.

Maturana, H. and F. Varela. *The Tree of Knowledge*, 1987.

Matza, D. *Delinquency and Drift.* New York: Wiley, 1964.

Mead, G. H. *Mind, Self and Society.* Chicago, IL: Chicago University Press, 1962.

Medvedev, P. and M. Bakhtin. *The Formal Method in Literary Scholarship.* Baltimore, MD: The John Hopkins University Press, 1978.

Melville, S. "Psychoanalysis and the Place of Jouissance," *Critical Inquiry* 13:349-70, 1987.

Menkel-Meadow. "Feminist Legal Theory, Critical Legal Studies, and Legal Education or 'The Fem-Crits Go to Law School,'" *Journal of Legal Education* 38:61, 1988.

Merry, S. "Concept of Law and Justice Among Working-Class Americans: Ideology as Culture," *Legal Studies Forum* 9(1):59-69, 1985.

Metz, C. *The Imaginary Signifier.* Bloomington, IN: Indiana University Press, 1982.

Meyers, M. "Predicting the Behavior of Law: A Test of Two Models," *Law and Society Review* 14:835-57, 1980.

Michalowski, R. *Order, Law, and Crime.* New York: Random House, 1985.

Mika, H. and J. Thomas. "The Dialectics of Prisoner Litigation: Reformist Idealism or Social Praxis?" *Social Justice* 15:48-71, 1988.

Miliband, R. *The State in Capitalist Society.* New York: Basic Books, 1969.

Milovanovic, D. "The Commodity-Exchange Theory of Law: In Search of a Perspective," *Crime and Social Justice* 16:41-49, 1981.

—— "Weber and Marx on law: Demystifying Ideology and Law — Toward and Emancipatory Political Practice," *Contemporary Crises* 7:353-70, 1983.

—— "Autonomy of the Legal Order, Ideology and the Structure of Legal Thought," in M. Schwartz and D. Friedrichs (eds.) *Humanistic Perspectives on Crime and Justice.* Hebron, CT: Practitioner Press, 1984.

—— "Anarchism, Liberation Theology and the Decommodification of the Juridic and Linguistic Form," *Humanity and Society* 9:182-196, 1985.

—— "Juridico-Linguistic Communicative Markets: Towards a Semiotic Analysis," *Contemporary Crises* 10:281-304, 1986.

—— "The Political Economy of 'Liberty' and 'Property' Interests," *Legal Studies Forum* 11:267-293, 1987.

—— *A Primer in the Sociology of Law.* Albany, NY: Harrow and Heston, 1988a.

—— "Jailhouse Lawyers and Jailhouse Lawyering," *International Journal of the Sociology of Law* 16:455-475, 1988b.

—— "Review Essay: Critical Legal Studies and the Assault on the Bastion," *Social Justice* 15:161-172, 1988c.

—— "Review Essay: Niklas Luhmann, A Sociological Theory of Law," *International Journal of the Sociology of Law* 16(3):399-408, 1988d.

—— *Weberian and Marxian Analysis of Law: Structure and Function of Law in a Capitalist Mode of Production.* Aldershot, UK: Gower Publishers, 1989a.

—— "Critical Criminology and the Challenge of Post-Modernism," *The Critical Criminologist*, 1-3, (December, 1989b).

—— "Law and the Challenge of Semiotic Analysis: A Review Essay of Bernard Jackson's *Law, Fact and Narrative Coherence*," *Legal Studies Forum* 14(1); 71-84, 1990.

—— "Images of Unity and Disunity in the Juridic Subject and the Movement Toward the Peacemaking Community," in H. Pepinsky and R. Quinney (eds.), *Criminology as Peacemaking.* Bloomington, IN: Indiana University Press, 1991a.

—— "Schmarxism, Exorcism and Transpraxis," *The Critical Criminologist* 3(4):5-6, 111-12, 1991b.

—— *Postmodern Law and Disorder: Psychoanalytic Semiotics, Chaos and Juridic Exegeses.* Liverpool, U.K: Deborah Charles Publications, 1992a.

—— "Re-Thinking Subjectivity in Law and Ideology: A Semiotic Perspective," *Journal of Human Justice* 4(1):31-54, 1992b.

—— "Subjectivity and Reality-Construction in Law," in D. Currie and B. MacLean (eds.), *Re-Thinking the Administration of Justice*. Halifax, Nova Scotia: Fernwood Publications, 169-181, 1992c.

—— "Borromean Knots and the Constitution of Sense in Juridico-Discursive Production," *Legal Studies Forum*, 17(2):171-92, 1993a.

—— "Lacan's Four Discourses," *Studies in Psychoanalytic Theory* 2(1):3-23, 1993b.

—— "The Decentered Subject in Law: Contributions of Topology, Psychoanalytic Semiotics and Chaos Theory," Paper presented at the Annual Meeting of Law and Society Association, Chicago, May 27-30, 1993c.

—— "Postmodern Law and Subjectivity: Lacan and the Linguistic Turn," in D. Caudill and S. Gold (eds.). *Radical Philosophy of Law*. New York: Humanities Press, 38-44, 1994.

—— "Dueling Paradigms: Modernist versus Postmodernist," *Humanity and Society* 19(1):1-22, 1995.

—— *Postmodern Criminology*. New York: Garland, 1997a.

—— (eds.). *Chaos, Criminology and Social Justice: The New Orderly (Dis)Order*. Westport, CT: Praeger, 1997b.

—— "Functions of Psychoanalysis in Criminology: A Comment on J. Lacan (and M. Cenac)," *Journal for the Psychoanalysis of Culture and Society*, 2(1), Spring, 1997.

—— "Lacan, Peirce and the Three Orders in Law," J. Levin and R. Kevelson (eds.) *Revolution, Institutions, and Law*. New York: Peter Lang, 105-125, 1998.

—— *Critical Criminology at the Edge*. Westport, CT: Greenwood Publishing Company, 2002.

Milovanovic, D. and J. Thomas, "Overcoming the Absurd: Legal Struggle as Primitive Rebellion," *Social Problems* 36(1):48-60, 1989.

Milovanovic, D. and S. Henry. "Constitutive Penology," *Social Justice* 18:204-24, 1991.

Milovanovic, D. and K. Russell (eds.). *Petit Apartheid in the U.S. Criminal Justice System*. Durham, NC: Carolina Academic Press 2001.

Moi, T. *Sexual/Textual Politics*. London: Methuen, 1985.

—— (ed.). *The Kristeva Reader*. Oxford: Blackwell Publishers, 1986.

Mohr, R. "Shifting Ground: Context and Change in Two Australian Legal Systems," *International Journal for the Semiotics of Law*" 15(1):1-24, 2002.

Morgan, G. "Paradigms, Metaphors, and Puzzle Solving in Organizational Settings," *Administrative Science Quarterly* 25:605-622, 1980.

References

—— "More on Metaphor: Why We Cannot Control Tropes in Administrative Science," *Administrative Science Quarterly* 28:601-607, 1983.

Morland, D. "Anarchism, Human Nature, and History: Lessons for the Future," in J. Purkis and J. Bowen (eds.), *Twenty-First Century Anarchism: Unorthodox Ideas for a New Millennium*. Washington, DC: Cassell, 8-23, 1997.

Morris, C.W. *Foundations of the Theory of Signs*. Chicago, IL: Chicago University Press, 1938.

Mossman, M.J. "Feminism and the Legal Method: The Difference it Makes," *Australian Journal of Law and Society* 3:30-52, 1986.

Muller, J. and W. Richardson (eds.). *The Purloined Poe: Lacan, Derrida and Psychoanalytic Reading*. Baltimore, MD: The John Hopkins University Press, 1988.

Munch, R. "The Law as Medium of Communication," *Cardozo Law Review* 13(5):1655-80, 1992.

Murray, E. *Imaginative Thinking and Human Existence*. Pittsburgh: Duquesne University Press, 1986.

Naffine, Ngaire. *Law and the Sexes: Explorations in Feminist Jurisprudence*. Sydney, Australia: Allen and Unwin, 1990.

Narogin, M. *Writing from the Fringe: A Study of Modern Aboriginal Literature*. Melbourne, Australia: Hyland House, 1990.

Newman, G. "Batman and Justice: The True Story," *Humanity and Society* 17(3):297-320, 1993.

Nandan, Y. (ed.). *Emile Durkheim: Contributions to L'Annee Sociologique*. New York: Free Press, 1980.

Nasio, J.D. *Five Lessons on the Psychoanalytic Theory of Jacques Lacan*. Albany, NY: SUNY Press, 1998.

Nelken, D. "Beyond the Study of 'Law and Society.'" *American Bar Association Research Journal* 2:323-38, 1986.

Nicholson, L. (ed.). *Feminism/Postmodernism*. London: Routledge, 1990.

Nietzsche, Friedrich, *Beyond Good and Evil: Prelude to a Philosophy of the Future*. Random House, 1966.

—— *Twilight of the Idols and The Anti-Christ*. Penguin Books, 1968a.

—— *Basic Writings of Nietzsche*, W. Kaufmann (ed.), Random House, 1968b.

—— *The Will to Power*. Random House, 1968c.

—— *Human, All Too Human*. Cambridge University Press, 1986.

Norris, C. "Law, Deconstruction, and the Resistance to Theory," *Journal of Law and Society* 15(2):166-188, 1988.

—— *The Contest of Faculties: Philosophy and Theory after Deconstruction*. New York: Methuen, 1985.

—— "Law, Deconstruction, and Resistance to Theory," *Journal of Law and Society* 15(2):166-187, 1988.

Norval, A. *Deconstructing Apartheid Discourse*. London: Verso, 1996.

Oakes, G. "The Verstehen Thesis and the Foundations of Max Weber's Methodology," *History and Theory* 16(1):11-29, 1977.

Oquendo, A. "Re-Imagining the Latino/a Race," *Harvard Black Letter Journal* 12:93, 1995.

Packer, H.L. *The Limits of the Criminal Sanction*. Stanford, CA: Stanford University Press, 1968.

Parsons, T. "The Law and Social Control," in W. Evan (ed.), *Law and Sociology*. New York: Free Press, 1962.

—— "Definitions of Health and Illness in the Light of American Values and Social Structure," in E. G. Jaco (ed.), *Patients, Physicians and Illness*. Glencoe, IL: Free Press, 1963.

—— *The Structure of Social Action*. New York: Free Press, 1968.

—— "The Life and Work of Emile Durkheim," in *Emile Durkheim, Sociology and Philosophy*. (Trans. D.F. Pocock.) New York: Free Press, xliii- lxx, 1974.

Pashukanis, E. "The General Theory of Law and Marxism," in P. Beirne and R. Sharlet (eds.), *Pashukanis: Selected Writings on Marxism and Law*. New York: Academic Press, 1980.

—— *The General Theory of Law and Marxism*. New Brunswick, NJ: Transaction Books, 2002.

Patterson, D. "Langdell's Legacy." *Northwestern University Law Review* 90:196-203, 1995.

Payne, S. "Aboriginal Women and the Law," in C. Cunneen, *Aboriginal Perspectives on Criminal Justice*. Sydney, Australia: The Institute of Criminology, 31-40, 1992.

Pearce, F. *The Radical Durkheim*. London: Unwin Hyman, 1989.

Pecheux, M. *Language, Semantics and Ideology*. New York: St. Martin's Press, 1982.

Peirce, C.S. *The Collected Papers of Charles Sanders Peirce*. (C. Hartshorne and P. Weiss, eds.), Cambridge, UK: Harvard University Press, 1931.

Peller, G. "The Metaphysics of American Law," *California Law Review* 73:1151, 1985.

—— "Criminal Law, Race, and the Ideology of Bias," *Tulane Law Review* 67:2231-2243, 1993.

Penther, P. "On Foreign Ground: Grand Narratives, Situated Specificities, and the Praxis of Critical Theory and Law," *Law and Critique* 10:211-235, 1999.

Pepinsky, H. *The Geometry of Violence and Democracy*. Bloomington, IN: Indiana University Press, 1990.

Pepinsky, H. and R. Quinney (eds.). *Criminology as Peacemaking*. Bloomington, IN: Indiana University Press, 1991.

Phillips, D. *Toward a Just Order*. Princeton, NJ: Princeton University Press, 1986.

Pickering, W.S.F. (ed.). *Durkheim: Essays on Morals and Education*. London: Routledge and Kegan Paul, 1979.

Pintore, A. "Law as Fact?" *International Journal for the Semiotics of Law* 4(12):233-53, 1991.

Pitkin, H. *Wittgenstein and Justice*. Berkeley, CA: University of California Press, 1971.

Podgorecki, A. *Law and Society*. Boston: Routledge and Kegan Paul, 1974.

Poulantzas, N. *Political Power and Social Class*. Atlantic Highlands, NJ: Humanities Press, 1973.

—— *State Power and Socialism*. London: New Left Books, 1978.

Pound, R. "The Need of a Sociological Jurisprudence," *Green Bag* 19:610-11, 1907.

—— "Mechanical Jurisprudence," *Columbia Law Review* 8:605-23, 1908.

—— "Law in Books and Law in Action," *American Law Review* 44:12-36, 1910.

—— *Jurisprudence*. St. Paul, MN: West Publishing, 1959.

—— *Social Control Through Law*. Archon Books, 1968.

Quinney, R. *The Social Reality of Crime*. Boston, MA: Little Brown, 1970.

—— *Critique of Legal Order*. Boston, MA: Little Brown, 1974.

—— *Class, State and Crime*. New York: David McKay, 1977.

—— *Bearing Witness to Crime and Social Justice*. Albany, NY: SUNY Press, 2000.

E. Ragland and D. Milovanovic (eds.). *Lacan: Topologically Speaking*. New York: Other Press, 2003.

Ragland-Sullivan, E. *Jacques Lacan and the Philosophy of Psychoanalysis*. Chicago, IL: University of Illinois Press, 1986.

—— "Counting From 0 to 6: Lacan, 'Suture', and the Imaginary Order," in P. Hogan and L. Pandit (eds.), *Criticism and Lacan*. Athens, Georgia: University of Georgia Press, 1990a.

—— "Lacan's Seminars on James Joyce: Writing as Symptom and 'Singular Solutions" in R. Feldstein and H. Sussman (eds.), *Psychoanalysis And...* New York: Routledge, 1990b.

Rajchman, J. *Truth and Eros: Foucault, Lacan and the Question of Ethics*. New York: Routledge, 1991.

Ramazanoglu, D. *Feminism and the Contradictions of Oppression*. London: Routledge, 1989.

Rapaport, H. 1990. "Effi Briest and La Chose Freudienne" in P. Hogan and L. Pandit (eds.), *Criticism and Lacan*. Athens, GA: University of Georgia Press.

Reardon, P. "Judge 'Misunderstood' Parody, Author Asserts," *Chicago Tribune*, 9, April 24, 2001.

Redding, R. "Socialization by the Legal System: The Scientific Validity of a Lacanian Socio-Legal Psychoanalysis," *Oregon Law Review* 75:781-802, 1996.

Reich, C. "The New Property," *Yale Law Journal* 73:733-87, 1964.

Reiman, J. *Justice and Modern Moral Philosophy*. New Haven, CT: Yale University Press, 1990.

Renner, K. *The Institutions of Private Law and Their Social Functions*. London: Routledge and Kegan Paul, 1949.

Rheinstein, M. (ed.). *Max Weber on Law in Economy and Society*. (Trans. E. Shils and M. Rheinstein.) New York: Simon and Schuster, 1967.

Rhode, D. "Feminist Critical Theories," in K. Bartlett and R. Kennedy (eds.), *Feminist Legal Theory*. Oxford: Westview Press, 333-50, 1991.

Ricoeur, P. "Creatity of Language," *Philosophy Today* 17:97-112, 1973.

—— *The Rule of Metaphor*. Toronto: University of Toronto Press, 1975.

Roach-Anleu, S.L. "Critiquing the Law: Themes and Dilemmas in Anglo-American Feminist Legal Theory," *Journal of Law and Society* 19(4):423-40, 1992.

Robinson, R. L. "The Shifting Race-Consciousness Matrix and the Multiracial Category Movement," *B.C. Third World Law Journal* 20:231-88, 2000.

Roermund, B. V. "Narrative Coherence and the Guises of Legalism," in P. Nerhot (ed.), *Law, Interpretation and Reality*. Boston, MA: Kluwer Academic Publishers, 310-54, 1990.

Rooney, J. "Polish Legal Semiotics," in R. Kevelson (ed.), *Flux, Complexity, and Illusion, Volume 6, Semiotics and the Human Sciences*. New York: Peter Lang, 375-90, 1993.

Rosenfeld, M. *Affirmative Action*. Cambridge, MA: Yale University Press, 1991.

Ross, T. *Just Stories: How the Law Embodies Racism and Bias*. Boston, MA: Beacon Press, 1996.

Rossi-Landi, F. *Linguistics and Economics*. Amsterdam, Netherlands: Mouton, 1977.

—— *Language as Work and Trade: A Semiotic Homology for Linguistics and Economics*, South Hadley, MA: Bergin and Garvey, 1983.

Rothschild-Whitt, J. "The Collectivist Organization: An Alternative to Rational-Bureaucratic Modes," *American Sociology Review* 44, 1979.

Rousseau, J. *The Social Contract*. Chicago, IL: Henry Regnery, 1954.

References

Rudmin, F. W. "Frege's Semiotic's Sampled: The Sense and Reference of the Verb 'Own,'" in R. Kevelson (ed.), *Law and the Human Sciences, Volume 3, Semiotics and the Human Sciences*. New York: Peter Lang, 357-73, 1992.

Rumble, W. *American Legal Realism*. Ithaca, NY: Cornell University Press, 1968.

Rusche, G. and O. Kirchheimer. *Punishment and Social Structure*. New York: Russell and Russell, 1968.

Russell, S. "The Critical Legal Studies Challenge to Contemporary Mainstream Legal Philosophy," *Ottawa Law Review* 18:1-24, 1986.

Russell, K. *The Color of Crime*. New York: New York University Press, 1998.

Ryan, W. *Marxism and Deconstruction: A Critical Articulation*. Baltimore, MD: John Hopkins University Press, 1982.

Salyer, L. "Captives of Law: Judicial Enforcement of the Chinese Exclusion Law," *Journal of American History* 76:91-117, 1989.

—— "The Constitutive Nature of Law in American History," *Legal Studies Forum* 15(1):61-64, 1991.

Salecl, R. "Crime as a Mode of Subjectivization: Lacan and the Law," *Law and Critique* 4(1):2-10, 1993.

Samuels, R. *Between Philosophy and Psychoanalysis: Lacan's Reconstruction of Freud*. New York: Routledge, 1993.

Sarre, R. "Mabo," *Humanity and Society* 18(1):97-104, 1994.

Saussure, F. de. *Course in General Linguistics*. New York: McGraw-Hill, 1966.

Sarup, M. *Post-Structuralism and Postmodernism*. Athens, GA: University of Georgia Press, 1989.

—— *Jacques Lacan*. Toronto: University of Toronto Press, 1992.

Sawiki, J. *Disciplining Foucault: Feminism, Power, and the Body*. London: Routledge, 1991.

Scheppele, K.L. "The Revisioning of Rape Law," *University of Chicago Law Review* 54(3):1095-1116, 1987.

Schneider, E. "The Dialectics of Rights and Politics: Perspectives From the Women's Movement," *New York University Law Review* 61:589, 1986.

Schroeder, J.L. "Law and the Postmodern Mind," *Cardozo Law Review* 16:805-89, 1995.

—— "The Hysterical Attorney: The Legal Advocate Within Lacanian Discourse Theory," *International Journal for the Semiotics of Law* 13(2):181-213, 2000.

Schulman, C. "Chaos, Law, and Critical Legal Studies," in D. Milovanovic (ed.), *Chaos, Criminology and Social Justice*. Westport, CT: Praeger Publishers, 123-137, 1997.

References

Schultz, E. *Dialogue at the Margins: Whorf, Bakhtin, and Linguistic Relativity.* Madison, WI: University of Wisconsin Press, 1990.

Schultz, V. "Telling Stories About Women and Work: Judicial Interpretations of Sex Segregation in the Workplace in Title V11 Cases Raising the Lack of Interest Argument," in K. Bartlett and R. Kennedy (eds.), *Feminist Legal Theory.* Oxford: Westview Press, 124-155, 1991.

Schum, D. *The Evidential Foundations of Probabilistic Reasoning.* New York: John Wiley and Sons, Inc., 1994.

Schutz, A. "Law and the Postmodern Mind," *Cardozo Law Review* 16:979-1002, 1995.

Schwartz, M. "The Value of Postmodern Theory to Critical Criminology: Violence Against Women and Corporate Violence," in R. Janikowski and D. Milovanovic (eds.), *Legality and Illegality.* New York: Peter Lang Publishers, 1994.

—— and D. Friedrichs. "Postmodern Thought and Criminological Discontents," *Criminology* 32(2):221-246, 1994.

Schwartz, R.D. and J.C. Miller. "Legal Evolution and Societal Complexity," *American Journal of Sociology* 70:159-69, 1964.

Schwendinger, J. and H. Schwendinger. "Defenders of Order? Or Guardians of Human Rights?" *Issues in Criminology* 5(2):123-57, 1970.

—— *Rape and Inequality.* Beverly Hills, CA: Sage Publications, 1983.

—— *Adolescent Subcultures and Delinquency.* New York: Praeger Publishers, 1985.

Searle, J. *Speech Acts.* Cambridge: Cambridge University Press, 1969.

Searle, J.R. (ed.). *The Philosophy of Language.* Oxford: Oxford University Press, 1971.

—— *Intentionality.* Cambridge: Cambridge University Press, 1983.

Selva, L. and R. Bohm. "Law and Liberation: Toward an Oppositional Legal Discourse," *Legal Studies Forum* 11:243-266, 1987.

Selznick, P. *Law, Society, and Industrial Justice.* New York: Sage, 1969.

Sellers, S. *Language and Sexual Difference: Feminist Writing in France.* New York: St. Martin's Press, 1991.

Shon, P. "Hey You C'me Here!" *International Journal for the Semiotics of Law* 13(2):159-79, 2000.

Silverman, K. *The Subject of Semiotics.* New York: Oxford University Press, 1983.

Sinclair, M.B. "Autopoiesis: Who Needs It?" *Legal Studies Forum* 16(1):81-102, 1992.

Smart, C. *Women, Crime and Criminology: A Feminist Critique.* London: Routledge and Kegan Paul, 1976.

—— *The Ties That Bind: Law, Marriage and the Reproduction of Patriarchal Relations.* London: Routledge and Kegan Paul, 1984.

—— "Feminism and Law: Some Problems of Analysis and Strategy," *International Journal of the Sociology of Law* 14:109, 1986.

—— *Feminism and the Power of Law.* New York: Routledge, 1989.

Smith, A.. *Laclau and Mouffe.* New York: Routledge, 1999.

Smith, D. "The Experienced World as Problematic: A Feminist Method," Twelfth Annual Sorokin Lecture, University of Saskatchewan, Saskatoon, January 28, 1981.

—— *The Everyday World as Problematic: A Feminist Sociology.* Toronto: University of Toronto Press, 1987.

—— "Sociology From Women's Experience: A Reaffirmation," *Sociological Theory* 10(1):60-87, 1992.

Smith, D.A. and C.D. Uchida. "The Social Organization of Self- Help," *American Sociological Review* 53:94-102, 1988.

Smith, P. *Discerning the Subject.* Minneapolis, MN: University of Minnesota Press, 1988.

Smith, P. "Feminist Legal Critics: The Reluctant Radicals," in D. Caudill and S. Gold (eds.), *Radical Philosophy of Law.* Atlantic Highlands, NJ: Humanities Press, 73-87, 1995.

Stables, W. "Law and Social Control in Juvenile Justice Dispositions," *Journal of Research in Crime and Delinquency* 24:7-23, 1987.

Stacy, H. "Lacan's Split Subjects: Raced and Gendered Transformations." *Legal Studies Forum* 20(3):277-293, 1996.

Stanley, L. and S. Wise. *Breaking Out: Feminist Consciousness and Feminist Research.* London: Routledge and Kegan Paul, 1983.

Stockdill, B. "Aids, Queers, and Criminal Justice," in B. Arrigo (ed.), *Social Justice/Criminal Justice.* Belmont, California: West/Wadsworth, 226-250, 1999.

Stockinger, P. "The Conceptual Representation of Action and its Normative Background," *International Journal for the Semiotics of Law* 1/2, 1988.

Stone, A. "The Place of Law in the Marxian Structure-Superstructure Archetype," *Law and Society Review* 19:39-67, 1985.

Strawson, P.F. "On Referring," *Mind* 59:320-44, 1950.

—— "Intention and Convention in Speech Acts," *The Philosophical Review* 73/4:439-60, 1964.

Strong, T. *Freidrich Nietzsche and the Politics of Transfiguration.* Berkeley, CA: University of California Press, 1975.

Summers, R. S. "Charles Sanders Peirce and America's Dominant Theory of Law," in R. Kevelson (ed.), *Peirce and Law.* New York: Peter Lang, 153-62, 1991.

Sumner, W.G. *Folkways.* New York: Ginn and Company, 1940.

Sumner, C. *Reading Ideologies: An Investigation into the Marxist Theory of Ideology and Law.* New York: Academic Press, 1979.

Swidorski, C. "Constituting the Modern State: The Supreme Court, Labor Law, and the Contradictions of Legitimation," in Caudill, D. and S. Stone (eds.), *Radical Philosophy of Law.* Atlantic Highlands, New Jersey: Humanities Press, 162-178, 1995.

Symposium: Critical Race Theory, *California Law Review* 82, 1994.

Taub, N. and E. Schneider. "Perspectives on Women's Subordination and the Role of Law," in D. Kairys (ed.), *The Politics of Law.* New York: Pantheon Books, 1992.

Teubner, G. "Substantive and Reflexive Elements in Modern Law," *Law and Society Review* 17(2):239-85, 1983.

—— "How the Law Thinks: Toward a Constructivist Epistemology of Law," *Law and Society Review* 23(5):727-57, 1989.

—— "The Two Faces on Janus: Rethinking Legal Pluralism," *Cardozo Law Review* 13(5):1443-62, 1992.

—— *Law as an Autopoietic System.* Oxford, UK: Blackwell Publishers, 1993.

Thomas, J. "Law and Social Praxis: Prisoner Civil Rights and Structural Mediations," in S. Spitzer and A. Scull (eds.), *Research in Law, Deviance and Social Control* 6:141-170, 1984.

—— *Prisoner Litigation: The Paradox of the Jailhouse Lawyer.* Totowa, NJ: Rowman and Littlefield, 1988.

Thomas, J. and D. Milovanovic, "Revisiting Jailhouse Lawyers," in S. Henry and D. Milovanovic (eds.), *Constitutive Criminology at Work.* Albany, NY: SUNY Press, 227-46, 1999.

Thomas, J. and S. Boehlefeld. "Rethinking Abolitionism: 'What Do We Do With Henry?' Review of de Haan, *The Politics of Redress*," in B. MacLean and H. Pepinsky (eds.), *We Who Would Take No Prisoners.* Vancouver, Canada: Collective Press, 1993.

Tiersma, P. *Legal Language.* Chicago, IL: University of Chicago Press, 1999.

Tifft, L. and D. Sullivan. *The Struggle to be Human: Crime, Criminology and Anarchism.* Orkney: Cienfuego Press, 1980.

Todorov, T. *Mikhail Bakhtin: The Dialogical Principle.* Minneapolis, MN: University of Minnesota Press, 1984.

Traugott, M. (ed.). *Emile Durkheim on Institutional Analysis.* Chicago, IL: University of Chicago Press, 1978.

Trubek, D. "Max Weber on Law and the Rise of Capitalism," *Wisconsin Law Review* 3:720-53, 1972.

—— "Complexity and Contradiction in the Legal Order: Balbus and the Challenge of Critical Social Thought About Law," *Law and Society Review* 11:529-69, 1977.

Turkle, G. "Rational Law and Boundary Maintenance: Legitimating the 1971 Lockhead Loan Guarantee," *Law and Society Review* 15:41-47, 1981.

Turkle, S. *Psychoanalytic Politics.* New York: Basic Books, 1978.

Tushnet, M. "Perspectives on the Development of American Law: A Critical Review of Friedman's 'A History of American Law.'" *Wisconsin Law Review* 1:81-109, 1977.

—— "Critical Legal Studies: An Introduction to its Origins and Underpinnings," *Journal of Legal Education* 36:505-17, 1986.

—— "Critical Legal Studies: A Political History," *Yale Law Journal* 100:1515, 1991.

Twining, W. *Karl Llewellyn and the Realist Movement.* London: Weidenfeld and Nicolson, 1973.

Unger, R.M. *Knowledge and Politics.* New York: Free Press, 1975.

—— *Law in Modern Society.* New York: Free Press, 1976.

—— *Passion.* New York: Free Press, 1984.

—— *The Critical Legal Studies Movement.* Cambridge, MA: Harvard University Press, 1986.

—— *False Necessity.* New York: Cambridge University Press, 1987.

United States of America vs. Jose Solis Jordan, U.S. District Court, Northern District of Illinois, Eastern Division, 1999.

United States of America v. Jose Solis Jordan, United States Court of Appeals for the Seventh Cricuit, Appeal from the United States District Court of the Northern District of Illinois, Eastern Division, 2000.

Uusitalo, J. "Abduction, Legal Reasoning, and Reflexive Law," in R. Kevelson (ed.), *Peirce and Law.* New York: Peter Lang, 163-85, 1991.

Valauri, J. "Peirce and Holmes," in R. Kevelson (ed.), *Peirce and Law.* New York: Peter Lang, 187-201, 1991.

Valdes, F. "Queers, Sissies, Dykes, and Tomboys," *California Law Review* 83:1, 1995.

—— "Foreword: Latina/o Ethnicities, Critical Race Theory, and Post-Identity Politics in Postmodern Legal Culture," *La Raza Law Journal* 1:11-35, 1996.

Van Ness, D. and K. Strong. *Restoring Justice.* Cincinnati, OH: Anderson Publishing.

Volosinov, V. *Marxism and the Philosophy of Language.* Cambridge, MA: Harvard University Press, 1986.

—— *Freudianism: A Marxist Critique.* New York: Academic Press, 1976.

Voruz, V. "Psychosis and the Law: Legal Responsibility and Law of Symbolisation," *International Journal for the Semiotics of Law* 13(2):133-58, 2000.

References

Vygotsky, L. *Thought and Language*. Cambridge, MA: Massachusetts Institute of Technology Press, 1962.

—— "Thought and Word," in P. Adams (ed.), *Language in Thinking*. Middlesex, UK: Penguin Books, 180-213, 1972.

Webb, J. "A Progressive Critique? The Contributions of Critical Legal Scholarship to a Marxist Theory of Law," *The Law Teacher* 19:98-102, 1985.

Weber, M. *The Methodology of the Social Sciences*. Glencoe, IL: Free Press, 1949.

—— *The Protestant Ethic and the Spirit of Capitalism*. New York: Charles Scribner's Books, 1958.

—— *The Critique of Stammler*. New York: The Free Press, 1977.

—— *Economy and Society*, (vols. 1 and 2). G. Roth and C. Wittich (eds.), Los Angeles, CA: University of California Press, 1978.

Weber, Marianne. *Max Weber: A Biography*. New York: John Wiley, 1975.

Werner, W. "The Unnamed Third," *International Journal for the Semiotics of Law* 12(3):309-31.

West, R. "Feminism, Critical Social Theory and Law," *University of Chicago Legal Forum*, 59, 1989.

—— "Jurisprudence and Gender," in K. Bartlett and R. Kennedy (eds.), *Feminist Legal Theory*. Oxford: Westview Press, 201-234, 1991.

White, J.B. *Heracles' Bow*, Madison, WI: University of Wisconsin Press, 1985.

Whitney, G.E. "The Place of Thirdness in Legal Reasoning," in R. Kevelson (ed.), *Peirce and Law*. New York: Peter Lang, 203-20, 1991.

—— "A Semiotic Model of Economic Theory," in R. Kevelson (ed.), *Law and the Human Sciences*. New York: Peter Lang, 445-65, 1992.

—— "A Peircian Perspective on the Legal Philosophy of Justice Holmes," in R. Kevelson (ed.), *Flux, Complexity and Illusion*. New York: Peter Lang, 407-29, 1993.

Whitt-Rothschild, J. "The Collectivist Organization: An Alternative to Rational-Bureaucratic Modes," *American Sociological Review* 44(4):509-527, 1979.

Whorf, B. *Language, Thought, and Reality*. J. Carrol (ed.). New York: John Wiley and Sons, 1956.

Wilden, A. *The Language of the Self: The Functions of Language in Psychoanalysis*. Baltimore, MD: The John Hopkins University Press, 1968.

Wilkinson, P. "The Potential of Functionalism for the Sociological Analysis of Law," in A. Podgorecki and C. Whelan (eds.), *Sociological Approaches to Law*. New York: St. Martin's Press, 1981.

Williams, C. and B. Arrigo. "Anarchaos and Order: On the Emergence of Social Justice," *Theoretical Criminology* 5(2):223-252, 2001.

—— *Law, Psychology and Justice: Chaos Theory, and the New (Dis)Order*. Albany, NY: SUNY Press, 2002.

Williams, J. "Deconstructing Gender," in K. Bartlett and R. Kennedy (eds.) *Feminist Legal Theory*. Oxford: Westview Press, 95-123, 1991.

Williamson, J. *Decoding Advertisement: Ideology and Meaning in Advertising*. New York: Marion Boyars, 1987.

Williams, R. "Taking Rights Aggressively: The Perils and Promise of Critical Legal Theory for Peoples of Color," *Law and Inequality* 5:103, 1987.

Williams, R. *Marxism and Literature*. New York: Oxford University Press, 1977.

Winant, T. "The Feminist Standpoint: A Matter of Language," *Hypatia* 2(1):123-48, 1987.

Winch, P. "Understanding a Primitive Society," *American Philosophical Quarterly* 1:307-24, 1964.

Wing, A..K. (ed.). *Global Critical Race Feminism*. New York: New York University Press, 2000.

—— (ed.). *Critical Race Feminism*. New York: New York University Press. 1997.

Winner, T. G. "Prague Linguistic Circle and the Humanities," in R. Kevelson (ed.), *Law and the Human Sciences, Volume 3, Semiotics and the Human Sciences*, New York: Peter Lang, 529-43, 1992.

Wittgenstein, L. *The Blue and Brown Books*. New York: Harper and Row, 1958.

Wolff, K.H. (ed.). *Essays on Sociology and Philosophy by Emile Durkheim et al.* New York: Harper Torchbooks, 1964.

Wright, E. "Thoroughly Postmodern Feminist Criticism," in T. Brennan (ed.), *Between Feminism and Psychoanalysis*. New York: Routledge, 141-152, 1989.

Young, T.R. "The ABC of Crime: Nonlinear and Fractal Forms of Crime," *The Critical Criminologist* 3(4):3-4, 13-14, 1991.

—— "Chaos Theory and Human Agency: Humanist Sociology in a Postmodern Age," *Humanity and Society* 16(4):441-60, 1992.

Zizek, S. *The Sublime Object of Ideology*. New York: Verso, 1989.

—— "The Limits of the Semiotic Approach to Psychoanalysis," in R. Feldstein and H. Sussman (eds.), *Psychoanalysis And...* New York: Routledge, 1990.

INDEX

A

Abel, R., 129
actus reus, 214
affirmative action, 52, 57, 58, 59, 60,
    62, 126, 259
African-American "fem-crits" (*see also*
    critical race theory, critical race
    feminism), 142
Ahonen, P., 197
Alberstein, M., 124
Althusser, L., 84, 206, 223, 229, 238,
    262
anarchists, 8, 23, 24
Andreski, S., 45, 66
anomie (*see* Durkheim, E.)
Aptheka, B., 262
Arrigo, B., 8, 25, 133, 143, 153, 191,
    193, 199, 201, 202, 203, 215, 223,
    226, 236, 237, 239, 240, 241, 246,
    247, 248, 250, 256, 257, 258, 260
Asch, M., 26, 236
Aubert, V., 164
autopoiesis, 155, 167, 170
autopoietic system, 167

B

bad faith, 131, 132, 133
Bakhtin, M., 206, 221
Balbus, I., 22, 87, 88, 102, 105
Balkin, J.M., 122, 133, 134, 153, 256,
    262
bandits, 7
Bannister, S., 60, 96, 102, 214, 218,
    238
Barak, G., 226, 247, 250, 262
Barenberg, M., 124, 125
Barthes, R., 186, 228, 229
Bartlett, K., 139, 142, 143, 144, 153,
    245, 246
battered woman's syndrome, 139
Baudrillard, J., 228

Baxter, H., 167, 183
Beirne, P., 5, 79, 84, 88, 103, 105
Bell, D., 147, 150, 153
Bendix, R., 47
Bennet, L., 203
Benson, R.W., 222
Benveniste, E., 209, 229, 230
Bernstein, B., 213
bipolar judge, 132
Black, D., 1, 8, 155, 170, 171, 172,
    173, 175, 176, 178, 179, 180, 181,
    182, 183, 184
    behavior of law, 155, 170, 173,
        175, 178, 180, 183, 184
    centrifugal law, 179
    centripetal law, 179
    conciliatory style, 172, 178, 184
    definition of law, 8
    jurisprudential model, 181
    morphology, 173, 178, 180
    penal style, 171, 175, 177, 178,
        184
    propositions, 174-180
    remedial style, 172
    sociological model, 111, 181
    sociology of the case, 155, 170,
        180, 181, 182, 183, 223
    stratification, 173, 174, 175, 178,
        180
    therapeutic style, 172, 177, 178
Black's Law Dictionary, 188, 192
Block, F., 85
Borch-Jakobson, M., 229
Borg, M., 170, 180
Bourdieu, P., 167, 214, 262
Bowles, S., 86
Boyle, J., 122, 123, 153
Bracher, M., 237
Braidotti, R., 250, 261
Braithwaite, J., 170